A TIME OF LITTLE CHOICE

Cover:

Illustration of dancers prior to a ceremony at Mission San Jose in 1806,
an ink wash by an artist with the Resanov Expedition
(courtesy of The Bancroft Library, University of California, Berkeley)

Ballena Press Anthropological Papers No. 43
Series Editor: Thomas C. Blackburn

A TIME OF LITTLE CHOICE

The Disintegration of Tribal Culture
in the
San Francisco Bay Area
1769-1810

by

Randall Milliken

A BALLENA PRESS PUBLICATION

General Editors: Sylvia Brakke Vane
Lowell John Bean

Volume Editors: Susan Cole
Karla Young

Ballena Press Anthropological Papers Editors:
Sylvia Brakke Vane
Thomas C. Blackburn
Lowell John Bean

Library of Congress Cataloging in Publication Data

A time of little choice: the disintegration of tribal culture in the San Francisco Bay area, 1769-1810 / by Randall Milliken.
  p. cm. -- (Ballena Press anthropological papers : no. 43)
Includes bibliographical references and index.
ISBN 0-87919-132-5 (alk. paper) : $32.95 --
ISBN 0-87919-131-7 (pbk. : alk. paper) : $24.95
  1. Indians of North America--California--San Francisco Bay Area--History--18th century. 2. Indians of North America--California--San Francisco Bay Area--History--19th century. 3. Indians of North America--Missions--California--San Francisco Bay Area. 4. Catholic Church--Missions--California--San Francisco Bay Area--History--Sources. I. Title.
E78.C15M55 1995
979.4'601--dc20
                                                95-22975
                                                   CIP

Copyright 1995 by   Ballena Press
                          823 Valparaiso Avenue
                          Menlo Park, CA 94025
      Orders: Ballena Press Publishers' Services
                          P. O. Box 2510
                          Novato, CA 94948

All rights reserved. No part of this book may be reproduced in any form or by any means without prior written permission of the publisher, except brief quotes used in connection with reviews written specifically for inclusion in a magazine or newspaper.

Printed in the United States of America.

Contents

	Tables	vii
	Figures	ix
	Maps	xi
	Preface	xiii
	Acknowledgements	xv
1.	Introduction	1
2.	The Tribal World	13
3.	Foreign Incursions, 1769-1776	31
4.	Christian Initiations, 1776-1784	61
5.	Mutual Accommodation, 1785-1792	85
6.	Social Transformation, 1793-1795	115
7.	Reconsideration, 1795-1799	137
8.	Regional Disintegration, 1800-1805	167
9.	Recapitulation, 1806-1810	193
10.	Conclusion	219

Appendixes

1. Encyclopedia of Tribal Groups   231

2. Yearly Mission Population Totals and Crude Death Rates   263

3. Yearly Baptisms by Tribal Group   269

4. Pertinent Manuscripts in Translation   275

Bibliographic Practices   321

Bibliography   323

Index   353

Tables

1. Some mothers who were baptized at Mission Santa Clara during the 1790s, with a log of the children they brought for baptism over the previous years. 130

2. Mission San Francisco men killed by Saclans on April 29, 1795, baptismal numbers of their widows, and information regarding the widows' subsequent husbands. 140

3. Mission San Francisco men killed by the Suisuns in January of 1804, baptismal numbers of their widows, and information regarding the widows' subsequent husbands. 182

4. Mission San Francisco men killed on the road between the Suisun and Carquin villages on February 7, 1807, along with information about their wives and any subsequent marriages of those wives. 206

5. Mission San Francisco Yearly Tribal Converts, Mission Births, Deaths, Crude Death Rates and Year-end Populations through 1810. 266

6. Mission Santa Clara Yearly Tribal Converts, Mission Births, Deaths, Crude Death Rates and Year-end Populations through 1810. 267

7. Mission San Jose Yearly Tribal Converts, Mission Births, Deaths, Crude Death Rates and Year-end Populations through 1810. 268

8. Yearly Baptisms of San Francisco Peninsula Tribes at Mission San Francisco between 1777 and 1800. 270

9. Yearly Baptisms of Marin Peninsula Tribes at Mission San Francisco between 1777 and 1810.   271

10. Yearly Baptisms of the Carquinez Strait and Northernmost East Bay Tribes at Mission San Francisco and Mission San Jose between 1777 and 1810.   272

11. Yearly Baptisms of the Southernmost East Bay Tribes at Mission San Francisco and Mission San Jose between 1795 and 1810.   273

12. Yearly Baptisms at Mission Santa Clara from the Rancheria Districts Designated by the Mission Santa Clara Missionaries between 1777 and 1810.   274

Figures

1. Graph of yearly baptisms of tribal people at three Bay Area missions, 1777-1810 — 6

2. Illustration of some items collected from Bay Area tribes by Langsdorff in 1806. — 17

3. Illustration of dancers at Mission San Francisco in 1816, probably recent arrivals from north of San Francisco Bay. — 29

4. Bar chart of year-end 1777-1785 populations at Mission San Francisco, showing a change in ratio of children (age 0-14) to adults (age 15 and over). — 82

5. Bar chart of year-end 1777-1785 populations at Mission Santa Clara, showing high number of children (age 0-14) relative to adults (age 15 and over). — 83

6. Illustration of a gambling scene in the Mission San Francisco village, by L. Choris in 1816. — 87

7. Illustration of tribal men arriving at the San Francisco Presidio under military escort, by L. Choris in 1816. — 105

8. Bar chart of year-end 1786-1795 populations at Mission San Francisco, showing a change in ratio of children (age 0-14) to adults (age 15 and over). — 132

9. Bar chart of year-end 1786-1795 populations at Mission Santa Clara, showing a change in ratio of children (age 0-14) to adults (age 15 and over). — 133

10. Graph of reported deaths at Missions San Francisco and Santa Clara during the winter of 1794-1795 in two week intervals. — 138

11.	Bar chart of yearly counts of married couples from four geographic regions who renewed their marriages at the three Bay Area missions between 1794 and 1806.	171
12.	Graph showing reported deaths during the epidemic of 1802 at the three Bay Area missions.	175
13.	Graph showing reported deaths at two of the three Bay Area missions during the measles epidemic of 1806. (Mission Santa Clara deaths were not reliably reported.)	194
14.	Illustration of dancers prior to a ceremony at Mission San Jose in 1806, an ink wash by an artist with the Resanov Expedition.	198
15.	Illustration of multiple sets of dancers performing in the plaza at Mission San Francisco in October of 1816, by L. Choris ([1816] 1932).	220
16.	Portraits of long-time Mission San Francisco neophytes, by L. Choris ([1816] 1932), including (1,3) Huimens, (2) a Huchiun, and a Saclan (4,5).	227
17.	Portraits of some new Mission San Francisco neophytes, by L. Choris ([1816] 1932), including (1) an Ululato, (2) a Numpali (may be alias for Caymus), (3) a Suisun, (4) an Olompali, and (5) a Cholvon.	227

Maps

1.	Geography of the San Francisco Bay Area and California.	15
2.	Contact-period language group areas of California and the San Francisco Bay Area.	25
3.	Routes of three key Spanish incursions into the San Francisco Bay Area between 1769 and 1776, as well as the locations of Spanish settlements through 1810.	33
4.	Tribal regions of the San Francisco Bay Area: northern perspective.	228
5.	Tribal regions of the San Francisco Bay Area: southern perspective.	229

Preface

Many books have been written about Central California Indians, but none of them provide specific information about the people who lived around San Francisco Bay at the time of the European invasion. None of them satisfy our curiosity about the nature of first contact and the subsequent 75 years of pre-Gold Rush San Francisco Bay Area Indian history. When I sought such a book in libraries, the closest work that I could find was the doctoral dissertation of James Bennyhoff, later published under the title *The Ethnohistory of the Plains Miwok*. Bennyhoff's book is a study of the locations, marriage patterns, and histories of the local tribal people of the Sacramento-San Joaquin River delta region, an area 50 miles inland from San Francisco Bay.

Bennyhoff employed a wide range of analytical tools in his study. Not only did he utilize historical diaries and reports, he also studied marriage patterns that were recorded in Franciscan mission records. Also, he examined the linguistic relationships between groups by analyzing women's names recorded in those same Franciscan records. Bennyhoff's study did not cover the local peoples of the San Francisco Bay Area, but it did provide a model for such a study. Feeling the need for such a work, I decided to apply Bennyhoff's techniques to the early records of the San Francisco Bay region, a decision that led eventually to the publication of this book.

Although it was my encounter with Bennyhoff's work which first drew my attention to the mission registers and to their potential value as a source of information on the tribal peoples of the San Francisco Bay Area, it was my subsequent study of Sherburne Cook's research that forced me to think about the process of missionization and its consequences. In 1943, Cook published the first really detailed, rigorous study of the interactions of Indians and Spaniards in California. I have since read and reread his publications—which are based upon a massive corpus of primary data—many times, and I am still learning new things from points that he made long ago.

Despite its rigor, however, Cook's work tends to be thematic, and is only occasionally directed toward the explication of sequential events on particular landscapes. As George Phillips, another California ethnohistorian, recently stated, "Cook...could not fully develop all the themes he identified, nor could he always support the generalizations he formulated" (Phillips 1993:xiii). In addition, our contemporary perspective tends to provide us with a more complex view of the contextual constraints on human actions than Cook presented. As a result of the Vietnam War and a myriad of other experiences in recent history, Americans are no longer the children of World War II who confidently understood the world in terms of monolithic forces of good and evil. We have learned a great deal about ambivalence, co-optation, and contradiction.

I hope that this book provides the reader with an understanding of the decision made by most people from the tribal areas to attach themselves to one of several missions around San Francisco Bay. The vast majority of them made that decision, contrary to what Sherburne Cook believed, in the absence of direct physical threat from the European intruders. Yet there can be no doubt that they made that decision during a time when changes in their world seemed to leave them little or no choice to do otherwise.

***

A few words are necessary regarding spelling conventions for American Indian language place names, personal names, and tribal names. Language group designations are spelled as commonly found in English language publications. These include Costanoan (Ohlone), Miwok, Patwin and Yokuts. However, many tribal, village, and personal names which are not commonly found in the literature present a problem. They were written by Spanish speakers who were trying to capture the sounds of languages foreign to them. Thus, many of those names appear in a variety of alternative spellings in the early texts, as different scribes tried to find Spanish letters to capture unfamiliar sounds.

When appearing in quotations from Spanish sources, California Indian personal names, village names, and tribal names are left as written in the original manuscript. In my own text, however, I have adopted standardized spellings, usually on the basis of the most common spelling found in the primary documents. For instance, Spanish writers variously referred to one tribe as "Chaclan," "Sacalan," "Saclan," and "Xatlan." I have standardized that spelling to Saclan.

Readers should thus follow Spanish orthographic rules in the pronunciation of unfamiliar Indian words which appear in this book. Bear in mind, however, that those words were spoken by people who had their own systems of vocal tone, inflection, and rhythm.

Acknowledgments

This book was originally prepared as a dissertation in anthropology at the University of California, Berkeley. It is the result of the nurturing comments of the members of my dissertation committee, Nelson Graburn, Eugene Hammel, Kent Lightfoot, and Gunther Barth. I offer them thanks for their help and apologies for my stubbornness in a few areas. The ideas in this book are also the result of my interaction with a larger community, including California mission register researchers Alan Brown, Bob Gibson, Alice Hall, Stephen Horne, Robert Jackson, John Johnson, Chester King, Steve Sanchez, and Charles Slaymaker. Special thanks go to the people who read draft dissertation chapters, among them Craig Bates, Edward Castillo, John Johnson, Daliel Leite, Elizabeth Leite, Tim Miller, Michael Nunley, George Phillips, Linda Anne Rebhun, and William S. Simmons.

I have also benefited from the insights of other students of California anthropology and history, including Lowell Bean, Tom Blackburn, Catherine Callaghan, Glenn Farris, David Fredrickson, Edna Kimbro, Don Miller, Peter Nabokov, Bev Ortiz, and James Sandos. I received financial and intellectual support over the past few years from Peter Banks, Gary Breschini, Rosemary Cambra, Matthew Clark, Stephen Dietz, Glenn Gmoser, Bill Hildebrandt, Miley Holman, Mark Hylkema, Tom Jackson, Norm Kidder, Pat Mikkelson, Robert Orlins, and Randy Wiberg, in their roles as representatives of various private companies and governmental agencies in California. In addition, I have received help in translating Spanish language documents from Elroy Avalos, Rigoberto Coloca-Rivas, Vivian Fisher, Carolyn Highley, Luis Carlos Rodriguez-Leiva, and Francisco Santamarina, and help on maps from Kathleen Smith.

Few people have been more helpful to me during my inquiry than the librarians of the many institutions around the San Francisco Bay Area. Thanks go to the staff and former staff of The Bancroft Library, University of California, Berkeley, especially Walter Brem, Vivian Fisher, Peter Hampf, Sheila O'Neil, and Irene Moran. Special thanks also to Julia O'Keefe of the Archives of the University of Santa Clara for all the times she put up with me when I showed up unexpectedly. Thanks also to the staff at the Oakland Genealogical Library of the Church of Jesus Christ of Latter Day Saints, to Jeffrey Burns of the Archives of San Francisco Diocese of the Catholic Church, to Steve Cavin of the American Academy of Franciscan History, and to Leslie

Masanoga of the San Jose City Archives at the San Jose Historical Society. Also, I thank Dennis Goodman, now retired as librarian at St. Mary's College, who first made it possible for me to study the Franciscan mission records.

I thank Peter Hampf, acting director of The Bancroft Library, for permission to reproduce the pictures used in this book, including the cover picture of native dancers rendered by George H. von Langsdorff at Mission San Jose in 1806. I also thank the following individuals for granting me permission to reproduce the quotations for which their institutions hold the copyrights: Nettie DeBill of Stanford University Press; Mitchel Postel of the San Mateo Historical Association; Rose Robinson of University of California Press; John Schwaller of the Academy of American Franciscan History; and William C. Sturtevant of the Smithsonian Institution.

***

Singular credits go to six people who are responsible for bringing this book to the light of day: Lowell Bean, who encouraged me to publish through Ballena Press; Tom Blackburn, who showed patience beyond the call of duty while editing the original manuscript; John Boring, who crafted the maps with more than professional attention; Susan Cole, who performed the final copy editing; Sylvia Brakke Vane, who shepherded the book to completion; and Malcolm Margolin, who convinced me that it was worth the effort.

Chapter 1

Introduction

> Today I buried Viridiana, the last of the adults who witnessed the founding of the mission; at that time she had been twenty-five years old. Everyone who saw the arrival of the ministers, the people from within a radius of six leagues [sixteen miles], have died; and of those who have been born since that time, rare are those who live (SFR-D 3516, [July 22, 1814, Ramón Abella].

In 1770 the political landscape of the San Francisco Bay region was a mosaic of tiny tribal territories, each some eight to twelve miles in diameter, each containing a population of some two hundred to four hundred individuals. By the year 1810, only forty years later, the tribal territories in all but the most northerly reaches of the San Francisco Bay region were empty. The change began when Spanish colonial explorers passed through the region in the year 1769. Soon after, in 1776 and 1777, the Spanish invaders founded the missions of San Francisco de Asís and Santa Clara, respectively. Over the succeeding decades people from one local tribe after another left their villages and moved to the missions.

The story of tribal disintegration in the Bay Area is a complex one. No two tribal groups were confronted by the choice to join the missions under exactly the same set of circumstances. There was, however, a common experiential thread over the forty years; each tribe left its homeland for the missions when a significant portion of its members came to believe that the move was the only reasonable alternative in a transformed world. They were not marched to the baptismal font by soldiers with guns and lances (cf. Cook 1943:74). Although many tribal people came to view themselves as culturally inferior, requiring the guidance of the foreign missionaries, not every tribal person was impressed by the Spanish invaders. Many people despised the missions. There people were subjected to paternalistic controls on their work schedules, on their sexual practices, their eating habits, their religious expression, all in ways contrary to indigenous values. Daily operations were maintained by threats of punishment in this life and an eternal afterlife. And the missions were breeding grounds for disease.

I argue in the following pages that ambivalence is the key concept in understanding tribal responses to the missions. Most people held mixed feelings of hatred and admiration toward the missions. They struggled with those feelings in a terrible, internally destructive attempt to cope with changes that were beyond their control. Eventually even those people who clearly rejected the values of mission life capitulated, because of changes in their tribal lands, disease, depopulation, and the accompanying collapse of intergroup alliances.

Context And Synopsis

Historic global processes that had been unfolding over several centuries were responsible for the appearance of the Spanish representatives of European mercantile power in the San Francisco Bay Area in 1769. Spain first claimed the Californias in 1542 when Juan Rodriguez Cabrillo explored the Pacific Coast, yet the Spanish had made no attempt to occupy Alta California (that part of California currently part of the United States of America) until the late 1760s. Russian and English expansion in the North Pacific (an expansion that might threaten the lucrative trade between the Viceroyalty of New Spain and the Philippine Islands) provoked Spanish authorities to look northward in 1769 and move to occupy the strategic bays along the coast of Alta California. Franciscan missionaries were to be the agents of the Conquista in Upper California, and effect the projected social transformation of the tribal peoples.[1]

The first missions were established at intervals near the California coast. Four military bases (presidios) were placed at strategic locations to defend the coast and to supply the missions with revolving squads of escorts. The Monterey Presidio and nearby Mission San Carlos Borromeo were established at Monterey Bay in the spring of 1770. San Francisco Bay Area populations encountered Spanish exploring parties between 1769 and 1776.

In the summer of 1776, the Yelamu people of the San Francisco Peninsula found the foreigners building two settlements on their lands, the San Francisco Presidio at the entrance to San Francisco Bay and the Indian mission of Our Seraphic Father San Francisco de Asís in a valley three miles to the

---

[1] See the works of Hubert Howe Bancroft (1884) and Charles Gibson (1988) for discussions of Spanish continental strategies. See Bancroft (1884) and C. Alan Hutchinson (1969) for discussions of Spanish plans for the development of Upper California. Francis Guest (1988) and Dianne Kirkby (1984) provide valuable discussions of the missionary mind set from two different points of view.

In this study I discuss the heated debates between the Spanish state and ecclesiastical bureaucracies over the division of governmental authority over missions and Mission Indians only insofar as they illuminate life as the Indians experienced it. Readers interested in the subject may refer to the works of Zephyrin Engelhardt (1912:117-120), Daniel Garr (1972), and Hutchinson (1969).

south. Within a few months the Tamien people, forty miles further to the south, encountered Spaniards constructing the mission of Our Seraphic Mother Santa Clara on their lands. By the end of 1777 the Spanish had also begun the small civilian settlement of San Jose near Mission Santa Clara.

For a local man or woman, the moment of first contact with a Spanish explorer's party or a missionary compound stretched the possibilities of the world, reformed and transformed it, and thus transformed the internal landscape of the self. The universe had suddenly conjured up human beings with purposes and technologies unlike anything the local people had been brought up to expect or understand. During the early days of Spanish settlement, local Indian people flocked to the missions to meet the Franciscan priests, feast with the newcomers, touch the myriad unknown objects brought by the foreigners, and watch the construction of strange buildings.

At both San Francisco and Santa Clara, Spanish soldiers soon killed local men who tampered with property and resisted punishment. Thus the Spanish right of occupancy was established by force. The first killings took place at Mission San Francisco, following a series of tense interactions in the fall of 1776. Conflict arose when Yelamu men took some Spanish items, shot an arrow near a soldier, and tried to kiss the wife of a soldier; possible aggressive behavior on the part of the invading soldiers during the same period was never documented. Eventually, a Yelamu man was shot to death by a soldier (Palóu ([1773-1783] 1926:4:135). Since the Yelamus probably included fewer than fifty adult males altogether, the death by firearms of a single man had sobering consequences. The Yelamu people never again directly confronted the Spaniards.

Violence erupted at Mission Santa Clara in the spring of 1777. Villagers from one of the Santa Clara Valley groups killed some mules that had been set to graze on the valley seed fields, and then took the carcasses to their village to eat. Spanish soldiers discovered the "theft" and entered the village as the meat was being prepared. The local men resisted the Spanish soldiers' attempt to arrest them by retiring to some brush and firing arrows. Three of the village men were shot to death.

Despite the killings, native teenagers joined the Christian communities at San Francisco and Santa Clara during their first two years of existence. It took many years, however, for the missions to build sizable communities. Most of the people who did join mission communities over the first four or five years came from local villages within a walking distance of one to two hours. Large groups of families from more distant tribes began to visit the missions only after tribal control over lands in the near environs of the missions gave way to Franciscan control.

The mission settlements created a new political dynamic in surrounding villages. When an individual became upset or angry with her or his life situation, the missions beckoned. When a village extended family felt that its interests were being ignored by other extended families, the option of moving to the mission existed. As the mission populations grew, Indian neophytes were given key roles in the new mission society. Some of the tribal elders must have worried that their families would be left out of the power structure in the new world unless they too joined the missions.

At the missions, people experienced an immediate and profound change in daily life. Before, both women and men had lived a varied hunting and gathering life under the leadership of family elders, with a great deal of individual freedom. That way of life was replaced by a narrow daily regimen of agricultural work under the direction of the priests and a hierarchy of overseers, consisting of acculturated Indians who were often from foreign lands. In the missions, people were beaten if they chose not to follow their leader's directions (Cook 1943:113-129; Fogel 1988:130-132; Guest 1983:20).

Extended family households gave way at the missions to isolated nuclear family dwellings. Teenage girls and unmarried women were separated from their families and confined at night in *monjerías*, isolated dormitories, in an attempt to impose the explicit Spanish sexual ethics of the time. The accumulation of refuse at the permanent mission villages was also unfamiliar; people could not follow the traditional practice of moving the entire village when refuse became a problem.

Mission death rates were incredibly high, especially among newborn babies and infants. Very few children born at the missions grew to adulthood. Various gastrointestinal diseases flourished in the crowded, unsanitary mission communities. Syphilis and tuberculosis came to be endemic, and occasional epidemics of measles and possibly influenza and typhoid fever ran through both mission populations and native villages (see Engelhardt 1912; Cook 1943:13-34; Jackson 1983, 1987; Webb 1952).

The majority of people lived a life of confusion and powerlessness within the mission system. One visitor wrote (in reference to the Christian Indian people at Mission San Francisco) that "all operations and functions both of body and mind appeared to be carried out with a mechanical, lifeless, careless indifference" (Vancouver [1792] 1798:21). Most of the Franciscan missionaries of the day, as well as some later authors, considered symptoms of depression to be proof of the stupidity and natural inferiority of the Indian people. Limited by their cultural chauvinism, the missionaries failed to see that they had undermined the peoples' sense of mastery, choice, and efficacy, important prerequisites for human health and happiness.

Native people who decided that they had made a mistake in joining a mission community, who returned to their village after they had been baptized, were forcibly returned. That policy had been instituted in California in 1775 by Junípero Serra:

> Last night they brought to me nine neophytes of this mission. I am sending four of these to Your Lordship.... The first three have deserted a number of times, and although they have been punished at various times, there is no sign of amendment.... I am sending them to you so that a period of exile, and two or three whippings which Your Lordship may order applied to them on different days may serve, for them and for the rest, for a warning, and may be of spiritual benefit to all (Serra [1748-1784] 1955-56:4:425).

The Franciscans of those times considered baptism to be an agreement by the Indian people to become their wards, or adult children. In their understanding, the universe included Earth, Heaven (a place of eternal happy life), Hell (a land of eternal torture for those who consciously rejected Christian moral behavior), and Purgatory (a place of suffering and expiation for some who would eventually go to Heaven). Physical force, the Franciscans believed, was a necessary tool to save Christian Indian souls for an eternal life in Heaven (see Cook 1943:57-64; Guest 1988:28).

The California missionaries used the Spanish military to bring back runaway Christian Indians less often than one might suppose. They relied instead on coopted non-Christian tribal leaders, paid with beads and blankets, to bring runaway Christians back to the missions. If that did not work, groups of Mission Indians were sent out to harass villages harboring runaways. Military squads did occasionally bring in runaways throughout the Spanish period, but they went out to hostile villages only when other methods failed.

Despite disease and humiliating treatment, the pace of mission recruitment in the San Francisco Bay region actually accelerated during the 1790s. This seems incredible to many of us today, since tribal people could not have failed to understand the negative side of mission life by that time. In fact direct resistance to the missions also increased during the 1790s. Late in 1793, as San Francisco Peninsula people were going to the missions in increasing numbers, Santa Cruz Mountains people of the Quiroste group attacked and burned buildings at Mission Santa Cruz to the south of the Bay Area. Then in 1794 and early 1795, soon after the Quirostes were defeated by Spanish soldiers, a huge group of adults joined the missions, more than in all the previous sixteen years combined (see Figure 1).

No event in the history of the Indian people of the San Francisco Bay Area is more difficult to explain nor more important to understand than the mass baptisms of 1794-1795. That mass social transformation becomes understandable when we look at it as the result of hundreds of decisions made by individuals within a context of steady deterioration in the level of tribal health, the failure

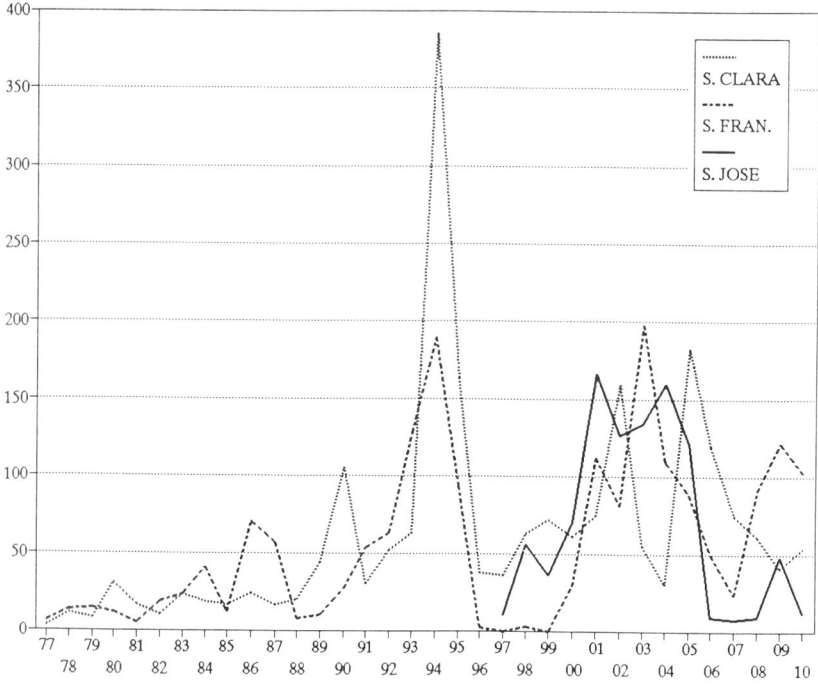

Figure 1. Graph of yearly baptisms of tribal people at three Bay Area missions, 1777-1810.

of the Santa Cruz Mountains resistance in 1793 and 1794, a crop-destroying drought in 1794, and an aggressive line of "hell and brimstone" preaching by newly arrived missionaries. This was a moment in history when so many individuals reached the same conclusion at the same time that a whirlwind of change swept up even the most doubtful individuals.

Between 1795 and 1810, a series of more distant tribes resisted the intrusion of the Spaniards and their Christian Indian allies. Some of those tribes tried to coax or intimidate their neighbors into joining their resistance. In each case, however, a direct attack by a group of fifteen to thirty mounted Spanish troops suppressed the threat of general insurrection. Each defeat of a local resistance leader was a spiritual defeat for all people who had hoped that they could define the terms of their relationship with the Europeans. It took only the arrest or killing of a few key resistance leaders for large numbers of their followers to succumb to the psychological pressure to accept Spanish domination as inevitable.

Indigenous peoples along the ever-widening mission frontier faced the same kinds of stresses that disoriented and demoralized those already within the missions. Villagers lived within an environment of ever-shrinking choices, disease, and the physical defeat of famous warriors. Frontier political groups actually became marginalized in terms of the socio-religious fabric of their inland neighbors, as they lost members through death and recruitment to the missions. Traditional religious rituals failed to prevent social and cosmological turmoil. Troubled people were always aware of the open invitation of the missionaries to come and associate with the powerful. Life in the missions, in the military bases, and in the town of San Jose became the yardstick by which people came to evaluate the meaning of their own lives.

Sources And Previous Research

An absence of accounts documenting tribal peoples' attitudes toward the Spaniards and their missions places unfortunate limits on this history. Only three native California Indian narratives exist regarding the mission period. All three narrators were born at missions south of the San Francisco Bay Area. The stories told by all three—Lorenzo Asisara ([1878] 1989, [1878] 1989a, [1890] 1892), Fernando Librado ([1912-13] 1979), and Pablo Tac ([1835] 1958)—relate to mission life rather than to life during the period of transition from village to mission.

In the early twentieth century, descendants of San Francisco Bay Area tribal peoples did share their memories with anthropologists. Most important among them were María Copa and Tom Smith of the Marin Peninsula and Angela Colos and Joe Guzman of the East Bay. All four were descended from people who had gone to Bay Area missions a century earlier (Kelly [1931-32] 1991; Harrington [1921]). However, none of their accounts pertained to the 1770-1810 period of missionization.

In order to reconstruct the initial contact situation and early mission experience, we are forced to rely upon the documents of the colonizing society. The western sources provide a weak substitute for the voices of native peoples themselves. The information they contain is shaped by the point of view of the dominant culture and the human need to justify one's behavior. We can only speculate about policies and events left unmentioned, and we find nothing whatsoever which honestly details the point of view of tribal Indian people. Nevertheless, the western sources are a window into the past, and as the only window, they gain in significance.

The diaries and letters of explorers and colonial administrators provide some glimpses into the context of tribal collapse. Important Spanish diaries that have been published include those of Gaspár de Portolá ([1769] 1969), Pedro Fages ([1772] 1969), and Juan Bautista de Anza ([1776] 1930), while the diaries of the visiting world travelers George Vancouver ([1792] 1798) and George von Langsdorff ([1806] 1814) are also of value. Most of the myriad bureaucratic reports and letters of missionaries and local Spanish military authorities used in the preparation of this book are referenced in Hubert Howe Bancroft's encyclopedic *History of California* (1884, 1885). Unfortunately, few of them have been published; for that reason, translations of twenty-four important primary documents are included in Appendix 4.

The most valuable (and hitherto underutilized) Spanish documents are the vital registers of baptism, marriage, and death that were kept by the missionaries at Missions San Francisco, San Jose, and Santa Clara. Between 1777 and 1810, 11,036 Bay Area Indian people were listed in the leather-bound mission baptismal registers. At each mission, the name, estimated age, and family ties of each newly baptized Indian person was recorded by a Franciscan missionary; in most cases the homeland or home village of the neophyte Christian was also noted (Merriam 1955, 1968, 1970). Christian Indian deaths and marriages were recorded in separate books. Mission registers document the patterns of tribal absorption into the San Francisco Bay missions, as well as fluctuations in mission mortality and population (see appendices 1-3).[2]

The amount of information in the mission registers is vast, but initially almost inaccessible. Dozens of references to members of a particular nuclear family may be found here and there through thousands of records from a given mission, and sometimes in the records of neighboring missions. An individual may appear as the subject of one baptism, as a parent or other relative in another, as a god-parent in still another. That individual may appear as a spouse in one or more marriage register entry and as a deceased person in a death register entry.

I used the genealogical technique called family reconstitution to sort out orderly relationships among the myriad bits of information in the mission records, to turn thousands of meaningless names into the stories of individuals and families, and to document individuals's lengths of life, number of marriages, number of children, and the ages at baptism, marriages, and death (Wrigley 1966). A computerized data base system was used to sort and manage the facts, and to document family links. The databases for the three pertinent Bay Area

---

[2] Ethnogeographic reconstruction from mission register data was initiated in Central California by James Bennyhoff (1977). He was able to reconstruct the ethnogeography of the Delta region of California's Central Valley and, to a lesser extent, of the San Francisco Bay Area, from the intergroup marriage patterns documented in these records. More recently, other scholars have used mission baptismal, marriage, and death records to further reconstruct the ethnogeography of local subregions within the Bay Area, including the Bodega Bay area (Slaymaker 1982), the Marin Peninsula (Tanner 1971), the Napa-Sonoma area (Milliken 1978), San Francisco Peninsula (Brown 1973; Milliken 1983), and the Santa Clara Valley (C. King 1978).

missions allow one to build an infinite variety of lists and reports. For instance, one can quickly produce lists of siblings by a given mother and/or father, or by common mother and father, lists of specific tribal members sorted by age, or lists of people sorted by their native names. Studies can be carried out of contradictory tribal identifications within sibling sets, of inter-tribal marriages, of length of life at the mission for specific tribal groups, and so on. These databases make the thousands of entries in the various vital registers available for studies of individual lives, of specific families and of aggregative demographic patterns.[3]

When arranged and analyzed with care, the mission register data can tell us something about the personal struggles of tribal people and new mission recruits as real human beings. Through family reconstitution from baptismal data, for instance, we learn that María Luisa Ruruesmain from the East Bay village of Genau lost all seven of her mission-born children shortly after their births. By cross-checking military reports with mission register data, we learn what the leaders of one group, the Saclans, did following their release from imprisonment in 1797. The following chapters will elaborate numerous such stories heretofore lost to history.

A large body of literature exists that deals with the institution of the Franciscan missions. Some histories of the missions have been written by scholars who felt that the mission period was an especially attractive moment in history (Engelhardt 1912, 1924; McCarthy 1958; Weber 1986). Sherburne Cook (1940, 1943, 1943a) took the opposite viewpoint. He systematically documented many of the negative aspects of the mission experience. Edith Webb (1952) provides a neutral description of the material lifestyle at the missions. Many other publications have also contributed to our understanding of the mission experience (Castillo 1989; Costo 1987; Guest 1979, 1983; Hoover 1989; Jackson 1983, 1984, 1987; Johnson 1988, 1989; Kirkby 1980, 1984; Meighan 1987; Phillips 1975; Sandos 1991).

Cautions And Reminders

Some readers may feel that this work blames the victims of tribal disintegration for their own oppression because it emphasizes the voluntary absorption of indigenous Bay Area people into the mission system. I do stress

---

[3] Two database formats were developed for storing and manipulating the mission register data. The first format combines baptismal data and death data. The second format records marriage register information. The databases contain fields for each of the standard pieces of information found in an individual's baptism record and death record, as well as "memo" fields for exceptional text.

the role that tribal and mission peoples played as agents of Spanish religious and civil authorities, a role that helped extend the caste system of the Spanish Empire throughout the San Francisco Bay Area. However, a detailed examination of the processes which coopt people into participating in the construction of their own prison *is not a matter of blaming the victims* (see Bettelheim 1958; Freire 1970; Nandy 1983).

If any blame is to be assigned in the history of Indian-Spanish interaction in Alta California, it must be allocated to the architects of the policy of forcibly returning runaways, the missionaries themselves, and to those in the Spanish government who supported that policy. The Franciscan missionaries in California do not come off so badly, however, when their attitudes and activities are compared with the attitudes and activities of most other agents of western expansion. The California Franciscans at least believed that they were preparing an impoverished people to live in a glorious afterworld; events in later California history suggest what the Anglo-American citizens of the United States would have done to the tribal peoples had they arrived in the Bay Area first. From 1848 through the 1860s, many American settlers went on a genocidal rampage against the Indians of interior California (Cook 1976:44-77; Heizer 1974a; Hurtado 1988; Rawls 1984).

The actions and activities of native women during the mission contact period are underrepresented in this book, largely due to the fact that most available primary documents were written by Spanish men. The majority of correspondence focuses on the hostile interactions between soldiers and native people. The extent to which powerful women were involved in tribal foreign policy will never be known.

The cut-off point of this history is the year 1810. Because of that, it falls short of a full discussion of the missionization process over the entire San Francisco Bay region. In 1810 the tribes in the northernmost portion of the Bay region were still intact. The groups on the northern shore of San Pablo Bay moved south to missions San Francisco and San Jose between 1811 and 1816. People from the more northerly Upper Napa Valley and Suisun Plain went to San Francisco from 1810 to 1822. Mission San Rafael, founded on the Marin Peninsula in 1817 and Mission San Francisco Solano, founded in the Sonoma Valley in 1823, absorbed people from further and further north until the missionization effort came to a final halt in 1836.

The decision to close this study at the end of 1810 is not, however, a completely arbitrary one. By that year all the villages in the southern and central portions of the San Francisco Bay region had been emptied. The San Joaquin Valley tribes had sent only a few individuals west to the missions by that year. The great migration of those tribes, which emptied the flat valley lands by 1828, began in earnest in 1811. The year 1810 also marks the beginning of the Mexican Revolution and, therefore, a new period in California mission history.

As a result of the revolution, few new priests arrived from Spain after 1810, the Spanish military was deprived of both leadership and pay, and Franciscans' plans to expand mission settlements into the San Joaquin Valley collapsed.

* * *

This book is about the independent nations that once lived in the Bay Area and their reaction to the Spanish presence. It is not a study of the Spaniards, or of their motives and plans as agents of western expansion into the San Francisco Bay Area. Spanish behaviors are discussed insofar as they redefined the universe of the native peoples and limited their options for action. Spanish military power thwarted every tribal attempt to drive the Spaniards out or to negotiate with them as equals. So native groups had little to say about the shape of the new order, the location of alien settlements, the distribution of new tools, techniques, and foodstuffs, or the appropriate integration of new customs and religious practices.

Day in and day out, throughout the mission era, ambivalent native villagers along the mission-tribal frontier struggled with a choice—find a place in the new mission system, or resist its attractions. The decision to reject mission life could be made a thousand times, but the decision to join a mission community could be made only once.

Chapter 2

The Tribal World

> The mode of life, arts, arms, in some of them various lines tattooed about the chin and neck, the way in which they paint themselves for war and for the dance, distinguish the different tribes.... They do not possess horses or canoes of any kind; they only know how to fasten together bundles of rushes, which carry them over the water by their comparative lightness.... They neither sow nor reap, but burn their meadows from time to time to increase their fertility (Chamisso [1816] 1932:85).

The San Francisco Bay region was thinly populated at the time of the Spanish entry. The land was divided among scores of independent tribes, associations of families that worked together to harvest wild plant and animal resources within fixed territories and to maintain yearly ceremonial cycles. Each tribe had its powerful families and its weak families, its renowned individuals and its unobtrusive individuals. Each tribe tailored the thematically similar religious concepts of the region to its own specific landscape, so that myth and ceremony became a unique constitution for local sovereignty. In fact, each tribe might be thought of as an independent, landholding religious congregation.[1]

The tribes around the Bay spoke dialects of five mutually unintelligible languages: Costanoan (also called Ohlone), Bay Miwok, Plains Miwok, Patwin, and Wappo. Most ethnographers and ethnohistorians treat those language groups as separate cultural units (Heizer 1974; Kroeber 1925; Levy 1978, 1978a; Margolin 1978). Such a linguistic group approach can create a misleading and overly simplistic view of the complex mosaic of cultural variation in the aboriginal San Francisco Bay Area. Although some cultural traits did covary with linguistic distributions, other traits were shared in restricted local areas by

---

[1] Many anthropologists consider the term "tribe" imprecise (Colson 1986; Fried 1975). Most California anthropologists refer to the contact-period political groups of west Central California as "tribelets," following Kroeber (1932). Yet "tribelet" has not taken hold as a term to describe similar multifamily landholding groups in other hunter-gatherer and agricultural societies. I find the term "tribe" to be useful and meaningful to lay audiences, and I hope that my specific description of political processes assuages readers who are uncomfortable with the term.

neighbors who spoke distinct languages. The most obvious cultural contrasts within the Bay Area were probably determined by geographic and ecological factors, and were the result of the differences that exist between the coastal, bay shore, interior valley, and riverine habitats (see Kniffen 1939).

Natural Landscape

The San Francisco Bay region consists of a varied landscape of estuaries, plains, rolling hills, and rugged ridge lands. Dominating the landscape is the Bay itself, a fifty-mile-long inland chain of salt water estuaries (see Map 1). The Bay is separated from the Pacific Ocean by ridges of the Coast Range, and has only one narrow opening to the Pacific, the quarter-mile-wide channel known as the Golden Gate. South of the Golden Gate, the Coast Range ridges rise gradually from low hills to 3500 feet in the Santa Cruz Mountains, while north of the Golden Gate they quickly rise to 2600 feet at Mount Tamalpais. On the east side of the Bay are the low East Bay hills, as well as the higher ridges of the Inner Coast Range, locally called the Diablo Range.

Numerous small streams meander down through the hills to the Bay or directly to the ocean. The majority of these streams can be waded easily at all but the wettest times of the year. They can be contrasted with the navigable Sacramento and San Joaquin rivers, which carry snow melt runoff through the broad Central Valley to the Bay from the Sierra Nevada Range, a hundred miles to the east of the Bay Area.

The varied topography of the San Francisco Bay Area produced a mosaic of different plant communities that was clearly discernible in the eighteenth century. Sloughs and marshlands edged the Bay in many places, especially around its southern and northern extremities. Grassland was the dominant terrestrial vegetational type. Open grasslands covered many inland valleys, as well as dry west- and south-facing hill slopes. A savannah of grassland and white oaks covered parts of the Santa Clara Valley, the Diablo Valley, and the many valleys further north surrounding San Pablo Bay. Live oaks and bay trees formed woodlands along creeks and on moist north-facing hill slopes everywhere in the region, while dark redwood forests covered areas of the Santa Cruz Mountains and the Marin Peninsula, where rainfall and fog were most abundant.

A Mediterranean climate prevails in western Central California, and cool wet winters alternate with warm and dry summers. Within that overall pattern, however, sharp contrasts exist between coastal and inland climates. Areas within three or four miles of the ocean are subject to a modifying marine influence, the effect of which lessons as one goes inland. In the inland valleys, summer days are usually warm and clear, while the coast may be covered by a

The Tribal World

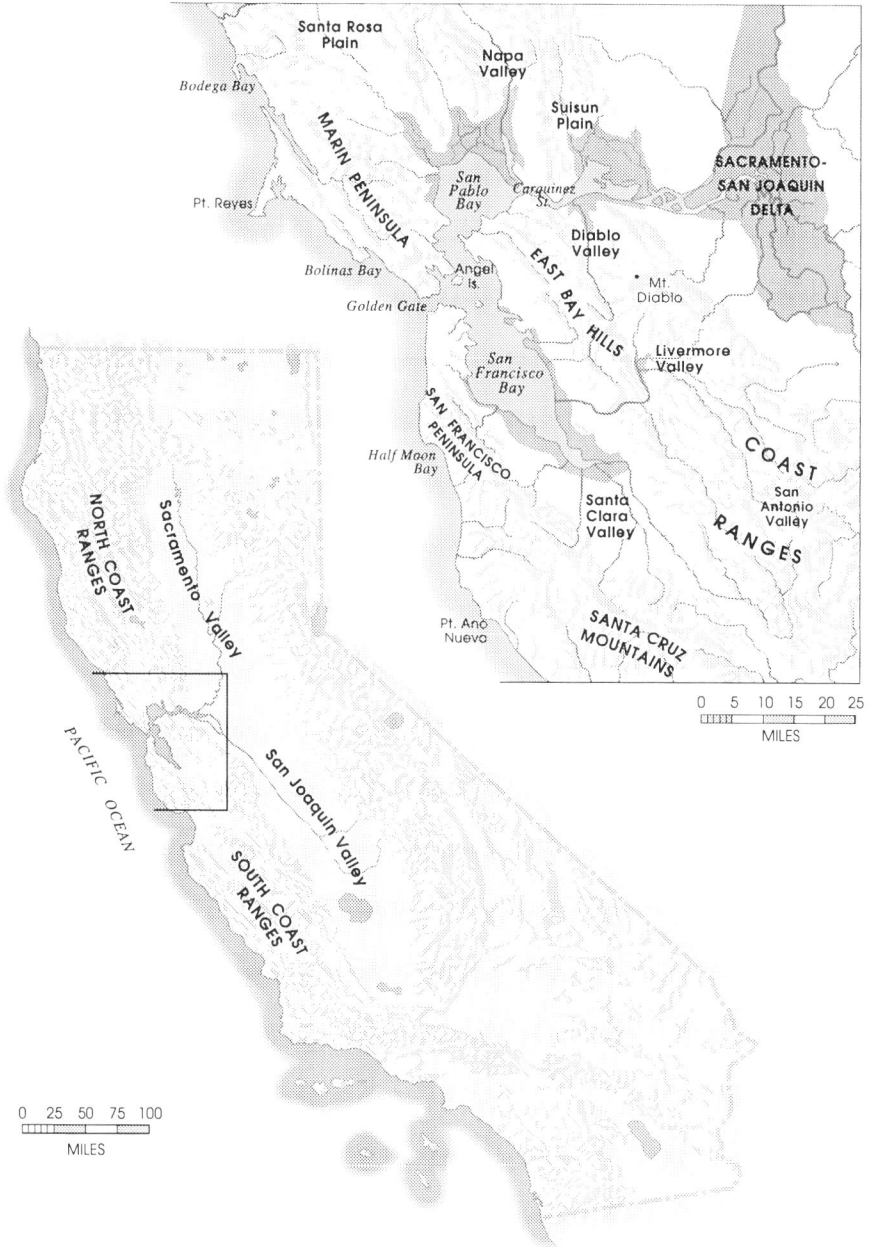

Map 1. Geography of the San Francisco Bay Area and California.

cool high fog. During the winter, the coastal areas escape the night frosts that occasionally fall upon the inland valleys.

Winter rain storms begin to move inland from the Pacific in October or November. Storm systems tend to last two to four days, and are separated by periods of cold clear days and frosty nights. In the eighteenth century, the first fall rains brought the native perennial grasses out of dormancy and triggered germination of a myriad of annual plants, while replenishing the small streams nearly dry from summer drought. Winter storms caused tiny streams to become raging torrents for a few hours, allowing runs of steelhead trout and silver salmon to move upstream to spawning grounds. Within and around the Bay, winter brought huge flocks of ducks and geese from nesting grounds as far away as Alaska. Herds of elk, which had spent the summer in the extensive marshlands around the estuaries, moved up into the hills. Seals and sea lions entered the Bay to feed on herring which spawned on the rocky beaches, and sea otters, whales, and porpoises abounded off the outer coast and within San Francisco Bay itself.

Beginning in March, the rain fronts become less frequent and the weather warmer, and a succession of spring wild flowers color the landscape. In the past, winter birds flew north, and others came from the south to feed and raise young in the marshes, woodlands, and grasslands. Mice, rabbits, and quail brought their young out to feed and grow. The freshwater marshes were especially productive in the spring, having trapped the nutrients washed downstream by the winter storms. By the middle of May, most soils were dry, and many grasses began to go dormant. Over the succeeding weeks one species of wild flower after another faded and became heavy with seeds. As the hillsides dried out, the elk moved down from the hills into the freshwater marshes.

Fire helped to maintain the grasslands and oak-grass savannas as the dominant types of vegetation in the region. During the dry months, people set slow-moving fires wherever there was enough dry ground fuel to burn (Crespí [1769] 1969:103; Menzies [1792] 1924:302). Burning increased the habitat for seed producing plants, increased deer browse, and kept the valley lands open for communal hunts (Lewis 1973; Blackburn and Anderson 1993).

Subsistence And Material Culture

People made their living by harvesting the plant, fish, and animal resources of their local environments, and augmenting them with food and tool-making resources received in trade from their neighbors. A sexual division of labor existed. Women harvested plant foods, involving an astounding variety of seeds, nuts, fruits, and bulbs, while men augmented the food supply by fishing and hunting for large and small game. A few important resources were obtained

The Tribal World

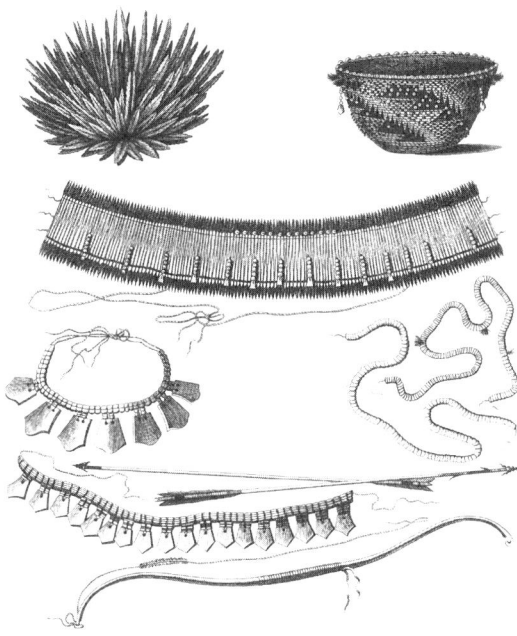

Figure 2. Illustration of some items collected from Bay Area tribes by Langsdorff in 1806.

from greater distances through an extensive indirect trading network. Trade items included obsidian or volcanic glass from the upper valley of the Napa River, shells from the coast, sinew-backed bows from the east, and tobacco, basketry materials, and ornamental pigments from various locations.

Acorns were an important source of carbohydrates for aboriginal Californians, as were the tiny seeds of grassland plants (e.g., California buttercup, chia, and red maids). The seed crops may have been the most important carbohydrate source in the Bay Area for much of the year. Father Francisco Palóu, founder of Mission San Francisco, wrote:

> The Indians of this locality live on the grass seeds of the fields, the labor of gathering them in season being relegated to the women, who grind and make the flour for the porridge. Among their seeds they have a black kind from the flour of which they make a *tamal*, in the shape of a ball the size of an orange (Palóu [1786] 1913:209).

Women also gathered and processed acorns, as well as hazelnuts, strawberries, blackberries, and soap plant root, depending upon the season (Palóu [1786] 1913:209).

Women spent a considerable portion of their time each year weaving baskets, which were necessary for gathering, storing, and preparing foodstuffs. Basketry work could be done at any season, in a large or small group, while supervising young children—another task for which the women were responsible. Basket manufacturing techniques varied from one local area to another (Mosher 1986). Unfortunately, relatively little is known about the subtle features of contact-period Bay Area basketry practices, because few local baskets survived into the modern era.

Men harvested most protein foods, such as fish, shellfish, and game. The people nearest to the sea relied as heavily upon fish and shellfish as upon terrestrial animals, while in districts further inland, hunting was more important. Larger animals were hunted with obsidian-tipped arrows and sinew-backed bows (Bates 1978:6). Traps were set for small animals, and antelope, deer, elk, quail, rabbits, and even grasshoppers were harvested in large numbers by communal drives. At Mission San Francisco in 1806, Langsdorff reported:

> One day we went out, accompanied by a party of twelve, and conducted by some thirty or forty Indians, to catch hares and rabbits. This is done by a peculiar kind of snare. Inside of three hours, without firing a shot, we had taken seventy-five, and most of them alive (Langsdorff [1806] 1814:179).

Houses in most places were small, hemispherical huts with bulrush or grass-bundle thatching (Palóu [1774] 1969:137; Vancouver [1792] 1798:13). These thatched houses sheltered anywhere from four to twenty-four nuclear or extended family members (Kelly [1931-32] 1991:177; Driver 1936:201). In areas adjacent to the few redwood forest habitats in the Bay region (e.g., the Marin Peninsula and Point Año Nuevo), people built small conical huts from redwood bark slabs (Crespí [1769] 1969:88; Heizer 1974a).

Women wore skirts of shredded plant fiber, occasionally with a deer skin back-skirt, while men usually wore no clothing at all (Palóu [1773-1783] 1926:3:258). Unlike most native North Americans, men in parts of the Bay region allowed their beards to grow (Palóu [1773-1783] 1926:3:266, 269, 277), and they decorated their pierced ears and pierced nasal septums with various ornaments. Women were commonly tattooed (see Figure 16, page 227):

> Some have only a double or triple line from each corner of the mouth down to the chin; others have besides a cross stripe extending from one of these stripes to the other; and most

have simple long and cross stripes from the chin over the neck down to the breast, and upon the shoulders (Langsdorff [1806] 1814:167).

Both sexes wore capes woven of feather and fur ropes:

> They also make for themselves garments of the feathers of many different kinds of water-fowl, particularly ducks and geese, bound together fast in a sort of rope, which ropes are then united quite close so as to make something like a feather skin.... In the same manner they cut the sea-otter skins into small strips, which they twist together, and then join them as they do the feathers (Langsdorff [1806] 1814:164).

Francis Drake's narrator reported in 1579 that the "king" of the people in the Point Reyes vicinity on the Pacific Coast of the Marin Peninsula wore "a Coat of Rabbit Skins reaching to his Waste" (*in* Kroeber 1925:276).

Population Density And Distribution

The rich and diverse ecosystem of the San Francisco Bay area sustained a very light population by today's standards, but a population that was actually dense for a nonagricultural society. The earliest Spanish explorers noted villages every three to five miles in most of the areas they passed through. Their descriptions indicate that the average village consisted of sixty to ninety persons. That is considerably smaller than the population sizes of contemporaneous villages in parts of the Central Valley and Santa Barbara Channel areas of California (which are estimated to have contained some 400-1000 inhabitants).

The largest reported Bay Area village, near Carquinez Strait, contained some four hundred people (Anza [1776] 1930:125; Cañizares [1775] 1971:96). Other villages that were noted as being "large" were located on San Francisquito Creek (250 inhabitants) and on the coast at Point Año Nuevo (200 inhabitants)(Crespí [1769] 1969:87; Font [1776] 1930:326, 366). Villages of about one hundred inhabitants were considered to be of "good size" (Anza [1776] 1930:133, 134), while villages with populations of around forty inhabitants were "not large" (Palóu [1773-1783] 1926:3:290).

Population density varied from one ecological zone to another within the Bay Area. The highest densities seem to have occurred along the southern and northern extremities of the shores of San Francisco Bay itself, where populations of approximately six people per square mile were found. Spanish explorer Pedro Fages described an especially concentrated area of villages on the Fremont Plain in 1772:

> Over the plain we spied several heathens, shouting out as though from joy at seeing us; we left five villages to our right, each of them having close to six houses of spherical shape, with considerable numbers of heathens living in them. Lying to our left hand were some villages; we could not make out very well what they were like, or how many houses were in them, since they were some way off (Fages [1772] 1969:120).

Similar habitats in the northern part of the Bay Area, which were mosaics of bay waters, marshlands, grasslands, and oak woodlands, also supported populations of six or more persons per square mile during the 1770s.

Villages were small and far apart on the wet Pacific Coast from Pescadero Creek north to the Golden Gate, and in the dry, rugged hill country of the easternmost Coast Ranges, overlooking the Central Valley. Mission baptisms suggest populations under two persons per square mile in these areas. The low population densities on the coast were probably the result of the relatively small seed-plant habitat and mammal populations in the coniferous forests of the coastal mountains. Population density in the eastern Coast Ranges was limited by sparse plant and animal resources and a lack of water in the summer months.

In many districts, village populations broke up and reconverged at various sites over the course of the year. Explorer Francisco Palóu noted evidence of seasonal movement in the San Andreas Valley a few miles from the bay shore on November 30, 1774:

> The first expedition that passed here did not give it a name on account of not finding any villages, while now, in the short stretch that we have traveled, we have found five large ones. From this it is inferred that the country is well populated and that the inhabitants move their villages readily from place to place (Palóu [1773-1783] 1926:3:272).

An entry in the *Libro de Bautismos* at Mission San Francisco mentions the seasonal movement of people on the central San Francisco Peninsula:

> Like all the aforesaid, they prefer to live at times along the tributaries of the San Mateo River, at other times at the aforesaid village [Olestura], as well as at Sycca. And they come up as far as Guriguri and San Bruno (SFR-B 178).

Spanish explorers noted abandoned villages at numerous places along the Pacific Coast, in the Santa Clara Valley, and in the East Bay area, as well as on the San Francisco Peninsula. Villages were moved because most resources were dispersed and only available for short periods of time.

Socio-Political Landscape

The lands around San Francisco Bay and the contiguous Coast Range valleys were occupied by scores of tiny tribes, each of which held territories some eight to twelve miles across (see Maps 4,5, pages 228, 229). Within each tribal territory lived a number of intermarried families that comprised a small autonomous polity of some two hundred to four hundred people. Members of the local groups hosted dances, pooled their labor during specific short harvest periods, defended their territory, and resolved internal disputes under the leadership of a headman. There were no higher levels of government in the region. The tiny nations were involved with one another in ever-changing alliances and conflicts.

In some areas of California, the families of a tribe shared a single central village location for much of the year; however, Bay Area tribe members lived most of the year in a more dispersed pattern. The Ssalsons of the San Francisco Peninsula, for example, lived contemporaneously at the three villages of Aleitac, Altagmu, and Uturpe. The Huimens of the southern Marin Peninsula also had three key villages, Anamas, Livangeluà, and Naique, on or near Richardson Bay. The Saclan villages of Jussent and Gequigmu were within a few miles of one another in the East Bay hills.

Early Spanish explorers and missionaries occasionally identified male village or tribal group leaders, and bestowed upon them the title of *capitán*. Evidence is contradictory regarding the amount of power the captains held. Their actions in community coordination and dispute settlement were probably constrained by a myriad of unwritten rules governing action in various specific circumstances. In the partially monetized society of Central California, grievances could be redressed through payment of shell money. Captains seem to have held the role of overseer in dispute settlements:

> No crime is known for which the malefactor cannot atone with money. It seems to be the law however, that in case of murder the avenger of blood has his option between money and the murderer's life. But he does not seem to be allowed to wreak on him a personal and irresponsible vengeance. The chief takes the criminal and ties him to a tree, and then a number of

persons shoot arrows into him at their leisure, thus putting him to death by slow torture (Powers 1877:177).

However, a captain's ability to impose settlements seems to have been limited. José María Estudillo stated that Bay Area natives paid no attention to their captains in carrying out their interfamily feuds:

> In their pagan condition they take up the bow and arrow at the least offence with one another; committing homicide with the greatest tranquility, without anyone giving the least reprimand, not even their own captains, whom they elect, or should I say retain, as the man they respect as the most valiant... Many of them make use of poisonous herbs to take the lives of those they hate. In this way the desire for vengeance, always the goal of the Indian, is satisfied (Estudillo [1809]).

Unfortunately, the Spaniards neither understood nor cared about the local rules for solving conflicts between the families within tribes, or the specific circumstances in which the captains would become involved in disputes.

Nor is much known about women's power in tribal and intertribal politics. The following statement concerning female leaders on the Marin Peninsula is our only detailed information about this important aspect of social life:

> There were two important female leaders. One (*hóypuh kulé(·)yih* or *hóypuh kul(·)éy·ih* 'woman chief') probably was more significant than data indicate. She handled the Acorn Dance, dominated the sünwele Dance, and was deeply involved in the Bird Cult. The second female leader (*máien*) was a genuinely key person: "máien bosses everyone, even *hóypuh*." Theoretically, she was head of the women's ceremonial house and *hóypuh* was head of the mixed dance house, "but máien did all the work." She bossed construction of a new dance house; had wood hauled for festivals; superintended preparation of fiesta food; sent out invitation sticks for dances, and, in some cases, selected the performers (Kelly 1978:419).

Since dances were the key expression of community life, there is no question that women wielded considerable influence in the community.

Foreign relations between tribes took the form of trade, warfare, and intermarriage. Territorial disputes and wife-stealing were the most commonly documented reasons for intertribal hostility:

> The land also provides them with an abundance of seeds and fruits...although the harvesting of them and their enjoyment is disputed with bow and arrow among these natives and their neighbors, who live almost constantly at war with each other (Fages [1775] 1937:70).

Most fights were individual ambushes or ritualized small group face-offs, but feuds sometimes grew into wholesale attempts to annihilate neighboring groups.

Despite their political divisions, the people of the Bay Area were tied together in a fabric of social and genetic relationships through intertribal marriages. Although most marriages took place between people from contiguous villages within the tribe (i.e., tribal endogamy), approximately ten percent of the adults in most villages had moved there from a neighboring tribe at the time of marriage (tribal exogamy). Such intertribal movement usually occurred between villages of adjacent groups that were only ten or twelve miles apart, although people occasionally moved to villages as far as twenty-five miles from their home.[2]

One foreign visitor to Mission San Jose, George von Langsdorff, mistakenly concluded that no intertribal marriages occurred at all:

> These people formerly lived in great enmity with each other...sparks of their ancient enmity still remain alive, and cannot be extinguished. For instance, the fathers never can prevail upon them to intermarry with each other; they will unite themselves only with those of their own tribe, and do not mingle in the society of the other tribes but with a certain kind of reserve (Langsdorff [1806] 1814:195).

There is abundant evidence of premissionization intertribal marriage in the mission records. There is also evidence that it was used by families as a conflict resolution mechanism, a technique that has been common in the past throughout the world (Boehm 1984). In future chapters I will present evidence involving two specific cases in which conflicts between missionizing tribelets were settled with accompanying intermarriages (Ssalson-Yelamu and Luecha-Tuibun).

---

[2] The missionaries at Mission San Francisco attempted to record the tribe of birth in the baptismal record entries of new adult neophytes. They were probably not always diligent about it, and therefore not always successful. However, enough newly baptized married couples were noted as being from different tribes for us to establish a pattern of at least minimal intertribal marriage (Milliken [1983]).

Langsdorff's misstatement does underscore an important point: long-distance intermarriage was limited in part because of the commitment people felt to their home territory and to their own way of doing things. The unfamiliar was disturbing and seemed dangerous. Intergroup marriages that did occur certainly gave the linked families enhanced positions in regional affairs.

Neighboring tribes were tied together by bonds of commerce and economic reciprocity as well as by bonds of intermarriage. One mechanism for sharing resources beyond the local tribal territory was the trade feast (Vayda 1967). Groups which found themselves with an over-abundance of some seasonally available resource invited neighboring groups to share in the harvest, and visiting groups reciprocated with gifts of shell beads. In addition to resource-specific trade feasts, tribes invited their neighbors to seasonal ceremonial dances. Trade feasts and regional dances reduced the chance that the people of one local valley might starve, while people just a few valleys away would have to discard extra food.

Regional dances provided opportunities to visit old friends and relatives from neighboring groups, to share news, and to make new acquaintances. People traded basket materials, obsidian, feathers, shell beads, and other valuable commodities through gift exchanges. Intergroup feuds were supposed to be suspended at the dances, but old animosities sometimes surfaced. All in all, such "big times" strengthened regional economic ties and social bonds.

Linguistic Landscape

Of the five languages spoken in the vicinity of San Francisco Bay—Costanoan (Ohlone), Bay Miwok, Coast Miwok, Patwin, and Wappo—the Costanoan (Ohlone) language was the most widespread (see Map 2). Costanoan (Ohlone) was spoken on the San Francisco Peninsula, in the Santa Clara Valley and in the mountains to both the east and west, and in much of the East Bay. The Bay Miwok language was limited to interior valleys of the East Bay, and perhaps reached the bay shore in the present East Oakland area. Tribes on the Marin Peninsula spoke dialects of the Coast Miwok language.

Although mutually unintelligible, Costanoan (Ohlone), Bay Miwok, and Coast Miwok are members of a single language family, Utian (Shipley 1978:84). The people on the north shore of Suisun Bay spoke the Patwin language, which was distantly related to the Utian languages. Those of the upper Napa and Sonoma valleys spoke the Wappo language, a language isolate that was unrelated to the others.

Ramaytush (San Francisco Peninsula), Tamyen (Santa Clara Valley), Chochenyo (most of the East Bay), and Karkin (Carquinez Strait) have all been suggested as distinctive linguistic Costanoan sub-groups within the Bay Area

The Tribal World

Map 2. Contact-period language group areas of California and the San Francisco Bay Area.

(Levy 1978:485). Such distinct groups did not exist in the past, and certainly reflect the amalgamation of later Costanoan speakers at the various missions. Linguist/missionary Felipe Arroyo de la Cuesta [1821-1837] carried out an elaborate study of the Costanoan dialects at Mission San Juan Bautista and took sample vocabularies at other missions. Arroyo stated that there were no abrupt language differences between neighboring Costanoan (Ohlone) tribes:

> Though they appear to speak distinct languages this is only accidentally true; that is, some of the words are different only because of the manner of pronunciation, in some cases rough, in others agreeable, sweet and strong. Hence it is that the Indians living in a circumference of thirty or forty leagues [eighty to one hundred and ten miles] understand one another (Arroyo de la Cuesta [1814] 1976:20-21).

Neighboring Costanoan dialects were probably no more distinct than colloquial American English and colloquial Australian English. Only by comparing widely separated dialects might one find differences as profound, for example, as those between the English and Dutch languages.

Linguists have also suggested that there were two languages, or at least two dialects, within the Coast Miwok-speaking area of the Marin Peninsula: Bodega Miwok and Marin Miwok (Callaghan 1970; Kelly 1978:414). Originally, the dialects of Coast Miwok may have varied along a gradual cline, as did the Costanoan dialects. Although now recognized as closely related, the Coast Miwok of the Marin Peninsula and the Bay Miwok of the interior East Bay area seem to have been mutually unintelligible languages (Callaghan 1971).

In addition to the Costanoan (Ohlone), Bay Miwok, Coast Miwok, Patwin, and Wappo languages, two other languages were spoken by tribes just beyond the San Francisco Bay Area. In the flat San Joaquin Valley to the east of the Bay Area, people spoke dialects of the Yokuts language, while just north of the Bay Area, on the Santa Rosa Plain, villagers spoke the Southern Pomo language.

World View And Ritual Practice

Bay Area people shared many beliefs about power, sickness, and healing with other native peoples throughout North and South America, beliefs that many today label superstitious:

> The Indians have some foolish practices when they go hunting and fishing which if they fail to practice they forgo the hunt

and the fishing. For instance, they plant a stick with feathers and seeds or they abstain from meat (Abella and Sainz de Lucio [1814] 1976:51).

Trained specialists performed rituals to maintain good relations with forces in the environment. Both women and men could be specialists, and they were usually older people (Amorós [1814] 1976:49-50).

People believed that specialized powers came to them through association with supernatural beings or forces. Anyone particularly good at anything, such as weaving, hunting, sports, gambling, singing, fighting, or healing, was assumed to be blessed by supernatural powers (Bean 1976). Dreams were a door through which invisible forces gave power to humans:

> Their principal superstition is their extremely obstinate belief in everything they dream about to such an extent that it is impossible to convince them of the unreality of their dream content (Durán and Fortuny [1814] 1976:51).

Although dreams were important, adolescents in west Central California did not seek dreams in directed vision quests (Applegate 1978; Benedict 1923).

Illnesses were thought to be caused by other people or by supernatural beings. Human enemies could use witchcraft to send invisible pains into a person (Merriam 1910:227). In addition, the spirits of places and objects could cause sickness or environmental problems if they were not honored by correct ritual means (Catalá and Viader [1814] 1976:50-51). Thus people were careful to make gifts at power spots:

> These oldsters make the rest believe that in order to prevent the devil from harming them they should offer him a little flour, which they eat, in a definite tree trunk, in this or that place (Manríquez and Escudé [1814] 1976:50).

Taboos also existed against speaking directly about the dead:

> These natives consider it very disrespectful to talk about their deceased parents and relatives.... In the course of a quarrel for greater vituperation they exclaim: "Your father is dead," and the flame of their fury grows greater (Amorós [1814] 1976: 59).

Healing was a process in which poison was turned back against a sorcerer or objects intruding into the body were removed (Catalá and Viader [1814] 1976:78). Some specialists used dances and songs to promote healing

(Amorós [1814] 1976:49), while others used herbal remedies (Durán and Fortuny [1814] 1976:79).

The concept of an afterlife, although present, was not linked with any idea of punishment or reward for one's life on earth:

> They relate that their departed relatives live in other lands or on the other side of the sea (depending on which side they are); that they play, etc., go about and dance; that they are happy, etc. (Durán and Fortuny [1814] 1976:145-146).

When people died they were either buried or cremated. The reasons for choosing one or the other are not certain; the two practices may have been a reflection of differences in social roles, or cremation may have simply been carried out by those families who were willing and able to take the time to gather the large amounts of wood that were required.

Oral narratives constituted both a means of educating the young and a primary form of entertainment. Unfortunately, only a few fragments of myths and stories are available for Bay Area groups (Kelly 1978, 1978a; Harrington 1921); the themes and characters in those stories place the Bay Area traditions in a group with the better documented traditions of Patwin and Eastern Miwok-speaking areas (Gayton 1935:595). The narratives indicate that the present events and places in nature were determined by the actions of a prehuman race of animal beings during a former mythological age.

The specific narratives of each group were linked to the local landscape, and served as a charter that established the group's origins and rights of ownership to a particular territory. Most of the Central California narratives that have been recorded seem to have been directed toward an audience of young men, in that they emphasize male skills and dependence upon knowledgeable older mentors. Some stories describe the occurrence of floods or wild fires as a consequence of avarice or rule-breaking. Many stress the dangers of interacting with neighboring peoples holding contrary allegiances (Barrett 1933; Gayton 1935; Gifford 1917; Kelly 1978; Merriam 1910; Radin 1924).

Dances comprised the main form of communal religious expression. Each local group had its own series of festivals. Every festival had its own set of specific dances, each with a unique set of costumes, accompanying songs, and choreography. During the most sacred dances, participants and costumes could only be touched by specialists, since they were thought to be invested with supernatural powers. No dance cycle details were documented for any of the groups around San Francisco Bay. Fortunately, the dances of the Coast Miwok-speaking people just to the north at Bodega Bay were still remembered by Tom Smith in 1932 (*in* Kelly [1931-32] 1991:224-315). Anthropologist Isabel Kelly

Figure 3. Illustration of dancers at Mission San Francisco in 1816, probably recent arrivals from north of San Francisco Bay.

wrote the following telling words about her attempts to write down Smith's knowledge of dances:

> If you could see what I am getting on dances, you would join my loud sobbing. It's simply grand, but I doubt if I emerge sane... And then—there's the perfectly horrible prospect of putting all this lovely ceremonial into skeletanized [sic] form. It is to weep! (Kelly [1931-32] 1991:xv).

The Bodega Bay dances shared many features documented for those of the Eastern Miwok-speaking tribes of the Sierra Nevada foothills (see Bates 1984; Gifford 1955). The common features of Bodega Bay and central Sierra Nevada dances were certainly shared by the people of at least the northern part of the San Francisco Bay region. We will never know how similar or different the more southerly dances of the San Francisco Peninsula and the Santa Clara Valley might have been.

* * *

The lifestyle of people in the Bay Area in the 1700s was very different from that of the city and suburban people who live in the region today. Because they lived off the seeds, fish, and animals of their local environments, details of daily life differed somewhat between coastal, bay shore, riverine, and interior valley homelands. Intermarried extended families grouped together in tribes which protected their tiny territories fiercely against the encroachment of neighbors. But adjacent tribes were also bound together by a complex web of intergroup marriages and trading alliances. Despite differences in language, artistic expression, and mythological history from valley to valley, general features of social structure, culture, and world view seem to have been shared throughout the region.

Chapter 3

Foreign Incursions, 1769-1776

	Spanish Actions	Tribal Actions
1769	October-November. Portolá travels San Francisco Peninsula.	Peninsula tribes guide and feed the strangers. Tuibuns or Yrgins are hostile.
1770	June. Monterey Presidio and Mission San Carlos founded 80 miles south of the Golden Gate.	Bay region people too far north to witness Spanish settlement at south end of Monterey Bay.
1770	November. Fages explores southern Bay Area.	East Bay groups exchange gifts with the Fages party.
1772	March-April. Fages explores East Bay to Carquinez Strait.	Alsons, Huchiuns, Carquins, Chupcans friendly with Fages. Tatcans terrified.
1774	November. Rivera explores north to Golden Gate.	Matalans annoyed by intruders. Peninsula groups welcome them.
1775	August-September. Crew of *San Carlos* explores SF Bay.	Huimens and Huchiuns offer friendship and curiosity.
1776	March-April. Anza explores Peninsula, East Bay, and northern San Joaquin Valley.	Peninsula villagers compete for Spanish attention, Yrgins show fear, Chupcans anger.

The Portolá Expedition, 1769

On a fall day in 1769, the Quirostes of Mitenne village at Point Año Nuevo on the Pacific Coast south of San Francisco Bay encountered a scouting party from the Spanish expedition commanded by Gaspár de Portolá. This was the first recorded meeting between San Francisco Bay region tribal people and European horsemen, although Coastal Central California people to the north and south had been visited by European ships prior to 1769.[1] On the day following their initial encounter with the horsemen, October 23, the people of Mitenne welcomed the full sixty-four-man Portolá party to their village. Spanish diarist Juan Crespí wrote:

> Here we stopped close to a large village of very well-behaved good heathens, who greeted us with loud cheers and rejoiced greatly at our coming.... These heathens presented us with a great many large black and white-colored tamales; the white tamales were made of acorns, and they said the black-colored ones were very good too. They brought two or three bags of the wild tobacco they use, and our people took all they wanted of it.... They almost all carry tall red-colored staffs, some with many feathers; they presented four of these staffs to Sergeant Don Francisco Ortega, who was the one they knew best because he had been the one who had explored this place with other soldiers (Crespí [1769] 1969:88).

Over the next few days the Spanish party continued north up the coast, through the lands of the Oljon, Cotegen, and Chiguan tribes (see Map 3).

All along the way local guides introduced them to the next people ahead (Crespí [1769] 1969:88-96). At San Gregorio Creek the Oljons were happy to greet and aid the Spaniards, as Crespí reported:

> As soon as we had reached this place...the whole of the big village here came over, all of them very well-behaved, fair, and well-bearded heathens, who received us with much kindness and pleasure.... They brought us large shares of big dark-colored tamales they make from their grass-seeds, and the soldiers said they were very good and rich when used in atole-mush. They were with us during almost all the time we spent here, very happy and friendly, bringing a new lot of

---

[1] The Pacific Ocean had been a Spanish lake for over two hundred years. Juan Rodríguez Cabrillo sailed north along the coast almost as far as Monterey Bay in 1542 (Bancroft 1884:76), and Francis Drake careened thirty miles north of the Golden Gate at Point Reyes for a number of weeks in 1579 (Bancroft 1884:82-94; Heizer 1974b). Sebastian Rodríguez de Cermeño visited the Pt. Reyes area in 1595 (Bancroft 1884:96; Meighan and Heizer 1952). Manila galleons annually sighted Cape Mendocino before heading south on their return voyages to Acapulco during the seventeenth and eighteenth centuries (Galvin 1971:2).

Foreign Incursions, 1769-1776

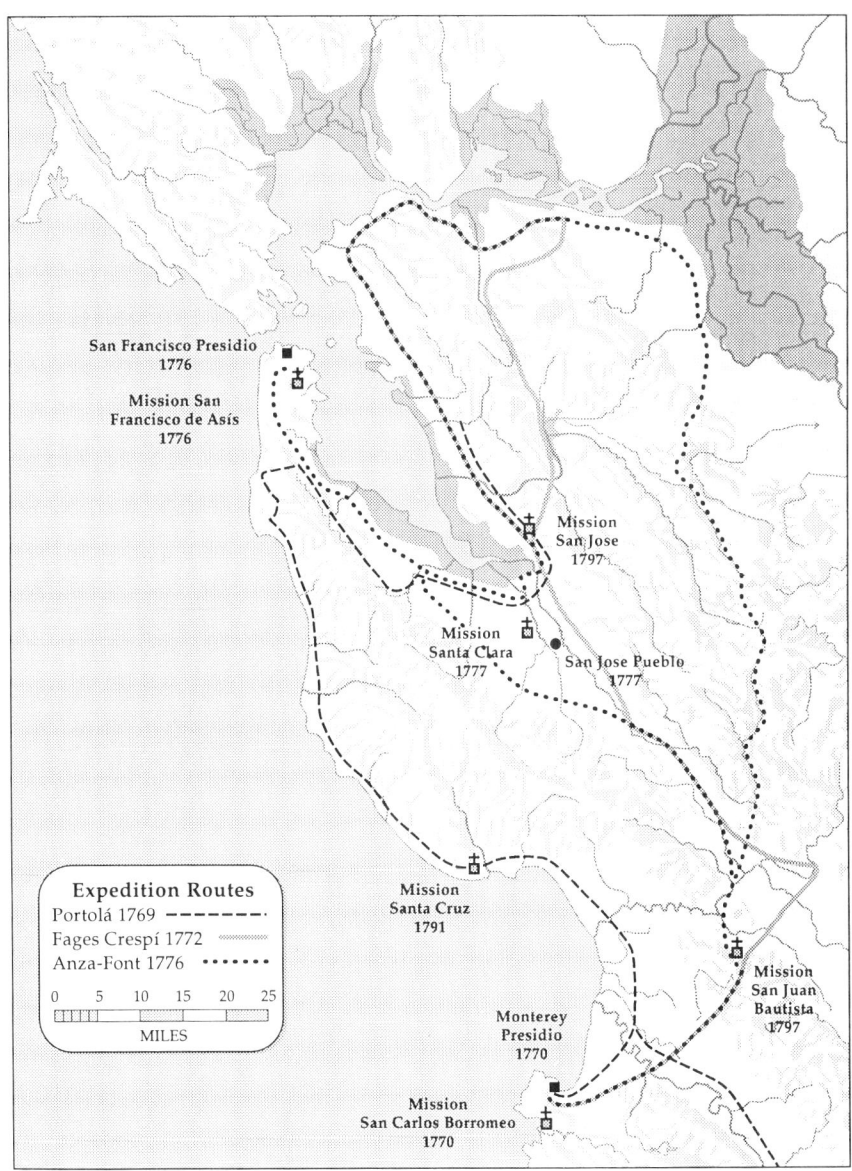

Map 3. Routes of three key Spanish incursions into the San Francisco Bay Area between 1769 and 1776, as well as the locations of Spanish settlements through 1810.

tamales again at every meal-time. Here the soldiers' pease ran out, leaving them with nothing but tortilla (Crespí [1769] 1969:90-91).

On November 4, the Portolá party crossed the Coast Range ridge and camped near the shore of San Francisco Bay in a valley claimed by the Ssalsons. The next morning Ssalson men brought them "dark-colored tamales and a sort of cherries, very fresh" (Crespí [1769] 1969:101). These men, as well as others from Ssalson and Lamchin villages, invited the Spaniards to come feast at their villages, only to have the strange expedition pass them by:

> We shortly saw a throng of heathens coming out of the mountains in a file: we counted forty-some men with bows and arrows, some having staffs painted with many colors, all hung with large bunches of feathers like wreaths hanging from them, and two of the heathens were laden with two very large rush baskets; they all came out upon the way in front of us.... They were insistent we should go to their village. At last after some time we took our leave (Crespí [1769] 1969:103).

As the newcomers continued south toward the Puichon towns, they were intercepted by still other people eager for them to come to their villages:

> On our going a short way two other heathens from another village came out to meet us and were also vehement that we should go to their village, which they gave us to understand was in that neighborhood. The governor gave them to understand we could not, that we had to go on, that if they wished they might visit us where we were going to camp. They were sorry for this, and left us, plainly offended that we would not go with them (Crespí [1769] 1969:103).

The offended people were probably Olpens from an area westward of the Spaniards' route.

The Portolá party camped on the bayshore plain, near three Puichon villages, from November 7 until November 12. The Puichons were delighted, but scouts sent out from the Portolá camp were not welcomed by people from unidentifiable tribes on the eastern shore of San Francisco Bay:

> They had met many heathens, but they seem wild and rude upon the other side of the estuary and would pay no attention to anything; they had spent about an hour stopping with one

heathen in order to pacify him; and if they gave any of them anything, either they would not take it, or if they did it was only to throw it away at once (Crespí [1769] 1969:106).

The San Francisco Peninsula groups all had plenty of advance notice of the approaching strangers, but it is possible that the East Bay people had no such warning, and the sudden appearance of strange men on horseback could have been alarming.

The East Bay people were not the first to react to the Portolá party with fear. A month earlier Portolá's scouts had frightened people at a Calendaruc village on the Pajaro River on Monterey Bay:

> These Indians had no notice of our coming to their lands, as was seen by the consternation and terror their presence caused among them: for some, amazed and confounded, scarce knowing what they did, ran to their weapons; others shouted and cried out; the women dissolved into tears. Our people did all they could to quiet them, and the sergeant of Loreto Presidio, who was in charge of the party, managed it with great difficulty by getting down from his mount and approaching them with signs of peace (Costansó [1769] 1969:73).

When the full Portolá expedition arrived at the Monterey Bay village two days later they found it abandoned.

The horse was the most incredible of all the curious and disturbing aspects of the invaders. The Rumsens at Mission San Carlos Borromeo on the Monterey Peninsula told the missionary Junípero Serra about his people's initial reaction to Spaniards and their horses:

> He asked him if he or his fellow countrymen, when they saw the officers and soldiers, had ever imagined a country where everybody wore clothes, etc.?

> He answered no, that they thought all countries were like their own. As regards the soldiers and the Fathers, after carefully looking them over, they had come to the conclusion that they were the sons of the mules on which they rode (Serra [1748-1784] 1955-56:2:87).

Much later, in 1827, the American trapper Jedediah Smith described a similar reaction to his horses in a first-contact situation in the northern Sacramento Valley, one hundred miles north of the Golden Gate:

Many Indians came as near the camp as I would permit and sat down. I gave them some presents.... They were under the impression that the horses could understand them and when they were passing they talked to them and made signs as to the men (Smith [1827] 1934:76-77).

Without doubt horses were initially the most intimidating symbol of the Spaniards' extraordinary, possibly supernatural, power.

The Portolá expedition left the Bay Area on November 12, 1769, retracing its route many hundreds of miles south to San Diego Bay. They completed the journey successfully, without deaths due to scurvy or starvation, only because they had been fed by the people of the San Francisco Peninsula (Bancroft 1884:155-162).

The Fages Parties, 1770, 1772

In 1770, the Spaniards established a town and mission on Monterey Bay, some eighty miles south of the Golden Gate. From Monterey they sent more exploratory parties north to San Francisco Bay, through an inland route up the Santa Clara Valley. The Matalans and Tamiens of the Santa Clara Valley first encountered the mounted Spaniards in November of 1770. Party leader Fages kept no record concerning these encounters, and mentioned native people only once in his brief diary of the journey:

> Up close to the lake we saw many friendly good-humored heathens, to whom we made a present of some strings of beads, and they responded with feathers and geese stuffed with grass, which they avail themselves of to take countless numbers of these birds (Fages [1770] 1969:119).

The goose hunters were Tuibuns at a lake on the Fremont Plain just south of Alameda Creek. The Spaniards went through their lands twice, first as they went north along the east shore of San Francisco Bay to the plain opposite the Golden Gate (presently North Oakland), and then again on their return.

In March of 1772, Pedro Fages again came up through the Santa Clara Valley into the East Bay. This time his party continued northward and eastward into the interior (see Map 3, page 33). Huchiuns on the southeast shore of San Pablo Bay received the alien visitors with great joy, as diarist Juan Crespí noted:

> We found a good village of heathen, very fair and bearded, who did not know what to do, they were so happy to see us in

their village. They gave us many cacomites, amoles, and two
dead geese, dried and stuffed with grass.... We returned the
gift with beads, for which they were very grateful, and some
of them went with us to another village near by (Crespí [1772]
1927:291).

All along the Carquinez Strait Huchiun-Aguastos and Carquins harvesting the spring salmon run welcomed the Spaniards:

On the banks of the other side we made out many villages,
whose Indians called to us and invited us to go to their
country, but we were prevented by a stretch of water about a
quarter of a league wide; and many of them, seeing that we
were going away, came to this side, crossing over on rafts,
and gave us some of their wild food (Crespí [1772] 1927:293).

The Chupcan people of the Diablo Valley first encountered the strangers on the following day, March 30, 1772:

As soon as we entered this valley four heathen shouted at us,
making signs that we should go and receive a bow trimmed
with feathers, the pelt of an animal, and arrows which they
had thrust into the ground. The captain went forward with a
soldier and received their present, returning it with beads,
with which they were well pleased (Crespí [1772] 1927:294-
295).

The Tatcans of the San Ramon Valley, southern neighbors of the Chupcans, may have been surprised by the approaching horsemen: "As soon as the heathen caught sight of us they ran away, shouting and panic-stricken without knowing what had happened" (Crespí [1772] 1927:298).

After leaving Tatcan lands, the Fages party of 1772 continued south, through the Livermore, Sunol, and Santa Clara valleys and on to Monterey, passing villages of friendly people along the way.

The Rivera Expedition, 1774

Bay Area tribes were left undisturbed from April, 1772 until the fall of 1774. During that two and one half-year period Spanish troops and Christian missionaries worked on the new presidio at Monterey Bay and on Mission San Carlos Borromeo on the nearby Carmel River. The Monterey Peninsula is some forty miles south of the Santa Clara Valley, just beyond the direct spheres of social interaction of the southernmost Bay Region tribes. However, indirect news about the Spanish settlements must have arrived in the Bay Region, passed northward from village to village.

In the late fall of 1774, a group of Matalan hunters in the upper Santa Clara Valley encountered a group of mounted Spaniards under the command of Captain Fernando Rivera y Moncada:

> We passed a patch of willows and cottonwoods, and now found running water in the creek. Here all at once there were heathens standing with their weapons in hand, [though] they made no show of them. In people such as these, who have no knowledge of others and live like wild beasts at bay, it is second nature to snatch them up (Rivera y Moncada [1774] 1969:133).

Rivera's expedition was looking for possible locations for a mission and military base on the San Francisco Peninsula. The party was not warmly received by hunters further along in the western Santa Clara Valley:

> In a little grove of those trees, about one in the afternoon, we came to three heathen with bows and arrows. Apparently they had been hunting, for we did not see in all that vicinity either villages or smokes, although on the plain we came across many well-beaten paths.... We passed not far from them and I called to them, but they did not wish to come near, even though I showed them some beads, but they made signs that I should throw them, which I did, but not even then did they approach. Seeing this, the commander alighted, took the beads, and gave them to them; we then went on our way, leaving them at their work (Palóu [1773-1783] 1926:3:262).

The Puichons on San Francisquito Creek, on the other hand, received the Rivera party warmly. On November 29, the Spanish party left them and continued north through Lamchin and Ssalson lands. Rivera distributed glass beads, ribbons, and tobacco to local captains all along the route (Palóu [1774] 1969:133-146):

> The chiefs would invite us to remain, but we left them with their wishes and happy over the beads, and continued onward; though they kept following us in bands from village to village, very happy and well-pleased (Palóu [1774] 1969:137).

Despite the warm welcome, Rivera noted an underlying apprehension on the part of the local men, who always kept the Spanish troops to their left side as they walked:

> So natural in man is the desire to have the advantage, that, as I have just now been observing of these savages accompanying us, they keep us always on their left-hand or bow side (Rivera y Moncada [1774] 1969:138).

In the event of trouble, right-handed men could most quickly aim their arrows toward people to their left.

Some insights into eighteenth century Franciscan methods of attracting followers from among native peoples emerges from Francisco Palóu's diary of this 1774 expedition:

> On the road a boy separated from them and approached me. He was a youth of about twenty years, of a reddish complexion, well-favored, with a little beard, and his face stained with ocher. He followed us the whole way through the valley, without leaving my side, and I noticed that he began to cry. When I asked him why he was crying he answered me, but I could not understand what he said, but I noticed that he put his hand on his breast and looked at me very tenderly, making signs that he would go with me....
>
> Every day we were in the neighborhood of his village he did not fail to come to visit us and bring others with him, with such demonstrations of confidence that as soon as he arrived he drew near me, and lifting my habit, covered himself with it, saying "Me Apam" "Thou art my father," which is the same word as those of Monterey use.... I told him I would return to live with them and would make him my son, showing him what was necessary for him to be this and to save his soul. It seemed to me that he understood, and showed signs of pleasure (Palóu [1773-1783] 1926:3:271-272).

This young man's fascination with Father Palóu illustrates how variable individual reactions were to the foreigners. Teenagers were especially likely to be in awe of the newcomers.

Francisco Palóu was devoted to helping Indian people achieve progress—as western society defined it—in ethical and material culture. Palóu, who had been a missionary in the Serra Gorda range of Mexico from 1750 through 1758, understood the value of material items in attracting converts. While among the Ssalsons Palóu wrote:

> I gave them presents of beads, and they ate of our food. I noticed that they took a special liking to the beans, and I took this opportunity to tell them that in our country we had these good seeds, and the kind from which the biscuit, better than theirs, is made; that I would return to live with them and would plant these seeds, and they would gather them in great abundance. I thought they understood me and were well pleased, for they replied that they would all get together and build their houses (Palóu [1773-1783] 1926:3:274).

Palóu knew that young adults were especially impressionable, and that parents were pleased by kind treatment toward their children. At a coastal Cotegen village during the return trip to Monterey he wrote:

> The heathen came with their present of some very large baskets of thick porridge.... Among them came a boy about twelve years old, son of the chief, whom I pleased with beads and other little gifts, with which his father seemed to be gratified, and the commander did the same (Palóu [1773-1783] 1926:3:290).

The Cotegens tried to guide the Rivera party inland to a village where a feast had been planned, but the Spaniards hurried south along the coast without heeding the invitation (Palóu [1773-1783] 1926:3:291-293).

The Ship San Carlos, 1775

On the morning of August 6, 1775, some Huimens at the southern tip of the Marin Peninsula discovered an alien boat and crew in the Bay. The Spanish naval vessel *San Carlos* had entered San Francisco Bay by moonlight the previous night and the ship's longboat crew was sounding the harbor near the town of Livaneglua for an anchorage:

> At this cove...there is a ranchería of Indians, who came out from their huts shouting and gesticulating to our men to come ashore. With the intention of taking soundings our men went a short way toward land, and on seeing this the Indians set up at the shore's edge a pole with a bunch of feathers at the top.

> Not being instructed to respond, our men kept well away; but the Indians, no doubt thinking it was mistrust that made them do so, sought to lessen it by throwing their bows to the ground and, first waving them round in the air, sticking all their arrows in the sand (Ayala [1775] 1971:81).

The *San Carlos* was a 193-ton two-masted brig, 58 feet in length. The thirty-man crew under Lieutenant Juan Manuel de Ayala had been ordered to chart the extensive estuary of San Francisco Bay. As the longboat crew continued to make soundings on that first day, three Huimen men ran to a steep point of land on shore:

> One of them, with high and rapid utterance and animated gestures, made a long harangue, directing it to our men. With a spyglass we saw them coming armed with bow and arrow, their bodies quite bare and coloured with a sort of dye that closely approached silver in hue. They were almost all the forenoon going from one place to another in hopes that the boat would come there, at times resting on their haunches and at other times moving from one part of the hill to another....
>
> The longboat set out a third time to approach the steep rock face of that same hill, so near as to inspect its point. The armed Indians, on seeing our men close by, hid themselves (perhaps in fear) among what oak trees they could find that would give them cover (Santa María [1775] 1971:21).

The *San Carlos* anchored between Richardson Bay and Angel Island, just across the channel from the present city of San Francisco (see Map 1, page 15). In the late afternoon a group of Huimen men came to the hill nearest the anchored ship:

> There appeared on a hill quite near us six Indians, among whom came two with sticks, doubtless in the nature of truncheons, which they carried to distinguish them from their retinue. One of these two made signs to the others to sit. He himself, standing, and shouting as loudly as he could and still speak clearly, was a long time holding forth to us. He seemed, from the manner of his delivery, to be telling us of their wanting us to meet them; and then he made signs for us to come ashore. No reply to match his impassioned plea was forthcoming, although from the ship we made answer with

signs that must have been more comprehensible to them than their strange speech was to us (Santa María [1775] 1971:23).

Again the longboat of the *San Carlos* set out to take soundings. Thinking that the boat was coming to visit them, the men came down to the shore, where they were joined by others returning from their village who were carrying heavy objects as gifts. The longboat failed to land and accept the items, so they left them on the shore and went home.

Near the end of the first day, Lieutenant Ayala went ashore and collected the gifts:

> This was a basketful of pinole (who knows of what seed?), some bunches of strings of woven hair, some of flat strips of tule, rather like aprons, and a sort of hairnet for the head, made of their hair, in design and shape best described as like a horse's girth, though neater and decorated at intervals with very small white snailshells (Santa María [1775] 1971:25).

Prior to the summer of 1775, Spanish exploration of San Francisco Bay had been limited to land expeditions in the southern area, the San Francisco Peninsula, and the East Bay area. The *San Carlos* stayed in the vicinity of Richardson Bay and Angel Island for a month while its longboat sounded the estuary northward into San Pablo Bay and eastward to Suisun Bay. Diaries of Lieutenant Ayala, first sailing master José Cañizares, and chaplain Vicente Santa María document a series of cordial, sometimes formal, interactions between Spaniards and the members of various local sovereign polities (Galvin 1971).

In the afternoon of the second day of the *San Carlos*' visit, a group of nine Huimens, three older men and six young men, came down to the shore. Chaplain Santa María went ashore to meet them, along with the sailing master, surgeon, and some armed sailors:

> As we came near the shore, we wondered much to see Indians, lords of these coasts, quite weaponless and obedient to our least sign to them to sit down, doing just as they were bid. There remained standing only one of the eldest, who mutely made clear to us with what entire confidence we should come ashore to receive a new offering which they had prepared for us at the shore's edge.

> Keeping watch all round to see if among the hills any treachery were afoot, we came in slowly, and when we thought ourselves safe we went ashore, the first sailing master in the lead. There came forward to greet him the oldest Indian offering him at the end of a stick a string of beads like a rosary, made up of white shells interspersed with black knots in the thread on which they were strung (Santa María [1775] 1971:29).

Any native Central Californian would have recognized the shell-festooned invitation string, which was knotted to indicate the number of days until an upcoming festival.

The Huimen captain led the foreigners over to the place where some baskets of food had been made ready. The ship's sailing master handed out some earrings and glass beads to the local men. Santa María wrote:

> It would have seemed natural that these Indians, in their astonishment at our clothes, should have expressed a particular surprise, and no less curiosity; but they gave no sign of it. Only one of the older Indians showed himself a little unmannerly toward me; seeing that I was a thick-bearded man, he began touching the whiskers as if in surprise that I had not shaved long since (Santa María [1775] 1971:31).

The young men looked to their elders for clues about proper behavior in this unprecedented situation:

> We noticed an unusual thing about the young men: none of them ventured to speak and only their elders replied to us. They were so obedient that, notwithstanding we pressed them to do so, they dared not stir a step unless one of the old men told them to; so meek that, even though curiosity prompted them, they did not raise their eyes from the ground; so docile that when my companions did me reverence by touching their lips to my sleeve and then by signs told them to do the same thing, they at once and with good grace did as they were bid (Santa María [1775] 1971:31-33).

The Huimen world was replete with rules governing correct behavior, rules whose breakage might bring disaster. The fact that one older man chided Santa María for failing to pluck his beard, however, suggests that their obedient cooperation resulted from courtesy and goodwill rather than awe. On the evening of the fourth day, August 9, the people of the nearest Huimen village found themselves being approached by a small group of the Spaniards:

> As soon as the Indians saw that we were near their huts, all the men stood forward as if in defense of their women and children, whom undoubtedly they regard as their treasure and their heart's core. They may have thought, though not expressing this openly to us, that we might do their dear ones harm; if so, their action was most praiseworthy.
>
> We were now almost at the ranchería. As we were going to be there a while, an Indian hustled up some clean herbage for us to sit on, made with it a modest carpet, and had us sit on it. The Indians sat on the bare ground, thus giving us to understand in some degree how guests should be received (Santa María [1775] 1971:41-43).

Santa María gave a religious lecture and sang part of a hymn, but was interrupted when people brought out some hot food. Later they gave out glass beads. Then, "as they saw that the moon was rising they made signs to us to withdraw, which we then did" (Santa María [1775] 1971:45).

On August 13, a group of men from a more distant village came to see the Spanish ship. They watched the ship from a hill until Father Santa María and some others took a boat to shore. Climbing the hill, Santa María came upon six men:

> Although at first they refused to join us, nevertheless, when we had called to them and made signs of good will and friendly regard, they gradually came near. I desired them to sit down, that I might have the brief pleasure of handing out to them the glass beads and other little gifts I had the foresight to carry in my sleeves. Throughout this interval they were in a happy frame of mind and made me hang in their ears, which they had pierced, the strings of glass beads that I had divided among them. When I had given them this pleasure, I took it into my head to pull out my snuffbox and take a pinch; but the moment the eldest of the Indians saw me open the box he took fright and showed that he was upset. In spite of all my efforts I couldn't calm him. He fled along the trail, and so did all his companions, leaving us alone on the ridge (Santa María [1775] 1971:47).

It is likely that the men fled in fear because they thought the small closed snuff box contained poisons such as those stored by sorcerers in bone tubes.

The *San Carlos* was moved one mile east to Ayala Cove on the north side of Angel Island on August 13. On August 15, the ship's longboat was sent out to chart San Pablo Bay. The Huchiun-Aguastos, who had been visited by the Fages-Crespí party three years earlier, saw the longboat on the bay. A group of fifty-seven people came down to meet it when it landed, and Sailing Master Jose Cañizares reported:

> There was in authority over all those Indians one whose kingly presence marked his eminence above the rest. Our men made a landing, and when they had done so the Indian chief addressed a long speech to them. He would not permit them to sit on the bare earth; some Indians were at once sent by the *themi* (which in our language means "head man") to bring some mats cleanly and carefully woven from rushes (Santa María [1775] 1971:51).

An elaborate feast was prepared for Cañizares's crew:

> Right away came atoles, pinoles, and the cooked fishes, refreshment that quieted their pangs of hunger and tickled their palates too. The pinoles were made from a seed that left me with a taste like that of toasted hazelnuts. Two kinds of atole were supplied at this meal, one lead colored and the other very white, which one might think to have been made from acorns. Both were well flavored and in no way disagreeable to a palate little accustomed to atoles (Santa María [1775] 1971:53).

When a much larger contingent of armed local men arrived from more distant villages, the Cañizares group experienced a moment of alarm:

> Fear obliged the sailing master to make known by signs to the Indian chieftain the misgivings they had in the presence of so many armed tribesmen. The *themi*, understanding what was meant, at once directed the Indians to loosen their bows and put up all their arrows, and they were prompted to obey (Santa María [1775] 1971:51-53).

The people of the San Pablo Bay village told Cañizares that they had previously "seen similar men, even on horseback," certainly the Fages-Crespí expedition of 1772 (Santa María [1775] 1971:51-55). Cañizares, who visited the Huchiun-Aguastos four times between August 15 and August 21, received the impression that the people wanted his men to come and live with them (Santa María [1775] 1971:55).

After they watched the *San Carlos* move from Richardson Bay to Angel Island on August 13, the Huimens stayed away from the opposite shore for nine days. Finally, on August 23, some Huimen men decided to venture on board the ship, for that morning two tule boats came out bringing four Huimen men and another man unknown to the Spaniards:

> Leaving their boats, they climbed aboard quite fearlessly. They were in great delight, marvelling at the structure of the ship, their eyes fixed most of all on the rigging. They wondered no less at the lambs, hens, and pigeons that were providently kept to meet our needs if someone on board should fall sick. But what most captivated and pleased them was the sound of the ship's bell, which was purposely ordered to be struck so we could see what effect it had on ears that had never heard it. It pleased the Indians so much that while they were on board they went up to it from time to time to sound it themselves. They brought us, as on other occasions, gifts of pinoles, and they even remembered men's names that we had made known to them earlier (Santa María [1775] 1971:59).

Although the first tongue of the Huimens was Coast Miwok, they communicated with the Spaniards on the *San Carlos* in the Costanoan language of their neighbors to the east and south (Santa María [1775] 1971:59). They were probably a multilingual people who spoke Costanoan in response to Spanish sailors who had learned Costanoan phrases at Monterey.

The man who had accompanied the Huimens to the ship that day was from a Costanoan-speaking tribe to the east, the Huchiun; he soon left the ship for his home area:

> They brought among their party an Indian we had not seen before. Soon after receiving our greetings he went away alone in his boat, leaving in another direction than the one they had taken (Santa María [1775] 1971:59).

The main party of Huimens left the ship at midday. They came back at seven o'clock the next morning, August 24, just as Father Santa María was about to say the morning prayer prior to celebrating Mass:

> I made signs to them to wait for me until I should be through and those who occupied the cabin should get up; but they couldn't hold their expectations in suspense so long, for while I was at my prayers in the roundhouse the Indian chieftain, seeing that I was putting them off, began calling the surgeon by his name and saying to me, "Santa María, Vicente, Father, *ilac*," which means "Come here"; and seeing that the surgeon did not leave his bunk, and that I did not come down, he came up to where I was reciting my prayers and, placing himself at my side on his kneecaps, began to imitate me in my manner of praying, so that I could not keep from laughing; and seeing that if the Indian should continue I would not be getting on with my duty, I made signs to him to go back down and wait for me there. He obeyed at once, but it was to set out in his boat with a chieftain, not known to us before, whom he had brought to the ship, and as if offended he left behind the daily offering of pinoles (Santa María [1775] 1971:61).

The Bay Region men were clearly not in awe of the Spaniards. They expected courteous conduct on the part of their visitors, but hard feelings arose due to conflicting definitions of courtesy.

Later, on the morning of August 24, just two and one-half hours after the first group left in anger, two other tule boats came alongside the *San Carlos*. The eight new visitors, Huchiuns from the East Bay area, opened the visit with a formal ritual:

> One of them, who doubtless came to the bow of his boat for the purpose, began to make a long speech, giving us to understand that it was the head man of the ranchería who came, and that he was at our service. This visit was not a casual one, for all of them appeared to have got themselves up, each as best he could, for a festive occasion. Some had adorned their heads with a tuft of re-dyed feathers, and others with a garland of them mixed with black ones. Their chests were covered with a sort of woven jacket made with ash-coloured feathers; and the rest of their bodies, though bare, was all worked over with various designs in charcoal and red ocher, presenting a droll sight (Santa María [1775] 1971:63).

Upon boarding the ship, the Huchiun men orchestrated a formal ceremony which seems to have symbolized intergroup solidarity:

> It was made clear to them who it was that commanded the ship, and they endeavoured to point out their leader to us. The chieftain of the ranchería had all his men, one after another, in the order of their importance, salute our captain; and when this ceremony was completed he begged us all to sit down, as the Indians also did, for distribution among us of their offering, which they brought to us in all tidiness. All being in their places in due order, the second chieftain, who was among the company, asked of another Indian a container made of reeds that he carried with him, in which were many pats or small cakes of pinole. It was given him, and having placed it beside him he indicated that he was to be listened to. With no lack of self-composure he spoke for quite a while, and then, opening the container, handed the pinole cakes to the first chieftain, who as soon as he received them handed them to our captain, making signs to him to distribute them among all the men of the ship, insisting, moreover, that he be the first to taste the pinole. The second chieftain was now very watchful to see if by chance anyone of the ship's company had missed partaking of the bread of hospitality [*pan bendito*]; he went up to the roundhouse, and several times stuck his head in the after hold; there was no limit to his painstaking inspection. After this our captain directed the steward to bring some pieces of pilot bread and gave them to the Indian head man, who distributed them with all formality among his party (Santa María [1775] 1971:63).

This ritual indicates that the Huchiun men considered the occasion to be a diplomatic contact between equals. The priest Santa María later shared what he considered to be his most valuable gift:

> We gave them glass beads and other little gifts, which they put in their reed container. This done, I brought out a representation of our holy father St. Francis, most edifying, and upon my presenting it to the Indians to kiss they did so with so much veneration, to all appearances, and willingness, that they stole my heart and the hearts of all who observed them (Santa María [1775] 1971:63).

That the Huchiuns were willing to act respectfully towards an object sacred to the Spaniards, people they clearly considered their equals, suggests that they considered that the Spanish ritual objects were likely to be responsible for the impressive material wealth which they saw all around them on the ship.

During the afternoon of August 24, 1775, the eight Huchiun men sat on the beach at Angel Island with Vicente Santa María, the Franciscan priest, sharing the sacred songs of the two cultures:

> They all crowded around me and, sitting by me, began to sing, with an accompaniment of two rattles that they had brought with them. As they finished the song all of them were shedding tears, which I wondered at for not knowing the reason. When they were through singing they handed me the rattles and by signs asked me also to sing. I took the rattles and, to please them, began to sing to them the "Alabado" (although they would not understand it), to which they were most attentive and indicated that it pleased them (Santa María [1775] 1971:67).

On the following morning, August 25, the same group of Huchiun men came back on board the *San Carlos*. Santa María wrote that the ship's crew spent some time learning their Costanoan words and writing them down. Santa María also wrote down the names of the men.

> Their chieftain was called *Sumu*; the second chieftain, *Jausos*; the others, *Supitacse* (1); *Tilacse* (2); *Mutuc* (3); *Logeacse* (4); *Guecpostole* (5); *Xacacse* (6) (Santa María [1775] 1971:67).

Twenty years later, four of those men would move from their East Bay villages to a Franciscan mission at San Francisco (see page 131).

Santa María's diary indicates that rivalry, even jealousy, was developing among the tribal people as the days passed. While the Huchiuns were still on the ship, some of the Huimens came on board:

> Soon after these Indians came to the ship there came eight others of our new friends, and at first it appeared that those of the one and the other ranchería did not look on each other with much friendliness, but our treating them all as equals made them friends and on speaking terms with one another (Santa María [1775] 1971:69).

With a truce in place, Santa María proceeded to teach everyone how to cross themselves. He remarked that "those under Sumu's command were better disposed toward these pious observances" (Santa María [1775] 1971:69).

Individual variations in personality, differences in curiosity, and a willingness to experiment, are bound to have an effect on the initial interactions between cultural groups.

The *San Carlos* remained at Ayala Cove until September 7. From August 23 onward, Indians in tule boats visited the ship every day, presumably from villages throughout the central San Francisco Bay region (Ayala [1775] 1971:84; Santa María [1775] 1971:61), but no more specific details were provided about the interactions. On September 7, with the charting of the estuary completed, the *San Carlos* hoisted sail to move to the Golden Gate. The rudder was damaged while the ship was attempting to lay in near Horseshoe Cove to await better weather outside the Gate, so it remained at the cove on the southern tip of the Marin Peninsula for another eleven days while repairs were made.

On September 11, Santa María made his second and final visit to a local village. Accompanied by a number of local people, a sailor, and the ship's surgeon, he walked the mile and a half to Livangelua, the main Huimen village:

> Our reception was such that on our approach all the Indian men and women living there came out and the *themi*, or head man, putting his arms over my shoulders, steered me to a council house in the middle of the ranchería. As soon as we reached the entrance, he made signs for me to go in first, then the surgeon and the sailor who had come with me. On going in by the small entranceway I said, "Ave Maria," whereupon five old Indians who were there said "Piré, piré," which means "Sit down, sit down." We sat down, and then all the Indians came in. After making the customary speech, I began handing out glass beads to all of them, which they received with much pleasure. While I was making this distribution, there came in three old women (who among them would sum up three hundred and fifty years), each with her little basket of pinole for us to eat; later they brought us water, which we drank (Santa María [1775] 1971:73).

The three old women were probably not over one hundred years old, but the point is well made that the village population included others beside children and young adults.

Santa María's final remarks underscore the good relationship between the Huimens and the crew of the *San Carlos* during the summer of 1775, while hinting at an inequality in their expectations for the future:

After this social affair, I set to inquiring their names and writing them down on paper. This gave them great amusement; for when I had finished, a number of them kept coming up and asking me how the names were spoken, and as I answered according to the paper they gave way to bursts of laughter. Thus we enjoyed ourselves that afternoon until we took our leave. The head man of this ranchería comported himself so politely that he came out with one arm around me and the other around the surgeon and went with us a part of the way until, taking leave of us, he went back to his ranchería and we returned to the ship, which was more than half a league distant. This is the manner in which these unfortunates have behaved toward us. What is certain is that they themselves seem to be asking a start at entering within the fold of our Catholic religion. Not to avail of this opportunity would be a lamentable misfortune (Santa María [1775] 1971:73).

The *San Carlos* sailed south to Monterey on September 18, 1775.[2]

Five days after the *San Carlos* left San Francisco Bay, on September 23, 1775, a fifteen-man Spanish land party arrived at the Golden Gate to provide help in the charting of the Bay. Finding that the *San Carlos* had sailed, the land party immediately returned to Monterey. Diarist Francisco Palóu had only the following brief comment to make regarding native peoples:

We returned to Monterey by the same road, not having suffered either in going or coming the least annoyance from the heathen, whom we found very peaceable and friendly, presenting to us their rude gifts of mussels and seeds, which were reciprocated with beads and some of our food (Paloú [1773-1783] 1926:4:43).

---

[2] The *San Carlos* was one of three Spanish naval vessels that were exploring the Pacific Coast in the summer of 1775. Another of the ships, the schooner *Sonora*, entered Bodega Bay to the north of the Marin Peninsula on October 3, 1775. The Bodega Bay people came out to a low hill near the ship's anchorage, from which they made speeches to the Spaniards on the ship for two hours. Finally, two men came alongside the ship in a tule boat and presented the Spaniards with feather ornaments, necklaces (*collares de hueso*, probably clam shell disk bead necklaces), and a basket of seed meal. In return, Captain Juan Francisco de la Bodega y Cuadra gave them handkerchiefs, mirrors, and glass beads. The *Sonora* sailed south to Monterey the following day (Campa [1775] 1943:130).

The Anza Expedition, 1776

In the spring of 1776, Spanish Army Colonel Juan Bautista de Anza led a group north from Monterey into the Bay Region to choose the precise sites for a military base and a mission (see Map 3, page 33). His group included Franciscan priest Pedro Font, eleven soldiers, and seven servants and muleteers. The diaries of the expedition indicate that by 1776 the local people were becoming increasingly familiar with the Spaniards and, in at least two places, increasingly antagonistic.

Matalan people of the southern Santa Clara Valley met the Anza party on March 25, 1776, and reacted with annoyance when the Spaniards did not stop with them:

> On seeing us they shouted amongst the oaks and then came out naked like fauns, running and shouting and making many gestures, as if they wished to stop us, and signaling to us that we must not go forward. Although they came armed with bows and arrows, they committed no hostility toward us.... Their method was to run, one behind the other in single file, until they got ahead of us, and then, halting, they began to shout and even to shriek, making many gestures and signs as if they were angry and did not wish us to go forward. Then, seeing that we continued on our way, without paying any attention to them, they again started to run to get ahead of us. Then they went through the same performance...although we understood nothing of what they said. And so they continued for about a league, when all but a few of them went away, then, finally, little by little even these left us and we saw them no more (Font [1776] 1930:323-324).

The Anza party was the fifth Spanish group to pass through Matalan lands since 1770. The Matalans were probably tired of the foreigners wandering through their lands without even stopping to acknowledge them, let alone exchange gifts and receive formal permission to cross through.

Some kind of war was going on in the spring of 1776 on the San Francisco Peninsula, possibly between the Lamchin and the Ssalson, for at Laurel Creek (in the present town of Belmont) Font wrote:

> We went still a little farther and came to a small village, from which came out several Indian men and women. The commander presented them with glass beads, and we stopped a little while with them. One of them was wounded in the leg by

> an arrow, and another stood with his bow and arrows making signs and gestures as if he were fighting, and pointing out the wound. From this we inferred that he was telling us how they were at war with other villages ahead, and was trying to persuade us not to go there because they were very warlike (Font [1776] 1930:328).

The twenty explorers continued north from that northernmost Lamchin village. They passed a Ssalson village on San Mateo Creek and camped about two and a half miles further northwest near another small village:

> At sunset some Indians were sighted on a hill. Then others came out and the first ones ran and afterwards came to the camp, and according to the signs which they made with their bows and arrows it seems that they wished to tell us that the others were hostile, but that we need not be afraid because they had already chased them away. These Indians were very friendly with us, and it seemed to me that they were saying that we must stay there.... At nightfall we bid them all goodbye (Font [1776] 1930:329).

There was no further discussion of this antagonism in the diaries of the Anza party.

On the following day, March 27, Anza entered the district of Yelamu, an area populated by about 160 people (and an area where the city of San Francisco, with hundreds of thousands of people, would eventually be located). Two local Yelamu men came to the Spanish camp at Mountain Lake:

> They were attentive and obsequious and brought us firewood. They remained at camp a while, but when the commander gave them glass beads they departed (Font [1776] 1930:333).

The Spanish party explored the entire San Francisco vicinity, including the village of Chutchui on Mission Creek, a hamlet of some sixty inhabitants.

The Anza party next retraced their steps down the Peninsula, then turned eastward across a part of the Santa Clara Valley that had not been traversed by the earlier Spanish expeditions. At a village of about one hundred people on Stevens Creek, they gave out beads to allay peoples' fear. One old woman, perhaps a shaman, reacted to the invaders as if they were spirit beings:

> One of the women, from the time when she first saw us until we departed, stood at the door of her hut making gestures like crosses and drawing lines on the ground, at the same time

talking to herself as though praying, and during her prayer she
was immobile, paying no attention to the glass beads which
the commander offered her (Font [1776] 1930:354).

The actions of the Stevens Creek woman suggest that some people viewed the
invaders as supernatural beings or sorcerers.

The Anza party of 1776 continued onto the bayshore plains of the East
Bay, which were Alson, Tuibun, and Yrgin lands. Local people reacted to the
party of traveling horsemen in a variety of ways:

> All along the plain we saw occasional Indians, some of whom
> fled on seeing us and others who waited for us. These latter
> the commander tried to win by giving them glass beads....
> One Indian who carried his provisions on the end of a pole
> invited us to eat some of them (Font [1776] 1930:357).

At Alameda Creek thirty men came up to them, speaking a language unlike any
they had yet heard:

> They came running, and before reaching us they raised an
> arm, extending the hand as a sign that we should stop.
> Yelling with great rapidity, they said: "Au, au, au, au, au, au,
> au, au, au, au, au, au," and then they halted, vigorously slap-
> ping their thighs. As they went yelling, one behind another
> and continued talking with great velocity and shouting, it
> seemed like something infernal. We gave them glass beads
> (Font [1776] 1930:358).

A little farther north a lone Yrgin man, walking along near San Lorenzo Creek,
was surprised and badly frightened by the Anza party:

> The last one whom we encountered discovered us about forty
> paces away, and although less than five steps from where he
> was there was a place where he might have hidden, such was
> his terror that he lay down in his tracks, or rather I think that
> he involuntarily fell down through fright. Since he and we
> were on the same trail, I reached the place where he was lying
> prone more dead than alive, without any particular movement
> of lips or limbs. I tried to relieve his fright and to get him to
> stand up, but for a long time I was unable to succeed, for he
> had courage enough only to take weakly some glass beads,
> most of which he let fall. Seeing this, I thought it best to leave

the unfortunate fellow alone, and if I had not done so I think
he would have died. We attribute this spasm to the fact that up
to that moment he had never had even a remote notice of us
or of any people other than those of his own kind (Anza
[1776] 1930:136).

This event occurred over six years after Portolá's scouts had first come through
Yrgin lands. The man had certainly heard about the previous explorations,
although he may not have believed the reports. His reaction is a further
reminder that individuals respond in a variety of ways to unique crisis situations.

On April 1, 1776, the Anza party camped near the large Huchiun-Aguasto village on San Pablo Bay where the explorers from the *San Carlos* had been so well treated the summer before. A group of thirty-eight men came out to meet them:

> At first they stopped and sat down on a small hill near the camp. Then one came, and behind him another, and so they came in single file like a flock of goats, leaping and talking, until all had arrived. They were very obliging, bringing us firewood, and very talkative (Font [1776] 1930:365).

On the following morning the men returned to invite the Spaniards to their village:

> At sunrise the ten Indians came, one behind another, signing and dancing. One carried the air, making music with a little stick, rather long and split in the middle, which he struck against his hand and which sounded something like a castanet. They reached the camp and continued their singing and dancing for a little while. Then they stopped dancing, all making a step in unison, shaking the body and saying dryly in one voice, "Ha, ha, ha!" Next they sat down and signaled to us that we must sit down also. So we sat down in front of them, the commander, I, and the commissary. Now an Indian arose and presented the commander with a string of cacomites, and again sat down. Shortly afterward he rose again and made me a present of another string of cacomites and again sat down. In this way they went making us their little presents, another Indian giving me a very large root of *chuchupate* [*Angelica* or *Lomatium* sp.] which he began to eat, telling me by signs that it was good (Font [1776] 1930:367).

Following the ceremony, reminiscent of the one which a Huchiun captain had orchestrated on the *San Carlos*, the local men accompanied the Spaniards to the nearby Huchiun-Aguasto village:

> After going a short distance we came to the village, which was in a little valley on the bank of a small arroyo, the Indians welcoming us with an indescribable hullabaloo. Three of them came to the edge of the village with some long poles with feathers on the end, and some long and narrow strips of skin with the hair on, which looked to me like rabbit skin, hanging like a pennant, this being their sign of peace. They led us to the middle of the village where there was a level spot like a plaza, and then began to dance with other Indians of the place with much clatter and yelling.
>
> A little afterward a rather old Indian woman came out, and in front of us, for we were on horseback, nobody having dismounted, she began to dance alone, making motions very indicative of pleasure, and at times stopping to talk to us, making signs with her hands as if bidding us welcome. After a short while I said to the commander that was enough. So he gave presents of glass beads to all the women, they regaled us with their cacomites, and we said goodbye to everybody, in order to continue on our way (Font [1776] 1930:368).

Upon leaving the Huchiun-Aguasto village on the morning of April 2, the Anza party proceeded eastward on a route overlooking the great fishing waters of Carquinez Strait. They saw some Carquin men sturgeon fishing with nets from their tule boats:

> We called to these Indians, offering to buy their fish from them. At first they paid no attention to us, but as soon as the commander showed them a colored handkerchief they came to the shore in a hurry, bringing two very large fish....
>
> The commander offered glass beads for them, but the Indians would not accept them at all, wishing to trade them only for clothing. Indeed, I did not see in any other place Indians like these, so desirous of clothing and so greedy for it that I was surprised, for they preferred any old rag to all the glass beads, which others are so fond of (Font [1776] 1930:372).

Leaving Carquinez Strait, the Anza party entered Chupcan territory in the Diablo Valley, using the same route followed by Fages in 1772.

The Chupcans, who had responded to Fages in a friendly manner (see page 37), came out to meet the Anza party in 1776 with a testing, hostile attitude:

> To the camp came many Indians who from all accounts were from a village not far away. Although they were apparently gentle they were rather impertinent, and they proved themselves to be somewhat thievish, especially in the matter of clothing, to which they were greatly inclined and attracted, manifesting themselves desirous of acquiring and possessing it. They showed themselves to be somewhat crafty and thievish, for as soon as one stolen thing was taken from their hands they stole another, and we did not have eyes enough to watch and care for everything. So we resorted to the expedient of putting them out of the camp and telling them goodbye in a good-natured way, but this did not succeed, and one of them even became impudent with the commander, who thus far had shown great patience with them. So, half angry, he took from the Indian a stick which he had in his hands, gave him a light blow with it and then threw the stick far away. Thereupon all departed, talking rapidly and shouting loudly, which I suspected was a matter of threatening (Font [1776] 1930:376).

Later that afternoon another Chupcan man visited the Spanish camp carrying a human scalp hanging from a pole, perhaps a sign of his people's continued anger (Font [1776] 1930:377). No further confrontations took place, however.

From the Diablo Valley, the Anza party moved eastward into the broad Central Valley, then south and west through the rugged inner Coast Range to the upper Santa Clara Valley, and then south to Monterey.

Overview of First Contacts

The indigenous people of the San Francisco Bay Region reacted in a variety of ways during their first encounters with the Spaniards. Curiosity and helpfulness were the most common initial reactions; in some areas, however, people showed great fear. By 1776, some tribes were reacting with increasing warmth, while others were exhibiting scorn.

Between 1769 and 1776, most people around San Francisco Bay clearly desired the glass beads and cloth given to them by the foreign visitors, and just as clearly respected the material wonders that the Spaniards had in their possession. Some young people displayed a certain amount of obsequiousness, but in most places older people clearly considered themselves to be the Spaniards' equals.

A vast discrepancy existed between the two cultures; there was a disparity in technology and an incongruity in world view. That discrepancy must be appreciated in order to understand the interactions that would unfold during the subsequent forty years. For instance, the Spanish missionaries believed that the world was the dramatic setting for a struggle between God and the Devil; God desired man's well-being, while the Devil attempted at every opportunity to undermine it. From the missionaries' point of view, all non-Catholic forms of veneration served the interests of the Devil. Even the most sympathetic of the Franciscan visitors, Vicente Santa María of the *San Carlos*, was unable to respect the symbols of native belief. During the *San Carlos*' stay off Angel Island, he discovered a religious shrine on Angel Island consisting of three feathered objects in a cleft in a rock:

> These were slim round shafts about a yard and a half high, ornamented at the top with bunches of white feathers, and ending, to finish them off, in an arrangement of black and red-dyed feathers imitating the appearance of a sun. They even had, as their drollest adornment, pieces of the little nets with which we had seen the Indians cover their hair.
>
> At the foot of this niche were many arrows with their tips stuck in the ground as if symbolizing abasement. This last exhibit gave me the unhappy suspicion that those bunches of feathers representing the image of the sun (which in their language they call *gismen*) must be objects of the Indians' heathenish veneration; and if this was true—as was a not unreasonable conjecture—these objects suffered a merited penalty in being thrown on the fire (Santa María [1775] 1971:49).

Vicente Santa María's destructive action expressed his fear of other forms of veneration and other cultural rules.

In some ways the native world view was similar to that of the Franciscans. Prosperity and health would vanish if people ignored the rules laid down by the First People. But no Devil deliberately tempted individuals to break rules; rule breakers were merely considered to be foolish and subject to disaster. Instead there were sorcerers, people who manipulated power to upset the well-being of others, who induced fear and hatred in the general population, just as presumed agents of the Devil provoked the fear and hatred of the Christians.

In contrast with the Spanish missionaries, many local people initially respected the new forms of worship practiced by the foreigners. Font documented a significant reaction to Spanish ritual practices in the Llagas Creek area south of the Santa Clara Valley:

> We found still standing the poles of the little bower erected in the journey which in September of last year was made by ship captain Don Bruno de Hezeta and Father Palóu, and in which Father Palóu said Mass, when they went to explore for a second time the port of San Francisco. We found that the Indians had made a fence of little poles around them, and in the middle had set up a thick post about three spans long, decorated with many feathers tied in something like a net, as if dressed, and with an arrow stuck through them. On one pole many arrows were tied and from another were hung three or four balls of grass like tamales, filled with pinole made of their seeds and of acorns, or of others of their foods which we did not recognize. In the middle of a long stake there was hung a tuft of several goose feathers, but we were not able to understand what mystery this decoration concealed (Font [1776] 1930:322).

Native California people assumed that the fundamental principles by which the world operated worked the same for everyone, even though external details might vary. The foreign technologies were different; so too, therefore, would be the objects of veneration and the ritual procedures. And so, at the time of initial contact, the local people were clearly ready and willing to incorporate the foreign forms into their own practices.

Chapter 4

Christian Initiations, 1776-1784

	Spanish Actions	Tribal Actions
1776	June. Mission of Our Seraphic Father San Francisco founded in Yelamu lands.	Yelamu people visit work sites until August 12, when they are attacked by the Ssalsons.
	December. Soldiers kill Yelamu man who threatens them.	Autumn. Yelamu men return to the mission site, clash with the Spaniards.
1777	January. Mission Santa Clara founded in Santa Clara Valley.	Spring. Three Tamien men killed by Spanish soldiers for butchering mules.
	June. First Santa Clara Valley baptisms during epidemic.	June 23. First baptisms at Mission San Francisco, three young Yelamu men.
	November. Pueblo of San Jose founded on Guadalupe River.	
1781		Two small adjacent village groups absorbed into Mission Santa Clara.
1784	Mission Santa Clara two-story adobe church completed.	Most local Yelamu family heads baptized at Mission San Francisco.

Mission San Francisco In Yelamu Lands

The northern tip of the San Francisco Peninsula, which was within Yelamu tribal territory, was the most desolate of the San Francisco Bay Region tribal landscapes. Much of the area was covered with windswept sand dunes and the scrubbiest of grasslands. Its creeks were small and it lacked extensive oak groves. The Yelamus, no more than 160 individuals, spent much of the year split into three semisedentary village groups. One group moved seasonally along Mission Creek, from Sitlintac on the Bay shore to Chutchui two or three miles further inland. The second group moved between Amuctac and Tubsinte villages in the Visitation Valley area, and a third cluster of families lived seasonally near the beach area facing the sea and the Golden Gate (Petlenuc).

The Yelamus were tied by marriage to villages on the east side of San Francisco Bay; two of the three wives of Yelamu tribal captain Guimas, for example, had been born on the east side of San Francisco Bay (Milliken [1983]:146). The Yelamu tribe probably played a key role in regional trade, moving obsidian and other goods from the north and east across the Bay and down the Peninsula, while bringing coastal shells to the East Bay.

In the month of June, 1776, a party left Monterey to establish a mission station and military base at the entrance to San Francisco Bay. In addition to fourteen soldiers, seven settlers, and missionary priests Francisco Palóu and Pedro Cambón, there were women and children and a retinue of thirteen young Indian servants, among them a native Rumsen Indian of Monterey who acted as interpreter. The servants drove the large mule train and a herd of 286 cattle (Palóu [1773-1783] 1926:4:118-119). Francisco Palóu, the supervising Franciscan missionary, documented the surprise the caravan prompted from villagers along the trail:

> We were well received by all the heathen whom we met on the road, who were surprised to see so many people of both sexes and all ages, for up to that time they had not seen more than some few soldiers, on the occasions when they went to make the explorations. And they were astonished at the cattle, which they had never seen before (Palóu [1773-1783] 1926:4: 119-120).

The people of Yelamu encountered the settlers, their mule train, and their cattle herd on June 27, 1776. The arriving party included seventy-five people, men, women and children, and was probably larger than any single Yelamu village aggregation.

The Spaniards set up fifteen tents near a lagoon in Mission Valley, at an unknown distance from the seasonal village of Chutchui:

> As soon as the expedition halted, a great many of the pagans came in, making signs of friendship and expressing their pleasure at our arrival. Their good will was greatly increased when they saw with what courtesy we treated them, and when they received the little presents which we gave them of beads and trinkets to attract them, and also of our food. They continued to visit us frequently, bringing us presents of small value, principally shell-fish and grass seeds (Palóu [1786] 1913:203).

While the people of Sitlintac, Amuctac, and other nearby towns came to get acquainted with the missionaries, the soldiers and settlers began cutting timbers for a mission station and moving the cattle onto convenient pastures near springs.

On July 26, 1776, the larger part of the Spanish party moved three miles northwest to begin constructing shelters and a chapel for the presidio of San Francisco on the south shore of the Golden Gate channel. The two priests were left with their five servants, six soldiers with families, and one settler with family. Palóu wrote:

> As the vessel had not arrived, we busied ourselves by exploring the country and visiting the Indian villages where we were always well received with every sign that our presence in the country was welcome. The people showed themselves courteous by returning the visits, whole villages coming in to see us and bringing us their little presents, which we tried to return in better kind and so win their affection (Palóu [1786] 1913:203).

On the August 12, six weeks after the Spanish arrival, the villages of the Yelamu were attacked and burned by people from the Ssalson tribe, some 12 miles to the south:

> The heathens of the villages of San Mateo, who are their enemies, fell upon them at a large town about a league from this lagoon, in which there were many wounded and dead on both sides. Apparently the Indians of this vicinity were defeated, and so fearful were they of the others that they made tule rafts and all moved to the shore opposite the presidio, or to the mountains on the east side of the bay. We were unable to restrain them, even though we let them know by signs that they should have no fear, for the soldiers would defend them (Palóu [1773-1783] 1926:4:135).

The attack was not the result of a minor feud. The Ssalsons attacked and burned not only Sitlintac, on the shore of Mission Creek, but also the other Yelamu villages as well (Palóu [1786] 1913:208).

The timing of the Ssalson attack leaves many unanswered questions. The Ssalsons may have been trying to do the Spanish a favor by securing for them complete control of the Yelamu lands. They may have been removing an impediment to their own easy access to the Spaniards. On the other hand, the attack may have been the result of a local feud that had nothing at all to do with the Spanish settlement.

The ship *San Carlos* returned to San Francisco Bay in mid-August of 1776 with a cargo of supplies for the extraordinary new settlements. It remained at anchor off the beach at the presidio site until October 21, with the crew supplying another thirty or so laborers. The area was a beehive of activity in the fall. A quadrangle was begun, consisting of connected single-story buildings, that measured 250 feet along each side. It included a chapel, a storehouse, and a guardhouse, as well as separate rooms for each family of officers, soldiers, and settlers. Walls were of timber, stakes, and mud, with tule thatch roofs. Other members of the invading party began building a church and living quarters three miles to the south in Mission Valley, probably at the site of the abandoned Yelamu village of Chutchui. Work also went forward to fence off corral areas for cattle and horse herds, and to spade meadows for wheat and vegetable crops.

Yelamu men who had survived the August Ssalson raid occasionally returned to the lagoon at Mission Valley during the autumn months. Palóu wrote that they came to hunt ducks, but they were probably watching the Spaniards and determining whether or not they could reinhabit their old village sites. On some of their visits the local men presented ducks to the newcomers and were given beads and Spanish food in return (Palóu [1773-1783] 1926:4:136). Back in the East Bay Huchiun villages where they were staying with relatives, the displaced Yelamu people must have continued to ponder the motives and objectives of the Spaniards and their own possible avenues of response.

Violence erupted between local men and the newcomers in December, following a series of hostile interactions to which we have only passing references, all from the Spanish point of view:

> In the last visits which they made in early December they began to disgrace themselves, now by thefts, now by firing an arrow close to the corporal of the guard, and again by trying to kiss the wife of a soldier, as well as by threatening to fire an arrow at the neophyte from the mission of Carmelo who was at this mission (Palóu [1773-1783] 1926:4:135).

A few days after the latter incident, the man who had made that threat visited the new mission with four companions. The Spanish sergeant ordered him arrested, dragged off to the guardhouse, and flogged. Two other local men heard his cries for help from the lagoon. They ran up to the guardhouse preparing to shoot arrows, but fled when muskets were fired into the air (Palóu [1773-1783] 1926:4:136).

On the morning after the Yelamu man was flogged the Spanish soldiers went down to the beach area at the foot of Mission Bay to find, arrest, and flog the two men who had tried to free their companion. There was a group of people camping at the beach who had returned from the East Bay, and the soldiers demanded that they point out the two who had fired arrows the day before. This was done, although the accused individuals denied responsibility.

The two men fled when the soldiers got off their horses and came toward them. The rest of the group backed off and began firing arrows, wounding a horse and one of the Spaniards:

> The sergeant, seeing this and that they did not stop shooting, ordered the men to fire, and the wounded citizen brought down one with a ball and he fell dead in the water of the bay (Palóu [1773-1783] 1926:4:137).

In this definitive clash the Spaniards proved that they had the power to kill anyone who directly confronted them. The method, which involved shooting tiny pellets over long distances, was reminiscent of native concepts of long distance killing through sorcery:

> The rest ran to take refuge among some isolated rocks not far away, whence they continued to shoot their arrows. The sergeant fired at them and at one shot the ball went through the leg of one of them and then pierced the rock, for they found the hole the next day, and signs that the Indians had taken out the ball, doubtless to see what it was that had made such havoc among them. As soon as the Indians among the isolated rocks saw one of their number dead and the other so badly wounded, they asked for peace, making the gesture of throwing their bows and arrows on the ground (Palóu [1773-1783] 1926:4:137-138).

The two men accused of trying to free their friend were captured and whipped, and the sergeant told them that he would kill them if they ever tried to attack the Spaniards again.

Mission Santa Clara In Tamien Lands

The foreigners settled a second San Francisco Bay Region location, this time forty miles south of the Golden Gate in the inland Santa Clara Valley, in January of 1777. On January 7, nine Spanish soldiers, together with one colonist from Mexico and one Franciscan missionary, went from the San Francisco Presidio to the broad valley they described as "pleasant to the appearance with extensive lands for wheat planting, and well suited to stock breeding" (Murguía and Peña [1777]). On January 21, another Franciscan priest arrived from Monterey with Indian helpers, a mule train of supplies, and livestock. The new arrivals brought along a huge inventory of work tools, priestly vestments, and church ornaments, riches which must have impressed the Santa Clara Valley villagers.

Mission Santa Clara lay at the northeastern edge of the Tamien tribal district, very close to the lands of three other tribes. Three large villages of over 120 inhabitants each lay within a four-mile radius of the Santa Clara Mission site; the native names of those villages are not now known. The missionaries at Mission Santa Clara gave each of them a Spanish designation—San Francisco Solano village of the Alson tribe a mile or two downstream at the mouth of the Guadalupe River; Santa Ysabel village of a different, unnamed tribe east of San Francisco Solano on the lower Coyote River; and San Joseph Cupertino village of the Tamien tribe in the oak grove about three miles to the southwest of the mission site. Still nearer to the site were two tiny hamlets—Our Mother Santa Clara, within a few hundred yards of the first mission site, and Our Patron San Francisco, perhaps another mile upstream on the Guadalupe River.

Within a few weeks of the founding of Mission Santa Clara, people from the local villages learned the cost of breaking the Spanish rules of appropriate interaction. The missionaries had brought with them a menagerie of tamed animals, including (by year's end) 117 cattle, 18 mules, 16 horses of the mission, other horses and mules of the soldiers, 20 sheep, 16 goats, four pigs, 20 chickens, and three roosters. The livestock were set out to graze on the fields that supplied the local tribes with greens, root crops, and seed harvests.

Diarist Francisco Palóu complained that the people of the Santa Clara Valley became "greedy and thievish" (Palóu [1786] 1913:213). Some local men killed some mules belonging to the soldiers of the Santa Clara escort, so additional soldiers were dispatched from the new San Francisco Presidio. The mounted Spanish soldiers of the late 1700s were well-armed, intimidating fighting men. They wore sleeveless overcoats made from four or five layers of sheepskin, capable of stopping arrows, and they carried oval shields made of two thicknesses of cowhide one hundred inches in circumference. The exterior of the shield was marked with the coat of arms of the Spanish royal house. The soldier's gun was carried in a sheath of well tanned leather, embroidered on the outside, and each man carried a belted cartridge pouch. Leather chaps were worn from waist to knee, and long boots protected the lower legs (Alvarado [1876]:1:56).

The response of the soldiers to the butchering of their mules was swift and its message clear:

> The corporal of the guard sent word to the lieutenant of the presidio, who immediately took the road with a detachment, and before entering the mission fell upon them in their villages at daylight and found them roasting the meat of the mules they

had killed. He attempted to capture them, and they hid themselves in the brush of a grove. The soldiers followed them, and seeing that they were firing arrows, they had to kill three, and with this example they stopped. They took some of the leaders to the mission and flogged them (Palóu [1786] 1913:161).

Despite the death of three men and the public whipping of others, Palóu stated that theft, especially of corn from the fields, continued to be commonplace at the new mission of Santa Clara.

First Mission Baptisms, 1777-1779

The first Christian baptisms in the San Francisco Bay Region took place among dying infants in Santa Clara Valley villages on June 6, 1777, almost a year after the missionaries came north to settle in the Bay Region. An epidemic of some undescribed disease ran through the Santa Clara Valley villages in late May and early June, killing mostly one- to two-year-old infants.[1] Parents in villages near the mission allowed the missionaries to baptize infants from June 6 to June 20.

Missionary priest Tomás de la Peña baptized two sick infants "with the delighted consent of their parents" in the hamlet he called Our Mother Santa Clara on June 6, 1777 (SCL-B 1, 2). Peña continued south up the valley that

---

[1] The symptoms of the spring 1777 disease in the Santa Clara Valley were not recorded, but the age distribution of those who died suggests that it was a bacterial disease from contaminated water. The epidemic was most acute among children under the age of four. Of twelve children under one year old baptized, eight survived; yet of thirteen children aged 1-2 baptized, only two survived. The age group from 1-2 is the one that is beginning to take in liquids and foods other than mother's milk. The epidemic was already occurring in every village on the floor of the Santa Clara Valley when the Spanish priests found out about it. Yet the attentive Father Palóu, who mentioned this epidemic in his biography of Father Serra, was not aware of similar problems elsewhere (Palóu [1786] 1913:213). This was the first epidemic recorded for the San Francisco Bay Area, although the fact that it did not strike adults suggests that it was not a new one to the population.

Many other waves of disease followed in succeeding years. The extent to which they spread among the tribes of west Central California away from the missions cannot be determined. Considerations about the nature of epidemic spread form the crux of an extensive debate about the depopulation of native North America (Ramenofsky 1987). One point of view holds that waves of disease decimated Indian populations, leaving only remnant populations to meet newly arriving European settlers (Dobyns 1966, 1983). Another argues that thin native population densities dampened the spread of initial epidemics ahead of the European frontier (Snow and Lamphear 1988). Recent studies indicate that some populations recovered rapidly following smallpox epidemics (Thornton, Miller, and Warren 1991).

day to the village he named San Juan Bautista, where he baptized five more children (SCL-B 3-7). Peña's partner, José Murguía, baptized thirteen infants and children at the village of San Joseph Cupertino, the main Tamien village to the southwest of Mission Santa Clara, on the same day. By June 22, 1777, the Santa Clara missionaries had baptized fifty-four children between the ages of a few months and nine years.

The Tamien families must have thought that the missionaries were attempting to heal the children by exorcising malevolent forces. There were no indigenous concepts equivalent to the notions of salvation or damnation, nor ceremonies that prepared one explicitly for an afterlife. Twenty-five of the children died before the end of the summer; what the parents thought about the missionaries' 46% success rate in healing we will never know.

While the epidemic was sweeping through the Santa Clara Valley villages, a number of young Yelamu people were undergoing Christian ritual training forty miles to the north at Mission San Francisco. During the spring they had overcome the fear caused by the shooting death of one of their people the previous December. They returned to their homeland to watch the missionaries and the four Christian Indians from Baja California work with the foreign tools, ploughs, axes, adzes, copper cauldrons, iron pans, bolts of cloth, and sewing needles. They were probably encouraged to help care for the foreign animals, the oxen, cattle, horses, pigs, mules, sheep, and chickens at the mission compound. Soon they were learning Roman Catholic rituals and chants, the mechanisms by which (in the minds of the native people) Spanish material power was maintained. In short, they were participating in a new adventure during an amazing and exciting time.

The first catechized neophytes baptized in the San Francisco Bay Region were three young Yelamu men. The ceremony took place at Mission San Francisco on June 24, 1777:

> They began to come to the Mission, attracted by presents and other inducements, until we were able to celebrate our first baptisms on St. John the Baptist's Day (Palóu [1786] 1913:20-8).

Twenty-year-old Chamis of Chutchui was the first Indian listed in the Mission San Francisco *Libro de Bautismos* (SFR-B 9). Chutchui was the local village site, and was located within a few hundred yards of the mission. Chamis's father had died years earlier and his mother was living at Pruristac on the coast with her new husband (SFR-B 313). The other males baptized that day were both nine years old—Pilmo (SFR-B 10), born at Sitlintac on the beach at the mouth of Mission Creek, and Taulvo (SFR-B 11), also from Sitlintac. Their fathers were also dead, their mothers not yet remarried (SFR-B 107, 143).

During the ceremony of baptism Father Palóu bestowed a Spanish name on each new neophyte. From the Spanish point of view, the three young Yelamu men crossed over into a new realm of possibilities and obligations at the moment of baptism. They were swearing fealty to a new deity who would give them eternal life in a wonderful, desirable place in the heavens. In return, the neophytes must struggle while here on earth to follow a particular set of rules in everyday behavior. The young people did not know it, but the Franciscan priests felt obliged to use force in order to make these new Christians live in accordance with their rules, in order to save them from Hell. Thus, at the moment of baptism, the missionaries saw themselves as legal secular guardians as well as spiritual mentors.

Teenagers and young children continued to be baptized at Mission San Francisco through the summer and fall of 1777. In many cases, one or both of the parents were dead. Some of the new neophytes may have been orphaned during the Ssalson attack on the local villages the year before. By the end of the year, 31 young Yelamu people were members of the Christian community, more than twice as many of which were young men (23) as young women (10).

Fewer young people were attracted to the catechism classes at Mission Santa Clara during that first year of 1777. On June 26, a man was carried to Mission Santa Clara by his relatives in the downstream village of San Francisco Solano (SCL-B 55); the man, christened Manuel, died that day (SCL-D 1). Over the summer and fall seven healthy children from nearby villages were baptized, and a group of five male teenagers went through a fall catechism and were baptized on December 18, 1777 (SCL-B 67-71). The missionaries summarized the year-end situation:

> There are presently at the mission thirteen Christians, seven adults and six children, attending catechism class, Holy Mass, etc. The others are in the villages with their parents, as they are still children. The majority of them have been excused from the ceremonies of the church. Many of them come over to the mission frequently. There are ten catechumens under instruction (Murguía and Peña [1777]).

Young people continued to be the main source of recruits at both missions in 1778 and 1779.

The children of some of the most important native families were among the earliest Bay Area Christian neophytes. Three children of Guimas, the Yelamu captain, were baptized at Mission San Francisco on January 31, 1778 (SFR-B 44, 46, 49). At Mission Santa Clara, four Tamien children of Aqui and his three wives were baptized in the summer of 1778 (SCL-B 97, 99-101). For the most part, however, the tribal status of the initial neophyte children and their families cannot be determined from the mission records. Some of the first neophytes may well have been from marginal families in the local ranking system.

The Christian marriage ritual was important to the missionaries; it was a sacrament of blessing for couples who chose to live together for the purpose of raising a family, and was a means of controlling and channeling the sexual behavior of young people. The first Church wedding of new neophytes in the Bay Region took place at Mission San Francisco on April 24, 1778, which was almost two years after the founding of the mission and ten months after the first baptism. The bride, fourteen-year-old Paszém, had only been a Christian for one month (SFR-B 56); the groom, Francisco Moraga (Chamis), age twenty-one, had been the first Mission San Francisco neophyte (SFR-B 7; SFR-M 7).

The second Christian wedding in the Bay Region took place at Mission Santa Clara three months later, on July 13, 1778, and was a wedding renewal ceremony for Riguis and Juinite, a middle-aged Alson couple from San Francisco Solano village who had been baptized the previous day under the new names of Pasqual María and Barbara María (SCL-M 3). The second marriage at Mission Santa Clara, on September 29, 1778, involved children of two prominent local families.[2]

Native people quickly learned about the importance the missionaries attached to sexual abstinence outside of marriage, and about the significance of the marriage ceremony in legitimizing monogamous sexual contact. Young unmarried neophytes at the missions usually found spouses in short order; boys, when they reached the age of seventeen or eighteen, and girls, when they were as young as fourteen or fifteen. Since young male neophytes far outnumbered young female neophytes in 1777, young girls who became Christians in that year and in 1778 were quickly married.

Baja California Indian men who had come north as servants to the missionaries were the grooms in three of the first nine weddings at Mission Santa Clara, and in four of the first eleven weddings at Mission San Francisco. María Rosa, who married a Baja California steward at Mission Santa Clara in April, 1779, was the daughter of Pasqual María and Barbara María from San Francisco Solano village (SCL-M 11). The daughter of the deceased Saunim,

---

[2] The first teenagers to marry at Mission Santa Clara were Antonio (SCL-B 71), a son of the woman Pagmite (SCL-B 146), and Ysabel (SCL-B 97), a daughter of the man Aqui (SCL-B 195) of San Francisco village (SCL-M 4). Antonio's sister Maria Clara (SCL-B 77) was the wife in the next marriage at Mission Santa Clara, to Joseph Rosario, Mission Indian from Baja California (SCL-M 6). Pagmite, mother of Antonio and Maria Clara, had probably been born in San Jose village, home of her own mother (SCL-B 178). She had borne Antonio by an early husband, Acchem, at Santa Ysabel village. After he died, Pagmite lived with Togues of Santa Ysabel (SCL-B 2103). Sometime soon before the founding of Mission Santa Clara, she married Tagsin (SCL-B 145) of San Francisco Solano village, a younger man. The villages mentioned belonged to three neighboring tribes. One may infer either that Pagmite was a marginal person or a very powerful woman.

who had been the oldest polygynous male at the nearby village of San Francisco Our Patron, also married a Baja California steward at Mission Santa Clara.

Very few married couples became Christians at either Bay Region mission in 1778 or 1779; however, some non-Christian families did move their habitations to the vicinity of Mission Santa Clara:

> Eight pagan families have joined the Christian families living next to the mission. Along with some unmarried young men they attend the catechism. All have made themselves houses of tule (Murguía and Peña [1778]).

Non-Christian parents and relatives of the newly baptized infants and teenagers gained access to mission goods and to the prestige of association with the Spaniards, without becoming embroiled themselves in the tedious work and study regime demanded of Christian neophytes.

In the early years, the missionaries sent to Mexico for stocks of clothing and household utensils with which to reward people who joined the missions:

> The Reverend Father Guardian was asked to charge against the missionary stipends by which His Majesty supports us only the most necessary items for ourselves, vestments, wine and wax for masses, chocolate, and powders. All the rest is to be used for cloths enough to cover those who will be converting to our Holy Faith, and for utensils for house and field, with the goal of putting into full motion this beginning, by which they will be able to maintain themselves (Palóu and Cambón [1783]).

The Franciscans gave presents and food to native families who moved to the new villages adjoining the missions and began taking the catechism classes. They also encouraged new neophytes to bring their relatives from more distant villages.

Indian-Settler Relations Through The 1780s

In late November of 1777, fourteen families of Spanish citizens from Mexico established the colonial pueblo of San Jose on the east bank of the Guadalupe River, four miles upstream from the first site of Mission Santa Clara. The pueblo was located in a boundary area between three tribes, the Tamiens, the "Santa Ysabel" group, and the Ritocsi group. In the early years of its existence, it was both a source of trouble and a source of opportunity for native peoples in the Santa Clara Valley. The settlers used nearby lands (that seemed to them empty) for herds and crops, without regard for the wild native crops that they destroyed in the process. On the other hand, the town provided an alternative source of Spanish material goods and foods for those native peoples who had no interest in the religious instruction offered by the missionaries.

The Spanish government established the town of San Jose to provide the local Indian people with a model of civil society, as well as to generate agricultural produce to support its military garrisons (Beilharz 1951). However, the government found it difficult to find families willing to leave Mexico and settle in an area that was considered a wild frontier. By way of inducement, each colonizing family was given household and farm supplies, two oxen, two cows, two horses, a mule, two lambs, and two goats. Conflicts with the settles were unavoidable. Their livestock and mission livestock multiplied rapidly after being introduced into the Santa Clara Valley. By 1780 the town of San Jose already had six hundred head of various large animals on the meadows between the Guadalupe and Coyote rivers (Bancroft 1884:331). The livestock grazed the herb and seed meadows which belonged to the women of the surrounding native towns, causing extensive damage to both root and seed crops.

By the fall of 1782, natives near the San Francisco Presidio and the pueblo of San Jose were killing cattle and horse. Departing Governor Felipe de Neve initiated a two-step policy toward the stock killers, which involved a violent initial response followed by friendly inducements:

> I have been obliged, in order to control this lawlessness, to make an example to one and all through moderate punishment, capturing the aggressors, bringing them to the presidio, and subduing them with eight or ten days in the blocks and twenty or twenty five lashes. This has generally worked with respect to the pagans. Upon verifying their rehabilitation they are admonished and regaled, treated to four quarts of maize each, or some garments, on my own account (Neve [1782]).

The irony of local Indian people being arrested and punished for the slaughter of animals grazing on their own lands is apparent.

Neve and future Spanish governors wanted to avoid widespread conflict with the surrounding native peoples. This was especially important in light of the fact that the Yuman people of the Colorado River had revolted and slaughtered Spanish settlers the year before (Forbes 1965). The keys to harmonious relations, from the Spanish point of view, were military readiness and friendly relations with the local tribal leaders.

A land dispute erupted between the settlers at San Jose and the Santa Clara Mission Indians in the fall of 1782. The priests at Mission Santa Clara represented the Indians, and petitioned the governor to remove the pueblo from the valley. When the new governor refused to do so, the missionaries filed a formal protest against him:

> Now the townspeople here under discussion have, as everyone knows, quantities of livestock, both large and small. And recent history has shown that, besides getting mixed up with the livestock belonging to the Indians from the mission, the animals, both large and small, belonging to the townsfolk have caused unceasing damage to the crops put in by the Indians (Murguía and Peña [1782] 1955:400).

When the Mission Santa Clara priests lodged their protest, in November of 1782, fewer than ten percent of the Santa Clara Valley people had joined the Mission Santa Clara community. Although the priests' concern at the moment was settler encroachment on lands used by Christian Indians, the thrust of their argument was to protect most of the lands of the Santa Clara Valley in trust for all Indians, both those yet to be missionized and those already missionized.

The Santa Clara missionaries noted in their brief that livestock were already damaging the wild crops upon which the native people depended:

> They will have to rely for their food on the herbs and acorns they pick in the woods—just as they used to do before we came. This source of food supply, we might add, is now scarcer than it used to be, owing to the cattle; and many a time the pagans living in the direction of the pueblo have complained to us about it (Murguía and Peña [1782] 1955:400).

In addition, they made the radical statement that the Indians had the right to slaughter trespassing cattle:

> All owners of such estates must keep them under close guard under penalty of paying for any damage done. And Indians are at liberty to slaughter such livestock as trespass onto their lands, without being subject to any penalty whatever (Murguía and Peña [1782] 1955:400).

The missionaries' protest was fruitless. The Spanish military authorities did not move the pueblo of San Jose; they did, however, insist that the settlers herd their livestock in assigned areas under supervision.[3]

Lieutenant José Joaquín Moraga of the San Francisco Presidio issued a ruling in 1782 sustaining the governmental point of view that any actions taken against settlers' fields and livestock by non-Christian Indians were criminal offenses:

> In the event that some pagans commit robbery or do damage to the fields or herds belonging to the pueblo, the aggressors will be identified and arrested with the least disturbance possible (Moraga [1782]).

In January of 1783, Moraga received word that non-Christian people from south of Mission Santa Clara had raided livestock. Moraga went to the village, probably in the upper drainage of the Guadalupe River, with eight soldiers and some settlers. He threatened the villagers until they turned over two men who had killed some horses (Moraga [1783]). The men were taken up to the San Francisco Presidio where they were held for "fifteen or twenty days, and given their lashings every three days" (Moraga [1783a]).

A tone of alarm runs through Spanish military correspondence during the winter of 1782-1783. Moraga's orders to the commissioner of the pueblo at the end of 1782 illustrate Spanish concerns regarding the strength and potential danger of the surrounding native peoples:

---

[3] Fathers Murguía and Peña ([1782] 1955) documented the illegal use of mission lands by settlers in a letter of November 1, 1782 to Governor Fages, in which they cited four sections of the *Nueva Recopilación de las Leyes de Indias*. A key section stated that missions were granted tillage land and common land for a full league (2.7 miles) surrounding neophyte Indian villages. They complained that Pueblo lands had been granted as close as one-third of a league (one mile) from the buildings of Mission Santa Clara. The two missionaries reiterated and elaborated their complaints in a letter to Father President Junípero Serra on November 2, 1782 (Murguía and Peña [1782a] 1955). Serra forwarded the complaints with his own supportive comments to his own superior, the Guardian of the Franciscan Convent of San Fernando, on December 8, 1782 (Serra [1748-1784] 1955:4:397).

Upon receiving the complaints of the missionaries at Santa Clara, Governor Fages moved rapidly to get the titles of settlers at Monterey in order. On December 2, 1782, he ordered Lieutenant José Joaquín Moraga to divide up the Pueblo lands, and on December 12 he ordered Moraga to give all the settlers title sheets (Fages [1782], [1782a]). In their letter of protest to Governor Fages on November 1, 1782 regarding the Indian right of property ownership around Mission Santa Clara, Murguía and Peña wrote, "It will serve as proof that physical force was used, and that they in no wise relinquish the right which they have to these lands and to the water supply on them—so truly theirs since they were born here, and in addition, these rights have been recognized in the said laws" (Murguía and Peña [1782] 1955:397).

Although the Indians of the environs of the pueblo are well-disposed and for now give no indication of disquiet, we should consider them enemies, all the more because we are surrounded by a great number of pagans. At any hour they could turn ugly, come to realize what they could do as a united group, and direct their will against our work (Moraga [1782]).

Moraga was aware of the Yumans' successful destruction of a series of Spanish settlements along the lower Colorado River in 1781. His December, 1782 directive included orders designed to reduce the possibility of a major incident between the settlers and the native villagers in the Santa Clara Valley:

No individual from the pueblo is to do harm to any native Indian, or to any of their villages. Anyone contravening these orders is to be imprisoned, if it is a grave crime, and I am to be informed, in order to settle the case. To avoid such problems, no one will be permitted to go alone to the villages. If it is proven that someone does such without the permission of the corporal (and then only in the situations discussed above), he will be severely punished (Moraga [1782]).

Moraga's edict spelled out procedures for interaction between tribal people and settlers:

When any person needs some pagans for their work on the more laborious pueblo projects, he will first give notice to the corporal [of the local military escort] who will arrange it, either accompanying him himself, or sending along a good soldier to request them through the captain of their *ranchería*. In no case are they to be brought in by force. Those who want to come are to be paid according to the work that they have done, so that they will return to their villages content (Moraga [1782]).

There is an implication here that settlers had been harassing villagers at times during the previous five years, when they needed workers, and that there had been incidents in which Indian workers had been cheated out of their pay.

Two other areas of conflict that Moraga wanted to avoid involved the sexual abuse of Indian women and petty theft by Indian men:

From this time forward the familiar intercourse which has been observed to occur between the households of the settlers and the pagan men and women is prohibited. When pagans are needed for work around the house, they are to be solicited with the same formality that has been spelled out in the article above. If it is necessary to employ the Indian women to mill grain or do other chores, they are to do it outside the doorway, in plain view, without being permitted to go inside (as has been done until now), inasmuch as this kind of familiarity leads to grievances against both populations (Moraga [1782]).

The regulations governing interactions between settlers and non-Christian Indians were developed further by Governor Fages in 1785, when a new commissioner took over at the pueblo of San Jose. Among the additional elements that Fages added was a comprehensive policy concerning punishment for settlers who abuse native people:

That they [non-Christian Indians] are to be paid according to their work, that they are not to be maltreated, nor done the least harm; anyone who ignores this order will be punished in like measure, giving satisfaction to the aggrieved Indian. If they shed an Indian's blood, or do him considerable harm, the aggressor will be put in prison forthwith. Testimony will be obtained immediately, the commissioner or the mayor making sure that the Indian is all right. If there had been legitimate reason for the harm, the man who did the damage will be held until the harmed man's captain is ordered to come in and is advised of the given reasons. If these reasons are found to be legitimate, no other punishment will be given (Fages [1785]).

The edicts issued by Moraga and Fages reflect the development of economic interactions between native people and Spanish settlers in and around the pueblo of San Jose.

Many Indian people looked upon the pueblo of San Jose as a positive place, a source of new material goods and of knowledge about the Spaniards, which could be gained without giving up behavioral autonomy to the missionary priests and their lieutenants. Patron-client relationships developed between native families and settlers throughout the 1780s, and these relationships made the missionary priests at Mission Santa Clara quite concerned:

There are innumerable pagans in all directions, whose conversion is being hampered by their frequent stays at said pueblo [San Jose], in which many of both sexes have taken up nearly full time residence, employed as servants and laborers

> by the citizens. And since they are not obstructed from living in their long held licentiousness and pagan custom, they are persisting in these ways and even learning other disgraceful vices which are proffered. They are content in being Christians by their names, which they receive at said pueblo. And, as through their work they receive their food, they refuse to take up the yoke of evangelism and the laws of Christianity. May God remedy this. With respect to all this, the damages which the mission causes to the pueblo are of minor consequence (Noboa and Peña [1788]).

The Indians from the villages on the east side of the Santa Clara Valley, those of Santa Ysabel and San Antonio, were encouraged to stay away from the mission by some of the settlers. According to Fermín Francisco de Lasuén, measures were necessary to halt the interaction[4]:

> They make use of them indiscriminately for all their house and field work. They are an immense hindrance to the conversion of the pagans, for they give them a bad example, they scandalize them, and they actually persuade them not to become Christians, lest they would themselves suffer the loss of free labor (Lasuén [1785-1803] 1965:168].

While numerous local Indian people were delighted with their special relationships with the settlers, the result was a developing hierarchy of Indian laborers supporting a Hispanic elite which did little besides give directions.

The San Francisco Presidio actually had a larger population than the Pueblo of San Jose for much of the Spanish period. For the tribal people nearby, it was an alternative source of goods and knowledge to the mission during the 1780s. But the presidio's influence on tribal people in the central San Francisco Bay vicinity was certainly more limited than that which the pueblo of San Jose

---

[4] Governor Fages promulgated a set of regulations regarding the interaction of Christian Indians, non-Christian Indians, and settlers in the area of Mission San Gabriel and the civil community of Los Angeles in 1787 (Mason 1975). It repeated many of the rules applied to the town of San Jose in 1782 and 1785. Some new language was included, such as that regarding the need to halt the "*pernicious familiarity* that is had in the pueblo *with the gentile Indians*" (Fages *in* Mason 1975:96). Fages specified that Indians who came from long distances to work at Los Angeles "will be permitted to stay all together by the side of the guardhouse, where they will be under the watchful eye of the sentinel" (Mason 1975:97). When missionary President Lasuén read the rules for Los Angeles, he recommended that they also be applied at the pueblo of San Jose (Lasuén [1785-1803] 1965:168).

had on the tribal people of the Santa Clara Valley. The presidio, unlike the pueblo, was isolated from many nearby tribal lands by the waters of the Bay.

Santa Clara Valley Baptisms, 1780-1784

At the close of the 1770s, the population sizes and age structures of the two mission villages were quite similar. Mission San Francisco had 113 neophytes, while Mission Santa Clara had 110 (Figures 4,5, pages 70-71). The core group of adult Christians at Mission Santa Clara was composed of people from the Alson village of San Francisco Solano, rather than the nearer tiny Tamien villages of Our Mother Santa Clara and Our Patron San Francisco. Mission Santa Clara was within a walking distance of an hour or two from at least four large villages representing four different tribes. The priests assigned young Christian couples to live in these surrounding villages, presumably to preach and pass out favors on behalf of the missionaries. Key families from the Tamien villages of Our Patron San Francisco and Our Mother Santa Clara might well have been satisfied with an association based on mere neighborliness, were it not for the fact that so many adults from the downstream Alson village of San Francisco Solano were moving to the mission village. Julian Julau (SCL-M 19), a thirty-year-old man from San Francisco Solano village, became the first Indian *alcalde* or captain of the Christian Indian community at Mission Santa Clara.

In 1780, the adults from Our Mother Santa Clara village and Our Patron San Francisco village were faced with the possibility that they might be left out of the emerging ranking structure at the mission. Aqui, the head of the leading family of Our Patron San Francisco village, together with one of his three wives, Omnisig, decided to become a Christian that summer (SCL-B 195, 196, SCL-M 26). One of the other men baptized and married that day was Caposte, a key person from the neighboring village of Our Mother Santa Clara (SCL-B 193, SCL-M 25). In November of 1781, Caposte's brother Sichcán joined the mission with one of his three wives, Tomolinguis (SCL-B 298, 299, SCL-M 51). As a consequence of these conversions, the two small local hamlets were effectively absorbed into the mission system, some five years after Mission Santa Clara was founded.

Following this spurt of conversions of individuals from the villages nearest to Mission Santa Clara, baptisms of adult married couples were infrequent through the 1780s. However, the married population of Mission Santa Clara grew anyway, due to the influx of teenagers who were married at the church a few weeks or months after baptism. An average of five teenage marriages per year took place at Santa Clara through the 1780s, which is about the number we might expect *en toto* from the lower Santa Clara Valley population, which was probably in the neighborhood of five hundred to seven hundred people. For most young people in the Santa Clara Valley during the 1780s, joining the mission and marrying there was becoming the accepted way of marking the transition to adulthood.

San Francisco Vicinity Baptisms, 1780-1784

At Mission San Francisco, competition between tribes was an element in conversions during the early 1780s, just as it had been at Mission Santa Clara. However, the San Francisco situation differed in that it involved villages from greater distances that sent multigenerational family groups to the mission. A wave of adult baptisms in 1782, 1783, and 1784 brought most of the Yelamu tribe and all the people of the small independent Urebure and Pruristac village groups into the Mission San Francisco community.

Most members of the population of the local Yelamu villages under the age of twenty were already baptized at Mission San Francisco by 1780. By that year, five older Yelamu married couples had also joined the mission, but most of the key elders had still not done so. Young Ssalsons, their recent past enemies from the south, began to appear to be baptized in 1780, and ended up comprising seventeen of the forty-one new neophytes that year. Children came up to Mission San Francisco from the south again in 1781, some from as far as the Puichon villages on San Francisquito Creek, halfway between San Francisco Mission and Santa Clara Mission. But by the end of 1781, no adult married couples from any group south of Yelamu had joined Mission San Francisco.

The state of warfare between the Yelamu and the Ssalson that had led to the burning of villages in August, 1776, was brought to an end by traditional means. Two marriages between young people from the two tribes took place at Mission San Francisco at the end of 1781. María Francisca of Chutchui, who was the Yelamu girl baptized back in 1777 and the sister of the very first neophyte of the mission, married Mariano, son of Guascan, a Ssalson widow. The wedding took place on December 19, 1781 (SFR-M 27). A week later Mariano's sister, María de los Remedios of the Ssalson, married Jacome de la Marca, son of the captain of the Yelamu village of Petlenuc (SFR-M 28). The missionaries at San Francisco wrote as follows:

> Some people from those villages [Ssalson] have come to be baptized and to live at this mission. They have married among those of this place.... With these conversions the continuous warfare in which they lived has ceased, with which both nations show themselves to be well pleased (Palóu and Cambón [1783]).

Many young adults from the Ssalson villages, from Urebure, and from Pruristac joined Mission San Francisco during the following year (1782), as did a few older couples from Urebure and Pruristac.

At the end of 1782, the San Francisco missionaries mentioned that they allowed non-Christian parents to keep their baptized children with them in their villages, a policy that was also current at Mission Santa Clara:

> All of the Indians counted in this census live below the bell tower of this mission, in a town of porous houses, except some children of pagans, who live with their parents in villages near the mission. They are brought for periods to the mission to be reacquainted with it, and then return to their towns. In this there is success in that others are brought to our Holy Faith and in that they voluntarily bring their children for baptism (Palóu and Cambón [1782]).

Families from tribes south of Yelamu could not walk to Mission San Francisco and return to their villages in a single day; thus far fewer people could make casual visits to Mission San Francisco than was the case in the Santa Clara Valley.

By the end of 1783, the San Francisco missionaries were complaining about their inability to get military escorts for overnight visits to preach in the more distant villages:

> Many more of them could be converted if we could but go out for awhile to visit them and preach to them; however, impediments placed by the military escort (who would have to stay out overnight away from the mission, due to the distance) hamper the main purpose of our having come here, even though God touches them to the heart (Palóu and Cambón [1783]).

Their preaching excursions were limited because of the rules that Pedro Fages and José Joaquín Moraga had instituted at the end of 1782 to avoid possible problems between the soldiers and surrounding native groups. These rules limited the priests but, in effect, also forced Indian peoples from the East Bay and the central San Francisco Peninsula to contemplate making the permanent move to the mission village where they could establish a relationship with the missionaries, the agents of the world's transformation.

There was a flurry of married couples from areas south of Yelamu joining Mission San Francisco in 1783, including some from the intermarried head families of the nearest groups south of Yelamu, the independent villages of Urebure and Pruristac. Xoyoxse, captain of Urebure, and his son were baptized with their young wives in March (SFR-M 58, 59); both wives were daughters of Pruristac captain Mossués. Captain Mossués and another important Pruristac man, Liquiique, were baptized with their wives in June (SFR-M 62, 63). By the end of 1783, there were as many adult neophytes from Pruristac and Urebure in the Mission San Francisco community as there were from the local Yelamu villages.[5]

On May 2, 1784, seven years after the first local Yelamu boys began attending the missionary catechism classes, Guimas, the Yelamu captain, and Huitanac, one of his three wives, joined the Christian community at Mission San Francisco. Eight other adult couples joined the neophyte community along with them, comprising the largest single group of established families to join either Mission San Francisco or Mission Santa Clara up to that time. It is probably no coincidence that Father Junípero Serra arrived two days later from Monterey to perform the confirmations.

Few adult married couples joined either Mission San Francisco or Mission Santa Clara in the late 1770s and early 1780s. In both places, it might be suggested, competition developed between village groups for the dominant position within the mission community. Married adults from the nearest villages became neophytes only after a few married adults from distant villages were baptized. Apart from these similarities, the dynamics of initial Christian conversion at San Francisco and Santa Clara were marked by contrast. In the Santa Clara Valley, many families brought their children to the mission for baptism, while remaining non-Christian themselves. At San Francisco, on the other hand, a significant portion of the local adults had joined their children as neophytes by the end of 1784 (Figures 4 and 5).

---

[5] In May of 1783, a key group of four older Yelamu women were baptized on the same day. One of them was Huitpote (SFR-B 313), the mother of the first San Francisco neophyte, Francisco Moraga (SFR-B 7), and of Maria Francisca (SFR-B 12), the Yelamu girl involved in one of the two marriages that ended the Yelamu-Ssalson hostility (SFR-M 27). Huitpote had been a cowife of the Pruristac man Liquiique (SFR-B 321), and had been living with him since at least 1769. She was forced into what we might call a "divorce" when her husband chose to marry his younger cowife before the church (SFR-M 63).

Huitpote was a key person in a network of intermarriages between Amuctac, Sitlintac, Pruristac, and the village of Halchis (probably the Jalquin tribe) on the east side of San Francisco Bay. Her two children by Liquiique (SFR-B 31, 32) married children of the deceased Amuctac key man Tossac (SFR-B 79, 83). Tossac's other child married into the family of the Halchis man Chique (SFR-B 310), as did one of Yelamu captain Guimas's children. Two of Chique's relatives married Baja men Diego Olvera and Cipriano Agraz (SFR-B 63, 61). This network of relationships suggests that Huitpote, as the mother of the first neophyte, played an important role in the interactions that had been bringing large numbers of Pruristac people up to Mission San Francisco prior to 1784.

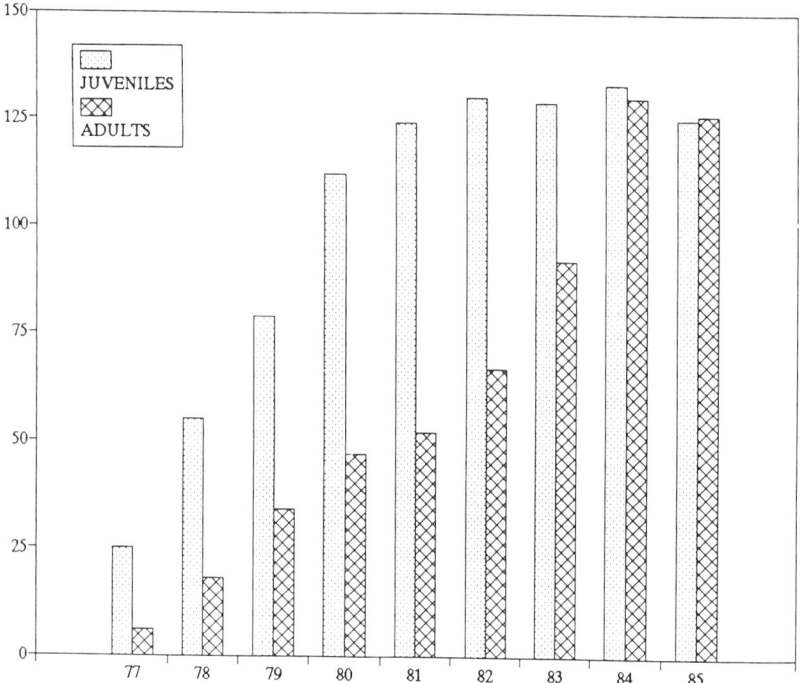

Figure 4. Bar chart of year-end 1777-1785 populations at Mission San Francisco, showing a change in ratio of children (age 0-14) to adults (age 15 and over).

In looking back at the 1777-1784 time period, it is not surprising that some Indian people joined the Franciscan mission communities. The foreigners must have seemed incredibly rich. For example, something as unremarkable to the Spaniards as a bolt of red cloth would have been an extraordinary object of wealth to Indian people, who placed great value on the small numbers of tiny red woodpecker scalp feathers that they might be able to gather over a period of years. Missionary Francisco Palóu wrote that the first neophytes were attracted to the missions through their interest in cloth, trinkets, and Spanish foods:

> They can be conquered first only by their interest in being fed and clothed, and afterwards they gradually acquire knowledge of what is spiritually good and evil. If the missionaries had

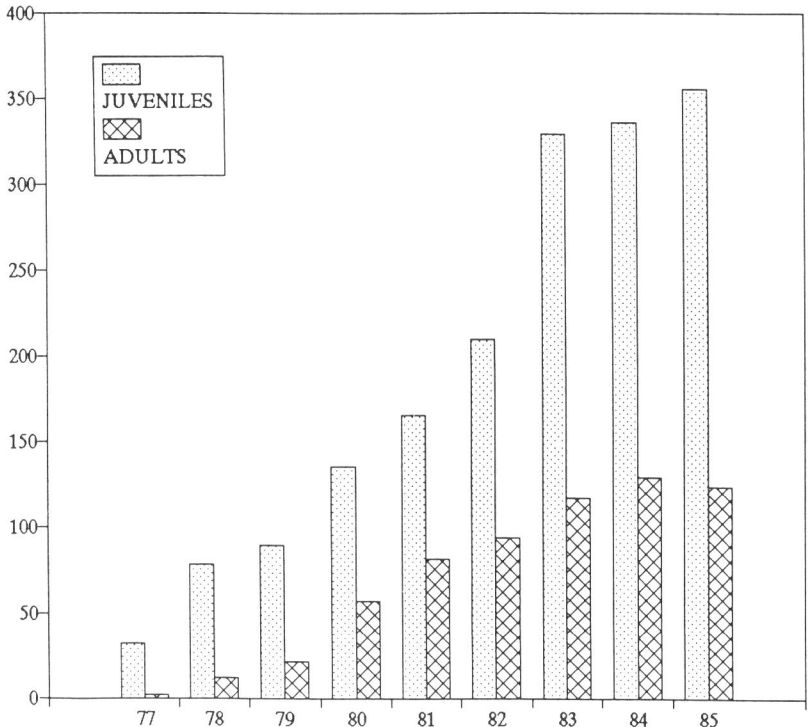

Figure 5. Bar chart of year-end 1777-1785 populations at Mission Santa Clara, showing high number of children (age 0-14) relative to adults (age 15 and over).

nothing to give them, they could not be won over (Palóu [1786] 1955:232).

The Franciscans offered themselves as gate-keepers and guides to the new world. However, it was not merely a pragmatic desire for the foreign material goods that attracted tribal people to join the missions.

Popular Catholic preaching in the late 1700s and early 1800s centered on the conflict between God and the Devil, and upon the ability of God and his missionary representatives to overcome the Devil's power. As late as 1884, stories were still being told of the powers of exorcism of one missionary, Magín Catalá, who came to Mission Santa Clara during the 1790s:

> While Fr. Magín was one day preaching, he told the faithful
> not to leave the church immediately after holy Mass, as he had
> a ceremony to perform. He emerged from the vestry after

Divine Service vested in surplice, stole and cope, and went through the kneeling multitude to the front door. There for some time he recited the exorcisms against evil spirits. Then he returned to the railing and informed the people that three legions of devils had come to harm them, but that they were now driven off (Engelhardt 1909:153).

The belief in a supernatural Devil has parallels with native beliefs about bear doctors and other types of malevolent sorcerers. By identifying native practices as a gift of the Devil, Franciscan preachers weakened commitment to deeply evocative ceremonies, and indirectly undermined the legitimacy of native leadership.

Metal utensils, tame livestock, and sailing ships could be interpreted as practical symbols of the Spaniards' positive relationship to the supernatural. However, not all native elders accepted the spiritual power of Roman Catholic ritual, as Father Gerónimo Boscana of Mission San Juan Capistrano documented in Southern California:

A *satrap*, or governor, of one of the rancherías, smilingly observed to the others, "See how this Padre cheats us! Who believes that the devil will leave us, by the sign of the cross? If it were to be done by dancing, as authorized by Chinigchinich, he would depart; but that he will do so, by the means which *he* says, I do not believe!" The others united with him in laughter, and appeared unimpressed with the efficacy of such ceremony (Boscana *in* Robinson [1846] 1925:328).

Reactions to the proselytizing Franciscans varied. But the disbelief in the efficacy of Catholic practice illustrated above was difficult to maintain in the face of disease and Spanish military strength.

* * *

The decision to join or not to join the mission was made by the individual through the application of logic. Family strengths, alliance responsibilities, assessments of future developments, and religious predilections were all elements in the decision. Most native people who stepped forward to become new neophytes had undergone a radical shift in perspective concerning the value of their own culture, and were affirming what they perceived to be the superior effectiveness of the Spanish way of life.

Chapter 5

Mutual Accommodation, 1785-1792

	Spanish Actions	Tribal Actions
1785		Climbing death rates at both missions. In March, epidemic at Mission Santa Clara.
1786	Outstation of San Pedro and San Pablo founded by Mission San Francisco at Pruristac.	Last Yelamu and Pruristac couples join Mission San Francisco community.
1789	Missionaries mention runaway neophytes for first time.	Tribal men begin going to Monterey as laborers.
1791	Mission Santa Cruz founded on coast south of Bay Area.	All coastal Chiguans and Cotegens at Mission San Francisco by year's end.
1792	George Vancouver visits Bay Area missions.	Charquin, a Quiroste leader, flees Mission San Francisco.

Mission Life and Death

The tile-roofed church at Mission Santa Clara, upon completion in the spring of 1784, became the dominant landmark of the broad, flat Santa Clara Valley. Within the church, the altar was decorated with five-foot tall paintings of Christian heroes and with finely made objects of metal and cloth, and the ceiling beams were worked "with designs carved as amply and neatly as possible" (Fages [1784]). The missionaries of Santa Clara Mission made the following comment on the communal lifestyle of the neophytes there:

> All of those listed in the preceding census live at the mission, where they attend the Mass and catechism (with the exception of some children, sons and daughters of pagan parents, inseparable from them due to their tender age), maintaining

themselves by the grain they sow communally and harvest under the direction and petition of the Father missionaries, who daily personally furnish their meals, to the healthy as well as the sick (Noboa and Peña [1784]).

A few years later, missionary president Fermín Lasuén described the daily spiritual instruction so central to these religious communes:

> They are instructed every day in Christian doctrine in the church, by a missionary, or in his presence by a well prepared Indian, once in the morning and another time in the afternoon. And many days this is repeated twice more for the children of both sexes at the missionary's door. This instruction is given alternatively in their respective languages and in Castilian. The youths take good advantage of these lessons; the middle-aged, good enough; but the really old ones learn only what they must, and then only with a lot of work (Lasuén [1793]).

The rhythm of everyday life in early California mission communities was described by French explorer Jean François de La Pérouse at San Carlos Borromeo, to the south of the Bay Region:

> The Indians as well as the missionaries rise with the sun, and immediately go to prayers and mass, which last for an hour. During this time three large boilers are set on the fire for cooking a kind of soup, made of barley meal, the grain of which has been roasted previous to its being ground. This sort of food, of which the Indians are extremely fond, is called *atole*....
>
> The time of repast is three quarters of an hour, after which they all go to work, some to till the ground with oxen, some to dig in the garden, while others are employed in domestic occupations, all under the eye of one or two missionaries.
>
> The women have no other employment than their household affairs, the care of their children, and the roasting and grinding of corn. This last operation is both tedious and laborious, because they have no other method of breaking the grain than with a roller upon a stone (La Pérouse [1786] 1989:85-86).

Figure 6. Illustration of a gambling scene in the Mission San Francisco village, by L. Choris in 1816. The adobe houses were constructed during the mid-1790s (courtesy of The Bancroft Library).

Cattle were slaughtered and meat was distributed each Saturday and on special feast days of the Roman Catholic Church (La Pérouse [1786] 1989:88-89; Menzies [1792] 1924:279); people were also allowed to augment their food supply with local wild foods:

> The Indian men are often permitted to hunt and fish for their own benefit, and upon their return they generally make a present to the missionaries of a part of their fish or game. But they proportion the quantity to what is strictly necessary for their consumption, taking care to increase it when they know that their superiors have any visitors or guests (La Pérouse [1786] 1989:90).

Until the late 1780s, it was often necessary to supplement mission-grown produce with wild produce from the surrounding countryside. In the year 1785, for instance, Mission Santa Clara did not have surplus grain to sell to the San Francisco Presidio. The president of the missions, Fermín Francisco de Lasuén, ordered Father Peña to sell the grain anyway. Peña was accordingly forced to send the neophytes out to harvest wild foods for their own survival (Guest 1973:163).

By the 1790s, supplementary wild harvests were more of a treat than a necessity at Mission Santa Clara. Except during a few years of drought or sudden population increase, it appears that food was not a problem for the mission villagers. British navigator George Vancouver commented upon the full storage facilities at Mission Santa Clara in November of 1792:

> The upper story of their interior oblong square, which might be about 170 feet long, and 100 feet broad, were made use of as granaries, as were some of the lower rooms; all of which were well stored with corn and pulse of different sorts; and beside these, in case of fire, there were two spacious warehouses for the reception of grain, detached from each other, and the rest of the buildings, erected at a convenient distance from the mission. These had been recently finished, contained some stores, and were to be kept constantly full, as a reserve in the event of such a misfortune (Vancouver [1792] 1798:19).

Mission women had some private property, although the missions were for the most part communal operations:

> The women raise some poultry about their huts, the eggs of which they give to their children. These fowls are the property of the Indians, as are their cloths, small articles of furniture, and implements of hunting (La Pérouse [1786] 1989:90).

Mission women worked together in groups, to a certain extent in the same way that they had worked in their tribal villages, although some new crafts were practiced. In 1792, Vancouver noted that the women at Mission Santa Clara wove woolen cloth of a higher quality than did the women at Mission San Francisco:

> Their occupations were the same, though some of their woollen manufactures surpassed those we had before seen, and wanted only the operation of fulling, with which the fathers were unacquainted, to make them very decent blankets (Vancouver [1792] 1798:19).

Men's work was much less varied in the mission community then it had been in native life. Men plowed, planted, and harvested, and provided the labor for building projects. They made the earliest living quarters and chapels of rammed-earth palisade construction, and later built living quarters, work spaces, granaries, and churches of adobe brick. In 1792 and again in 1795, groups of skilled craftsmen—such as masons, millers, carpenters, tanners, shoemakers, tailors, blacksmiths, weavers, and saddlers—were sent up from Mexico to teach their crafts to the most cooperative Mission Indian neophytes (Bancroft 1884:615).

The amount of work expected of the neophytes by most missionaries was not great, in and of itself (Cook 1943:94). For women, the amount of daily physical labor may actually have been lighter in the missions than in the traditional gathering economy. A labor problem did exist, however, with respect to the radically altered nature of authority over daily behavior. Native people did not always agree that certain work was needed, and they certainly did not believe that another person had the right to make them work when they did not want to. Yet at the missions, under a caste-based hierarchy of overseers, people were beaten if they did not follow directions (Cook 1943:113-129; Guest 1983:20).

None of the radical departures from traditional village life was more disturbing than the separation of unmarried females from extended family living situations:

> The married couples listed above in the census live in a town contiguous to the other mission buildings, a town formed of six rammed-earth palisade walled houses and the rest of thatch roofed huts, the adult bachelors in a room and the unmarried women in another with a door and key which is locked at night (Noboa and Peña [1784]).

The *monjería*, the institution of isolating unmarried women in a separate locked room at night, drew the following comment from La Pérouse:

> An hour after supper, they take care to secure all the women whose husbands are absent, as well as the young girls above the age of nine years, by locking them up, and during the day they entrust them to the care of elderly women. All these precautions are still inadequate, and we have seen men in the stock and women in irons for having eluded the vigilance of these female Arguses, whose eyes are not sufficient for the complete performance of their office (La Pérouse [1786] 1989:91-92).

Vancouver also commented on the institution of the *monjería*. At Mission San Francisco in 1792 he wrote:

> The women and girls being the dearest objects of affection amongst these Indians, the Spaniards deem it expedient to retain constantly a certain number of females immediately within their power, as a pledge for the fidelity of the men, and as a check on any improper designs the natives might attempt to carry into execution, either against the missionaries, or the establishment in general (Vancouver [1792] 1798:11).

The institution of the *monjería* may have been effective as a form of insurance against revolt, as Vancouver suggested, but its conscious purpose was to keep unmarried girls and women from engaging in sexual liaisons.

Health conditions in the missions were poor from the beginning. The native people were being introduced to diseases that came from everywhere in the world through the medium of the yearly visits of the supply ships from Mexico. These new diseases thrived not only because the population was immunologically unprotected, but also because of the crowding and squalor that existed in mission communities:

> These miserable habitations [thatched huts], each of which was allotted for the residence of a whole family, were erected with some degree of uniformity, about three or four feet asunder, in straight rows, leaving lanes or passages at right angles between them; but these were so abominably infested with every kind of filth and nastiness, as to be rendered not less offensive than degrading to the human species (Vancouver [1792] 1798:13).

At both Mission San Francisco and Mission Santa Clara death rates between 1780 and 1784 were nearly double that which one would expect in a native village—and those were nonepidemic years (see Tables 5-6, pages 266, 267).

In 1784 some new disease began taking lives at Mission Santa Clara. The symptoms of Sixto Antonio, a man who died at Mission Santa Clara in the summer of 1784, were described as taking the form of "a malignant fever which suddenly attacked his head and caused a very serious delirium which made him unable to make his last confession" (Peña [1786]). The description, though vague, eliminates the possibility that the epidemic involved a pustule-causing disease such as smallpox, or a dysentery-causing disease such as cholera.[1] It could have involved one of any number of diseases, including the "English sweats," encephalitis, influenza, or typhus (Ackerknecht 1965; Burnet and White 1972).

Mortality increased dramatically at both missions in 1785. At Mission San Francisco the crude death rate for 1785 climbed eighty percent above that of the previous year, although there was no particular concentration of deaths in any short period of time. At Mission Santa Clara, the death rate in 1785 was more than triple that of an aboriginal village. Twenty-five people died in the month of March, 1785, alone. They represented both sexes and all age groups. No clues as to cause, or causes, of the deaths can be found beyond the 1784 description of Sixto Antonio's symptoms.

At San Francisco mortality rates leveled off from 1786 through 1791 (the average yearly crude death rate was 100 per 1000). At Mission Santa Clara, on the other hand, mortality continued to climb during that 1786 through 1791 period (with an average yearly crude death rate of 160 per 1000). Although we lack direct proof, we should expect that the high death rates were the result of a wide array of diseases. The physician with the La Pérouse expedition provided an illuminating description of the diseases which plagued the Indian population at Mission San Carlos Borromeo in 1786:

> Sore throats, catarrhs, pleurisies, and peripneumonies, are the ordinary diseases of the winter season.... When these diseases have attained a certain degree of violence, they commonly degenerate, through this improper treatment, into chronical disorders; and they who have survived their effects under the development of their first character do not fail to end their days shortly in phthisis, or pulmonic consumption.
>
> Ephemeral and intermittent fevers, and dyspepsia, are chiefly remarkable in spring and autumn....

---

[1] The Mission Santa Clara and Mission San Francisco death rates jumped in 1785, shortly after a smallpox epidemic spread through many parts of North America in 1782-1784 (Decker 1991). Among those who died in the Bay Area were a larger than normal number of Hispanics: José Dominguez (January), Francisco Aruz (March), and Maria Josefa Romero from the pueblo of San Jose, as well as José Ramos and José Joaquín Moraga from the Presidio and Mission of San Francisco. This suggests that some virulent, uncommon disease like smallpox was at work in the Bay Area. But no increase in death rates occurred at Mission San Carlos in Monterey in 1785, nor was there any short dramatic rise in the monthly death rates at San Francisco, such as would have occurred in a smallpox epidemic.

> The diseases most general in summer are fevers of various kinds, putrid, petechial, inflammatory, and bilious, together with the dysentery.... The diseases most formidable are the inflammatory and bilious fevers, the progress of which is so violent, that the patient has rarely strength to resist them.
>
> Besides these various diseases, the inhabitants of California are liable to nervous fever, rheumatism, prurient eruptions, ophthalmia, syphilis, and epilepsy....
>
> Neither are infants at the breast exempt from all the infirmities to which that early stage of life is naturally liable, excepting rachitis, or rickets of which I did not see a single instance. Like Europeans, however, they are subject to the pains of dentition, chaps, convulsions, whooping cough, worms, cholic, diarrhoea, marasmus, strabismus, &c. (Rollins [1786] 1798:270-271).

Such situations—high mortality rates due to a wide variety of fevers and diarrheal diseases—were not unique to the California missions in the seventeenth and eighteenth centuries. Those were times of increased communication between Europe, Africa, and America, and thus of repeated epidemic outbreaks worldwide, especially in urban areas with concentrated populations of poor people (Dobson 1989:418). But the death rates at missions Santa Clara and San Francisco over the decades between 1780 and 1830 were among the highest continually sustained death rates anywhere.

Social Control in the Missions

The Franciscans coordinated and directed work in the missions through Hispanic *mayordomos* and native *alcaldes*. Governor Neve inaugurated the role of *alcalde* in 1777 as part of the process of preparing the Indians to take over their own town management. As originally conceived, the *alcaldes* were to have complete secular power in the mission villages, a situation that Junípero Serra, the first president of the Upper California missions, bitterly opposed (Beilharz 1951:28-29). The system was later modified to give the missionaries ultimate control after a number of clashes occurred between missionaries and *alcaldes* at various missions in 1778. Fages's order of 1787 describes the institution in the 1780s:

> At the completion of its first five years, each mission must choose one or two *alcaldes* [mayors], and the same number of *regidores* [advocates], according to the number of Indians that have been converted.... Although these authorities are granted some powers, they are necessarily subordinate to the missionaries, without whose direction they would not be able to exercise their powers. Nor are they given the power to bring charges against them, since they are subordinates (Fages [1787]).

The politics of work-crew supervision must have been complicated. A dominance hierarchy involving privileges and favors, with insiders and outsiders, undoubtedly developed among both the women and the men in the mission villages.

Tension underlay the power relations in these emerging mission village hierarchies. During the year 1786, a series of investigations and trials involving a missionary began which hint at such tensions. In March of 1786, two of Mission Santa Clara's Baja California Indians, Plácido Ortiz and Anecleto Valdez, together with Antonio, a local man from Santa Ysabel village, accused Father Tomás de la Peña of having murdered four Indians at Mission Santa Clara during the year 1784 (Guest 1973:159-170). Extensive investigations followed, and testimony was taken from the two missionaries and from seventeen Indians at Mission Santa Clara.

Witnesses initially reported that Father Peña killed Sixto Antonio with a hoe. Said one man, "I was standing on a little pile of unthreshed wheat and I saw Father Peña give many blows with the iron of a hoe to someone who was watering the crops" (Guest 1973:167). Peña said that it was true that he had taken a hoe from Sixto Antonio in the field, but only in order to show him how to use it correctly. Sixto Antonio had died, said Peña, from a malignant fever "as the result of a serious epidemic illness which has not ceased at the mission for the last two years" (Peña [1786]). The death of Sixto Antonio is listed in the Mission Santa Clara *Libro de Difuntos* on July 28, 1784, without comment as to cause (SCL-D 160).

Governor Fages initially concluded that Father Peña had been overly severe in punishment, that he had punished some Indians with his own hands, and that "one or the other" had died as a result (Fages [1786]). But subsequent investigations engendered so much contradictory testimony among the Indians that Fages changed his mind, and concluded that the three main accusers among the Indians had manufactured the whole thing. Fages then had the three arrested for perjury, and they spent ten years under arrest at the Monterey Presidio (Guest 1973:170). Eventually some of the Indian witnesses admitted that they had lied. They explained that they had done so because (1) they had been pressured by Plácido and Antonio, and (2) they were angry with Father Peña (Talamanca y Branciforte [1795]).

The episode seems to have resulted from a power struggle for control of the Mission Santa Clara community. The Plácido faction had controlled the mission food distribution system, and the priest broke that control:

> At one time Plácido had been manager of the storehouse and granaries. But when proof was supplied that he had been guilty of graft, he lost his position of eminence, and the keys to these important buildings were taken away from him. The Indians who had testified in favor of Plácido's allegations against Peña were friends of his, men who were indebted to him for the stolen goods they had received (Guest 1973:164).

The Plácido faction represented the families that had originally lived at the site of Mission Santa Clara. Plácido and his wife María Rosa from the nearby village of Our Patron San Francisco were the preeminent couple at Mission Santa Clara in 1783, as indicated by the fact that they were placed at the head of the list in the 1783 mission census. Antonio (the local man who was Plácido's accomplice) and his wife were the highest local Indian couple listed in the 1783 census (Noboa and Peña [1784]). Antonio's wife Lorenza Ynez was the daughter of Aqui, former leader of Our Patron San Francisco village.[2]

The shakeup that led to Plácido's loss of power must have been a traumatic event in the Mission Santa Clara community. After the deportation of the faction leaders, Father Peña retained the support of at least some elements of the Santa Clara Valley Indian community. When Peña went down to Mission San Carlos Borromeo for a few months in 1787, Father Noboa wrote to tell him that the non-Christians had stopped coming to catechism classes. "Continuously, I find myself confronted with the same old questions the pagans ask; 'Where is Father Tomás: When will Father Tomás come back?'" (Guest 1973:169). We

---

[2] Five Baja California natives married at Mission Santa Clara, Joseph Rosario of San Francisco Borja (SCL-M 6), Anecleto Valdez of San Fernando de Velicata (SCL-M 7), Plácido Ortiz of San Ygnacio (SCL-M 11), Francisco Gragiola of San Ygnacio (SCL-M 21), and Esteban of San Francisco Borja (SCL-M 22). They were the foremen and most important people at the Mission village during the earliest years.

Two of those Baja Californians played key roles as leaders of the anti-Peña faction. Both were married to women from Our Patron San Francisco village. Plácido's wife María Rosa was a daughter of Riguis and Juinute, the first baptized couple at Mission Santa Clara, from Our Patron San Francisco village (SCL-M 3). Anecleto's first wife, Maria Catharina, had also been from Our Patron San Francisco village (SCL-M 7). The local man, Antonio, who played such a prominent role, was married to Lorenza Ynez (SCL-M 4), daughter of Aqui, the captain of Our Patron San Francisco village.

do not know the extent to which the respect stemmed from fondness as opposed to fear.

Spanish Military Activity In Tribal Areas

As more and more people joined the missions from places more than an easy day's walk away, a problem arose concerning the desire of neophytes to come and go between homeland and mission. After the Yuma victories on the Colorado River in 1781, neophytes were made to carry a pass whenever they left their mission communities, no matter whether it was to go on visits to their home villages, to go out to gather supplementary wild foods, or to go to another mission at the behest of a missionary. The pass rule was proclaimed by Governor Neve in 1783:

> Thoroughly persuaded that the good order and tranquility of these provinces, to which I aspire, depends in large measure upon the care and vigilance with which missionaries and political authorities supervise the life and customs of its inhabitants of whatever condition or quality they may be; and knowing full well from experience that the ease with which they travel from one place to another without passes or any document which shows their destination, makes it easier for evildoers to be confused with the good, I have ordered...that no Indian nor other resident shall leave his place of habitation without official license (Neve [1783]).

New neophytes sometimes decided that they wanted to go back to their old way of life. Those who did so were considered runaways by the missionaries and the Spanish military government. Father Serra had initiated the practice of the forcible return of runaway Christian Indians at Mission San Carlos Borromeo as early as 1775 (Serra [1748-84] 1955-56:4:425). La Pérouse commented upon the lack of freedom that resulted from the decision to join a mission:

> It must be observed that the moment an Indian is baptized, the effect is the same as if he had pronounced a vow for life. If he escapes to reside with his relations in the independent villages, he is summoned three times to return; if he refuses, the missionaries apply to the governor, who sends soldiers to seize him in the midst of his family and conduct him to the mission, where he is condemned to receive a certain number of lashes with the whip (La Pérouse [1786] 1989:82).

People who came to the missions from great distances were more likely to flee than people from the nearer villages. They missed their homelands and hoped that they could avoid pursuit when they fled. Governor Fages commented on the impulse to return home in 1787:

> We note that the pagans that aggregate at these missions are generally people from their local environs. Those whose native lands are farther than six or seven leagues [16 to 20 miles], or those who have not been baptized are hard put to remain at the missions. They usually give no other reason for not becoming Christians than the large distance at which the find themselves (Fages [1787]).

The first Bay Region runaway mentioned in an extant record was Francisco Xavier Ritus, age twenty-seven, of Mission Santa Clara (SCL-B 1127). He seems to have fled Mission Santa Clara in the spring of 1788, only three or four months after he was baptized. His return in February of 1789 was noted in the Mission Santa Clara *Libro de Casamientos*, in which it was reported that his Christian bride, Buenaventura María Liliole, "has been living now for nearly one year in concubinage with said Francisco Xavier, a runaway from the mission" (SCL-M 166).

The earliest extant documentation of Mission San Francisco runaway Christians is found in a death register entry in the year 1789:

> During an expedition undertaken in search of some Christians from the outstation of San Pedro and San Pablo, Diego Olvera privately baptized an Indian child of about one year's age, who was on the verge of death (SFR-B 725).

There may have been earlier runaways in the 1780s, as well as earlier expeditions by mission stewards to bring them back, but none are mentioned in the surviving military correspondence.

It may seem remarkable that people who fled the missions could not easily disappear into the native populations that surrounded the tiny areas of Spanish settlement, but it really was impossible for runaways to hide for long. Native Bay Region people did not see themselves as "Indians," members of a unified ethnic group. They found their identity as members of specific tribes. Due to historical enmities among neighboring tribes, new neophytes could only flee to a limited number of places. Furthermore, the missionaries had their own committed followers who were in contact with the informational network that linked non-Christian villages:

> The chief of the alcaldes was called the general. He knew the names of each one, and when he took something he then named each person by his name. In the afternoon, the alcaldes gather at the house of the missionary. They bring the news of that day (Tac *in* Phillips 1975:29).

Considering the relatively light population in the countryside in the Bay Region, it was fairly difficult for people to keep their whereabouts hidden from the Spaniards and their native informers.

The Spanish officers under Governor Fages tried to return runaways to their missions without upsetting the local villagers. Fages documented his policy of minimal disruption, and the reasons for it, in a letter to his successor in 1791:

> The repeated flight of neophytes from the missions has led to serious injuries during the sorties of search parties of troops, due to the poor leadership of troop commanders. For this reason I have avoided such sorties as much as possible, relying instead on other means to bring them in. The most efficacious is for the Fathers to send other reliable Indians to petition for them from the captains of the *rancherías*, who, by virtue of this courtesy and some small gift, send them back or bring them back themselves. In those cases in which this method has proven unworkable, some troops are sent with the same purpose. I have sent them under precise orders, in order to obviate such untoward consequences as may arise in the mountains. That is where the fugitives usually lodge themselves, and where it is necessary to dismount and lead the horses on foot in order to arrive at the *rancherías*, due to the ruggedness and unevenness of the footing (Fages [1791]).

Fages wished to use his own troops to bring in runaways only as a last resort, and then only with orders to take extreme care. Fages's next statement from the same document provides the key to the entire Spanish colonial enterprise of dominance:

> The pagans could venture some lamentable transgression there which would undermine the maintenance of that critical concept of authority among the innumerable mass of Indians who surround us, and of respect for our weaponry, without which they would disavow our friendship, which is an important element of our policy of conquest (Fages [1791]).

Fages clearly understood that the slowly expanding Spanish usurpation of tribal lands and tribal authority was taking place within a context of native belief in the invincibility of his troops.

Due to strict laws that were enforced by Spanish military personnel, Indian people in the Bay Area were unable to trade for firearms from any source during the Spanish period. So far as is known, no Bay Area Indian ever had a gun between 1777 and 1810. Spanish fears of arming the non-Christian villagers went beyond the control of firearms; for example, when some people near the town of San Jose were able to trade with Spanish settlers for some metal axes in the spring of 1790, Governor Fages ordered the commissioner of San Jose to negate the trade:

> That no one is to go to the villages, except to look for livestock, definitely not to look for sea otter pelts. That you take back any axes that the pagans have, paying them for them (Fages [1790]).

Two weeks later Fages reiterated that the non-Christians were to be compensated for the confiscated axes:

> That you confiscate the axes of the pagans, redeeming them on the accounts of those who gave them out, sold them, or traded them. Warn everyone that nobody is to go to the villages without your orders. No one is to give them axes, plow blades, or other weapons or iron tools. That you will pay the Indians without fail (Fages [1790a]).

Horseback riding by Indians was also outlawed, again for security reasons; however, that rule was modified because the missionaries needed Indian cowboys (Guest 1973:157).

As early as 1784, military officials at the San Francisco Presidio wanted to move the growing government cattle herd from nearby overgrazed land onto recently vacated tribal lands south of the mission. The governor wrote that such a move would result "in grave harm to the Indians" (Fages [1784b]), and the move was not allowed. But three years later, in 1787, the missionaries complained that the Christian Indians of Mission San Francisco were seeing their fields cut to pieces and their *pinole* seeds despoiled (Cambón and García [1787]). The Presidio herds were moved south to the Royal Ranch near Monterey in 1791, and in 1797 a new royal ranch was established on the abandoned lands of the Urebure group (Bancroft 1884:707).

At Mission Santa Clara the missionaries also complained about environmental deterioration. Late in 1787, the cattle and plantings of the settlers of San

Jose were destroying the greens that the Santa Clara Valley Indians were accustomed to eating:

> There is an abundance enough of grain for the Indians to be supported, but the lack of greens, as a result of the citizens of the pueblo of San Jose having cleared all the fields for their houses, their plantings, and their irrigation ditches, deprives them of it for their *pozole* and *atole* throughout the winter season, it being impossible to procure it at said season (Noboa and Peña [1788]).

By 1790, the problem of overgrazing was such a cause of antagonism between the non-Christian villages and the Spanish settlers at San Jose that Lieutenant José Argüello ordered the settlers to keep their cattle together as a single herd (Argüello [1790]).

Whenever Indians did kill livestock, the Spanish authorities pursued and punished them. In the spring of 1790, twelve Matalan men tried to kill a mare near San Jose. The ten who were captured were sent to work at the San Francisco Presidio. Regarding the other two, Argüello reported:

> I gave Corporal Macario orders to the effect that as soon as he gets word that the two who had gotten away are back at any of the villages near the Pueblo, he is to go get them with six or eight men, two or three of his own and others he should ask for from Corporal Pacheco. He is to be sure that they are sent up to this presidio (Argüello [1790]).

The Spanish military had become a regional police force. Local resistance leaders, who were perceived by the Spanish military as being lawbreakers, were quickly dealt with before they could build a reputation for successful opposition.

Some native people who joined the missions continued to participate in the intergroup feuds being carried out by their non-Christian relatives. When Santa Clara Mission Indians joined their non-Christian relatives in such a dispute in 1788, they found that both their independence and their judgement were to be overridden by Spanish authorities:

> The pagans of the village adjacent to Mission Santa Clara had fought with the people from the hills. Some Christians of the mission joined the altercation. Because of it he sent Sergeant Amador. Upon arrival at the mission he found that the Father ministers had punished two or three Christians who had gone to see the encounter. He immediately went out through the

> neighboring villages to reprove the ringleaders and to tell them that if they invite Christians to join in their future fights, they will be punished. He also reproved the Christians (Argüello [1788]).

Without the ability to call on their Christian relatives to help them, the ever shrinking tribal village populations were increasingly vulnerable to the attacks of more distant tribes that had scores to settle.

The Spanish military attempted to extend their legal jurisdiction beyond the Indians who were living at the missions to the non-Christian people living in proximity to the Pueblo of San Jose:

> He verified that a pagan named *El Caporal*, who works at the Pueblo, was found to be putting a group together to go make war on some other pagans over a woman. He was seized and given a few lashes. After three days under detention he was put at liberty (Argüello [1788]).

In 1790, Governor Fages instructed the commissioner of the pueblo of San Jose to use his police powers to eliminate the native practice of raiding distant villages for women:

> When some pagans come together due to being beset by others from whom they have stolen women, you should persuade them that they should return them, making them understand what evil this is and that if I find out about it I will be angry and will come with many soldiers to punish them. By the same token, if those from distant *rancherías* come to rob those in your vicinity, petitions will be sent to their captains with similar admonishments. But in those cases where they keep those women over time and have children with them, just let them be. The pagans are free, anyway (Fages [1790]).

Another example of the introduction of Spanish authority, again in the area of male-female relations, was mentioned in a directive from Governor Fages to corporal Macario Castro at the town of San Jose in May, 1790:

> That he call upon the Indians and their captain who beat up an Indian woman and warn them that if they repeat it they will be punished (Fages [1790c]).

In general, the Spanish military knew and cared little about what was going on among tribal factions. Their interference was probably limited to protecting those native families who had developed patronage relations with key families of settlers or soldiers. The policy for maintaining regional peace and harmony depended more upon the threat of military force than upon its continuous use.

When the Spanish soldiers did move against non-Christian Indians, they did so with such brutal force that the most highly respected male leaders in the villages were at times humiliated. Father Peña's response during the investigation against him in 1786 describes the soldiers' tactics:

> On occasion soldiers have used their weapons against the pagans without having encountered resistance. At times the pagans have been left abused by the cruel punishment of being hung from a tree by one foot, by scarifying their buttocks with swords. The same soldiers hang them and then beat them with staves, each one taking a turn (Peña [1786]: 46-47).

The authority of village captains and elders deteriorated in the face of the successful Spanish military efforts at regional social control. Even those leaders who cooperated with the Spanish by accepting bribes to return runaways or supply laborers to the town were admitting that power and prestige flowed out of the presidio and the pueblo to the surrounding people.

Baptisms during the Late 1780s

Throughout the 1780s and early 1790s, people kept moving to the missions, despite the obvious drawbacks of mission life. Disease and environmental deterioration contributed to the pressures to abandon tribal life:

> They have no other doctors than these same missionaries, who equally see to it that nothing is lacking for the pagans, who frequently come, now with their little children, now to visit their Christian relatives and to be catechized. Many come to pass the time. The shortage of their wild foods renders them distressed and needy (Noboa and Peña [1784]).

There was no unaltered tribal life in the villages that were in contact with the missions. When they viewed themselves in the "mirror" of the Christian communes, some people in the nearby native villages saw their own lives as wanting.

In 1786, the missionaries at Mission San Francisco opened the outstation of San Pedro and San Pablo at the site of Pruristac village, twelve miles down the coast from Mission San Francisco. The station consisted of a full quadrangle, with chapel, granary, and work and living rooms. Its purpose was to reduce the crowded conditions at San Francisco and to provide a base of operations closer to the coastal villages further south. In addition, the farm raised critically needed supplemental crops (Cambón and García [1787]). The San Pedro outstation drew new members to Mission San Francisco from down the coast as far as Point Año Nuevo during the remainder of the 1780s and the early 1790s. At the same time, people from the bay shore of the Peninsula went up to Mission San Francisco itself.

Only a small number of people from the East Bay moved to Mission San Francisco through the late 1770s and 1780s. Most were teenagers or unattached adults related to the Yelamu people. One of the earliest was María Rosa, from "Halchis in the mountains," who married the Baja Indian mission servant Cipriano Agraz in 1779. Her wedding was of considerable significance within the caste system at the mission. It took place on the same day as the marriages of two other mission servants from Mexico, Diego Olvera and Raymundo Morante, to local women.

On August 12, 1785, a missionary at San Francisco reported that Lower California native Cipriano Agraz had been killed in the East Bay:

> The Christian Indians who had been gathering wild seeds on the other shore brought the news that on the sixth the pagans who live to the south of that territory had killed the Indian Cipriano Agraz of the Mission of Santa María in Baja California, now married and residing in this Mission of Our Patron San Francisco with María Rosa de Viterbo, Indian of this mission (SFR-D 145).

The people on the east side of the bay to the south of Mission San Francisco were the Jalquins, probably the people of Cipriano's own wife María Rosa.[3]

---

[3] Cipriano's wife, María Rosa de Viterbo, was from Halchis (probably Jalquins) in the East Bay hills. A few months after Cipriano was killed, on January 5, 1786, she married the Spanish widower José Manuel Valencia (SFR-M 102); she died in December of 1787 without having had any children. The wedding of María Rosa was one of only two Spanish-Indian marriages at San Francisco Mission during the Spanish period. The other local woman to marry a Hispanic man was María Soledad (SFR-B 102) of Urebure, who married in succession Sacarias (SFR-B 962) of the Huchiuns (Genau village), Ygnacio Yguera of Mexico (SFR-M 508, June 25, 1795), José Anecleto Barbosa of Mexico (SFR-M 999, November 6, 1805), and José Antonio Aguilár of Mexico (SFR-M 1047, September 29, 1806). She had no children.

We know nothing about the specific animosities that led to Cipriano's death. The Jalquins would be major players in an East Bay uprising against the Spaniards a few years later, from 1795 to 1802. This 1786 event may well have contributed to the tensions that led to that later conflict.

Most of the people from the nearer East Bay villages were content to make no more than occasional visits to Mission San Francisco during the 1780s. Among those who did become neophytes were some young people who came from great distances, and who were married at the mission so quickly that we must assume their marriages had been previously arranged. Nazaria Saqénamaie came from "the other shore in the place they call Juris, of the Carquin family" in July of 1787 (SFR-B 658). She was already the wife of a Huchiun man who had been baptized in 1786 (SFR-B 504), and she renewed her marriage with him at the mission on the day she was baptized (SFR-M 155). In 1788, Blandina Guaiámay came from "the village of Ssogoréate at the port of *La Assunta* near the mouth of the large river of Our Father San Francisco, of the Aguasajuchiun family" to marry Bonifacio from the East Bay village Chinau the next day (SFR-B 708, SFR-M 182, SFR-B 194). Bonifacio, age seventeen, had been a neophyte at San Francisco Mission since he was nine years old.

Mission Santa Clara was surrounded by many more large villages than was Mission San Francisco, yet relatively few of the Valley's adults chose to be baptized during the late 1780s. Instead, most couples continued to take their children to the mission for baptism and to raise them in their home villages. As a result, the ratio of adults to children was much lower at Mission Santa Clara than at Mission San Francisco throughout the 1780s and early 1790s.

The adults that did join Mission Santa Clara came from villages that are now nearly impossible to locate. The missionaries referred to most of them by using one of ten generic Christian names, four of which were becoming district names identified with the cardinal directions: Santa Agueda (north), San Carlos (south), San Bernardino (west), and San Antonio (east). Prior to 1790, the largest number of adults to join Mission Santa Clara came from the village that the priests called San Francisco Solano.

During the summer of 1790, eleven couples were baptized from the San Carlos district alone. Unlike the San Francisco Solano people, however, the San Carlos district people probably came from a number of different villages. New neophytes in 1790 that were identified as San Carlos people were probably from villages of the Ritocsi tribe or from any number of groups in the Santa Cruz Mountains.

Widening Economic Impacts

Even native people who had no desire to join the missions were interested in obtaining Spanish manufactured goods. The only thing they could offer in trade was their labor. Non-Christian Indians had worked for settlers at the town of San Jose since its inception. By 1790, Governor Fages [1790a] was still having to remind the commissioner of the town that citizens were not allowed to go by themselves to native villages to negotiate for laborers. Fages also moved in 1790 to stop an emerging peonage system under which some settlers were advancing loans to Indians with future labor as security:

> They cannot be told that they should work for a certain person towards a specific end. However, under your direction and with the knowledge of the captains, they are to be assigned to work, the men as well as the women, with everything absolutely regulated in accordance with the specific guidelines. In accordance with them, when they fulfill the duties of their work, they are to be given just compensation. Make sure that no pay advances are given, so that they will always be free to work where you send them (Fages [1790]).

Rules protecting the rights of tribal Indians and controlling their hiring through tribal captains eased the work of the military by minimizing disputes between the Spanish settlers, and between the settlers and the Indians.

A new opportunity arose for tribal men in and around the Santa Clara Valley to participate in wage labor in 1789. Governor Fages decided to upgrade the buildings of the Monterey Presidio (Fages [1793], Appendix 4, 2). He decided to hire Indians from the vicinity of San Jose because they were learning Spanish and were familiar with the type of labor necessary, unlike many of the non-Christian villagers from the hinterlands between Monterey and Santa Clara.

Fages described the deals that he made with numerous village captains from the Santa Clara Valley and the lands to the east and north in the winter, spring, and summer of 1790 in the following way:

> I first called together their captains and leaders. I proposed that they send groups of five, ten, fifteen, or twenty men, according to the number of people that they had and that they could do without for the defense of their lands. I promised to reward them with blankets, shirts, glass beads, and shells. They agreed to the pact, and in groups of eighty to one hundred they arranged with the commissioner of the town and the commander of the guard to give them an escort of a

Figure 7. Illustration of tribal men arriving at the San Francisco Presidio under military escort, by L. Choris in 1816 (courtesy of The Bancroft Library).

> corporal and four soldiers to accompany the groups for security. The corporal gathered up and held the bows and arrows of each person, in order to avoid all trouble. The escort conducted them over the twenty leagues [fifty-four miles] which separates Monterey from the town of San Jose, in order not to disquiet the pagans they encountered along the road (Fages [1793], Appendix 4, 2).

The tribal men who went to work at Monterey worried about the safety of the families they had left in their villages:

> They made a specific request to the commissioner regarding the protection of the towns and the women they left behind in the villages, guarding against the tremendous abuse which they are in the habit of doing to one another whenever they see their spouses left behind. At their arrival provisions were given them on the king's account, but it was not much, because most of them brought seed meal, rabbits, fish, wild fruit and other foods from their homes. When they arrived

> they were allowed a day or two of rest, given food to relieve their fatigue, as were those who left to return to their homes. The morning fare was a normal portion of beef, those at midday and in the afternoon a sauce pan of hot corn meal mush and beans (Fages [1793], Appendix 4, 2).

Native laborers were treated well at Monterey. Fages needed to create a good impression upon them so that more work crews would be willing to go to Monterey in the future:

> To please them upon their return, I met with the captains of each group and asked them if they had experienced any problems, if things had gone well, and if they would come again when they were requested. All responded "yes" in one voice. Then they were given back the bows and arrows which I had kept in custody. I gave each person a small cotton blanket valued at five or six reales, on the king's account. And on my own account I gave the captains four to six strings of glass beads and to the rest two or three strings of glass beads. I permitted them to go to the beach to gather shells, which they greatly value to work into the coinage with which they trade and the adornments which they and their wives wear. They were sent off in this way. I appointed a corporal and four soldiers to escort them to their lands. One or two cattle were slaughtered for the road. And while they were pillaging the meat, two mules were loaded with the two half loads of shells, relieving them of the weight. The troop leader was advised to take whatever road they wished and to treat them with the utmost humanity. In this way, so in conformity with the customs of these people, they were kept well pleased (Fages [1793], Appendix 4, 2).

When a group contracted from one village returned home from Monterey, another contracted group was brought in. That group was expected to stay and work at Monterey for the period of a single "moon" (Fages [1790a]). A succession of groups went to Monterey in late April, late May, and late June.

San Jose military commissioner Macario Castro had trouble finding local non-Christian men for the Monterey projects in late July of 1790. According to a letter of complaint from Governor Fages on July 22, Castro broke up a dance at a non-Christian village in order to round up workers. When they arrived at Monterey the governor wrote:

Clara remained non-Christian. People brought their children to nearby Mission Santa Clara for baptism, and thus were able to develop ties to the Franciscans without giving up their personal autonomy.

Some new elements were introduced into the lives of Bay Area Indian people during the period between 1785 and 1792. Infant mortality rates, which were already high before the Spaniards arrived, rose alarmingly in both mission populations, and may have been skyrocketing in nearby non-Christian villages as well. Environmental degradation intensified as a result of livestock grazing and the suppression of controlled burning. A missionary priest at Santa Clara was accused of beating four people to death. People of the region discovered that neophytes who quit their mission were considered escapees. Mission stewards visited villages to pressure the captains into forcing runaway neophytes to return.

The excitement and novelty of first contact had certainly worn off by the early 1790s. Despite the negative aspects of mission life, a seed of change had been planted and was growing. If traditional culture could be described as a single fabric that was spread across the region, one might think of the missions as foreign objects worrying holes in that fabric, causing it to fray and slowly unravel.

Chapter 6

Social Transformation, 1793-1795

	Spanish Actions	Tribal Actions
1793	January. Missionaries visit Quiroste villages down coast.	February. Quiroste leader Charquin harbors Christians.
	May. Military raids Quirostes and captures runaways.	Spring. Lamchins, Puichons and remaining Ssalsons join missions.
		December. Quirostes attack Mission Santa Cruz.
1794	January. Soldiers raid Quirostes, capture resistance leaders.	
	July. Father M. Fernández harasses Santa Clara area villages.	September. Coastal adults baptized at Mission Santa Clara.
		October 31. Key Santa Clara Valley faction joins Mission Santa Clara.
	November 2. H. Sal confers with upset Santa Clara Valley headmen.	November-December. Mass migration to missions from Pacific Coast, Santa Clara Valley, and East Bay.

The First Resistance Movement

The first active resistance to Spanish power in the Bay Area was led by Charquin (SFR-B 1002), a leader of the Quirostes in the area of Point Año Nuevo, down the coast from San Francisco. Although he did not fight Spanish soldiers until early 1793, Charquin had harbored fugitive neophytes since November of 1791.

Charquin was baptized as Mateo in mid-November of 1791 at the San Pedro outstation. He was among a mixed group of Quirostes from Point Año Nuevo, and Oljons from San Gregorio Creek. At age sixty he was the oldest male in the baptismal group of November 18, and was the first adult that was baptized that day (SFR-B 1002). Directly behind him in order of baptism was Lachi, known through indirect sources as the captain of the Oljons (SFR-B 1003; see also SFR-B 569, 674). From this I presume that Charquin was the Quiroste captain. According to Hermenigildo Sal, "He didn't even remain at the mission for eight days" (Sal [1793], Appendix 4, 1). The reasons that Charquin became upset and fled the mission are undocumented; Captain Lachi and the Oljon people stayed.

Part of the explanation for the varied reactions of the Oljons and Quirostes in November 1794 must lie in individual personality differences, but another part lies in the differing places of the two tribes in preexisting regional power alliances. Charquin's Quirostes had been the largest, most powerful group on the Pacific Coast between the Golden Gate and Monterey Bay. Yet when Charquin went up the coast to San Pedro, he had no relatives already in the mission system, while his northern neighbor, Oljon captain Lachi, had ties by marriage to one of the most important Christian families at Mission San Francisco—that of Pruristac captain Luciano Tiburcio Mossués (SFR-B 319).[1] At San Pedro in November, 1791, the Quiroste leaders found themselves outsiders in a new network of ranking and power relationships.

Charquin and his followers retreated into the rugged country behind Point Año Nuevo in late 1791, lands that were equidistant from missions San Francisco, Santa Clara, and Santa Cruz. From there he invited dissatisfied neophytes to join him.

> Not even when the missionaries sent out messengers for him did he return. On two occasions endeavors were made to apprehend him. On one of them he retreated into the mountains and on the other he took up arms against the Christians of the mission. This has caused him to become insolent, inasmuch as he is increasingly fearsome in the eyes of the Indians (Sal [1793], Appendix 4, 1).

Most of the neophytes at the coastal outstation of San Pedro were withdrawn up to San Francisco in the early spring of 1792, perhaps in response to Charquin's activities. But Charquin's faction did not hold complete sway over the coast. Oljons and Quirostes continued to come north to join Mission San Francisco in

---

[1] Oljon captain Lachi actually had somewhat indirect marriage ties to the Christian captain of Pruristac. Suiquim, one of Captain Lachi's four wives in the 1780s, brought her three-year-old son by Lachi up to the San Pedro outstation for baptism on October 25, 1789 (SFR-B 756). She herself was baptized on November 25, 1789 (SFR-B 761). Two days later, on November 27, 1789, she married Onofre (SFR-B 92), a son of Pruristac captain Luciano Tiburcio Mossués (SFR-M 199). At the time of Lachi's baptism, therefore, Onofre was the stepfather of Lachi's son.

1792. Quirostes were also baptized at Mission Santa Clara during that year, under the district designation "San Bernardino."

On January 6, 1793, Mission San Francisco servant Diego Olbera baptized a twenty-two year old woman on the verge of death "at the Quiroste village in the mountains" (SFR-B 1165). Olbera was probably in the area trying to convince Charquin and his followers to return to the mission. Instead, relations degenerated further. A major confrontation developed in the Quiroste community just a month later, when two young couples, recently baptized at Mission Santa Cruz, visited Charquin's village:

> On the fifteenth of this month [February, 1793] Corporal Miguel Pacheco, in charge of the escort of Santa Cruz Mission, reported...that two Indians of the Charquin's *ranchería*, who had been baptized, went back there with a license to visit. Because they had become Christians he wanted to kill them and take their wives. Although they fled that day, they returned by night to look for their wives. Upon discovering them, Charquin took away their weapons. They had to return alone to their mission (Sal [1793], Appendix 4, 1).

The two couples had been baptized and married at Santa Cruz on February 17, 1793 (SCR-M 31, 32). Both of the women involved, Tuiguimemis and Miscamis, were twenty years of age, and were from the village of Mitenne of the Quirostes (SCR-B 189, 190). The husbands—Uetex, twenty-two years old, and Vayas, nineteen years old, who had gone back to Mission Santa Cruz when their new wives were taken from them—were also from Mitenne (SCR-B 186, 187).

During the eighteen years that the Spanish military had been present among the tribes of the Bay Area, its leaders had tried to avoid direct confrontations that might result in losses and a resultant weakening of its authority. But the success of Charquin goaded the soldiers into action. Sal's letter of February, 1793, requested orders to move against Charquin:

> The Reverend Father Friar Baldomero Lopez told him [Sal] that Charquin had finally given them enough to endure. The commander of the presidio of San Francisco concluded that he also would no longer allow such excesses (which had continued, notwithstanding the consideration with which they had tolerated his behavior). He desires to go under cover of darkness to capture this Indian and give him what he deserves, regardless of the obstacles presented by the impregnable reaches of the mountains in which he pulls together his forces.

> It was known that said Charquin had in his power about twenty Christians of the Mission of San Francisco, including women and children, and allowed none to leave him. Consequently, in regard to what he has reported, he hopes to receive a directive for action as soon as possible (Sal [1793], Appendix 4, 1).

No diary survives stemming from any successful expedition against Charquin, yet indirect evidence exists that one did take place, and that it occurred in late April and early May of 1793. An entry in the Mission San Francisco *Libro de Difuntos* on May 3, 1793 recorded the death of two children of runaway families at the mountain Quiroste village of Chipletac (SFR-D 541, 542), and just a few days later, on May 6, 1793, ten Accsagis couples from the same region were baptized at Mission San Francisco. Charquin seems to have been captured at that time.

At the same time that the Santa Cruz Mountains confrontations were taking place, migration to the missions from the bay shore side of the San Francisco Peninsula was actually on the upswing. From January through May of 1793, forty-six Bay shore Puichon, Lamchin, and Ssalson couples moved north to join Mission San Francisco. At the same time, ten Puichon couples went to Mission Santa Clara. A number of Olpen people, Santa Cruz Mountain people inter-married with both bay shore and coastal groups, also went to the missions in 1793. Charquin's resistance faction was forcing people to make decisions, and to declare their allegiances. So many were opting for the missions that most members of the Bay shore population of the San Francisco Peninsula were Christians by the end of 1793.

Quiroste resistance did not end with the capture of Charquin in the spring of 1793. On December 14, 1793, Quirostes took part in a direct attack on Mission Santa Cruz, the only attack on a mission north of Monterey ever reported during the entire Spanish era. Upon hearing of the incident, Father President Lasuén wrote from Monterey:

> I have found out for certain that on the night of the fourteenth of last December the pagan Indians, and some Christian Indians, from the rancherías to the northwest of that mission made an assault on the guard, wounded the corporal in the hand, and another soldier in the shoulder, and set fire to the roof of the corral for the lambs, and the old guard house. The corporal fired a few shots, and with that they withdrew without serious injury to either side (Lasuén [1785 1803] 1965:299).

The attack on Mission Santa Cruz was a continuation of the ongoing history of the Charquin resistance. Concerning the cause of the December attack, Father Lasuén wrote:

> The motive they have given is this, that the soldiers had taken away to San Francisco various Christian Indians belonging to that place who had been fugitives from there for some time, and that they had taken a Christian Indian woman away from a pagan man, and it was he who was the principal instigator and leader of the disorder (Lasuén [1785-1803] 1965:299).

Clues exist to suggest that the Quiroste anger resulted from mission penetration into traditional family control of marriage. When the Spanish troops had raided the Quirostes and captured Charquin the previous spring, they had returned the two young neophyte women (SCR-B 189, 190) mentioned in the quote above to their Christian husbands at Mission Santa Cruz. One of the leaders of the December 1793 attack was Ochole, the father of one of those two young women. Ochole may have joined his non-Christian son-in-law in attacking the mission because the missionaries assisted his daughter in renouncing her husband as well as her culture.

Squads of soldiers were dispatched to Mission Santa Cruz following the Quiroste raid, one group from San Francisco under Pedro Amador, and another from Monterey under Pablo Cota (Arrillaga [1793]). During the next six weeks, Cota sent out mission Indians to track down the people who had attacked Mission Santa Cruz. On January 28, 1794, Second Lieutenant Perez-Fernández, the officer in charge at San Francisco Presidio, wrote to the governor:

> The nine Indians who, at the orders of Ensign Pablo Cota, went out searching for the heathen Ochole on January nineteenth have not returned as of the twenty-eighth (Perez-Fernández [1794a]).

Later, on February 1, 1794, Perez-Fernández learned that Cota's Indian auxiliaries had returned from the back country to Mission Santa Cruz:

> The nine Indians who went into the mountains on orders of Second Lieutenant Pablo Cota have returned. They brought in eight prisoners, including the ringleader called Pella. He believes it to be important that they be sent down to Monterey (Perez-Fernández [1794b]).

On February 3, 1794, Father President Lasuén ([1785-1803] 1965:300) wrote that five Christians and a large number of non-Christians had been sent from

Santa Cruz to Monterey for punishment. Perez-Fernández wrote on February 1, 1794 that the Indians were still angry, "that the pagans of the mountains are making arrows to go fight against the mission" (Perez-Fernández [1794b]); however, no subsequent attack seems to have taken place.

Ochole was eventually baptized at Mission Santa Clara on December 5, 1794; from there he seems to have been sent to the San Francisco Presidio (SCL-B 2718). In April of 1796, Ochole and Charquin (the latter having been recaptured after escaping from the Santa Barbara Presidio in 1795) were moved from the San Francisco Presidio down to Monterey "in shackles for atonement" (Sal [1796d]). Eventually they were shipped to the San Diego Presidio; both men died in prison in 1798 (SCL-D 2032; SFR-D 1189).[2]

Spanish Power, Tribal Ambivalence

The arrests of the Mission Santa Cruz attackers did not end the turmoil that roiled the south San Francisco Bay landscape; in fact, that continued to grow. The priests at Mission Santa Clara were growing concerned. The mission settlements were getting larger, and the priests were beginning to lose their personal control of the mission communities. In March of 1794, the Santa Clara missionaries reported new episodes of native cattle rustling:

> At the foot of the mountains at one side of San Jose Cupertino Creek [Stevens Creek] are some pagans who have been eating livestock. He has given orders to try and capture them with the help of the party that is bringing cattle down to Santa Clara (Perez-Fernández [1794d]).

---

[2] Charquin's name was not mentioned between the time the complaint was lodged against him in January, 1793 (Appendix 4, 1) and August, 1794, at which time he was a prisoner at the Santa Barbara Presidio (Arrillaga [1794a]). Thus I assume he was first captured in the May, 1793 raid. Charquin escaped from the Santa Barbara Presidio on June 10, 1795. At the time the governor wrote, "He orders that the Indian Mateo Charquin, who has escaped from the Santa Barbara Presidio, be taken. When that is done transfer him securely to this presidio [Monterey]" (Borica [1795e]). Charquin's escape took place at a time when a major revolt was taking place at Mission San Francisco (see Chapter 7). No records detail the date and context of his recapture before April, 1796. Charquin died at the San Diego Presidio in the spring of 1798 (SFR-D 1189). Ochole also died at the San Diego Presidio, a few months earlier, as reported in the *Libro de Difuntos* of Mission Santa Clara on January 6, 1798 (SCL-D 2032). The circumstances of their deaths were not reported.

This incident occurred only four weeks after Commander Perez-Fernández' February 1 warning regarding arrow making and other signs of hostility among some Santa Cruz Mountains people.

In response to the reported loss of cattle, a Spanish corporal and some troops raided a village in the hills on the west side of the Santa Clara Valley, but found it empty. Two days later one of the wanted men went in to Mission Santa Clara to explain that they had merely feasted on a cow that had already been killed by a bear:

> Father Noboa said that it was probably true, since the animal was one of the recently fixed yearling steers that had recently wandered off. So the summoned pagan was found innocent. However, he was held in the stocks for ten days as punishment for failure to report the death of the steer (Perez-Fernández [1794e]).

But as soon as one group was punished, another group took some livestock:

> At sunrise on the eleventh there arrived word from the corporal of the same escort, Miguel Pacheco, that on the night before four Christian Indians had taken horses from the herd of the guard, and gone out to rob and kill cattle, the meat of which the corporal confiscated from the village and brought to the Fathers. He placed the four Christians under detention and immediately sent Corporal Peralta with a soldier to bring them up to the presidio. He was back at the mission by midnight (Perez-Fernández [1794e]).

On the same day, March 11, 1794, the sergeant of the San Francisco Presidio arrived in the Santa Clara Valley for a completely different purpose—to hire tribal villagers to work on a new gun emplacement at Fort Point, the cliff on the south side of the Golden Gate:

> Sergeant Pedro Amador arrived at the mission shortly before [Peralta], with the intention of going over to the pueblo to solicit pagans for work on the fort. On the twelfth he wrote me that the four Christian Indian prisoners had incriminated fifteen pagans in the cattle-killing affair. He awaited my directions to fall upon these pagans with his soldiers and some auxiliaries from the pueblo (Perez-Fernández [1794e]).

The San Francisco Presidio commander directed the sergeant to go out after the fifteen non-Christians:

> Losing no time, I despatched another man to tell him to go ahead, and when they are caught, to transfer them to Corporal Peralta along with the four Christians, then continue with his original mission. He returned today [March 15] with only twenty-two contract laborers, unable to find more. He told me that he had gone with fifteen men, troops and settlers, in search of the accused pagans. They found the village empty, but captured four of them in a nearby village. Those four and the four Christians are now prisoners here at the Presidio. They have confessed to me that they, and the others that were not caught, killed several head of cattle (Perez-Fernández (1794e]).

Perez-Fernández, not averse to using convict labor, put the captives to work on the new fortifications at San Francisco. By bringing the cattle thieves up to the presidio, he felt he was combining punishment, productive work, and resocialization.

To the Santa Clara missionaries, the cattle theft incidents were anything but typical. Father Noboa sent a message of continued alarm to the governor on March 14, 1794:

> It is good that the present crime has been punished, but even to go out and investigate can lead to terrible consequences. You see, I, who am carefully watching, see the villages swelling in numbers, with more and more Christians. They and the pagans are very full of themselves. If you ask me, the situation is about to erupt, just as it did in Sonora. They are almost completely united, and I judge, not with good will (Noboa [1794]).

Father Noboa had been at Mission Santa Clara for ten years, so his perception of danger cannot be taken lightly.

In the midst of the ferment in the late winter and early spring of 1794, the military authorities at San Francisco Presidio were trying to get their new fortifications built. In addition to using the prisoners, they hired twenty-two non-Christian villagers from the vicinity of the pueblo of San Jose. Each man was given a cotton shirt and a blanket at the start of work. Two of the freely hired villagers ran away after three days. The other twenty ran away after having worked for fifteen days, leaving their shirts and blankets behind (Perez-Fernández 1794f). Second Lieutenant Hermenegildo Sal then sent his sergeant to find non-Christians who really wanted to work. By April 30 work was proceeding on the new battlements at the presidio with the aid of the eight cattle killers (who had not fled), thirty-three newly hired non-Christian laborers, and another thirty Christian laborers hired out by Mission San Francisco (Sal [1794]). Sal was hopeful that the new group of hired tribesmen would return home happier than the previous group:

> They are quite content as they are being well treated. He is confident that when they return to their village they will speak well of the way we dealt with them (Sal [1794]).

On July 29, 1794, Governor Arrillaga ([1794a]) received word that a man named Meve, brother of the infamous Charquin, had arrived at Santa Clara Mission asking for forgiveness and asylum. Governor Arrillaga ordered him taken prisoner: "In case the missionaries deny him to us, the corporal should enter the church and bring the culprit out, forgetting all the niceties, because his was not a crime that is given ecclesiastical immunity" (Arrillaga [1794a]). Meve, who was nicknamed *El Calvo* ("Baldy"), was arrested and exiled to prison at the Presidio of San Diego. Meve and his brother Charquin were considered especially worthy of comment by departing Governor Arrillaga; in his report to the incoming governor, Diego de Borica, in August of 1794, Arrillaga noted:

> Item 24. Two men are imprisoned at the Santa Barbara Presidio, a settler and a Christian Indian from San Francisco named Charquin, the latter for running away and for sheltering other runaway Christians in his village.

> Item 25. In the Presidio of San Diego are three Indians, two pagans and a Christian.... [One of the pagans] is a captain of a village in the mountains adjoining San Francisco, named Meve or El Calvo. I imagine that you will find one year at the presidio will suffice him as punishment, while two years will be appropriate for the one that is at the presidio on the [Santa Barbara] Channel, who is his brother (Arrillaga [1794b]).

No earlier record concerning the man Meve has been found. We can surmise that he was wanted for participating in the resistance movement with Charquin more than a year earlier.

The appearance of Meve seeking asylum in the Mission Santa Clara church corroborates other evidence that suggests that there was a growing crisis among tribal groups over a wide area in the summer of 1794. Meve's surrender suggests that any remaining coastal factions advocating direct resistance to missionization were in a state of disarray and confusion. The collapse of a once strong center of resistance swung ambivalent factions within the still large regional tribal populations toward an acceptance of the inevitability of Spanish authority.

Another new element during the summer of 1794 was the arrival of two new priests, fathers Manuel Fernández and Magín Catalá, to Mission Santa Clara. These men brought a new, aggressive attitude to the Christian attack on tribal culture. Manuel Fernández came to Santa Clara on or around July 13, 1794. He had a tough and belligerent personality, judging by his actions in California (Geiger 1969:85). For example, an agitated Gabriel Moraga, commissioner for the town of San Jose in 1794, wrote a letter of complaint to José Argüello in Monterey at the end of October:

> I inform you that as a result of a number of trips that the Reverend Father Manuel Fernández, minister of the Mission of Santa Clara, has made to the villages in the neighborhood of this town, the pagans have abandoned the towns and retired into the mountains. It is common knowledge among these Indians, and verified by the reports of soldiers who accompanied said religious, that he severely threatened the Indians who refused to become Christians, and with some he even went beyond threats to actual punishment. As a confirming example, when he arrived at the cornfield of the soldier Ygnacio Soto (who is here at this moment), the priest called to one of several pagans who was harvesting corn. Because the man did not come over to him immediately, he asked a soldier who was with him for his lance and proceeded to severely horsewhip the Indian with it (G. Moraga [1794], Appendix 4,4).

Neither the soldiers nor the townspeople of San Jose appreciated Father Fernández' aggressive behavior. Fernández blurred the line in his preaching between threats of heavenly punishment and threats of earthly punishment for those who did not heed the call:

> After this and other actions, the pagans truly believed the Father's threat that he would burn the villages of all those who had said they would go to be baptized but failed to do so (G. Moraga [1794]).

Perhaps Fernández' told them that they would burn in Hell after death if they refused to become Christians. On the other hand, it is certainly credible that he did threaten their villages, given his other documented violent actions.

The other new priest, Magín Catalá, arrived at Santa Clara on September 1, 1794. Catalá, schooled in a pre-Enlightenment form of Catholicism, believed himself to be an exorcist of devils:

> One night Fr. Magín visited a sick person in an Indian rancheria. On the following Sunday, while preaching, he related that on this occasion he had discovered a legion of evil spirits there; that he had exorcised them and had commanded them not to go to the neighboring village, whereupon they had disappeared. The holy man then exhorted his hearers to fortify themselves against the machinations of the devil by reciting the Rosary of the Blessed Virgin, and thus to prevent the evil spirits from taking possession of their hearts (Engelhardt 1909:153-154).

Whether due to the arrival of the two new priests, or to other causes, the period of accommodation, slow mission growth, and local resistances was coming to an end.

Two weeks after Father Catalá arrived at Mission Santa Clara, and two months after Father Manuel Fernández' arrival, a group of six Santa Cruz mountain couples, consisting of Olpens and Quirostes, were baptized in a single group by Father Fernández on September 20, 1794. This was the first large group from the western mountains and coast to come over to Santa Clara, and the first coastal group to appear anywhere after Meve's arrest. Subsequent baptisms in November suggest that the rest of the coastal and mountain villagers had been preparing to move to Santa Clara, or at least were discussing the possibility in the late summer.

Most of the villagers of the Santa Clara Valley had been content for the past seventeen years to share the valley with the Spaniards and with those of their relatives who had become neophytes in the Santa Clara Mission. By late September 1794 it was clear that such a relationship could not continue. Suddenly they faced the prospect of a massive immigration of mountain and coastal tribesmen to Mission Santa Clara, people who could eventually capture the prominent positions in the mission community. In addition, they were coping with the consequences of a seed crop failure induced by drought. Finally, the new missionaries were going from village to village threatening everyone with the imminent fires of Hell if they did not become Christians.

I surmise that the villagers of the five tribes in and around the Santa Clara Valley broke into three factions in response to the crisis. One faction decided that Father Manuel was correct, and that they should join the mission out of fear of the Spanish religion. A second faction also wanted to join the mission, but as a political expedient, in order to block its takeover by the Quirostes and their coastal allies. The third faction wanted to drive out the

Spaniards and all the Indians who supported them. I also surmise that most people were only weakly affiliated with one faction or another; they were confused, did not know what to do, and were ready to move in any of a number of directions.

Sometime in early October of 1794, a group of forty-five tribal people from the big villages around Santa Clara began attending catechism classes. These classes included individuals from every nearby village, including an elder from Santa Ysabel who was said to be ninety years old, one from San Bernardino who was said to be eighty, and another from Santa Agueda who was said to be seventy. Others, however, were working actively to convince them and many waverers not to become Christians. When Father Fernández heard about the resistors, he struck again:

> One pagan inhabitant of the town, called *El Mocho* ("The Cripple"), came to me to complain that said Father [Fernández] had gone to his village and, because he would not go to the mission and because he was accused of dissuading his relatives, had ordered him tied up and whipped, first with a halter rope, and subsequently with a leather riata. The Indian was left in such bad condition that he came in supporting himself by a cane, unable to stand upright, with waist and buttocks covered with swollen wounds (G. Moraga [1794], Appendix 4, 4).

This was too much for the anti-mission faction. The most alienated local traditionalists threatened retaliation.

On the night of October 29, 1794, two days before the planned baptismal ceremony for the forty-five-person Santa Clara Valley catechism class, a man was caught near the pueblo of San Jose either planning insurrection or attempting to work sorcery against the Spaniards:

> It came to pass shortly after sunset last night that citizen Ygnacio Castro came upon, a short distance out behind his house, a pagan Indian armed with bow and arrows, whom he could not identify because he was completely covered with paint. Castro set about interrogating him. Among other things the Indian said, as if taking pity on him, that he should get his wife and children away from town, because the pagans were very angry. Many had gotten together, including those from very far off, and determined to come and kill all the people of the pueblo and of the mission. This man was going that night to tell the pagans whom the Father had brought in not to

become Christians. Then Castro commiserated with him and persuaded him by flattery to come and see me. When the Indian resisted, Castro grabbed him by the hair and shouted to citizen Pedro Romero, who was his nearest neighbor. But the Indian's resistance was so strong that by the time Romero arrived, he had escaped (G. Moraga [1794], Appendix 4, 4).

The activist faction that wanted to kill the Spaniards was probably a small one. Most of the non-Christians of the Santa Clara Valley, hearing of the potential conflict, became frightened and moved up into the mountains to the east:

> Soberanes and the previously mentioned Romero, who arrived yesterday, told me that from the Laguna Seca hither they observed tracks of many Indians heading toward the mountains to the east, and the same has been observed in this area.
>
> I remain fully vigilant. Beginning tonight I will see that everyone keeps his horse saddled, that the few arms that are here are ready, that the pueblo is patrolled, and that everything is in such a condition that any surprise will be avoided until I receive supplies from you (G. Moraga [1794], Appendix 4, 4).

Moraga's report was penned on Thursday, October 30; on the following day, October 31, the members of that first big local catechumen class were baptized by Manuel Fernández at Mission Santa Clara (SCL-B 2567-2612). No attack took place upon them or upon the settlers.

On the day that the baptisms took place, José Argüello responded from Monterey to Moraga's alarm by ordering Second Lieutenant Sal to go down from San Francisco, investigate, and evacuate the missionaries, if necessary:

> Upon carrying out those orders, call upon the captains with all due respect. Once they understand that the object of their ire has been removed, they will calm down. In that case, convey a sincere message to set the record straight, that we do not want to cause them any trouble so long as they are not causing us any trouble, nor do we want to make Christians of them by force or intimidation. Tell them the governor has ordered the Father who harassed them to leave. Finally, take all necessary measures to quiet them, and to admonish them for having fled into the mountains, since they should have shared their complaints when the problem arose by sending two or three men down to Monterey to talk with the governor. I count upon

> the efficiency with which you will apply prudence and wisdom to this situation, which is so extraordinary in its circumstances....
>
> If, Heaven forbid, the Reverend Father Manuel refuses to leave the mission, order the corporal of the escort of his mission to refuse to escort him on any of his journeys (Argüello [1794]).

Sal rushed down to the Pueblo of San Jose, arriving at daybreak on Saturday, November 1. Mission Santa Clara seemed calm; forty-five people, including some elders, had been baptized the day before without incident. On November 2, 1794, Sal wrote back to Argüello:

> I inform you that I arrived at the Pueblo at daybreak on the first of the month. As soon as they heard about my arrival some of the pagans appeared. I immediately arranged to send some of them to bring in their people and captains. Before mid-day three of the captains presented themselves to me. I spoke with them and they are since said to have been calming their people, with the effect that some have cooled off. Today I am awaiting the arrival of three or four other captains who are coming in with their people. I have adopted measures to regale them and gift them to the best of my ability. There is not the least indication that they fear that I am aware of a revolt afoot (Sal [1794a], Appendix 4, 6).

Whatever the possibility had been for full scale war before Sal arrived at Mission Santa Clara, no further problem ensued.[3] Sal may have undercut the power of resistance factions by assuring the tribal captains that Father Fernández would not be allowed to harass them in the future. I also suggest that most of the native leaders had been ambivalent about both the desirability and the possibility of driving out the Spanish. At the conclusion of this incident

---

[3] On Tuesday, November 4, 1794, Lieutenant Argüello at the San Francisco Presidio forwarded the reports he had been receiving from the Santa Clara Valley to Governor Borica in Monterey. In his cover letter Argüello wrote that Corporal Moraga had made too much of the original situation. But Argüello also noted that the Missionary President Lasuén had been informed and had agreed to send a letter to Manuel Fernández asking him to "moderate his zeal" (Argüello [1794a], Appendix 4, 7). Fernández stayed on at Mission Santa Clara until April, 1795, worked at Mission San Francisco through August of 1795, then at Mission Santa Cruz from October 1795 through October 1798.

Mass Migration In The Winter Of 1794-1795

During the next few weeks that followed the November 2 meeting between the Santa Clara Valley captains and Hermenegildo Sal, people began moving to Mission Santa Clara from all directions. Some of the Santa Cruz Mountains and coastal people were probably already in catechism classes. Thirty-three Quiroste and Solchequi adults were baptized on November 12 and 13; seventy more were baptized between November 27 and December 5. A good portion of the remaining adults from San Jose Cupertino village, the main Tamien town on the west side of the Santa Clara Valley, were with the latter groups.

Between December 10, 1794 and May 2, 1795, 360 more people were baptized at Mission Santa Clara. The Franciscans sent extra missionaries from Monterey to help with the brief catechism classes. People of all ages and sexes poured into Mission Santa Clara from every village in the Valley, from up the San Francisco Peninsula at San Francisquito Creek, and from the headwater areas of the Guadalupe River and Los Gatos Creek to the south. Between December 13 and December 27, sixty-two people from the Fremont Plain area in the East Bay joined Mission Santa Clara, and more people from that area went down to Mission Santa Clara after the first of the year, early in 1795.

The new neophytes at Mission Santa Clara included people who had been bringing their children for baptism to Mission Santa Clara throughout the 1780s (Table 1), but other families also appeared who had never brought their children for baptism. The absorption of so many families quickly brought the child to adult ratio in the Christian population at Mission Santa Clara down to less than one to one (see Figure 9, page 133).

The massive influx was not confined to Mission Santa Clara. Entire Huchiun village populations were crossing the bay to Mission San Francisco in the fall of 1794. Potential catechumens were being ferried across San Francisco Bay from the eastern shore by November 4, if not earlier. The November 4 date is established because of a tragedy that occurred that day:

> The Fathers of the mission of San Francisco sent Indians of the mission by sea in tule balsas to the Islands opposite the mouth of the port, and to the opposite shore on the fourth of this month in order to conquer pagans. One of the balsas was carried outside the port by the currents, and wrecked upon the

Lieutenant Sal was the real captain of the entire western part of the Bay Area, the person who could give orders and see that they were carried out.

Table 1. Some mothers who were baptized at Mission Santa Clara during the 1790s, with a log of the children they brought for baptism over the previous years.

Mother	Children's bapt.#'s	sex	age at baptism		date of baptism	date of death	age at death	
Yonaset								
	SCl-B 1719	F	38	years	7-12-1790	9-07-1790	38	years
	SCL-B 21	M	1	year	6-08-1777	7-01-1777	1	year
	SCL-B 199	F	1	year	7-16-1780	5-11-1788	9	years
	SCL-B 352	F	5	days	5-15-1780	8-31-1783	1	year
	SCL-B 720	F	2	months	4-21-1785	5-06-1799	14	years
	SCL-B 796	M	5	years	9-29-1785	11-10-1788	8	years
	SCL-B 1156	F	2	months	3-23-1788	10-30-1789	2	years
	SCL-B 1350	F	2	months	5-17-1789	4-24-1806	17	years
Rasmamis								
	SCL-B 2597	F	30	years	10-31-1794	2-10-1803	38	years
	SCL-B 320	M	8	days	12-17-1781	1-04-1829	48	years
	SCL-B 783	F	10	days	8-27-1785	9-23-1786	1	year
	SCL-B 1090	F	5	days	8-05-1787	8-28-1787	1	month
	SCL-B 1329	M	6	months	4-29-1789	11-16-1789	1	year
	SCL-B 2330	F	7	days	6-13-1793	9-14-1794	1	yerar
Jasuam								
	SCL-B 2731	F	40	years	12-05-1794	8-02-1796	42	years
	SCL-B 406	M	4	years	9-01-1782	12-31-1786	8	years
	SCL-B 407	M	2	years	9-01-1782	9-26-1815	35	years
	SCL-B 1182	M	1	month	6-21-1788	12-06-1789	1½	years
	SCL-B 1751	F	8	days	7-31-1790	11-04-1791	1½	years
	SCL-B 2196	M	8	days	10-03-1792	11-16-1794	2	years
Jaquete								
	SCL-B 2738	F	50	years	12-05-1794	10-16-1801	57	years
	SCL-B 151	M	18	months	11-16-1779	5-13-1788	10	years
	SCL-B 211	M	6	months	8-13-1780	4-18-1817	37	years
	SCL-B 639	M	10	days	3-29-1784	5-23-1784	2	months
	SCL-B 927	F	5	days	8-15-1786	11-23-1786	3	months
	SCL-B 1241	M	8	days	10-18-1788	9-16-1792	4	years
	SCL-B 2173	M	7	days	8-26-1792	9-17-1834	42	years
	SCL-B 2550	F	5	days	10-09-1794	11-30-1796	2	years
Chalsim								
	SCL-B 2882	F	30	years	12-22-1794	5-27-1806	41	years
	SCL-B 646	F	20	days	5-03-1784	6-11-1786	2	years
	SCL-B 968	F	1	months	9-20-1786	11-08-1806	20	years
	SCL-B 1252	M	2	months	12-08-1788	8-26-1792	4	years
	SCL-B 1963	M	10	days	8-31-1791	9-18-1792	1	year
	SCL-B 2743	M	4	months	12-09-1794	1-18-1796	2	years

Farallon Islands. Two of the four crew members succeeded in swimming back to shore. The other two perished (Perez-Fernández [1794g]).

One of the drowned ferrymen was Bonifacio, the young Huchiun man from the Genau directly east of San Francisco, whose wife had come to the mission in 1788 from the Huchiun-Aguasto village near the entrance to Carquinez Strait (SFR-D 704, 705).

Forty Huchiun children were baptized on Friday and Saturday, November 14 and 15, 1794; their parents were baptized on November 18 (twenty-four people) and November 26 (twenty-nine people). In prior years, catechumen parents were usually baptized at least three weeks after their children. Either these new neophytes had been catechized in their home villages, or shorter emergency procedures were in place. It is worth noting that three of the new Christians at San Francisco on November 26 were among the men whose names had been recorded when they visited the ship *San Carlos* in August, 1775, nineteen years earlier (Supitaxe, age fifty; Guilicse, age fifty; Mutacxe, age forty, all Huchiuns).[4]

On November 20, Commander Perez-Fernández wrote to Governor Diego de Borica that the priests at Mission San Francisco wanted him to break standing orders and provide them with an escort, to go via Santa Clara "northward on the opposite shore as far as the mouth of the harbor, to make conquests among the pagans" (Perez-Fernández [1794g]). Perez-Fernández informed the governor that he had turned down the missionaries' request for three reasons:

> 1. Because it is nearly unknown country; there are indications that the people who live there are contrary.
>
> 2. I do not believe that a single religious and two or three soldiers are a strong enough party to cross and remain overnight in unknown territories.

---

[4] Ship's chaplain Vicente Santa María ([1775] 1971) had recorded the visit of the following men to the *San Carlos* on August 24, 1775: "Their chieftain called Sumu; the second chieftain, Jausos; the others, Supitacse (1); Tilacse (2); Mutuc (3); Logeacse (4); Guecpostole (5); Xacacse (6)." Besides the three men baptized at Mission San Francisco on November 26, 1794, three others of the 1775 visitors can be accounted for. Logeacse was baptized on January 12, 1803, from the Huchiun-Aguasto (SFR-B 2562). Xacacse was probably the same man as Ratacsse, a Huchiun baptized at age fifty on September 20, 1803 (SFR-B 2848). Second chieftain Jausos had died before 1794. His son Royute was baptized in mid-January of 1795 as part of the third cluster of Huchiun migrants during that winter (SFR-B 1696). Captain Sumu of the 1775 group was never identified in a baptismal record.

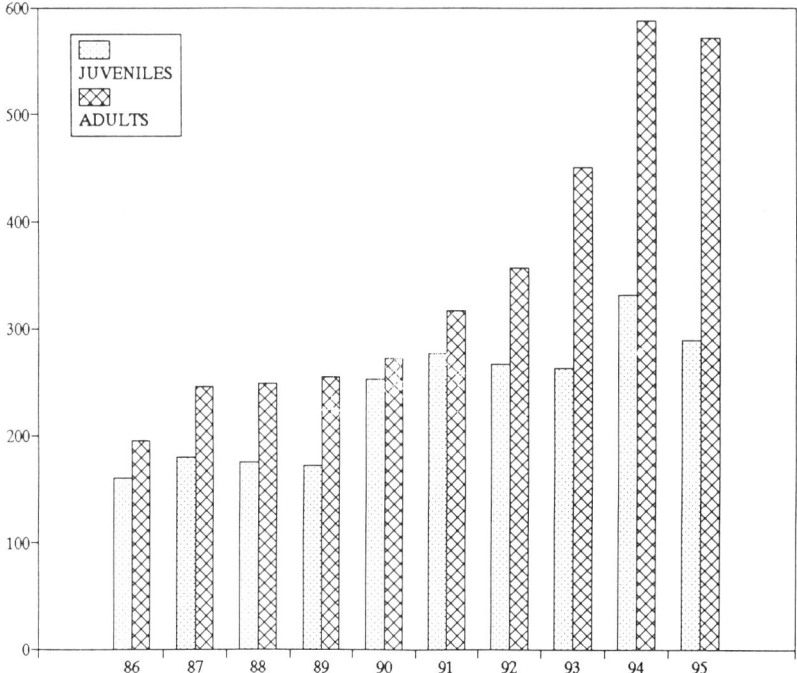

Figure 8. Bar chart of year-end 1786-1795 populations at Mission San Francisco, showing a change in ratio of children (age 0-14) to adults (age 15 and over).

3. Although the Reverend Fathers believe it to be an opportune moment, because the pagans are without food, having lost their harvest due to the severity of the drought, which facilitates drawing them in, I do not have the resources to send out an expedition of such magnitude (Perez-Fernández [1794g]).

Governor Borica recognized the volatility underlying the wave of change, a change which the missionaries certainly saw as a miracle; he sent a return letter to the San Francisco Presidio on December 3:[5]

---

[5] The transcribed notes of Borica's [1794] December 3, 1794 letter indicate that it was sent to the commander at Santa Cruz. This may have been a transcriber's error. The context of the information suggests that it should have been written to Perez-Fernández at San Francisco Presidio. Perhaps Perez-Fernández was visiting Mission Santa Cruz at the time. At any rate, the original letter cannot be checked, as it was destroyed in the San Francisco fire of 1906.

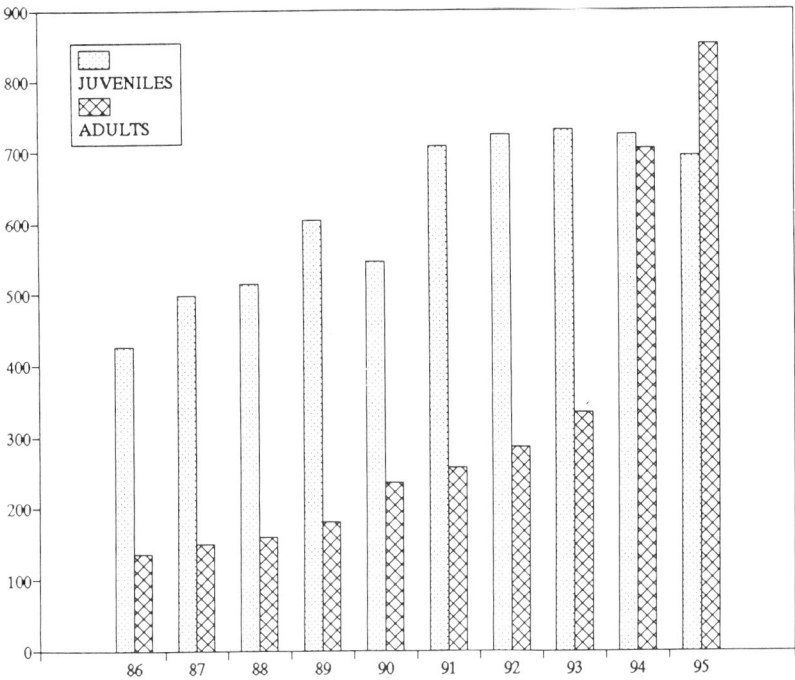

Figure 9. Bar chart of year-end 1786-1795 populations at Mission Santa Clara, showing a change in ratio of children (age 0-14) to adults (age 15 and over).

Under no circumstances are soldiers ever to go out from their guard stations overnight, whether it be to accept converts or for any other purpose. The Fathers can do whatever they like. Go to Mission San Francisco and let the Father know the orders that pertain to these situations, and commend the commander of the escorts there, as well.

The zeal of the Religious for the salvation of souls stimulates them to attract the unhappy pagans who live in darkness to our Religion by all possible methods. So they use whatever means they see fit, although some of their methods are fruitless. There is no doubt, in view of what just happened to the Indians that they sent by sea to catechize, that in the future they should abstain from similar conquests or undertakings (Borica [1794]).

Actually, the missionaries did not need to cross to the East Bay. Huchiun families, joined by Saclans, continued to join the catechism classes throughout December of 1794 and the early months of 1795.

The Saclans, southern neighbors of the Huchiuns, must have been trying to decide how to respond as the Huchiuns were crossing the bay in November. A Saclan group was baptized in mid-December; seventeen children were baptized on December 15 (SFR-B 1531-1547), followed by forty-two adults on December 18. Groups of Huchiun and Saclan people of various sizes were baptized all through the winter and into the spring of 1795. At least thirty Huimens from the southern tip of the Marin Peninsula, spouses and companions of the Huchiuns, were mixed in with the last large baptismal groups in this mass movement, in early 1795. There were also newcomers from more distant parts of the East Bay, including three Carquins, one Chupcan, and eight Tatcans. These people went to San Francisco with the Saclans.

The Mission San Francisco population jumped from 628 at the end of October, 1794, to 1095 at the beginning of May, 1795. The level of religious instruction that could have been provided for so many new people must have been absolutely minimal. Among the new tribal converts were far fewer children than one would expect, resulting for the first time in a preponderance of adults over children in the mission population (see Figure 8, page 132).

Huge numbers of people went through wedding ceremonies moments or hours after being baptized. The priests at Santa Clara married eighteen couples on October 31, 1794, sixteen couples on November 15, ten on November 30, sixteen on December 6, sixteen on December 11, and so on through March 25, 1795. At San Francisco, fifteen couples were married on November 8, 1794, twelve on November 18, ten on November 25, seven on December 13, seventeen on December 18, and many more through March 10, 1795. Mission mass marriage procedures were described to Hubert Howe Bancroft many years later:

> Men and women were...ranged in separate lines in the presence of the mission people, and harangued by the padre, with the aid of an interpreter, on the merits and responsibilities of marriage. Each person was asked whether he or she wished to be married, and every one saying aye was ranged in a separate line of his or her sex. Any man or woman who admitted having had sexual connection was placed apart to be married to her or him with whom that connection had been, to be married whether they were willing or not. The rest of the men were then asked, one by one, which of the women opposite they chose to marry. If the selected woman showed unwillingness to accept the man, he had to choose again (Bancroft 1888:227-228).

During the mass immigration of 1794-1795, most of the adults in the Santa Clara Valley were renewing their existing marriages. Many women were left without spouses, however, when their husbands were forced to marry only one cowife. Some of the individuals in the large baptismal blocks never remarried at the mission. This most commonly occurred among women aged forty and older and men aged sixty and older (SCL-B 2675-2681, 2914-2917; SFR-B 1520-1524, 1583-1590, 1748-1753).

The Forced Conversion Question

Some scholars have argued that the emigration of 1794-1795 took place because the Spaniards shifted their policy toward missionization from persuasion to forced conversion. That conclusion is not supported by the historical evidence. No troops were used to bring non-Christians to the missions during the 1790s. There is some evidence to the effect that Christian Indian squads harassed non-Christian villagers, but the evidence also suggests that Christian Indian groups were not strong enough to enter villages and force people to march to the missions in the numbers that appeared for conversion in the winter of 1794-1795. The argument for overt forced conversion, on the part of the Spanish military or the Mission Indians, misrepresents the dynamic situation that existed in 1794 and underestimates the power of cultural hegemony, reinforced by indirect violence.

The main argument in favor of forced conversions during the 1790s turns upon interpretations of the terms *conquista* and *empresa* in contemporary correspondence (Cook 1943:75). Commander Perez-Fernández ([1794g]) at the San Francisco Presidio wrote that the priests wanted to make *conquistas* in the fall of 1794; this was a term used in Hispanic America to refer to victories over the Devil through baptisms. Governor Borica wrote that the missionaries wanted to engage in *empresas*, a word that has been mistranslated as "impressments," but which should be read as "undertakings" in English (cf. Cook 1943:74). Borica ([1794]) actually wrote that Mission Indians were crossing the bay in the fall of 1794 to "*catequizar*," or prepare potential neophytes for baptism. In their role as evangelizers, Mission Indian catechists probably did claim that droughts and diseases were caused by offended Christian supernaturals. But Mission Indians did not cross the bay in sufficient numbers to physically force entire village groups to cross over to the mission in the winter of 1794-1795.

An ecological explanation must also be considered for the massive conversions of 1794-1795 (see Coombs and Plog 1974). A report during the fall of 1794 mentioned a drought and a loss of seed crops among the tribal peoples of the area (Perez-Fernández [1794g], see page 132). Perhaps low seed yields did contribute to the physical and psychological stresses to which Bay

Area village groups were subjected. However, low harvests were only one of the factors which caused people to leave their homes for the missions in huge numbers.

The concept of culture helps us to understand how sovereign peoples can voluntarily give up their autonomy and subjugate themselves to foreigners. Each individual internalizes his or her culture, a culture that consists of a complex structure of ideas about the external world together with rules for living in that world. Groups share a culture insofar as their members share ideas and rules. This template of expectations and rules is at once strong and malleable, fragile and brittle. Under conditions of rapid change, which do not conform to cultural expectations and can not be predicted, the individual can become shocked and confused (Wallace 1957).

* * *

Events in the Bay Area were unfolding for which the traditional culture had not prepared people. Infant mortality had been increasing for years, to the point where people must have known that their populations were not being replaced. Trading networks and feud alliances were being disrupted by the disappearance of groups from the landscape. Traditional rituals did not prevent the increased deaths, the military defeats, or the crop losses of 1794, nor did they bring the skills and goods associated with Spanish culture. Native peoples scrambled to find stable reference points, but the world no longer fit within their complex cultural template. They were left in a state of disorganization and confusion.

When the lives of native peoples in the Bay Area were disrupted, they tried to deal with the new situations using old concepts. One such way to regain stability was to transfer faith to a new set of unseen spirits and the rituals those spirits were said to prescribe. The missionaries offered just such a new set of rituals, as well as training in the new technology. Under these circumstances of doubt and ambivalence, only a slight nudge in one direction could trigger a mass reaction, and start a movement. In the fall of 1794, once a few key groups decided to go to the missions, that movement began. It quickly gathered force and swept up those people who had been wavering about the missions or rejecting their call completely. On the surface, this was a religious conversion movement; it might be more realistic, however, to call it a psychological disintegration movement.

Chapter 7

Reconsideration, 1795-1799

	Spanish Actions	Tribal Actions
1795	April 29. Mission Indians sent to bring back Saclans, attacked and seven killed at Napa.	Mid-April. Small Saclan group flees Mission San Francisco during epidemic. Summer. Hundreds flee Mission San Francisco.
1797	June 10. Mission San Jose founded in southern East Bay. July 16-17. Amador attacks Saclans and Huchiuns, arrests resistance leaders.	June 20. Huchiuns drive Raymundo's posse out of their lands. August. Paleños begin hemp project near town of San Jose.
1798	June. Taunan threat to Mission San Jose quieted by visit from Spanish troops.	June. Some Saclan and Huchiun escapees return to Mission San Francisco.

Disease, Flight, And Death

In April, the peak of spring, weakening Pacific storm fronts bring only occasional rains, and longer days and warming temperatures trigger blooms of orange, yellow, and purple wildflowers on the green hills and flatlands. The soil is soft underfoot. Warblers glean insects among the catkins of newly-leafed oak trees, while in the marshes green shoots push up through the tangled brown mat of the previous year's bulrush and cattail stems.

Conditions were anything but pleasant in the neophyte village at Mission San Francisco in April of 1795. The new neophytes were having second thoughts about their decision to leave their homelands. Long term problems of social organization, work conditions, and hygiene were aggravated by the near doubling of the population over the previous winter. The population jump also led to a food shortage, a problem which had not occurred since the earliest years of the mission. The poor conditions combined with feelings of homesickness to awaken the new neophytes' repressed doubts about their decision to join the "modern" world.

An epidemic of unknown cause struck Mission San Francisco in March of 1795. Deaths began to increase dramatically on March 21, peaked during the week of March 26-April 1, and continued at a high rate through the last week of April (Figure 10). Death rates were abnormally high for all age groups except male adolescents. Unlike the epidemics which swept through the California missions in 1802 and 1806, this one was limited to Mission San Francisco. Typhus, a fairly slow-moving disease that is passed from person to person in drinking water and food, was the likely culprit. Typhus has a long history of occasional local flare-ups in Mexico and North America (Ackerknecht 1965:32).

A group of new Saclan neophytes left Mission San Francisco on *paseo* (a sanctioned vacation to their homeland) in mid-April, 1795. When they failed

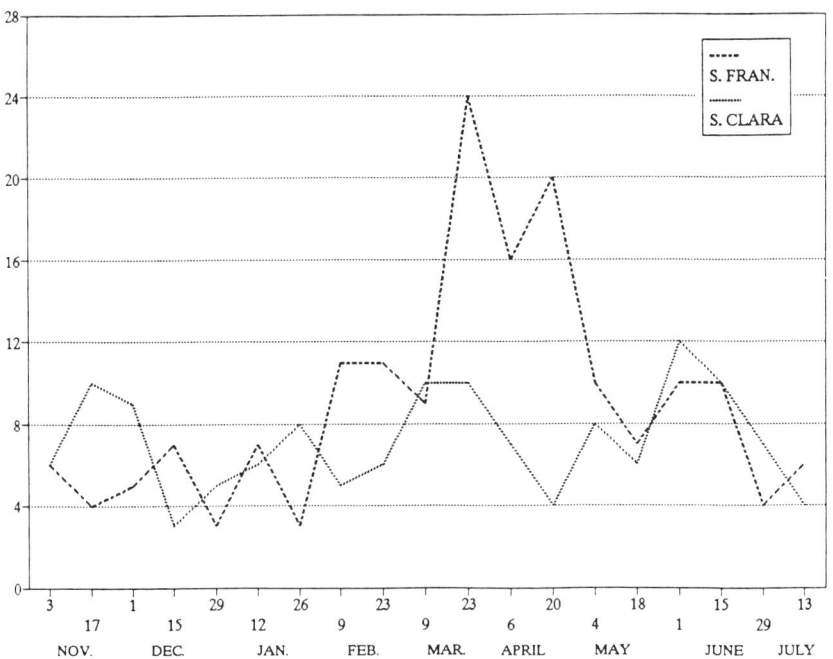

Figure 10. Graph of reported deaths at Missions San Francisco and Santa Clara during the winter of 1794-1795. (Each point reflects the count for a two week interval beginning on the date noted.)

to return by April 27, missionary Antonio Dantí sent a group of fourteen other Mission Indian men to bring them back:

> He advised that they bring with them only some short ropes in order to tie up the Christians and so to bring them back. He did not permit them to bring their bows and arrows, assuring them that the pagans would not be able to do any harm to the Christians (Borica [1795a]).

Included in the posse were the *alcaldes* of the Mission San Francisco village, Pasqual (Yelamu) and Rogerio (Huchiun), as well as three other longtime Christians, and nine new Huchiun and Saclan neophytes.

The runaway Christians had gone with non-Christian Saclans and Jalquins to a dance at the Chimenes *ranchería*, according to information received by Governor Borica. The Chimenes were mentioned in no other historical record. Borica ([1795c]) vaguely located them in the northern part of the Bay Area. The name probably derives from a village name of the Napa tribe, Tciménukme.[1] Father Dantí's posse seems to have followed the fugitives to the Saclan villages in the East Bay hills, and then followed them northward across the Carquinez Strait to the lower Napa River area.

In the early afternoon of April 29, the Mission San Francisco posse approached the Chimenes village. The fugitive Saclan men and their allies emerged from the dark of the Chimenes dance house and attacked the new arrivals. By the time the fight was over, seven posse members were dead:

---

[1] Correspondence documenting the gathering at the Chimenes provides only general clues as to their location. Governor Borica's report indicates that it was "near the Port of Bodega," that it was "no less than thirty leagues [eighty miles]" from the presidio, and that it took travelers twenty-two hours to go there from the land of the Saclans (Borica [1795b], Appendix 4, 10). A distance from the presidio of eighty miles due north would place them in the present Cloverdale area on the Russian river, which is impossibly distant. I believe that Borica, who in 1795 knew nothing about the interior lands north of San Francisco Bay, guessed at the distance to the village after interviewing Oton.

To reach the North Bay from Saclan country, one must cross either the half-mile wide Carquinez Strait or the two-mile wide San Pablo Strait. In the early twentieth century, Samuel A. Barrett (1908:293) was told that there had once been a village called "Tciménukme" on the Napa River at the present town of Napa. Tciménukme was far to the east of Bodega Bay. But it was in the northern area and was reachable by a twenty-two hour walk, including a boat crossing of Carquinez Strait, from the Saclan country. The only non-Saclan or Jalquin person known to have gone to the Chimenes in 1795 was Cesario, who was identified in a later document as a member of the Napa tribe (Abella [1818-1822], Cesario, #1835).

> Upon their arrival, men armed with bows and arrows emerged from the dance house with such force that they broke down its walls. They began at once to fire arrows, yelling, "These men are our enemies." Faced with such violence, the *alcaldes* tried to calm them down, telling them that they came neither to fight nor to do any harm. They paid no attention, but continued to fire arrows until they killed the seven. Six of the new Christians had fled at the start of the altercation, upon the orders of the *alcaldes*. The declarant himself got away at great risk, inasmuch as arrows were flying all around him (Borica [1795c], Appendix 4, 10).

Of the eight mission men who were involved in the direct confrontation, only Oton (SFR-B 614), a young Huchiun man, survived. Oton was married to the daughter of Romualdo Guimas, missionized captain of the Yelamu group. Four of the seven mission men who were killed were longtime Christians, among them Oton's stepfather Juan José Lecmese, and the two mission *alcaldes*, Pasqual Baylon and Rogerio. Also killed were three new neophytes who had been baptized the previous November and December, a Huchiun and two Saclans (Table 2).

A few years later some of the Saclan attackers provided details about the fight to Spanish investigators. An investigating officer's version of resistance

Table 2. Mission San Francisco men killed by Saclans on April 29, 1795, baptismal numbers of their widows, and information regarding the widows' subsequent husbands.

Death #	Name	Bapt. #	Tribe	Age	Wife Bapt.#	Wife's Next Husband Bapt.#	Tribe	Wedding
1056	Rogerio*	350	Huchiun	29	16	**		
1057	Santiago	270	Huchiun	22	297	132	Lamchin	10-08-96
1058	Juan José	210	Huchiun	44	482	**		
1059	Pasqual Baylon*	27	Yelamu	36	1019	127	Lamchin	5-07-97
1060	Guadencio	1395	Huch/Sac	23	1670	470	Ssalson	1-09-98
1061	Lioncio	1475	Huchiun	27	1489	**		
1062	Buenaventura	1764	Saclan	36	1676	**		

*These two men were the *alcaldes* at Mission San Francisco.
**In these four cases the wife died between 1795 and 1797 without having remarried.

leader Potroy's (SFR-B 1765) testimony follows:

> Upon my pointing out that his relatives and countrymen in the village where he had been arrested accused him of having been the prime instigator of the killings, he responded that it is true that he had helped to kill the seven Christians and that he had also helped to set fire to Rogerio, one of the seven (Argüello [1797c], Appendix 4, 13).

A Jalquin man involved in the resistance, Caguas (SFR-B 2374), also provided details:

> It is true that when one of the seven deceased, named Ventura, fled, he intercepted him and killed him with a single arrow (Argüello [1797c], Appendix 4, 13).

The posse member whom Caguas killed, Buenaventura (SFR-B 1764), had been standing next to Potroy in the baptismal line at Mission San Francisco just ten weeks prior to the Chimenes confrontation. We can assume that Buenaventura and Potroy had been friends, if not relatives; in fact, in the small world in which these events took place, everyone involved on both sides of the fight had been known to one another.

When Oton and the six survivors who had fled prior to the confrontation returned to Mission San Francisco, Father Dantí attempted to suppress the news of the killings:

> Having presented himself to the Father, the Indian related what had happened. At this he [Father Dantí] replied that he was a liar. But as the Indian insisted on the truth of the sad occurrence, the Father said to him, "Then be careful about what you say to any soldier or the commander will find out. Be careful to say nothing." But the occurrence was already known to all, as the women were crying inconsolably (Perez-Fernández [1795], Appendix 4, 9).

Governor Borica in Monterey reacted with alarm upon receiving word of the aggressive actions of the Saclans, and ordered the guard of Mission San Francisco on alert:

> Make sure that the troops of the escort are vigilant round the clock, because although one might dismiss the rumors that are floating around to the effect that the Chaclanes want to strike the mission, we should at all times go about our business as though the enemy were really in view (Borica [1795]).

The governor felt that his troops were not strong enough to go out and arrest anyone at the time:

> My best efforts would allow me to send no more than twenty men from the various companies without neglecting other important responsibilities (Borica [1795c], Appendix 4, 10).

The governor also had broad strategic reasons for not wanting to engage in a war with tribal peoples from the north. He was aware that one of Vancouver's ships had landed at Bodega Bay in 1792:

> As for the argument against punishing the Chimenes, they live near Port Bodega, where in the course of time they could do quite a lot of harm to us as declared enemies, were some foreign nation to attempt to establish themselves there (Borica [1795c], Appendix 4, 10).

The Spanish military did not attack the runaway Saclans or the Chimenes during the summer of 1795.

When word of the killing of members of the Christian posse was received, people began to abandon Mission San Francisco in large numbers. By the end of the summer of 1795, at least 280 Indian people had fled the mission. According to Second Lieutenant Perez-Fernández:

> They have slipped out a few at a time, going off in different directions. It has come to such a pass that even the very natives of San Francisco, San Mateo [the west bay shore], and San Pedro [Pacific coast], long time Christians who have never before run away, are found to be missing from among the inhabitants (Perez-Fernández [1795a], Appendix 4, 11).

This flight was the largest threat yet to the hegemony of the Spaniards in the Bay Area.

The following year, 1796, the governor launched a military inquiry into the causes of the massive desertions from Mission San Francisco. He had received a complaint from missionary José María Fernández to the effect that the Indians' unhappiness had been the result of especially abusive treatment by Father Antonio Dantí and Father Martín de Landaeta (Engelhardt 1912:501). At a September, 1796 inquiry conducted by newly arrived Coronal Pedro Alberni, three soldiers testified that the problems at Mission San Francisco under the administration of missionaries Antonio Dantí and Martín Landaeta had been "the three *muchos*, which are much work, much punishment, and much hunger"

(Amador *in* Alberni [1796]). Diego Olbera, a servant at Mission San Francisco since its founding twenty years earlier, confirmed the stark picture. He contrasted the conditions under fathers Dantí and Landaeta with those under previous Franciscan priests (Olbera *in* Alberni [1796]).

Mission president Fermín Francisco de Lasuén came up from Monterey in September, 1796 to conduct his own investigation. His letter to Governor Borica indicates that the priests at San Francisco had been pushing the Indians to complete mission projects, including new adobe row-houses to replace the grass shelters in the mission village:

> I am not trying to make saints out of the Fathers who have been in charge of this mission. They may have gone to extremes in disciplining. I have neither witnessed them, nor heard about them, nor received any reports about them. What is said about the work cannot be denied. It is evidenced by the big projects accomplished in a short time, for much of it was forced labor. I reprimanded them, and placed them under obligation to be more forebearing (Lasuén [1785-1803] 1965:401).

In the same letter, Lasuén disagreed with the military officers' conclusion that food shortage, overwork, and punishment caused the flight in 1795. He attributed it to a fear of disease:

> Of those who ran away and crossed the bay, these have come back: three men, a woman with a nursing baby that has been baptized, and a girl of sixteen or seventeen who is receiving instructions with a view to baptism. They report that they did not run away, and the others are not staying away, because of fear of punishment or aversion for the work; rather, they fled through fear of a contagious and fatal disease that broke out here (Lasuén [1785-1803] 1965:402).

Alberní's investigations among his soldiers had not identified disease as a factor in the mission's abandonment; however, upon being asked by Argüello why they had fled Mission San Francisco in 1795, fourteen of twenty-three Huchiun men interviewed later mentioned either their own sickness or the death of a relative as one motive for flight (Argüello [1797d], Appendix 4, 14). Actually, neither Alberní nor Lasuén were incorrect regarding motives for the 1795 flight; eight of the fourteen men who mentioned sickness and death as the cause of their flight indicated that the sickness and death were connected with hunger. The following statement is an example:

> Magin—He testified that he left due to his hunger and because they had put him in the stocks when he was sick, on orders from the *alcalde*.[2]

The heavy punishments administered by Father Dantí and by various Indian overseers were also given as motives in fourteen responses:

> Claudio—He declares that he fled because he was continually fighting with his brother-in-law Casimiro and because the *alcalde* Valeriano was caning him every time he turned around, and when he was sick this same Valeriano made him go to work.[3]

> José Manuel—He testifies that when they went to bring wood from the mountains Raymundo ordered them to bring him water. When the declarant wouldn't do it, this same Raymundo hit him with a heavy cane, rendering one hand useless. He showed his hand. It was a little puffed up, but had movement. That was his reason for having left the mission.[4]

> Homobono—He testifies that his motive for fleeing was that his brother had died on the other shore and when he cried for him at the mission they whipped him. Also, the *alcalde* Valeriano hit him with a heavy cane for having gone to look for mussels at the beach with Raymundo's permission (Argüello [1797d], Appendix 4, 14).[5]

---

[2]This was Llucal, who was born in 1754, and was probably a Huchiun (SFR-B 1484). His wife, and a child born in 1788, lived through the epidemic and the period of flight (SFR-B 1416, 1454).

[3]This was Ssojorois, who was born in 1736, and was from the "other shore" (SFR-B 463); his son Bonifacio had been one of the two ferrymen who drowned while transporting Huchiun people across the Bay in November, 1794 (SFR-D 704). The brother-in-law, Casimiro, was a Ssalson, as was the *alcalde* Valeriano (SFR-B 490,442).

[4]This was Tolensa, who was born in 1768, and was a Huchiun (SFR-B 1158). His wife had returned to the mission in September, 1796, at which time their three-month old child was baptized (SFR-B 1882).

[5]This was Sumipocsé, age forty-one, who was from Josquizara, a Huchiun ranchería (SFR-B 504). One of his two children, Diego, had died at the very beginning of the epidemic, on January 20, 1795 (SFR-B 758, SFR-D 730).

It is clear from the testimony of the runaways that "too much sickness" was not an alternative to "too much work, too much hunger, and too much punishment." Instead, it was an additional cause for the mass flight.

The Franciscan missionaries were for the most part unable to admit the existence of the ethical questions associated with their work. Father President Lasuén wrote the following to his own superior in Mexico after his visit to San Francisco:

> At the beginning of last month I returned from San Francisco, a place to which I was obliged to go because of the gravest and most trying problem I ever faced in all my life. The Reverend Fathers Fray Diego García and Fray José María Fernández had plotted with fanatical zeal to expel Fray Landaeta from that mission. The Indians joined in the conspiracy, and the officers of the presidio, Alberni and Argüello, joined it or tended that way. For this purpose they collected accounts of different unbecoming incidents that took place at different times in the past, giving them the appearance of cruel, enormous, and monstrous crimes, and these they attributed to Fathers Dantí and Landaeta (Lasuén [1785-1803] 1965:404).

Father José María Fernández, whom Lasuén criticized, had only been in California since June. He resigned from California mission service a year later, after further difficulties at Mission San Francisco. When he left he wrote:

> If I had been listened to last year, all this danger would have been avoided. But no one believed me. I was taken for a fraud, a troublemaker. I was accused of conspiring with the secular authorities for sinister purposes. I am quitting because I am choked to the core with feelings, but I declare that for all these grievances I ask for justice in God's court, and if He keeps me healthy, in the appropriate court of men (Fernández [1797]).

Missionaries unquestionably differed from one another in their attitudes toward the local people and in their administrative capabilities. José María Fernández seems to have been the most sympathetic of the Spanish priests in the Bay Area to the rights of the local people. Among those priests who stayed and worked within the mission system, some certainly had a more positive influence on the experience of Indian neophytes than others.[6]

After the great influx of new neophytes that occurred during the winter of 1794-1795, food supplies were taxed and authoritarian leadership was out of control. These conditions combined with poor hygienic controls to provide ideal conditions for the outbreak of contagious diseases. But neophytes had tolerated poor general health conditions, enforced alien work regimens, and the imposition of coercive social controls for many years. The unique additional element that existed at Mission San Francisco in 1795 was the fact that the village was filled with large numbers of new neophytes who had not truly converted to a faith in the mission system, and who were in a labile psychological state.

The Chimenes battle was a catalyst for the mass flight of the population of frightened new neophytes. It also ignited a serious threat to Spanish hegemony over the many Bay Area tribes, and kindled opposition to the Spanish presence that lasted until 1801.[7] Not a single tribal couple appeared at Mission San Francisco for baptism from the day the killings were reported until March, 1800, which is a period of almost five years (SFR-B 2036, 2039). No similar mass flight or ongoing resistance occurred again in west Central California until the late 1820s.

Disputes and Patronage at Santa Clara

At the time that the Saclans began their resistance to the missions, tribal villages were already empty west of the pueblo of San Jose and Mission Santa Clara. Non-Christian villages existed in the mountain valleys to the east, on the Fremont Plains to the north, and in the Laguna Seca area along the Coyote

---

[6] Father José María Fernández' criticisms ran counter to the "common sense" point of view of most of his brethren; therefore, they considered him insane. Father President Lasuén described him as "a good religious whose mind was somewhat deranged" (Geiger 1969:84). Upon their return to Mexico, Father Fernández and Father Antonio de la Concepción Horra (who himself had been declared insane in California) presented a memorial of protest against the conditions in the Alta California missions in civil court in 1798. Their protest led to a series of investigations which lasted through 1802 (Engelhardt 1912:549-555; Geiger 1969:123-124; Guest 1973:218-248). Government investigators supported the mission administration; they found nothing particularly abnormal nor disturbing in the workings of the California missions.

[7] Historians who have discussed the Saclan resistance and the subsequent flight of a quarter of Mission San Francisco's population include Bancroft (1884:708-709), Cook (1957), Cutter (1950:81-82), Engelhardt (1912:499-500), and Guest (1973:207-217). None of these authors examined mission register information concerning the individuals that were involved, and only Cook (1957) documented the continuing struggle between the Saclans and the Spaniards through 1801.

River to the south. The people in Mission Santa Clara catechism classes on April 29, 1795 were from the southern East Bay "Santa Agueda" district (Alsons, Tuibuns, and Causens). They went through the baptismal ceremony over the weekend of May 2-3. Baptisms at Santa Clara came to an abrupt halt after that weekend, a halt that is attributable to a region-wide reaction to the Saclan success in the Chimenes battle.

Tribes near the Santa Clara Valley probably retreated somewhat from the Spanish communities following the Saclan success, although an interest in the material items that were available in the pueblo of San Jose and their ties to relatives at Mission Santa Clara continued to draw them to the Spanish-controlled communities. So while Huchiuns, Saclans, and their near neighbors in the East Bay continued to completely reject the missions throughout the remainder of 1795, 1796, and early 1797, a few couples from tribes farther south were baptized at Mission Santa Clara during those years.

When a Spanish surveying party went onto the Fremont Plain just north of the town of San Jose in search of possible new mission sites in November, 1795, most villagers fled (Sal [1795]). Yet this was not a first-contact situation by any means; villages from the vicinity had been sending immigrants to Mission Santa Clara for over fifteen years. Their nervousness was almost certainly the result of the Saclan victory six months earlier. However, Tuibuns on lower Alameda Creek did visit the Spaniards:

> Without our asking they told us that the land flooded where we were, that on the other side the land shows itself to be rich, and that one can work most of these plains with ploughs without iron. The pagan populations is shown to be substantial, there are paths everywhere crossing to the estuary, most of them heading into the mountains and on to the Valley of San Jose [Livermore Valley] that lies toward the rivers (Sal [1795]).

In the context of the ongoing difference of opinion within villages and within individuals regarding cooperation with the Spaniards, the Tuibuns who visited the Spaniards' camp saw a practical benefit in such cooperation.

In May of 1796, Indians were again needed for work on the Monterey Presidio. The mass baptisms during the winter of 1794-1795 had reduced the number of non-Christian people living in the Santa Clara Valley, and thus diminished the labor supply for settlers at the pueblo and for military projects at the presidios. Hermenegildo Sal had to send extra goods to the commissioner of the pueblo of San Jose in order to get workers at Monterey:

> I send you thirty blankets with townsman Dolores Mesa in order to increase your chances of sending me some people to work for one month at the presidio, offering the women a flannel jacket and

> some cloth for making garments. Tell them they will be well taken care of and treated. If it be necessary, reward one or two captains with a blanket in order to facilitate getting workers. Set it up so that they do not get their pay beforehand, or they will run away with it (Sal [1796b]).

Although costs had gone up, tribal men were found for work projects. The last group recruited for Monterey was obtained in September, 1796:

> The group of Indians that are here now will finish on the twenty-fourth of this month. I hope that you can send me twenty pagans by the twenty-third or twenty-fourth. If they come we will finish this year's work. Now I must repeat to you the payment that must be given. You should gratify the captains if you find it necessary, as was done with Patricio, by giving a blanket (Sal [1796c]).

During the middle and late 1790s, Indians continued to have problems with the citizens of San Jose regarding fields and livestock in the Santa Clara Valley:

> It would not be difficult for everyone to take necessary measures to eliminate the robberies which the Indians, pagans and Christians, are committing at harvest times, to watch out for the security of the population, and to keep enough men on duty with the guard for any eventuality (Borica [1796]).

In a report in August, 1796, the governor stated that overgrazing, in the context of three straight years of drought, was destroying pasture lands (and therefore Indian seed harvest lands and wild animal grazing lands). He admitted that it was these conditions that forced Indians to rob cattle and grain fields:

> Because of the lack of pastures I have distributed the cattle far from the center of the ranch. I do not have sufficient men to round them up and count them. It is clear that great losses have been sustained due to the severe drought of the past three years and due to the fact that Indians, pagan and Christian, prodded by hunger, have stolen them (Borica [1796a]).

Arrests for the killing of cattle and horses were common:

> On the twenty-eighth [of January 1796] Luís Peralta, in charge of the escort of Mission Santa Clara, reported that he rounded up four

Christian Indians upon receiving word from the commissioner of the pueblo of the death of some mares and cows.... These Indians may be of use. He asks authorization for Luís Peralta to send them to work at his presidio [San Francisco] (Sal [1796a]).

Labor on projects at the presidios continued to be the main form of punishment for Indians who broke Spanish laws:

That you punish the Indians Fermín and Mariano with work at your presidio [San Francisco], keeping them on rations and without wages and giving them sacks for cover (Borica [1796]).

In late June of 1797, the citizens of the pueblo complained that tribal people had killed two mares. Again the governor authorized the local authorities to organize a sortie to punish horse killers:

You will bring together fifteen or twenty men and fall upon them by surprise. Find out who the offenders were. Right there in front of their companions give each one twenty five lashes. As you come up to the village you are not to trample any pagans. Only fire to round them up, to apprehend the criminals and to punish them, and then only if they take up arms to fight against our men. But do not shoot to kill. Do not permit the settlers to bring in any of the pagans for labor by force. If they need Indians they are to pay them according to custom (Borica [1797]).

The citizens of the pueblo needed native workers for their water ditch construction and other projects in the summer of 1797. Because most of the local villagers in the vicinity of the pueblo had by then joined the mission, the settlers had to range far to the south and east to find willing workers. This problem was noted in a letter by commissioner Ygnacio Vallejo to the governor:

I bring to Your Lordship's attention the fact that a number of parties of armed men from the pueblo have been going out to solicit pagan Indians to work on the lower ditch.... They obtained pagan volunteers in the village for the project. Moreover, he says that of the five parties that went out with this goal, only two conducted fourteen pagans back. And the citizens asked that those be distributed to them to work on the lower ditch in order to encircle the wheat fields (Vallejo [1797]).

The constant intercourse between Spaniards and tribal people provided opportunities for trouble, and not just between settlers and Indians. During one of Commissioner Vallejo's 1797 hiring expeditions, his non-Christian native guide had an unexplained confrontation with another local tribesman:

> During their march they came across two Indians who were out hunting in the middle of the plain. When the party came up to them to get information regarding the whereabouts of the rest of the people of their village (a place which was still a good distance farther on), one of the two, the oldest, immediately fired an arrow at the Indian guide whom the party had brought along. He attacked him without provocation. Seeing this action, and that the man was taking up another arrow in order to continue firing, Ygnacio Castro jumped his horse between them. The pagan fired just as he did so, striking the horse and killing it. The arrow entered the chest via the esophagus (Vallejo [1797]).

The struggle between the hunter and the guide seems to have been provoked by some previous incident between them:

> It is inferred that there was some grievance between these two and the pagan guide that our party had brought along, since no sooner had they run into one another than they tried to kill each other.... He also said that they pursued the aggressor, who "fled like a quail" (Vallejo [1797]).

This incident may reflect tensions between factions in favor of working with the Spaniards and factions opposed to such accommodation. On the other hand, it may have resulted from a feud that had nothing to do with the Spaniards.

The Spanish government had a new purpose for hiring tribal workers in 1797. It had decided during the mid-1790s to subsidize the production of hemp as a cash crop in order to support its frontier operations. With the villages of the Santa Clara Valley nearly empty, the commissioner sought wage laborers from Captain Pala's hill tribe in the "San Antonio" district, directly to the east of the Santa Clara Valley:

> He asked the pagan captain Pala for two young Indians to be taught hemp culture. The captain offered him all the people that he might wish, if only they would be excused from supplying workers at the presidios. While they have been away on those projects their women and seed crops have been harmed by other pagans (Vallejo [1797b]).

The Paleños, who had been raided while their men worked at the Monterey Presidio, were quite happy to work for the Spaniards nearer to home.[8]

> [Vallejo] promised to propose their offer to the governor. He thinks he will be able to teach these Indians quite easily, as they have always had a good relationship with the pueblo and the presidios (Vallejo [1797b]).

Governor Borica agreed to the plan, and by late August Pala's people joined the hemp growing enterprise:

> Corporal Mateo arrived and they are going to make hemp culture first-priority. The Indian volunteers were gotten quickly. They are quite happy to leave off from the other projects and tasks that they so abhor (Vallejo [1797c]).

By September there were more tribal people who wished to work on the hemp project than were needed by the Spanish authorities, as Commissioner Vallejo complained on September 26, 1797:

> [Vallejo] says they are working in the hemp fields. They do not lack pagan workers. Twenty more arrived this morning. Having nothing for them to do, he persuaded them to work for the townspeople, among whom they were divided up. He says that he is being careful, that he knows they should be well treated and paid punctually (Vallejo [(1797d]).

The main article of payment received by Indian laborers seems to have been flannel cloth (Sal [1800]).

By 1797, the settlers were beginning to spread onto lands still used by native peoples along Coyote Creek to the east of the pueblo. Citizen Larios requested water out of Coyote Creek to nourish his cornfield (Vallejo [1797]), but the governor refused his request:

---

[8]Captain Pala was first mentioned in a brief segment of a July 29, 1795 directive by Governor Borica ([1795d]) to the commissioner of the pueblo of San Jose regarding the distribution of blankets. The note does not clarify the context of the comment. Pala (SCL-B 4252) and his wives Sorsor (SCL-B 4261) and Hunsum (SCL-B 4279) brought their children to Mission Santa Clara for baptism between 1783 and 1797 (SCL-B 453, 634, 716, 891, 1093, 1223, 1933, 3255, 3437, 3477).

That the settlers are not to plant the lands along the Coyote so long as the Indians have not been converted at the mission (Borica [1797]).

The settlers were also encroaching westward from San Jose onto the Indian lands of Mission Santa Clara. Ongoing arguments over land use between the missionaries and the settlers were coming to a head.

In January, 1797 the Spanish citizens came up with a plan to move the entire town of San Jose from the east bank of the small Guadalupe River to the mission lands on its west bank. Gabriel Moraga outlined five reasons for moving the pueblo; these were to avoid periodic inundations, to be closer to the mission, to get lands for new settlers to farm, to be closer to wood supplies, and to reduce the risk of attack (presumably by the angry Saclans to the north).

The Franciscans opposed the plan to move the pueblo and opposed any and all expansion of the settlers' holdings in the Santa Clara Valley. They cited the subsistence needs of the Indians and, just as importantly, the Indians' ownership of the land under Spanish law. The missionaries Magín Catalá and José Viader wrote:

> The King Our Lord has declared it to be his will that all the land that is estimated necessary would belong to the natives, without anyone predominating or being favored against the sovereign will. It is known that Mission Santa Clara presently maintains 1434 Christians, and in addition to these there are more than 4000 pagans who have their villages roundabout. Who would deny that these lands will be necessary for their livelihood when it comes to pass that each of them receives their allotment and leaves the community to live, and then must live from the products of tilling and ranching...?
>
> Finally, Lord Governor, I propose to you that already these natives, neophytes as well as pagans, have behaved well during these conversions [to an agricultural Christian society]. They know that those called "people of reason" and "settlers" do not support this process. They have come to understand that the settlers are usurping the lands which God had given to their fathers. Finally, I myself can swear to having heard the pagans complain among themselves regarding the injustices and evident outrages that the settlers practice in wanting to appropriate lands that belong neither to these settlers nor to anyone else (Catalá and Viader [1797]).

The pueblo of San Jose was not moved. A compromise boundary was drawn which gave some mission lands to the south of the pueblo to the settlers, but retained all lands to the west of the Guadalupe River for the mission and its native inhabitants. The spread of Hispanic land use on the west side of the Guadalupe River was thus halted for the entire Spanish period. But the ultimate issue of land ownership was left unresolved.

Mission San Jose and the Saclans

In May of 1797, Alson and Tuibun villagers on the Fremont Plain gathered at the old village site of Oroysom to watch Mission Santa Clara neophytes, Spanish soldiers, and Franciscan missionaries begin laying the foundations for The Mission of the Glorious Patriarch, Saint Joseph. At least seventy Santa Clara neophytes were reassigned to the new Mission San Jose. They were relatives and former neighbors of the people who still lived in the native villages in the vicinity, and people baptized at Mission Santa Clara from the "Santa Agueda" district.[9]

Mission San Jose was dedicated with elaborate ceremony on June 9, 1797 (McCarthy 1958:49). The site that was chosen was only thirteen miles north of Mission Santa Clara. The new mission would certainly have been built further inland, in the Livermore or Diablo valleys, were it not for Spanish concern about the hostile Saclans (Borica [1797d], Appendix 4, 16). The Spanish authorities sent two Mission Indian interpreters, a Bay Miwok speaker and a Costanoan speaker, with an escort of three Spanish soldiers, through the non-Christian villages in the East Bay to announce the new construction (Argüello [1797]).

Meanwhile, at Mission San Francisco, two missionaries were activating a new plan to get runaway Huchiuns to return to that mission. More than thirty Mission San Francisco neophyte men crossed to the East Bay by tule balsa under the direction of Baja California Indian Raymundo El Californio on July 20, 1797.

---

[9] The priest who founded Mission San Jose stated that it was built at "Oroysom, alias San Francisco Solano" (SJO-B, title page). Of the seventy resettled Mission Santa Clara neophytes documented in the Mission San Jose Registers, fifty-seven had been from "Santa Agueda" at baptism, ten had been from "Santa Ysabel," one was from "San Bernardino," and only one was from Mission Santa Clara's "San Francisco Solano" district. Other evidence suggests that the "San Francisco Solano" people at Mission Santa Clara were from a village in the Alviso area across the sloughs to the south of Mission San Jose. The seeming contradictory uses of the place name might be explained if Alviso and Mission San Jose were the southern and northernmost areas occupied by a single tribelet, the Alsons.

> Upon their arrival on the other shore they found some Christians in three villages of the pagan Cuchillones. They were all ages and sexes. He retreated to the beach with them, worried that the rest of the Indians would soon be returning from a dance. While he was trying to embark, he was impeded by a struggle with the Christian runaways that he had gathered up. In the meanwhile the rest of the Indians arrived from the dance. Although our people were intimidated, they succeeded in getting to their tule balsas. Two who lagged behind were attacked by the pagans and obliged to jump into the bay. They were picked up by their companions, one of them having received a flesh wound to the head (Borica [1797d]).

It is clear that Raymundo's group attempted to force Christian escapees to return to San Francisco; it is also clear that Raymundo was lucky to escape with his own life.

> In view of this opposition Raymundo the Californian decided to order the Christians to return to the mission. But a storm came upon them, dispersing all the balsas. He had to return, as did four others, to the same enemy shore from which he had just departed. Seeing that the boats were falling apart, he decided to abandon them. They went on foot along the shore of the bay until they came opposite to San Francisquito. There they came upon a village of pagans who supplied them with tule from their own houses in order to construct new balsas. With these they had the good fortune to arrive back at their mission. Over the next few days the rest of the boats arrived with the other Christians, <u>without anyone having been lost</u> (Borica [1797d]).

Neophyte Bibiano Guitchu, who had fled Mission San Francisco in 1795 and was living at a Huchiun village, described the incident and the strong hatred many East Bay people felt toward Raymundo:

> Raymundo arrived at the beach where the declarant was hunting sea otters. The minute he saw him he became angry, saying that he was a brave man and that he greatly regretted that he did not have his bow and arrows with him and that he [Raymundo] was going to die as soon as they could tie him up and hang him. He said all this because he believed that they had entered his hut and stolen his gear. As soon as Raymundo and his companions ordered him to shut his mouth, he did so. Presently he went away to his

hut to look for his weapons. At that time the pagan villagers began to arrive. By the time he got back, Raymundo and his party had already embarked. Asked why he wanted to purchase the murder of said Raymundo, offering glass beads and other goods for his death, he responded that he had not done that, and that all the pagans had wanted to try to kill him (Argüello [1797c], Appendix 4, 13).

Raymundo's interest in raiding the East Bay may have had as much to do with revenge as with saving souls. He was the brother-in-law of Rogerio, one of the Mission San Francisco *alcaldes* that had been killed at the Chimenes village in 1795.

The Saclans and Huchiuns were not ready to tolerate Spanish encroachment into the East Bay area. By June 29, 1797, rumors spread among the work crews at the Mission San Jose site that "Indians from where Raymundo had gone" (the Huchiuns) wanted to attack the Indian workers at the site (Miranda [1797a]). On July 3, word came to Mission San Jose that tribal people from the northeast, the Livermore Valley, were also "getting ready to come and attack any pagans that are working here" at the Mission San Jose site (Miranda [1797b]). By July 6, the rumor was afoot that a consortium of tribesmen also intended to attack the pueblo of San Jose (Argüello [1797a]).

The well-known Sergeant Pedro Amador arrived at the Mission San Jose site on July 7. He received a report from a Mission Santa Clara neophyte, Tilomeno, that the Saclans had sent emissaries to threaten a nearby group—probably his people, the Causens:

> The Christian Tilomeno told the troop leader that they had witnessed some pagans arguing with a pagan captain who lives near the mission, telling him and his people not to work at the mission nor get involved with it. Their own captains had said that if these [nearby people] worked at the mission they would have to kill them, as well as the Fathers and the soldiers. The pagan captain responded to these other pagans that they had better not try to kill the soldiers, as they do not sleep at night and continually go about on horseback with their muskets ready to protect those who are working here. This pagan captain then told the visiting Christians that he would come to work at the mission with his people when they had finished gathering their wild seeds. With that the other pagans left very upset. It is definite that many *rancherías* are joining together. They are manufacturing arrows.

> Those two pagans are from the villages of the Sacalan, those who committed the offenses against the Christians of San Francisco. All of them are neighbors of the people of the Valley of San Jose [Livermore Valley], from that area of the bay shore across from San Francisco (Amador [1797]).

These disagreements and threats between tribal captains remind us that there were factions both within and between tribes that held varying viewpoints on the proper response to the new Spanish expansion into the East Bay.

In early July, other tribal peoples from the hills east of the Santa Clara Valley were renewing their raids on the horse herds of the Pueblo of San Jose. The situation was about to explode. But, as had occurred on most previous occasions, when the situation reached a critical point it was the Spanish forces that erupted. Sergeant Amador went with a squad of soldiers to the pueblo, and then made the following recommendation to his superiors:

> Of the threats by the pagan that killed Castro's horse, they are working on the problem. Troop leader Vallejo went out, as per your instructions, to punish the man, which was necessary to set the pagans straight. I think the same is necessary with the rest of the pagans, the Saclans, because they have the idea that we fear them. This is the source of the threats they are making. It is clear that they do not appreciate the sincerity and prudence with which you have tolerated them. However, you will not lack for representatives to send to put down these pagans if you decide that is what is needed. In case you decide to cut the threads of this malignant cancer which these pagans are spreading, as you better than anyone well understand, I would consider myself the least of your representatives. In the best spirit I offer myself to take care of this situation, placing every ounce of my intelligence and my experience to the purpose. With your permission I will bring a party of fifteen or twenty men. At the same time we will gain another benefit by bringing in the Christians who are living among the pagans. I remain with the guard here awaiting that which it seems to you best to do (Amador [1797]).

At the time that Amador was recommending that the Spaniards go on the offensive in the East Bay, the total Saclan population was probably less than 130, a figure that includes 50 or so runaway neophytes. Their allies, the Jalquins, may have had 170 people, while the Huchiuns and Huchiun-Aguastos probably numbered 400 people, a figure that includes 150 Mission San Francisco escapees.

Arrest of Saclan Leaders

On July 10, 1797, Governor Borica sent word from Monterey that Pedro Amador should gather his forces and attack the Saclans:

> Amador will go with twenty retired veteran soldiers and townspeople and two active soldiers to the village of the Sacalan, fall upon them at daybreak and capture the ring-leaders of those who participated in the deaths of the seven Mission San Francisco Christians in 1795. He should bring them, as well as any runaway Christians found among them, back to San Jose. In this expedition he is to avoid any loss of blood. Only if the pagans take up arms against our people in a way that risks wounding someone will gunfire or lances be used, and then only to the minimum extent necessary to achieve control (Borica [1797]).

Amador sent to San Francisco Mission for two Christian Indian interpreters and guides, presumably Huchiun and Saclan men, on July 12. On the evening of July 13, his party headed north, traveling only at night.

At dawn on July 15, 1797, twenty armed Spanish horsemen struck the Saclan village of Jussent, probably located in the present Moraga or Lafayette area of central Contra Costa County. The Spaniards were surprised to find that the village had been divided into three separate house clusters. They approached the middle house cluster, which contained about fifty men and women (probably no more than twenty of whom were adult males capable of fighting). The Saclans had prepared ditches beforehand to keep the soldiers from charging through the village on horseback.

As the mounted Spaniards approached them, the men began to fire arrows; they refused to lay down their weapons upon Amador's demand. Soon they killed a soldier's horse and wounded two other horses:

> Seeing this opposition, we used our weapons in order to subdue them so that they would surrender. Seven were killed, for they refused for two hours to give up. Finally, it was necessary to dismount and throw them back with swords and lances, for they have some wells in the middle of the village which are like walls and which can be strongly defended (Amador [1797a], Appendix 4, 12).

Thirty Saclans, neophytes and non-Christians, were finally brought under control by the Spaniards. The soldiers then entered the two nearby sub-villages, but most of their inhabitants had already fled. Only two more people were added to the group of prisoners.

> Having carried out an investigation and having ascertained the guilty ones and the Christians, I made it clear to the rest, through the interpreters, that we did not wish to do them any harm. They said they wanted to obey and that they well understood that we had no evil intentions. I liberated the pagans and we set forth toward the region of the Juchillones (Amador [1797a], Appendix 4, 12).

After releasing those non-Christians who had shown no resistance, the Spaniards continued northward with their prisoners. Along the way the re-grouped Saclan men from the other villages came forward. Amador wrote:

> We had gone but a short distance when there began to assemble a great many Indians, uttering shrieks and cries, so that we had to go into line of battle again. Falling upon them, we killed one person, and with this they retreated (Amador [1797a], Appendix 4, 12).

The Spanish posse continued north toward the Huchiun towns, and probably spent the night in the valley of San Pablo Creek.

At dawn on July 16, the Amador party entered one of the Huchiun villages near San Pablo Bay. They demanded all runaway Christians and any others that might be implicated in the attack on Raymundo just three weeks earlier:

> We struck the first, second, and third village in the same morning. As we reconnoitered the Indians of the last village, which is very large, the inhabitants were just about to open hostilities. But being admonished by the interpreters that we had not come to harm them but to hunt for Christians, they were pacified (Amador [1797a], Appendix 4, 12).

These raids took place in villages that might have been anywhere from the western entrance of Carquinez Strait south and west to the plain in the present city of Richmond.

> We returned to the first village with the Christians and pagans and there assembled all those who had been concealed in the three villages. Having separated out all those we had caught and were

taking with us, we set forth on our return journey (Amador [1797a], Appendix 4, 12).

The captured Saclans, less than a score of people, watched as Amador's men used interpreters and informers to sort out the neophytes and the non-Christian resistance leaders from among the Huchiuns. Eventually the posse started back south, herding eighty-three Christian Indians and nine non-Christians charged with murder or assault. It took them two and a half days of travel along the bayshore plain to reach Mission San Jose.

Amador kept the captured Saclans and Huchiuns at Mission San Jose from July 18 until July 23. They arrived back at Mission San Francisco on July 26, after a three-day walk around the southern bay (Vallejo [1797]; Espí and Landaeta [1797]). Most of the neophytes were sent directly to Mission San Francisco, but four Christians and nine non-Christians implicated in past altercations were taken to the Presidio.

The fight was by no means gone from those Saclans—numbering at least one hundred other people—who remained on their lands. On July 26, a captain from a Livermore Valley tribe arrived at the Mission San Jose construction site, and told the corporal of the guard that he wanted to be baptized, but that other pagans threatened "to kill him as well as the soldiers, if they became Christians" (Miranda [1797b]). Again Sergeant Amador was sent from the San Francisco Presidio to Mission San Jose (Argüello [1797b]):

> August 2—A Christian Indian returned today who had gone out with permission. He brought news that the pagans were saying that they were aware that the sergeant had come in response to the warning the pagan Saclans had issued before. These pagans sent word that they wanted to come in to become Christians, but that they were fearful of the sergeant. The Christian told them that the sergeant did not want to harm them. Also he told them, regarding those other who had warned them, that they are not to make trouble for the Christians (Amador [1797c]).

On the following day the captain of an unnamed "river" tribe sent his own emissaries to Pedro Amador:

> On the third three pagans arrived to say that they were asked by their captain, who had heard that the sergeant was here from a Christian who had gone to them with permission, to go and see if he were very angry. They were very afraid. I told them that I was not angry with them, nor was our Great Captain angry, rather that he loved them greatly and if he ever heard that we were causing them trouble, that he would cause trouble for us. They say that they are near the rivers and that they wish

to receive counsel from here because they fear the Saclans because they told them [the Saclans] that they wanted to become Christians. I told them if they came in they would come to no harm, that whatever they wanted to do they should notify us, that we would defend them. With that they left quite happy, and since that time I have had no problems (Amador [1797d]).

No further threats from the Saclans were reported during the summer of 1797—nor were there any baptisms at the new mission until September.

On August 9, 1797, the captive Saclan and Huchiun men were put on trial at the San Francisco Presidio. In the absence of any true civil authority in the territory of Upper California, the trial was run according to Spanish military court procedure. The recorded testimony of the tribesmen suggests a mixture of proud rejection of Spanish authority and fearful evasion of responsibility for past violence (Argüello [1797c], Appendix 4, 13). Potroy of the village of Jussent was implicated as the leader of the Chimenes attack in 1795. All of the accused men were found guilty, the Huchiuns that were involved in the attack on Raymundo El Californio in 1797, as well as the Saclans involved in the earlier Chimenes affair.

The convicted Saclans and Huchiuns received sentences from Governor Borica On August, 26 1797. Potroy received seventy-five lashes (twenty-five apiece on three distinct occasions) and one year in shackles for leading the 1795 attack at the Chimenes village. Caguas received fifty lashes (twenty-five apiece on two occasions) and eight months in shackles. The rest received two or four months in shackles, in addition to twenty-five lashes. The only exception was Joxanssea, a Christian who claimed that he had not been involved in the 1795 incident; he received two months in shackles, but no lashes. The four Huchiun men who had driven Raymundo out of the East Bay the previous June received twenty-five lashes and one or two months in shackles (Borica [1797c], Appendix 4, 15).

The captured resisters blamed Captain Ojyugma of Juuquili, a Jalquin village, for instigating the most recent threats against Mission San Jose.[10]

---

[10] Juuquili is identified as being a Jalquin village on the basis of baptismal information on Carues, one of the men arrested for the 1797 killings. He was identified as a Saclan at the time of his arrest. During the 1797 hearing, Carues stated that he was from Juquili. At his baptism in 1802, Carues was identified as a Jalquin, as were three other members of the 1797 Saclan resistance group (SFR-B 2752). Although the evidence is contradictory, it is assumed that Spanish knowledge of East Bay tribal geography increased with time. Jalquins and Saclans, who were lumped together in 1797, were recognized as being separate by 1802. The Jalquins were almost certainly the same tribelet as the people called Yrgins at Mission San Jose. Captain Ojyugma was probably the same man as Justino Huyumja, a fifty-year old Jalquin baptized at Mission San Francisco on January 30, 1802 (SFR-B 2352).

Potroy stated:

> It is true that the pagans had been uniting in order to go attack the new mission of San Jose. The ringleader in that was the captain called Ojyugma of the village of Juuquili, which is about three leagues [eight miles] away from the place Sergeant Amador went (Argüello [1797c], Appendix 4, 13).

The people of Ojyugma's village received a visit from Pedro Amador on August 20, 1797:

> He went out on August 20 at eight in the evening to look for the Oiyugma village. He headed straight for that of Juquili and came upon the village at daybreak. He did not find the captain that he sought. He made some excuses about looking for him and another man—mainly to trade them blankets for sea otter skins. In this way he got them to bring him directly to the captain, who he was then able to draw out of the *ranchería* along with three other men by means of these promises. He escorted them to the mission—them only. He says that these villages are ten leagues [twenty-seven miles] away from the mission and opposite the beach.

> He continues, saying, "On arriving at the mission I let them know through the interpreters that the Lord Governor, who is the Great Captain, governing us as well as them, loves the pagans very much and is desirous of their well-being. He has ordered me to find out whether or not it is true, as stated the Cuchillones and Sacalanes that I had brought to Mission San Francisco, that Oiyugma had brought together an assembly to come and burn the mission and kill the soldiers. Said captain responded that he has said nothing nor become involved in any such thing—that those who are his enemies have invented all these lies and that they are always trying to kill him."

> The other three said that they did not know anything. In fulfillment of his promise he gave them a blanket each. "To Captain Oiyugma I gave a blanket in your name, as well as some glass beads which the priests gave me. They were rendered quite content by this as well as by the idea that I passed on to them that you recognized him as great captain, that he should take care that they do not make trouble amongst one another, nor should the other three. With that they went along very happily. The priests gifted them and remained with them that they be made Christians and to pass

along any other information they might learn to the corporal of the escort of Mission San Jose" (Amador [1797e]).

Captain Ojyugma was either a resistance leader who had second thoughts as a result of Spanish intimidation, or he was a member of a faction at odds with the Saclan resistance leaders. One way or the other, the situation illustrates the difficulty that native leaders had in maintaining a united stand against Spanish expansion.

The first baptism at Mission San Jose, on September 1, 1797, was performed by a Mission Santa Clara priest and recorded in the baptismal book of the latter mission (SCL-B 3431). It was performed for the newborn child of a Causen family transferred back to the new mission from Mission Santa Clara. The next day, a twenty-four year old Jalquin woman, Gilpaye, became the first tribal person baptized by the new Mission San Jose missionaries (SJO-B 1). She married a transferred Mission Santa Clara neophyte from "Santa Ysabel" on September 24.[11] Between September 4 and September 24, a score of children and teenagers from the nearby Alson and Causen villages and from the more distant Souyens were baptized at Mission San Jose; a few other Alson and Tuibun adults joined the new mission later in the fall.

Approach and Avoidance, 1798-1799

In the spring of 1798, zealous evangelizers from Mission San Jose angered the captain of the Taunans in the hills about twenty miles northeast of the Santa Clara Valley. Commander Argüello at San Francisco got word of potential trouble on April 6:

> From Mission San Jose they have said that in one of the nearby villages they are amassing arrows and inviting people everywhere to join them in an attack on said mission. He has sent out a sergeant and six soldiers in anticipation of problems (Argüello [1798]).

---

[11] Gilpaye's baptism and marriage occurred only a few days after the diplomatic interactions between the Spaniards and Captain Oiyugma of the Jalquins. Oiyugma had promised to send people from his village to join the missions, yet no Jalquins other than Gilpaye and her child were baptized at Mission San Jose until June, 1999. I suggest that her marriage was arranged as a gesture of peace by Oiyugma.

Sergeant Pedro Amador arrived at Mission San Jose later in the week to investigate the rumor of an impending attack. He sent word to the governor on April 11 that it was all a misunderstanding:

> He sent some Indians out to the village to find out, through dissimilitude, if they plan to attack the mission. He has drawn out the following facts. The Indians had gone to the river [San Joaquin?] to get shafts in order to kill deer, inasmuch as this is their livelihood. They feared that the soldiers were after them because they killed a horse. Also, the minister of the mission asked him [Amador] for men to go out to another village eight leagues [twenty-two miles] distant. He has refused until he learns the governor's will (Amador [1798]).

While Amador was conducting his investigation at Mission San Jose, Commander Argüello at San Francisco learned that the Mission San Jose priests were hiding the fact that they had visited the Taunan village on April 2:

> He received word about the minister's expedition into pagan lands. That all his standing orders are to be followed, no force is to be used to bring pagans in from their villages. The *alcalde* forwards word to Amador from San Jose that on April 2 the minister went to the Colorado [a creek deep in the Coast range mountains]; upon seeing this they fled because they said [the priest's party] wanted to baptize them. The corporal of the guard is to be reminded of his duty [regarding such expeditions] as well as of his punishment if he fails to carry it out (Argüello [1798a]).

Argüello's letter reflects the army's continuing annoyance with missionaries who upset tribal people. Sergeant Amador went out to the Taunan village himself on April 13, 1798; his subsequent report suggests that more than one group was gathered there:

> From one of their captains he reclaimed the horse they killed, which belonged to Castro. He brought about twenty-six of them, including children, back with him to the mission at their insistence, because they wanted to become Christians. Others remained out in order to return to their homes (Amador [1798a]).

Twenty-one of the Taunan children who returned to Mission San Jose with Amador were baptized on April 17, 1798 (SJO-B 59-79). Over the next two weeks, twelve Taunan adults were baptized, yet none of them were the parents of any of the twenty-one children (SJO-B 80-91); those parents did not join Mission San Jose until the winter of 1803-1804, five years later (SJO-B 999-1135 range).

In June, the governor received new reports that Taunan leaders were threatening Mission San Jose, so Sergeant Luís Peralta was sent to Mission San Jose to investigate (Argüello [1798c], Appendix 4, 17). The extant paraphrase of the sergeant's report reads:

> On the seventh [of June] he went with six men to Mission San Jose. The corporal there informed him that the Father of the mission permitted some Indians to go to their *ranchería*. Two of them did not come back. They told said corporal (through their captain), that these two had gone to another *ranchería*, and that the captain of the latter was furious because his people had been permitted to become Christians. He was thinking about finishing them off, then going on to the mission. Another pagan had told him that they had killed a soldier, but that is not possible because no one is missing. He has taken precautionary measures. He asks that he be appointed to negotiate peace between the two captains (Peralta [1798]).

Sergeant Peralta ([1798a]) visited the hostile Taunan village, where everyone denied that they had any antagonism toward surrounding tribes or toward the missions. He concluded that the rumors of trouble were false.

Forty-eight Saclan and Huchiun Christian runaways turned themselves in at the San Francisco Presidio While Peralta was at the Taunan village in June of 1798. They came in with two mission people who had gone across the bay on *paseo* (Borica [1798]). Lieutenant José Argüello received them:

> He did not punish them since they came in voluntarily; that he sent them with two soldiers to their nearby mission, where they were well received and immediately given clothing (Argüello [1798b]).

In October of 1798, another thirty-three mission Saclan escapees were returned to Mission San Jose by the corporal of the guard there (Borica [1798a]). Although they had originally been baptized at Mission San Francisco, they were allowed to join the population of approximately two hundred people then living at Mission San Jose. They were allowed to remain at Mission San Jose "because of the horror with which they regard the mission of San Francisco" (Borica [1799]).

The year 1799 came and went with few recorded developments. More than a dozen people fled Mission San Jose in April; some of them were Saclans running away for the second time (Barcenilla [1799]). During the summer, a few Souyens from the Livermore Valley and Taunans from the mountains took children to Mission San Jose for baptism (SJO-B 200-206). In September, another runaway Saclan woman returned to Mission San Francisco with her young child (SFR-B 1997). More than a hundred immigrants were baptized at Mission Santa Clara. At least four groups were well represented: Santa Ysabel, Taunans, and Paleño's from the eastern hills, and Matalans from the south.

By the end of the 1790s, the territory under native control had receded to encompass only the north and east sides of the Bay and the hills east of the Santa Clara Valley. Mission Santa Clara, which had grown to include some 1400 people, was in effect the largest village of native Californians in west Central California. Mission San Jose, although relatively small, was beginning to attract large numbers of catechumens, and had a population of 188 new neophytes (plus a few score of resettled Mission Santa Clara neophytes). Despite an aversion to mission life that had intensified since the flight of 1795, people were still being attracted to the missions because they wished to maintain ties with neophyte relatives, and because they coveted the cloth, beads, and blankets that were becoming symbols of prestige in villages farther inland.

Tribal people also continued to be attracted to the Pueblo of San Jose in order to work for trade goods. Captains such as Pala acted as middlemen in the hierarchical arrangement of patronage and dependence that existed between natives and newcomers. They were probably men of political skill and personal charisma, and were almost certainly traditional tribal leaders rather than marginal individuals taking advantage of the new socioeconomic situation. The Spanish military kept a careful eye on the situation so that these leaders did not gain too much power. Lieutenant Hermenegildo Sal, for example, wrote the following observation to San Jose commissioner Macario Castro in 1800, regarding El Chato, a non-Christian ally of one of the citizens of the pueblo:

> According to that which the pagan Indian El Chato says, citizen Larios gave him the sword in order to defend himself against a rabid wolf. Moreover, he gave him a horse to go from one area to another. I have brought this practice to a halt, but I give more credence to the Indian's word than to that of Larios.... I told him that neither Christian Indians nor pagans should have any use for a horse. This order should be posted at the guard station, that anyone who goes against this measure will be forcefully placed in a pair of shackles by you and sent to me at the presidio (Sal [1800a]).

By denying non-Christian Indians access to weaponry, horses, and practical property rights, the Spaniards were ensuring a future in which the Indian people of Central California were to become landless laborers, comprising a class of people with a status below that of the poorest of the *gente de razón* from Mexico.

***

As the eighteenth century was drawing to a close, opposition factions in tribal villages continued to resist Spanish intrusions into the East Bay hills and into the hills east of the Santa Clara Valley. Among them were escaped Christian and non-Christian Saclans, allied with some Jalquins. But neither they nor any other group caused the Spaniards the kind of fear that they had felt in the months immediately following the Chimenes incident. Pedro Amador's victory against the Saclans in July of 1797, and Luis Peralta's intimidation of the Taunans in 1798, combined to solidify the Spaniards' feelings of confidence. The point had been driven home to the frontier tribes that small groups of forty or fifty warriors, armed only with bows, lacked the power to protect their borders against Spanish invaders.

Chapter 8

Regional Disintegration, 1800-1805

	Spanish Actions	Tribal Actions
1800	April. Amador raids Saclans.	Jan.-Feb. Some Saclans return to Mission SF. Other Saclans kill two neophytes.
1802	Epidemic hits Mission SC in July, Mission SF in August.	Spring-Summer. Surge of bay shore and Livermore Valley people to Mission SJ.
1803		Spring. Significant Marin Peninsula migration to Mission San Francisco.
1804	January. Mission SF Saclans invade Suisuns, some killed.	May. Some Tuibuns plot revolt at Mission San Jose, without result.
	Fall. Soldiers raid interior twice, "Monte del Diablo" named.	Fall. Chupcans flee north to the Suisuns.
1805	January 20. Spaniards attack Luechas, kill 11 men.	January 15. Luechas kill a Spaniard, wound Father Cueva.
		March. Luecha women marry Alsons at Mission Santa Clara.
	October. L. Argüello leads 32 day raid through coast ranges.	June-Dec. Hundreds of migrants from Diablo Range to Mission Santa Clara.

Collapse of the Saclan Resistance, 1800-1802

Very few native peoples moved to the missions over the five year period from the time of the Chimenes affair in 1795 until the autumn of 1800. Remnant groups from the Santa Cruz mountains and areas just south of the Santa Clara Valley did keep joining Mission Santa Clara during those years, and at Mission San Francisco, the last tribal elder from the Peninsula groups allowed herself to be baptized on June 19, 1800:

During this Feast of the Body of Christ in 1800, the baptism of pagans on this side of the estuaries has come to a conclusion (to the great honor and glory of God), as today the last person was baptized, a woman of sixty years age, known by the name La Comadre ["Aunty"] among enlightened people and Indians alike (Ramón Abella, SFR-B 2073).

However, the cultural conquest of the Peninsula was not as yet quite complete. The last significant block of Puichons were baptized at Mission Santa Clara two months later, on August 8, 1800 (SCL-B 3963-3976). Among them was Toles (SCL-B 3963), father of Mission Santa Clara alcalde José Domingo (SCL-B 3963).

Most of the remaining runaway Huchiun and Saclan families returned from the East Bay to Mission San Francisco early in 1800. Huchiun and Saclan children, some belonging to runaway neophyte parents, were baptized together with young Guaulens and Habastos from the Marin Peninsula.[1] Weddings took place on February 12, February 25, and March 27, and involved widowed Saclan, Huchiun, and Huimen neophytes who had been away since 1795 (SFR-M 608-611, 614-615, 617-618).

New baptisms of non-Christians took place at Mission San Francisco on March 7, 1800, after a hiatus of almost five years. The people involved were Huchiuns, who almost certainly were relatives of the returning runaways. During the same period (January through March of 1800), seventeen married couples joined at Mission San Jose; they were Tuibuns, Causens, Pelnens, and Taunans from the vicinity of Mission San Jose.

In February of 1800, some Saclan men killed an Alson man who had been a Christian at Mission San Jose for five months and a Taunan man who had just been baptized at Mission San Jose on January 21, 1800 (SJO-B 210, 211). They also killed a non-Christian captain from an undocumented group, fulfilling a warning that they had made a month earlier that they would kill people who cooperated with the Spaniards at Mission San Jose (Amador [1800]; Argüello [1800]). The killings happened at the same time that other Saclans were returning to Mission San Francisco, and therefore indicate that new factional divisions had developed within the tribe.

---

[1] The following children of returning runaway Huchiuns were baptized at Mission San Francisco in January of 1800: Melchora (SFR-B 2009, parents SFR-B 1767, 1719), Santiago (SFR-B 2010, parents SFR-B 1642, 1667), Ramón (SFR-B 2011, parents SFR-B 1631, 2028), and Juan Crisostomo (SFR-B 2014, parents SFR-B 1728, 1736). In February Crisanto (SFR-B 2025, parents SFR-B 1481, 2040), Fulgencia (SFR-B 2026, parents SFR-B 1830, 2059), and Ramón (SFR-B 2027, father SFR-B 1108) were baptized. Arsenio (SFR-B 2037, parents SFR-B 1830, 2059) was baptized on March 7, 1800, the same day as Piti and Usete, the first married couple to be baptized from the Huchiun lands since the spring of 1795.

Spanish troops responded to the deaths with their most protracted police action in the Bay Area to date (Argüello [1800]). Sergeant Pedro Amador led a party of fourteen soldiers in a six-day sortie to native villages north and east of Mission San Jose that lasted from April 7 to April 12:

> Left Santa Clara on the seventh—arrived at the location of the village he sought. It was not there—it had been moved.
>
> On the ninth they found it. The Indians fled to the mountains from where they threatened, but did not attack. With the best horses a few of those who took up arms were caught. Sword and lance had to be employed to control them, and a captain was killed. The rest ran off. Then the expedition retired from the village and waited about three hours, in order to be sure that the Indians were not going to attack and because it was not easy to get to the place where they were. The expedition then descended to the plain of San Jose [Livermore Valley] where it awaited the return of the corporal and four soldiers sent to take ten captive Indians to the garrison at San Jose.
>
> At three in the afternoon on the tenth the corporal and four men returned. They traveled all night to reach the villages.
>
> On the eleventh he fell upon the seven villages to gather up twenty-one Christians who were delivered by their captains. None of the pagans wanted to become Christians. In two of the villages the pagans almost took up arms. Amador ordered them to get the rest ready and "I made them pay for their insults. I burned all their arrows and bows. I made them see that they were no match for us and that they received that punishment due to their audacity in wanting to take up arms against us."
>
> On the twelfth he arrived at San Jose, where the commander took statements from the pagans he had captured initially. Two Christians said that, of those who came in, only one is among those who helped to kill the Christians, along with the other captain who died, and the other man who succeeded him as captain, who was the one who got a lance through the body because he faced the soldiers with rocks after his arms were taken from him. "Upon his being stabbed with the lance I tried to remove it with my hands, but it remained in his body because the pole had broken off."

He arrived on the fifteenth back at San Francisco (Amador [1800]).

Amador returned the twenty-one Saclan Christians to the missionaries at Mission San Francisco; they comprised the last significant group of the 1795 escapees.[2]

Ten non-Christian Saclan men were brought before Commander José Argüello at the presidio of San Francisco, incriminated in the previous February's killings:

> He inquired among the pagans by means of interpreters, and found out that seven of the ten were from the village where they had taken up arms against the sergeant. One captain especially gave them quite a lot of trouble. He states that this man had helped to kill the two Christians and a pagan. He set the others free, ordering that they be given fifteen to twenty lashes each (Argüello [1800]).

The men that were found guilty were sent to the Monterey Presidio and then by ship to Loreto, Baja California (Alberní [1800]); their eventual fate is unknown.

The rate of adult emigration jumped dramatically in 1801 all along the mission frontier. All three missions received a large influx of complete family groups (see Figure 11). By the year's end, 109 married couples had renewed their marriages at the missions, which was the largest number to do so since 1794. Mission San Jose was the primary absorption center for the new migrations. In January of 1801 alone, twenty-one couples became Christians, equaling the total number of marriages recorded during the previous year. The couples consisted of Alsons and Tuibuns from the local villages on the Fremont Plain. Most of the remaining Alson and Tuibun villagers joined the mission from April through August of 1801. They brought with them some Pelnens, Souyens, and Taunans from just over the hills to the east.

At Mission San Francisco, twenty-two married couples were baptized in the spring of 1801, consisting of Huimens from the Marin Peninsula and Huchiuns from the northern East Bay. At the same time, significant portions of village populations went to Mission Santa Clara from the *Paleños* to the east and the Matalan in the Laguna Seca area to the south. By the end of summer, 1801, the flat plains from the Santa Clara Valley north all along the east side of San

---

[2] Most of the Saclan returnees of 1800 never again fled Mission San Francisco. However, one of them—Hugolino—did flee again, to live among the Chupcans, where he remained until the winter of 1810 (SFR-B 1558; son SFR-B 4063, subsequent wife, SFR-B 4108).

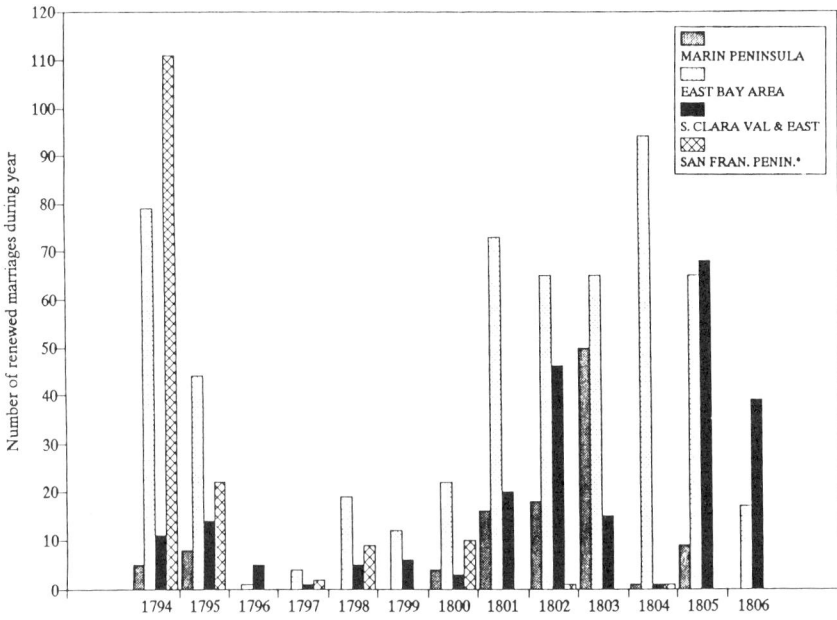

Figure 11. Bar chart of yearly counts of married couples from four geographic regions who renewed their marriages at the three Bay Area missions between 1794 and 1806. (*San Francisco Peninsula count includes western Santa Clara Valley people.)

Francisco Bay to the present Richmond area were devoid of native villages, with the exception of the San Leandro Creek Jalquin (Yrgin) region.

During the spring and summer of 1802, 224 people moved to Mission Santa Clara. Among the forty-four married couples were some of the longtime suppliers of labor to the settlers and military. Pala, leader of the hemp-growing Paleños, joined Mission Santa Clara on April 4, 1802 (SCL-B 4251), and Aloc, a key leader of one of the hill tribes east of Mission San Jose, was baptized at Mission Santa Clara on May 8, 1802 (SCL-B 4289). Most of the new neophytes at Santa Clara were from the San Carlos district to the south (consisting mainly of Matalans from the Laguna Seca area, where the towns of Coyote and Morgan Hill now stand).

The intensive absorption of East Bay tribal people continued unabated into 1802. In January and February, twenty-one Jalquin families moved to Mission San Francisco; they were intermarried with Seunens (SFR-M 694-696) and Tatcans (SFR-M 715, 720). The four Jalquin men who had been among the six non-Christians arrested and punished in 1797 for the 1795 killings (Otseit,

172   *A Time Of Little Choice*

SFR-B 2319; Carues, SFR-B 2372; Jovocsia, SFR-B 2374; Caguas, SFR-B 2375) were members of the group. They had been released at various times in 1798, after having served their sentences in irons, and had returned to live in the Jalquin villages along San Leandro and San Lorenzo creeks. Also in this group was the mother of 1795 Saclan resistance leader Potroy, Crispula Sacnete (SFR-B 2356, age sixty). She was accompanied by her Saclan husband, Crispulo Chumculis (SFR-B 1770), a runaway from 1795. With these Jalquin and Saclan baptisms in the spring of 1802, the Saclan resistance truly came to an end.

Deteriorating Health Conditions

Mission mortality rates fluctuated wildly from year to year at the end of the 1700s and the beginning of the 1800s. A general trend of steadily increasing mortality underlay the fluctuations at Mission San Francisco throughout the period. The pattern was a little different at Mission Santa Clara, where mortality peaked at incredibly high rates during the 1780s, and actually fell during the 1790s. Unfortunately, by 1800, the death rate at Mission Santa Clara still averaged around 100 per thousand, which was nearly twice as high as the aboriginal mortality rate (see Tables 5-7, Appendix 2).

Newly opened Mission San Jose immediately surpassed the two older Bay Area missions in its death rate. From 1798-1800, the mortality rate there averaged 160 per 1000; it then rose to 195 per 1000 in the 1801-1805 period (excluding the epidemic year of 1802).

Populations of the missionized tribes shrank rapidly as a consequence of both the high death rates among the migrants themselves and of the tremendously high death rates among their mission-born children. For instance, thirty-eight different women each had a child at Mission San Francisco during the two-year period 1796-1797; eighteen of these children died before they reached the age of one. Thirteen of the twenty children who did reach the age of one died before they reached the age of three. Only two of the thirty-eight children lived until their tenth birthday (SFR-B 1907,1922). Infant mortality was also very high at Mission Santa Clara and Mission San Jose.

High death rates were not merely the result of occasional flare-ups during epidemics. They were chronic, caused by food- and water-borne diseases that were endemic in the villages and, increasingly over time, the indirect effects of endemic syphilis. Syphilis was blamed for a large portion of the mortality in every medical report stemming from California during the period. Pedro Fages in a 1791 report noted its spread northward from the Baja California missions:

> The declining state of the population of the old missions is due
> to contagious syphilis, which has infested these parts for many

years. And since the florescence and progress in which it is found among the people of the new establishments will be well enough understood [from the attached reports], you will agree that steps must be taken immediately in the many families in which it occurs (Fages [1791]:154).

The symptoms of syphilis were graphically described by Russian visitor George von Langsdorff in 1806:

> The most frightful of all the diseases here is that which is but too well known in every part of the world.... It is almost universal both among the Spaniards and Indians, and occasions so much the greater devastations among them, as they themselves resolutely reject all medical assistance for it. Spots upon the neck, with many other horrible and disgusting deformities, consumption and death, are the usual consequences of it. Opthalmia, rheumatic pains, swellings at the corners of the mouth, and chronical diseases of many sorts which I observed, may also I believe be pretty generally referred to the same origin (Langsdorff [1806] 1814:210-211).

Women with untreated primary or secondary syphilis (those stages which occur within the first year or so after infection) miscarry fifty percent of the time and deliver congenitally syphilitic and weakened infants fifty percent of the time. In latent stages, the percentage of affected births drops off to ten percent (Murphy and Patamasucon *in* Holmes et al. 1984:352). Women can be reinfected and go through the vulnerable initial stages again and again. Postpartum infections are also high for syphilitic women, and often result in subsequent infertility (Moore and Spadoni *in* Holmes et al. 1984:763). The missionaries treated the symptoms of syphilis with poultices and ointments designed to dry up sores; these were essentially useless remedies (Valle 1973).

Female death rates were higher than male death rates at the Bay Area missions. Among adults, death rates for adult women were almost twice those for males. This fact resulted in a steady change in the ratio of men to women in the mission settlements during the late 1790s and early 1800s. In 1796, the ratio of adult women to adult men at Mission San Francisco was approximately one to one; by 1800, there were 255 men but only 205 women at Mission San Francisco. Similar changes took place at the other missions.

An epidemic involving an unidentified disease struck Mission Santa Clara and Mission San Francisco in 1802; it had come to the Bay Area from missions in Southern California. The epidemic first hit the Santa Barbara Channel area, where it was labeled *dolor del costado* (Tápis [1803]), in the spring of 1801. It first struck in the north at Mission San Carlos Borromeo in January of 1802, where it was called *peste* (SCA-D 1407). It spread north to Mission San Juan Bautista in March and to Mission Santa Cruz in April.

The *peste* first struck the Bay Area at Mission Santa Clara in July 1802 (see Figure 12). Cook (1943:19) collected various descriptions of its symptoms, which he listed as "*fuertes dolores de cabeza*" ("terrible headaches"), "*cerramiento de garganta*" ("throat swollen shut"), "*pulmonía y dolor de costado*" ("pneumonia and pain in the side"), "*fuertes calenturas*" ("strong fevers"), and "*toz y dolores de cabeza*" ("cough and headache"). Such a wide range of symptoms might be produced by a number of diseases. Cook (1943:19) suggested that the disease involved was pneumonia or diphtheria, while Valle (1973:144) thought that the symptoms suggested scarlet fever or diphtheria. It might also have been an especially virulent consumptive form of tuberculosis.

At Mission Santa Clara six of the first eleven deaths involved unmarried young women between the ages of thirteen and twenty. The oldest woman in the first group to die was Constancia, the wife of *alcalde* Luís Antonio.[3] She may have been in charge of the *monjería*, the unmarried women's quarters, in which case it is probable that she and the unmarried girls caught the disease from a visiting woman from a more southerly mission. The disease soon spread to both sexes and all age groups, although preadolescent and adolescent boys were the least hard hit. Ninety-three people died during July, which was the worst month. Deaths continued at a much higher rate than normal for two more months. Thirty-three people died in August, and another thirty-seven died in September.

The *peste* struck Mission San Francisco around the eighteenth of August, 1802. The deadliest phase there lasted only two weeks, which was half

---

[3] The following people were the earliest to die at Mission Santa Clara during the *peste* epidemic of the summer of 1802:

ID	Date	Name	Sex	Age	Status
SCL-D 2766	July 6, 1802	Constancia	F	Age 31	*alcalde's* wife
SCL-D 2767	July 6, 1802	Maria Fabiana	F	Age 14	not married
SCL-D 2768	July 6, 1802	Ana María	F	Age 15	not married
SCL-D 2769	July 6, 1802	María Cesaria	F	Age 13	not married
SCL-D 2770	July 7, 1802	Plautila	F	Age 15	not married
SCL-D 2771	July 7, 1802	Praxedis	F	Age 13	not married
SCL-D 2772	July 8, 1802	Ansano	M	Age 49	widower
SCL-D 2773	July 8, 1802	Agueda	F	Age 17	married
SCL-D 2774	July 8, 1802	Martiniana	F	Age 16	not married
SCL-D 2775	July 8, 1802	Florido	M	Age 20	married
SCL-D 2776	July 9, 1802	Clara Montefalco	F	Age 20	married

Note the preponderance of teen-aged and young adult females. Presumably they slept together in the *monjería*, an ideal environment for the spread of disease.

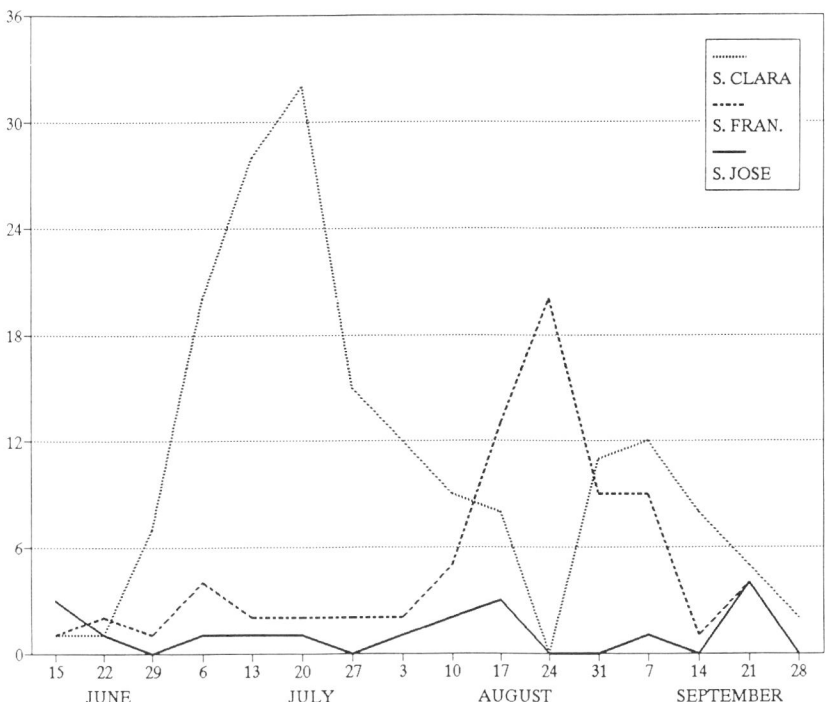

Figure 12. Graph showing reported deaths during the epidemic of 1802 at the three Bay Area missions. (Each point reflects the count for a one week interval beginning on the date noted.)

as long as it had lasted at Mission Santa Clara. However, as at Mission Santa Clara, the highest death rates were concentrated among adolescent girls, adult women, and (to a lesser extent) adult men. Josefa María, the wife of Mission San Francisco foreman Diego Olbera, died on August 14, 1802, a few days before the first flare-up of deaths. As the wife of an important person at the mission, she might well have been sent to Mission Santa Clara to help tend the sick the month before, and may therefore have brought the *peste* back to Mission San Francisco.

At Mission San Jose no dramatic increase in death rates occurred at any time during 1802. This suggests that the *peste* did not appear at that mission.

Without question, diseases such as the *peste* penetrated tribal lands away from the missions. In December of 1802, the priests at Mission San Francisco listed the deaths while away from the mission of eight Christians, "who at various times in August, (on account of the *peste*) had fled" (SFR-D 1562). However it was syphilis, rather than occasional intense epidemics, that probably contributed most significantly to population collapse in the tribal lands. Endemic syphilis acted to reduce fertility and increase infant mortality in the native populations. Tribal groups that arrived at the Bay Area missions from the early 1800s forward brought with them a lower number of children per adults than would be expected in a healthy population.

Marin Peninsula Contact and Emigration, 1783-1803

The Coast Miwok-speaking tribes of the Marin Peninsula first began immigrating to Mission San Francisco in significant numbers in 1800. During the twenty-four year period from 1776 to 1800, only thirty-five Marin Peninsula villagers had moved south across the Golden Gate. Before the 1800-1803 wave of emigration from the area is discussed, however, we will examine the small amount that can be determined about interactions between the Spaniards and native peoples on the Marin Peninsula during the 1776-1799 period.

The first Marin Peninsula people to move to Mission San Francisco were a couple from Livaneglua, the main Huimen town, which was located where the town of Sausalito is found today. The couple, Juluio and Olomojoia, brought their children for baptism during the spring of 1783 (SFR-B 305, 325). They returned in February of 1784 with Motupa, Juluio's eleven-year-old daughter by his other cowife. Juluio and Olomojoia were baptized and married at Mission San Francisco—as members of the large group that included Yelamu captain Guimas—on March 5, 1784.

A few more Huimens appeared in the baptismal records at San Francisco later in the 1780s. It is remarkable that none of them seem to have had family ties to the Yelamu people of San Francisco, considering the great number of marriage ties that existed between Yelamu and the East Bay Huchiuns. The strong currents of the Golden Gate may have been dangerous for the native tule balsas, limiting direct north-south travel and interaction.

In 1790, the English captain John Colnett laid over at Bodega Bay, fifty miles north of the Golden Gate, to repair his ship (Wagner 1931:337). Spanish authorities, in fear of possible English settlement, made a weak attempt to occupy the Bodega Bay in 1793. In April, Juan Bautista Matute took the ship *Sutil* to Bodega Bay, where he awaited the arrival of an overland party of eleven soldiers under Felipe de Goycochea. Goycochea did not leave San Francisco until August. He crossed the Golden Gate to a disembarkation point at Richardson Bay on August 5, 1793, then headed northward to the Guaulen village at Bolinas Lagoon. Goycoechea later wrote:

> Some settlements of natives on this shore of the lagoon were noted, about twenty of whose inhabitants followed us, manifesting much wonderment at the horses and much fear. When spoken to by the interpreter, however, they lost their fear and offered to go forward with us, and this they did (Goycoechea *in* Wagner 1931:342).

With their Guaulen guides, the Spanish party continued thirty miles north to Tomales point, passing nine villages along the way:

> Although the Indians accompanying us told us that these were prepared to give us battle, we passed by all of them without noticing any of the inhabitants in any warlike demonstration (Goycoechea *in* Wagner 1931: 342).

Local people, probably Segloques, contacted Captain Matute at Bodega Bay, then ferried him across the mouth of Tomales Bay to meet with Goycoechea on Tomales Point. During the next two days, Goycoechea explored Point Reyes, swung eastward into Olema territory, and arrived at Bodega Bay late in the evening of August 10, 1793.

By the time Goycochea arrived at Bodega Bay the *Sutil* had sailed for Monterey. The sailors had left some chickens and pigs with the local Yoletamal people of the Bay; the horses ridden by the Goycoechea party were even more remarkable to the Yoletamals:

> We passed the night without unsaddling all the horses, as the people from six settlements had come to visit us. They were much delighted and asked me to remain another day so that all the natives roundabout could see our horses. I told them that I would not leave very early, so as to allow time for them to come, but that I could not stay all day because I had nothing for my animals to eat (Goycoechea *in* Wagner 1931: 344).

Goycoechea's diary does not document his return route very well, nor does it provide the names of the villages or tribes through which he passed. He does state that all of the people that he encountered north of the Golden Gate spoke the same language, that they made their living by fishing, and that they were poor in seed crops. He also made the following observation:

> Neither do the people seem to be very warlike, although they preserve little harmony amongst themselves, even at short

distances those of some settlements do not go to others because of fear (Goycoechea *in* Wagner 1931:345).

In terms of the more visible aspects of their everyday behavior, the Marin Peninsula people were like those the Spaniards had been dealing with for years on the south side of the Golden Gate.

Thirteen Huimen couples joined the mass immigration to the missions during the winter of 1794-1795. They and their children were baptized at Mission San Francisco, together with some Huchiuns. A number of Huimens had been among those who had fled from Mission San Francisco after the Chimenes encounter in the spring of 1795. However, not all of them had fled, as their marriages at the mission during the late 1790s (SFR-M 509, 514) corroborate. Those who had fled stayed away from Mission San Francisco, along with their East Bay neighbors, from the spring of 1795 until January, 1800.

On January 28, 1800, five teen-aged Guaulen girls and one boy were baptized at Mission San Francisco (SFR-B 2015-2020). The oldest girl in the group, Taulmain, married widower Juan Antonio Guecuecmele, a returning Huimen runaway neophyte, the next day (SFR-M 608). Other Marin Peninsula people went through catechism lessons over the next few weeks. Soon twenty-five Habastos, four Huimens, and two more Guaulens were baptized. In addition, others married neophytes; two more Guaulen girls and two Habasto girls, for example, married Huimen neophyte widowers, while two Habasto women in their thirties immediately found husbands among the neophytes of the San Francisco Peninsula (SFR-M 615, 617, 618, 621, 622, 627). Marriage to a neophyte apparently was an important way for a vulnerable woman and her powerless tribal relatives to establish a secure place for herself within the Mission San Francisco community.

In the spring of 1801, twelve Huimen couples, three Habasto couples, and one Guaulen couple joined Mission San Francisco. Huicmuse, aged 20, who was christened Marin (SFR-B 2182), was one of the new neophytes. He became an important member of the neophyte community, and his name was eventually bestowed upon the Marin Peninsula. Two more Guaulen couples were baptized that summer, but—as had happened the year before—there were no baptisms in the fall.

Another Marin Peninsula contingent, consisting of eighteen married couples in addition to some children and single adults, went to San Francisco during the spring of 1802. Five Guaulen couples from the Pacific Coast came between January and April, as did the first Tamal couple from the valleys just to the north of Mount Tamalpais, the highest peak on the Marin Peninsula (SFR-M 716-718, 723-724).

The *peste* passed through the Bay Area missions in the summer of 1802. No Marin Peninsula immigrants were baptized that summer or fall, but the largest group of Marin Peninsula people to date went to San Francisco during the winter of 1802-1803. Among the forty-nine married couples were the last significant group of Huimens and Guaulens, a few Habastos and Tamals, and the first Olemas and Omiomis from farther to the north. Baptisms again declined during the summer of 1803, but in September the last large group of Habastos from the San Rafael area were absorbed into Mission San Francisco, together with a few Huimen stragglers.

By the end of 1803, the Huimen, Guaulen, and Habasto villages on the southern Marin Peninsula were empty. During the 1800-1803 period of migration, 275 Marin Peninsula adults moved to Mission San Francisco. They brought with them only 192 infants and young people under the age of fifteen. Since a normal native population should have included 250-275 people under the age of fifteen, it is probable that chronic diseases like syphilis, as well as epidemics like the *peste*, were crippling their ability to maintain their population.

The 1801-1803 Marin Peninsula migrations completely altered the mixture of language groups at Mission San Francisco. Coast Miwok was a rarely heard language at the mission in 1800; Costanoan (Ohlone) was the dominant native language, while Bay Miwok from the East Bay was also commonly heard. By the end of 1803, however, only forty-three percent of the 1070 Mission San Francisco neophytes spoke Costanoan, while another fifteen percent spoke Bay Miwok from the East Bay. Coast Miwok was spoken by forty-two percent of the mission residents. Coast Miwok had become the codominant native language in the Mission San Francisco community in three short years.

East Bay Emigrations and Insurgencies, 1802-1804

The *peste* epidemic during the summer of 1802 did not dissuade villagers from the interior valleys east of San Francisco Bay and south of Mission Santa Clara from moving to the missions. By November of 1802, large groups were again joining Mission Santa Clara from tribes in the San Carlos district to the south. The *peste* did not appear at Mission San Jose, where multitribal groups from the Livermore Valley area were pouring in during the summer and fall of 1802. All in all, the year 1802 saw the baptism of 130 married couples at the three Bay Area missions, which was a higher number than the previous year. From the point of view of the Franciscans at Mission San Jose, it was the most successful year for tribal absorption of the decade.

Native migration to the missions continued apace in 1803, although it was slow during the summer months at all three missions. In September of 1803, a large portion of the Huchiun-Aguastos from the southeast shore of San Pablo Bay went to Mission San Francisco, and the last big group of bayshore Jalquins went down to Mission San Jose. Significant portions of the Pelnen, Seunen, and Souyen populations from the Livermore Valley also moved to Mission San Jose during the fall of 1803. By year's end, the tribal population of the Livermore Valley had been significantly reduced.

As the year 1804 began, tribes along a wide frontier looked south and west across empty lands to the missions. The boundary ran from the Olemas, Tamals, and Omiomis on the Marin Peninsula to the Huchiun-Aguastos and Carquins on Carquinez Strait, then to the Tatcans of upper San Ramon Creek, the Pelnens, Seunens, and Souyens of the Livermore Valley, the Taunans of the hills south of Livermore Valley, and finally to the Asirins and Tayssens east of the Santa Clara Valley.

In 1804, Marin Peninsula villagers suddenly stopped going to Mission San Francisco; three Huimens were baptized in April, and one Olema person in June, but that was all. During the same year, ninety-four East Bay couples joined Mission San Francisco and Mission San Jose. Some dramatic event may have taken place that brought an end to the Marin Peninsula emigration, but nothing is documented. Mission San Francisco turned its attention to the East Bay.

A new center of resistance to Spanish hegemony arose between 1804 and 1810 among the Suisuns, a Patwin-speaking group from the north side of Carquinez Strait, thirty-five miles northeast of Mission San Francisco. It is ironic that their resistance began with the killing of former Saclan resistance leader Verecundo Juscule and several other Saclan and Jalquin men in 1804.

The entire Tatcan tribe of the San Ramon Creek area just west of Mount Diablo moved to Mission San Francisco in January, 1804. On January 25, 1804, a group of fourteen men—consisting of six Saclans, four Jalquins, two Huchiuns (one married to a Saclan), a Seunen (married to a Saclan), and a Puichon—left the mission to go on *paseo* into the East Bay; they never returned. Their deaths were verified and noted in the Mission San Francisco *Libro de Difuntos* in April (see Table 3 below). The following note was included with the entry listing their deaths:

> On January 25, 1804 a party left here for the other shore to the east of the mission at about ten in the morning. Shortly afterward a strong storm came up. Fourteen men went on this occasion. In the days immediately after we received reports that everything seemed fine. We heard nothing more until, three weeks having passed, we heard that the party went far

beyond the strait of the Carquines to the village of Suyusuyu...[illegible four word phrase].... It is not possible to affirm whether they died by drowning or at the hands of the pagans, as the incident has caused everyone to stop talking. But I am inclined to believe that they died by drowning. If the pagans had killed them, their relatives would have told me about it. Four Christians from another party said that on March 7 they [the former group] definitely left the area directly across the bay (SFR-D 1759).

Verecundo Juscule, who nine years earlier had been a resistance leader at the Chimenes battle, was among the men who died on this trip. Verecundo and the other thirteen neophytes may have gone into the Suisun lands in pursuit of relatives who had fled ahead of them. Mission register sources indicate that at least two runaway Saclan neophytes were living at this time with the Chupcans, close allies of the Suisuns (SFR-B 4022, 4063). The evidence suggests that the former Saclan resistance leaders had undergone a complete conversion in an attempt to regain their psychological balance after their 1797 defeat. They had themselves become agents of mission hegemony.

At Mission San Francisco, the widowed spouses of most of the men in the 1804 party soon remarried. Although many of their new spouses had ties to the deceased husbands, some were old neophytes from Peninsula tribes, especially the Puichons (Table 3). We are reminded that these re-marriages, as well as the thousands of other marriages that were recorded in Bay Area mission records, were meaningful unions that were an inextricable part of the complex web of interfamily relationships that was beyond either the purview or interest of the Franciscan missionaries.[4]

Another violent encounter took place between Mission Indians and tribal people in mid-February, 1804. Members of a tribe from the mountainous country between Mission Santa Clara and the San Joaquin Valley under Captain Joscori drove a group of Mission Santa Clara Christians off their land, killing a mission *regidor* in the process. The Spanish governor wrote to the viceroy in May, 1804 about the incident:

---

[4] Five of the nine Saclan and Jalquin widows of the 1804 group married longtime San Francisco Peninsula neophytes (Table 3). The widow of Verecundo Jusculé married a Puichon man who may have been a brother or close relative of the only Puichon who lost his life with Verecundo --long-time Christian Juan Regis (SFR-B 610). The Puichon man who died with Verecundo in 1804 was Pedro Armengal (SFR-B 609), who had stood next to Juan Regis during the baptismal ceremony for sixteen San Francisco Peninsula adults that took place on January 25, 1787. The man who stood behind Juan Regis at the time of baptism in 1787 was a Huchiun, Pascasio (SFR-B 611). Pascasio married the widow of Reginaldo, another of the men who died in the 1804 incident.

Table 3. Mission San Francisco men killed by the Suisuns in January of 1804, baptismal numbers of their widows, and information regarding the widows' subsequent husbands.

Death #	Name	Bapt. #	Tribe	Age	Wife Bapt.#	Wife's Next Husband Bapt.#	Tribe	Wedding
1759	Pedro Armengal	609	Puichon	39	918	1195	Lamchin	5-04-04
1760	Timoteo	1159	Huchiun	34	2130	**		
1761	Simpliciano	1640	Huchiun	34	1952	**		
1762	Anacario	1550	Saclan	30	1568	1198	Lamchin	7-27-04
1763	Tiberio	1710	Saclan	23	1716	3011	Carquin	5-09-04
1764	Tisano	1722	Saclan	23	1730	51	East Bay	7-27-04
1765	Trazon	1805	Saclan	55	1809	1149	Huchiun	10-23-04
1766	Teodorico	1708	Saclan	33	1714	874	Lamchin	7-05-04
1767	Reginaldo	2314	Seunen	25	2326	611	Huchiun	9-17-04
1768	Honorato	2315	Jalquin	27	2327	**		
1769	Arron	2378	Jalquin	22	2331	892	Lamchin	5-08-04
1770	Verecundo*	1738	Saclan	59	2264	610	Puichon	7-27-04
1771	Nicasio	2434	Jalquin	42	2435	498	Ssalson	3-21-05
1772	Cayo	2377	Jalquin	22	(bachelor)			

* Verecundo Jusculé was one of the leaders of the 1795 Saclan resistance.
** In these three cases the wife made no subsequent marriage.

> The commander at San Francisco advises me that the priests of Mission Santa Clara sent out twenty Christians in solicitude of some runaways. The pagans killed the leader of the party. The rest fled to save themselves. I do not have enough troops to punish this insult (Arrillaga [1804]).

The people who killed *Regidor* Jorge, and drove out his party of fugitive hunters, were probably the Tayssens of the rugged Orestimba Creek country, whose captain, Joscora, was eventually baptized at Mission Santa Clara in February 1806 (SCB-5048). *Regidor* Jorge was from the mountains south of the Santa Clara Valley (SCL-B 2029, SCL-D 3247).

Before the Spanish government could send out troops to the southeast in response to the killing of Jorge, rumors of possible insurrection began to spread at Mission San Jose. In June of 1804, a group of closely related Tuibun Christians tried to organize a revolt at Mission San Jose. One of them was reported to have said, "It will not be long before we kill the soldiers and the Fathers. Then we will have plenty of livestock and wheat to eat" (Peralta [1804], Appendix 4, 18). The plotters made contact with others in the mission village, especially some recently baptized Taunan men. Once word of the plan spread around the village at Mission San Jose, the soldiers of the guard found out about it:

> As a result of the murder of a pagan by the Christians of Mission San Jose, there grew up a kind of mutiny or conspiracy whereby those same Christians planned to kill the priests and guard and burn down the mission (Argüello [1804]).

The plot of June, 1804 was discovered just as the last of the large factions of the western Livermore Valley tribes were beginning catechism classes at Mission San Jose. Commander Argüello at the San Francisco Presidio sent his sergeant to break up the rumored plot:

> Upon receiving notice, I determined to send a sergeant with what troops I could spare. Under my instructions he went immediately to said mission and took testimony from the imprisoned ringleaders and accomplices in the intended transgression (Argüello [1804]).

The four men accused of organizing an insurrection were shipped to the San Francisco Presidio as prisoners. Sent along with them was León, a former Taunan tribal leader who had refused to join the plot. Commander Argüello informed Governor Arrillaga of his actions:

> Having castigated the least culpable and having left the rest of the Indian population well admonished, quiet, and calm, he returned to the presidio with four of the principal rebel leaders and one other man (Argüello [1804]).

León's arrest illustrates the police tactics employed by the Spanish; they realized that they did not need to directly punish everyone involved in potential resistance to their authority, they needed to punish only those who were held in the highest esteem within the native community:

> The other man, I am informed, was only guilty of having been asked to participate. But since he is the most highly respected among his countrymen due to things he accomplished as a pagan, it seems to me advantageous to keep him for a few days punishment in the presidio, then send him back to his mission well advised regarding good conduct. I am keeping the four so to speak principal rebels prisoners here until I receive a judgement from Your Grace (Argüello [1804]).

The ease with which the revolt was discovered and foiled illustrates the difficulty that neophytes had in organizing opposition to the mission hierarchy. The mission Indian community was filled with psychologically divided people. Some individuals were consistently opposed to the Spanish authorities, others consistently identified with them, and still others wavered in their position. There was no shortage of informers concerning any overt attempt at resistance.

In June of 1804, the killers of the neophyte Jorge of Mission Santa Clara remained at large and unpunished. Furthermore, the Mission Santa Clara missionaries complained that tribal resistance had stimulated a new round of flight:

> The Fathers of the missions cry for assistance regarding runaway Indians who hole up as fugitives. They complain that because I do not go out looking for them it lowers the morale of the others, who then flee. Finally, Father José Viader of Mission Santa Clara is upset with me regarding the killing of the Christian George by the pagans of the mountains. I informed you about this last February 28. I found myself without forces when it happened, and as I still do not have them, I have been unable to do anything (Argüello [1804]).

The situation was reminiscent of that which had existed during the summer of 1795, after the runaway Saclans killed seven people from Mission San Francisco. People once again held mixed feelings about the choices that they had made to move to the missions, and members of a mission population were once again ready to interpret successful opposition as a sign that they, too, should change their minds and flee.

By the late summer of 1804, the Spanish military had pulled together enough troops to raid various interior East Bay villages that were hiding escaped Christians and accused criminals. The nearest tribal groups at the time were the Chupcans near Suisun Bay; the Volvons, Ssaoams, and Luechas of the inner Coast Range eastward of the Livermore Valley; and the Juñas and Tayssens deep in the mountains east of Santa Clara.

The first Spanish punitive expedition in 1804 set out in September under Luís Peralta. During their sortie the party approached the Chupcan village on Pacheco Slough (where the town of Concord is presently located), which harbored runaway neophytes, and pinned its inhabitants down from the landward side. The villagers slipped out of their village on Pacheco Slough in tule boats during the night, and almost certainly crossed Suisun Bay to find refuge among the Suisuns, with whom they were intermarried. The members of the Peralta party, who lacked guides familiar with the Chupcans' capabilities, were surprised to find the village empty the following morning. They renamed the village site "*Monte del Diablo*," or "Thicket of the Devil," since they believed that it could only have been the latter's intervention that had made it possible for the Chupcans to escape them. The place name was later applied by American settlers to nearby Mount Diablo, which was the dominant mountain peak in the central Coast Ranges (Ortiz 1989).

The soldiers returned to the San Francisco Presidio after their raid, complaining that they were unable to find the Indian people they sought "for want of good guides" (Peralta [1804a]). A second Spanish police raid occurred in October of 1804; the expedition returned to the San Francisco Presidio before October 26:

> The second expedition made by Sergeant Peralta in pursuit of the pagan Indians who killed the Christian Jorge did not succeed in capturing them. They did succeed in seizing eleven Christians of Mission San Jose and Mission San Francisco. After giving over the women and children to the Fathers, they arrived at the Presidio with thirty-two troublemakers (Argüello [1804a]).

If the October sortie captured runaways from both Mission San Francisco and Mission San Jose, while also seeking the men who killed Jorge of Mission Santa Clara, presumably on Orestimba Creek, it must have covered an extensive area in the interior valleys east of San Francisco Bay and the Santa Clara Valley. Unfortunately, no diary or extended report remains. The expedition seems to have returned to the Chupcan lands in the lower Diablo Valley, since a Chupcan infant (SJO-B 1290) was baptized at Mission San Jose on October 26, 1804, the day that Peralta returned from his second raid.

Luecha and Volvon Opposition, 1805

By the winter of 1804-1805, many of the tribes on the very eastern edge of the San Francisco Bay area, in the hill country overlooking the San Joaquin Valley, were ready to move to the missions. While Peralta was out in the hill country in October of 1804, about half of the Ssaoams of the east side of the Livermore Valley were baptized at Mission San Jose. The remainder of the Ssaoams must have been moving to Mission San Jose at that time, for they were baptized there at the end of the year and during the first months of 1805. Among those Ssaoams were some in-married spouses from the Luechas, their neighbors to the south, and from the Volvons, their neighbors to the north.

As a group, the Luechas were not ready to give in to the Spaniards in the winter of 1804-1805. In January of 1805, they attacked a Mission San Jose party, wounding a Franciscan priest and killing the mission *mayordomo* and three Christian Indians. This was a dramatic event, the first time an "enlightened person" was killed by tribal people in the San Francisco Bay Area, and the first time a Franciscan priest had been wounded.

The missionary priest, Father Cueva, left Mission San Jose with his escort on January 13 or 14, ostensibly to visit an Asirin village to hear confessions and baptize the sick. Yet very few Asirins were still non-Christians at the time; most had joined Mission Santa Clara. A letter in which the corporal of the guard at Mission San Jose had ordered soldier Ygnacio Alviso to go no further than the Asirins, suggests that the soldiers were aware that Father Cueva actually desired to proselytize in tribal areas more remote from the mission. The native guides missed the canyon of Arroyo del Valle, which was the route to the Asirins, either deliberately or accidentally, and continued on to the canyon of Arroyo Mocho, near or within Luecha territory. One report states that the party lost its way in the Livermore Valley in one of the dense ground fogs which occasionally grip the winter landscape. Whatever the case, the Luechas found foreigners in their territory and attacked them:

> The guide led them to a village of pagans, telling them they were Christians. Those from the village began to fire arrows with great enthusiasm—soon they got support from two other villages. They killed Ygnacio Higuera and two of our Indians. Father Cuevas took an arrow in the eye and Joaquín Higuera another in the thigh. The pagans killed all the saddle horses, and those of the remuda as well. They kept firing arrows at the Father and the soldiers from midday until about dusk. The soldiers lost everything but their leather jackets, shields, and muskets. This took place yesterday, and some Indians brought back word on foot. This morning the Father and soldiers arrived on horses that had been sent out for them (Sanchez [1805], Appendix 4, 19).

The four men killed by "the pagan Luechas" were Mission San Jose *mayordomo* Ygnacio Higuera of Sinaloa (age 47), Tuibun neophytes Claudio (age 30) and Victor (age 28), as well as Yrgin neophyte Lucano (age 29) (SJO-D 537-540).

Commander José Argüello at San Francisco blamed the incident on the Mission San Jose priest, Father Pedro de la Cueva:

> Complaint is made regarding the temerity with which Father Cueva, recently arrived from Mexico, ignored the council of a soldier who had recognized that they were placing them

Regional Disintegration, 1800-1805

selves in danger. Being carried away by his authority, he forced his will upon the others (Argüello [1805]).

On January 20, 1805, a punitive force of eighteen soldiers and fifteen townspeople left the pueblo of San Jose for the Luecha lands (Argüello [1805]). According to Peralta's report:

> On the twenty-second he arrived at the point where the criminals had committed the crime. They did not find a single soul. They looked for the bodies, finding only that of the steward buried in a gully. Due to the rains that had recently fallen, it was impossible to find the trail by which the Indians had fled. The expedition went on into the mountains. They came upon and seized two pagan Indians. From them they verified the location of the village they sought.
>
> On the twenty-third in the afternoon they left for the place identified by the pagans. "We came upon it and came charging in with swords drawn. As we came upon them they were taking up arms. They began to fire. We struck them down, and five of the delinquents were killed at that place. The rest, with their women, fired at us from some ravines, one group from a nearby grove of trees. Presently everyone charged the grove" returning their fire because they had fired, thus killing five of the delinquents, including two captains "and a little girl struck by accident." The grove was searched. "Twenty-five head, among them children and adults, all women, were brought out." Four adult males were also caught, two of them wounded. It is believed that some men suffering from gunshot wounds remained in the grove. After sunset the party retired to where they had left the horses, bringing the prisoners with them.
>
> On the twenty-fourth they returned to the grove to see what they could find. Finding nothing, they returned. They recovered the body of the steward. They searched again [for the other bodies]. Not finding them, they retired.
>
> On the twenty-seventh they freed one of the Indian men who had proved himself to be innocent (Peralta [1805]).

At final count, eleven Luecha men were killed in Peralta's raid, and four men captured (Arrillaga [1805]); many others escaped. Twenty-five non-Christian

Luecha women and children were brought in to Mission San Jose, presumably as hostages. Nine Luecha children were baptized at Mission San Jose by the wounded Father Cueva on February 6, 1804. The Luechas who remained at large were not given the time to try to rebuild their normal village way of life; another Spanish expedition entered their territory in mid-February. When runaways in surrounding hill villages heard that Luís Peralta was coming again toward their lands to hunt them down, most of them came down out of the mountains to meet him. As the extant paraphrase of Argüello's report states:

> He ordered Sergeant Luís Peralta to return with another expedition into the mountains where the Indians were who had gone against Father Cueva. The expedition turned out well, in that before they even reached the mountains most of the runaways gave themselves up to their missions of San Jose and Santa Clara. Since then some pagans have asked to be baptized. One captain from the big village on the San Joaquin River called Pescadero came to give Sergeant Peralta assurances that neither he nor his people had taken part in the attack against Father Cueva and his escort.
>
> Peralta returned on the twenty-second, bringing two Christians who had been involved in the crime. They have been imprisoned along with the four pagans.
>
> He recommends that the Christians be exiled to some distant Presidio for a few years (Argüello [1805a]).

Three of the adult Luecha women captured in the initial raid went through catechism and were baptized on March 2, as part of a larger group of fifty-two people from the Livermore Valley environs. Prison terms at Santa Barbara or San Diego were recommended for the four non-Christian Luecha men who were arrested (Argüello [1805b]); however, no documents listing the punishments meted out in this case have been discovered. As the spring gave way to summer, a few more Luechas were baptized, but at Mission Santa Clara rather than at Mission San Jose, probably because two of the neophytes that they had killed in January were Tuibuns, which was one of the dominant groups at Mission San Jose. Tuibun anger would have made Mission San Jose seem particularly unattractive to any Luecha who was considering the move to a mission.

The solution to the tensions that existed between the Luechas and the Mission Indian communities was to arrange for intermarriages to take place; this is an important mechanism for restoring good relations in feud-based societies the world over. Consequently, two Luecha women, whose husbands had probably been killed by the Spanish party on January 20, married Mission Santa Clara widowers from the "Santa Agueda" district—Tuibuns or Alsons—on August 7, 1805 (SCL-M 1201, 1206).

The Luecha attack and Spanish counterattack did not slow down the pace of emigration out of the interior valleys of the East Bay during the spring of 1805. In March, the last large factions of Livermore Valley Souyens and Seunens were baptized at Mission San Jose. Some Volvons from east of Mt. Diablo were baptized at Mission San Francisco in the same month. In May, a large portion of the Volvons went to Mission San Jose, which was enjoying its fifth consecutive year of heavy immigration from the north and east.

In late May of 1805, Governor Argüello was informed of yet another plot to drive the Spaniards out of the East Bay, this time involving neophytes and catechumens from the Seunens and Volvons:

> In Mission Santa Clara a Christian Indian was captured on the roof of the Fathers' rooms. With him had come a pagan from the *ranchería* of the Seunens, to check out the entrance. They schemed to burn down Mission Santa Clara and kill the Fathers that very night. Their object had been to bring together the *rancherías* of the Bolbons and Seunens, a great number of pagans. All this was related by the Indian prisoner. Another five implicated Christians were also taken into custody (L. Argüello [1805]).

Most of the Seunens had moved to Mission San Jose in 1803 and 1804, and at least fifty Volvons were in catechism classes at Mission San Jose in the spring of 1805. Forty-four Volvons were baptized between May 22 and May 30. The parents of some of the Volvon children who were baptized at the time left Mission San Jose without becoming neophytes. Among them was a man by the name of Poyl, who was eventually baptized at Mission San Francisco in March of 1806 along with the Seunen man Polecs (SFR-B 3327, 3326); these two individuals may have been the leaders of the near revolt of 1805 (see Appendix 1, Volvon).

In response to the Seunen-Volvon threat and the continuing Luecha insurgency, the Spanish government mounted the longest and most thorough campaign yet attempted in the San Francisco Bay area. The government sent out a party of twenty-two soldiers under Luís Argüello some time around May 13, 1805. The party, which departed from Mission San Jose, stayed out for an entire month, sweeping through every valley and flatland area in the interior Coast Ranges from Mt. Diablo on the north to Pacheco Pass (opposite Carnadero, near Gilroy) on the south:

> [This letter] is accompanying the expedition diary of Second Lieutenant Luís Argüello, who during the thirty-two days that he took in fulfilling his commission, surveyed "all the mountains of San Jose and Santa Clara, as far as opposite *El Carnadero*, penetrating the rivers, plains, and swamps, without encountering problems with the native populace"—as a result proving false the news that the pagans wanted to burn the mission of San Jose. The accusers stated that they had uttered the threat in order to be freed from the whippings that were continually given them by the Fathers of the mission (Argüello [1805d]).

The area covered extended seventy-five miles from north to south and contained approximately 1700 square miles of the most rugged territory in Central California.[5]

During the extended sortie, the Spanish party probably visited villages ranging from those of the Chupcans in the north to those of the Tayssens in the south. They once again struck the Luechas. They remained in tribal areas until June 15, when they returned to Mission San Jose with thirteen runaway Christians and another nine non-Christians who had been implicated in various crimes against Spanish law. The surviving paraphrase of the report reads:

> On the journey he visited the village of the celebrated Joscori—he captured everyone except this captain.
>
> Among the pagan captives were six men involved in the assassination of the Christian George [in February of 1804].
>
> Having solicited all the prisoners regarding whether they had been baptized, they were turned over to the ministers of San

---

[5] Sherburne Cook was certain that the May-June, 1805 expedition under Luís Argüello went into the San Joaquin Valley. "Argüello must have gone into the valley, otherwise there is no sense to the mention of the rivers, tule swamps, etc. Further, 32 days is a long trip, hardly to be spent in the coast ranges" (Cook 1957:245). The context within which the trip took place, however, involved troubles with Seunen, Volvon, Chupcan, Luecha, and Tayssen peoples, all groups west of the San Joaquin. The territories of those groups were certainly the main areas that were searched. Tule swamps existed in the Diablo Valley and Livermore Valley, and there were small plains and flatlands back in the San Antonio Valley and elsewhere. The mention of "rivers" does suggest that the party visited San Joaquin River villages, probably in a search for runaway Christians from the eastern hills who were hiding with relatives on the river.

Jose and Santa Clara with the recommendation that the Fathers be moderate in their punishment of the six (Argüello [1805d]).

Most of the tribal men and the Christian runaways wanted by the Spanish military were now captured, including those who had been involved in the killing of Mission Santa Clara *regidor* Jorge back in February of 1804.

By early June, 1805, additional families of Luechas and Tayssens were pouring into Mission Santa Clara, even before Luís Argüello's expedition had returned. In August, more Volvons from the Mount Diablo area—the spiritual landmark of the region—were baptized at Mission San Francisco. Another third of the Volvon population remained non-Christian until the spring of 1806. The Carquins and the Chupcans were the only East Bay groups that were still intact at the end of 1805. They and the remaining non-Christian Huchiun-Aguastos had certainly withdrawn to the north side of Carquinez Strait by the end of 1805.

***

During the 1800-1805 period, the East Bay and southern Marin Peninsula valleys were emptied of people, as villagers trekked to the three Franciscan missions in existence at the time. Continual migration over those years erased almost a score of tiny sovereign groups from the face of the earth. Although migration was unceasing, it was neither steady nor smooth. Over those six years families were torn by arguments and indecision regarding the possibility of moving to the missions, and individual minds were changed again and again. Some people fought the Spaniards, and some fled to live with relatives in more distant groups. No one could stay where they were and remain unaffected. Everyone along the mission-tribal frontier faced the imperative to modify their way of life in a rapidly changing world.

Chapter 9

Recapitulation, 1806-1810

	Spanish Actions	Tribal Actions
1806	March 28-May 19. Russian expedition under Resanov visits San Francisco Bay.	Mid-March. Measles strike missions San Jose and San Juan Bautista. Mid-April. Measles strike missions Santa Clara and San Francisco.
1807	Summer. Cholvons hired as laborers at San Jose Pueblo.	Feb. 4. Suisun drive out large Mission San Francisco posse, kill twelve invaders.
1808	Sept.-Oct. Moraga explores Sacramento Valley.	Spring-Summer. Surge of middle Marin Peninsula emigrants to Mission SF.
1809	Spring. Alaskan sea otter hunters throughout SF Bay.	Spring-Summer. Olemas, Tamals to Mission San Francisco.
1810	May 22. Moraga attacks and burns a Suisun village. August and October. Spanish parties raid San Joaquin Valley.	Jan.-Feb. Carquins move to Mission SF. Suisuns kill four Carquin neophytes. June-Sept. Surge of San Joaquin Valley people to Mission Santa Clara.

A Measles Epidemic and Russian Visitors

The period between 1806 and 1810 began with the worst epidemic of the Spanish era in California. One quarter of the mission Indian population of the San Francisco Bay Area died of the measles or related complications between March and May of 1806 (see Figure 13). At the time the measles struck, big groups of Tayssens and Luechas were in catechism classes at Mission Santa Clara. Mission San Jose catechism classes were much smaller, composed of a few Luechas and some of their eastern neighbors from the big Cholvon villages along the San Joaquin River. At Mission San Francisco that spring the

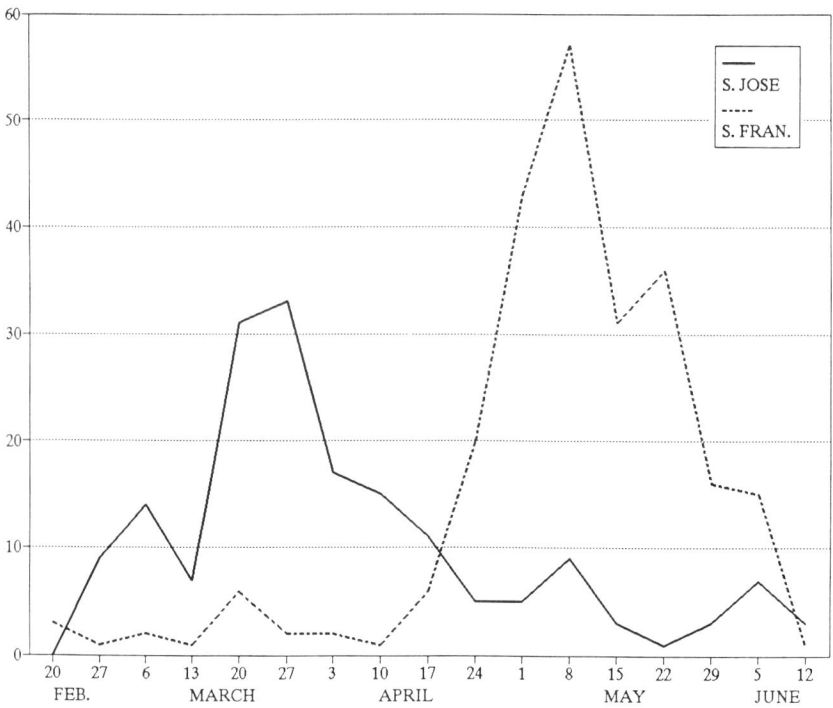

Figure 13. Graph showing reported deaths at two of the three Bay Area missions during the measles epidemic of 1806. (Mission Santa Clara deaths were not reliably reported.)

last Volvons from the Mount Diablo area were being baptized.

Measles had appeared at Rosario in Baja California in June of 1805 (Ruíz [1805]); it then spread northward, reaching the Bay Area in the spring of 1806. It struck at Mission San Jose and Mission San Juan Bautista farther south in the first week of March. In late March, it appeared at coastal Mission Santa Cruz; in early April it reached San Carlos Borromeo, in mid-April Mission Santa Clara, and it finally struck at Mission San Francisco on April 24. The east-to-west movement of the epidemic suggests that it reached the Bay Area missions via tribal populations in the San Joaquin Valley.

The rapidly spreading disease struck Mission San Jose in early March of 1806. There it raged for six weeks. Nearly three-quarters of the children under five years of age died in those few weeks, as well as nearly half of the adult women and nearly one quarter of the adult men. Overall, some thirty percent of the mission inhabitants died. The epidemic came to an end in the middle of April.

It is not easy to follow the epidemic's progress at Mission Santa Clara, because the *Libro de Entierros* for Santa Clara that spring is a confused mass of undated and delayed entries. The epidemic began sometime in early April and continued through the end of May. In addition to the 230 people who were listed in the Santa Clara death register for the year, another seventy deaths may not have been recorded.[1] The Santa Clara mortality rate was at most twenty percent, which was lower than at Mission San Jose, but it still entailed a horrible loss of life.

While the measles epidemic raged at Mission San Jose, a Russian exploratory expedition under Count Nikolai Petrovich Rezanov entered San Francisco Bay. The Russians landed at the San Francisco Presidio on March 28, 1806 (Langsdorff [1806] 1814:150). Diarist George von Langsdorff later described the daily life of the Mission Indians:

> The works to which the [neophytes] are principally employed are husbandry, tending the cattle, and shearing the sheep, or in mechanical trades, as building, preparing tallow and soap, or making household utensils; also in the transport of provisions, and other objects of necessity, from one mission or presidency to another. The most laborious employment, which is grinding the corn, is left almost entirely to the women; it is rubbed between two quadrangular oblong stones till ground to meal....
>
> The cattle, horses, and sheep, do not require any particular care and attention. The herds are left out in the open field the whole year through, and only a sufficient number are kept in the neighborhood of the establishment to serve their immediate wants....
>
> All the husbandry work is performed by oxen: the horses are kept for military service and for the use of the ecclesiastics, or for the transport of provisions and other objects from one

---

[1] The 1806 year-end population at Mission Santa Clara that is listed in the annual report is less by seventy-two people than the same population as determined by subtracting the death entries for the year from the 1805 year-end population (Bowman 1958:147). Scores of deaths were noted in the *Libro de Difuntos* for late March, late April, and early May. Yet no deaths at all were listed at Mission Santa Clara for the two-week period between April 1 and April 15. The priests may have failed to record seventy-two deaths that occurred during that two-week period, because of the stress resulting from the disaster.

mission to another: in the latter service some mules are also employed (Langsdorff [1806] 1814:168-170).

Langsdorff gained the impression that the neophytes were allowed to continue their dances and sports at the missions:

> They are permitted to retain their former habits and customs, as far as they are not inconsistent with their new religion. In their dances, their amusements, their sports, their ornaments, they are freely indulged (Langsdorff [1806] 1814:171).

With regard to the foodstuffs provided in the missions, Langsdorff wrote:

> Their principal food is a thick soup made with meat, vegetables, and pulse. This is portioned out three times in the day, morning, noon, and evening, in the quantity of about a German measure [three English pints] to each person. At the hour of eating, every family goes with a vessel of some kind to the kitchen, when as many measures are served to each person as there are persons belonging to it. I was present at the time of delivering out the soup, and it appeared to me incomprehensible how any one could three times a day eat so large a portion of such nourishing food. According to what we are informed by our cicerone, between forty and fifty oxen are killed every week for the community, besides which, meal, bread, maize, pease, beans, and other kinds of pulse, are distributed without any stated allowance (Langsdorff [1806] 1814:160).

Langsdorff held the native culture in contempt. He attributed the ability of the Spanish to keep so many people under control to the kindness of the missionaries and to the natural inferiority of the Native Californians:

> When it is observed that two or three monks, and four or five soldiers, keep in order a community of a thousand or fifteen hundred rough uncivilized men, making them lead a wholly different course of life from that to which they had been accustomed, without any spirit of mutiny or insurrection appearing among them, it must be supposed that the cause is to be found principally in the mildness and forbearance with which they are treated, in the paternal care and kindness extended towards them. I must, however, also attribute it in

> a great degree to the extreme simplicity of these poor creatures, who in stature no less than in mind are certainly of a very inferior race of human beings: I believe them wholly incapable of forming among themselves any regular and combined plan for their own emancipation (Langsdorff [1806] 1814:168).

Langsdorff recognized the role that traditional intertribal enmities played in allowing the missionaries to control so many people with the help of so few Spanish soldiers:

> Every now and then attempts at escape are made. On such occasions, no sooner is any one missed than search is made after him; and as it is always known to what tribe the fugitive belongs, and on account of the enmity which subsists among the different tribe, he can never take refuge in any other (a circumstance which perhaps he scarcely thought of beforehand), it is scarcely possible for him to evade the researches of those who are sent in pursuit of him (Langsdorff [1806] 1814:171).

He also described the punishment for flight from the missions:

> He is almost always brought back again to the mission, where he is bastinadoed, and an iron rod of a foot or a foot and a half long, and an inch in diameter, is fastened to one of his feet: this has the double use of preventing him from repeating the attempt, and of frightening others from imitating him (Langsdorff [1806] 1814:171).

Langsdorff's information reinforces impressions gained from earlier travelers and Spanish documentary sources regarding mission conditions and the tribal jealousies that limited native resistance.

Father Pedro de la Cueva of Mission San Jose arrived at San Francisco in mid-April to negotiate a grain sale to the Russians. The measles epidemic was coming to an end at his mission. Cueva, who was described as a "gay and cheerful" man, told the Russians that his Indians were busy grinding grain for trade:

> The difficulty of the land transport, the small number of converts at St. Joseph, and a disease hitherto unknown in New California, the measles, which had broken out this year, and had for some weeks attacked great numbers of the Indians,

198   *A Time Of Little Choice*

occasioned very great delays in furnishing us with the supplies we had agreed for (Langsdorff [1806] 1814:188).

Father Cueva invited the visitors to come and visit Mission San Jose, and told them that he would entertain them with a "dance of the Indians" (Langsdorff [1806] 1814:192).

The Russian party arrived at Mission San Jose late in the evening on Sunday, April 20. On Monday morning, April 21, Father Cueva suspended work and ordered preparations for a feast and dance:

> He therefore now announced that they were to have a holiday from their work, that they might dress themselves in their very best attire, and prepare for a dance. For this purpose he distributed a number of ornaments among the best dancers, who immediately withdrew with them to make the necessary preparations (Langsdorff [1806] 1814:192).

It is worth noting that the sacred ceremonial dance regalia was in the possession of Father Cueva. In traditional culture, the dance regalia would have been under

Figure 14. Illustration of dancers prior to a ceremony at Mission San Jose in 1806, an ink wash by an artist with the Resanov Expedition (courtesy of The Bancroft Library).

the care of the most highly esteemed older dance society leaders; Father Cueva had assumed that role.

> The dancers assembled towards noon in the large court of the mission; they were divided into companies; some were distinguished above the rest by particular ornaments and by a particular kind of song which they sung. One of these divisions consisted of the inhabitants of the coast, the other were people from the more inland tribes.... (Langsdorff [1806] 1814:195).

One of the dance sets resembled the Sierra Miwok *Pota*, in which two groups act out a battle between opposing supernatural forces:

> About two o'clock we sat down to a very good dinner, and afterwards went again to see the Indians, who were still occupied with their dancing, and were now going to exhibit a mock fight. A large straw figure represented the enemy, and a number of the men, armed with bows and arrows, sprung and danced about with frightful gestures and contortions to defy their adversary, who, if he had been able, would have done the like. One of them at length gave a signal, and at the same moment the straw figure was pierced with a vast number of arrows, and the man who personated the chief was carried off in triumph (Langsdorff [1806] 1814:196).

The people of Mission San Jose were more likely to have been celebrating their survival during the measles epidemic on that Monday than honoring the Russian visitors.

The measles epidemic struck Mission San Francisco on Thursday, April 24 (SFR-D 2060). On April 28, Father Landaeta wrote the following to Father Peña in Mexico:

> The measles have wreaked havoc upon the Indians of this province, but none at all upon the *gente de razón*. We missionaries here find ourselves with about four hundred sick. Until now no one has died except the cook Andres, but I think that some of those who are down will die. We have taken the precaution to collect them into four large groups, maintaining

them with regular meals and *atole*. But all of our efforts cannot counter the thousand stupid actions which send them to the cemetery (Landaeta [1806]).

The epidemic reached its peak at Mission San Francisco in May. Mortality rates surpassed those of the worst periods at Missions Santa Clara and equalled those at Mission San Jose. Mortality among infant males was seventy percent, while not a single little girl under five years of age lived through the epidemic. Almost half of the adult women at Mission San Francisco died, although only twenty percent of the men died.

The Russians were still at the port loading the grain they were purchasing when the measles struck at Mission San Francisco. About 150 people died at Mission San Francisco while they were there, yet Langsdorff's only written comment was a complaint that the epidemic slowed the arrival of grain. The Resanov expedition sailed out of San Francisco Bay on May 19, 1806, while the measles epidemic was still going strong at Mission San Francisco.

The epidemic persisted for six weeks at Mission San Francisco, lasting until the week of June 1-7, 1806. It then spread north to the remnant villages of the southern Marin Peninsula, carried by frightened runaway Christians. A death register entry on June 12, 1806 reads:

> The Huimen neophytes informed me that the man named Luchesio has died among the pagans, where he had fled, probably in complete fear. His death was the result of the measles (SFR-D 2280).

In the short run, the measles epidemic frightened tribal people enough to bring recruitment to a halt; however, by 1807, large groups were once again migrating to the missions. In the long run, the epidemic was just one more demoralizing pressure on the native villagers.

Turmoil on the Marin Peninsula

The measles epidemic of 1806 probably caused the near cessation of migration from the Marin Peninsula during 1806 and 1807. However, a group of thirty-two Olemaloque and Libantone people did go to Mission San Francisco from the Point Reyes area in July of 1807. Their arrival at San Francisco coincided with the appearance of Alaskan sea otter hunters on the Marin Peninsula, brought there by American (United States) and Russian ships.

Native Alaskan hunters were reported off the outer coast "in front of the Port" on February 14, 1807 (Arrillaga [1807]). They had been left on the Farallon Islands to hunt sea lions by the Boston ship *O'Cain*, which was working under contract to the Russian-American Company at Sitka. In March, another Boston vessel under Russian contract, the *Peacock*, anchored at Bodega Bay while its Alaskan contract hunters took otters in Olemaloque lands on the Marin Coast. Some of the hunters even came into San Francisco Bay. Governor Arrillaga was upset to hear that the Americans and Alaskans were building shelters at Bodega Bay in early May (Arrillaga [1807a]), but the *Peacock* left in that month to join the other American ships off Baja California (Ogden 1941:50).

A large surge of Olemas, Tamals, and Omiomis emigrated from their villages on the central Marin Peninsula for Mission San Francisco during 1808. Altogether, 142 Marin Peninsula people joined Mission San Francisco during the year. In April of 1808, some of the new neophytes brought in a report that runaway Olema neophyte Gavino Aichicacú had been killed by *Americanos* (SFR-D 2548).[2] Since no Boston vessels were on the California coast in 1808, Gavino was probably killed the year before by someone from the Boston ship *Peacock*.

In the winter of 1808-1809, a veritable Alaskan invasion of the Marin Coast took place.[3] The Russian ship *Kodiak* arrived at Bodega Bay in the late fall of 1808 with 130 native Alaskan sea otter hunters, 20 native women, and 40 Russians aboard. In late January and early February of 1809, numerous Olema and Olemaloque families migrated to Mission San Francisco. No information is available regarding the extent to which their move was influenced by the arrival of the Alaskans.

In early February, 1809, the Alaskan otter hunters brought fifty canoes into San Francisco Bay by way of a portage across the northern headlands of the Golden Gate (Ogden 1941:57-59). Mission San Francisco Indians captured a man from "Onolasca or Coudiac" on Angel Island at the end of the month (Arrillaga [1809]). This man told the Spanish authorities that the Russian ship *Neva* was at Bodega Bay and that construction was going on there. On March 25, 1809, ten Spanish soldiers attacked some Alaskan natives camped at San Bruno, killing four men and arresting two more who were badly wounded. However, this setback did not stop the unauthorized hunting. On March 31, 1809, Father Sainz de Lucio of Mission San Francisco was upset to the point of being fearful:

---

[2] Soon after the Americans killed Gavino Aichicacú in April, 1808, the Mission San Francisco priests gave the name Gavino to an Olemaloque man, Tabalchucha (SFR-B 3585). Gavino Tabalchucha was a young adult, about the same age as Gavino Aichicacú. The new Gavino may have been a relative or friend who came forward to take the place of the slain man in the mission community.

[3] In October, 1808, Alexander Baranov, director of the Russian-American Fur Company, ordered his assistant Ivan Kuskov to hunt off the California coast during the coming winter months. He directed Kuskov to winter at Drakes Bay or Bodega Bay (Baranov [1808] 1989:170-171).

> For this year we will not need to find merchants for sea otter pelts, since the Russians and English have relieved us of the trouble of catching them. They have made themselves masters of the bay. They have more than forty little "jayague" canoes, with which over the past three months they have gone freely wherever they wished, with so little respect that I truly fear them (Sainz de Lucio [1809]).

Alaskan natives continued to hunt otters in the Bay during April. The Russian ship, which seems actually to have been the *Kodiak*, remained at Bodega Bay through August of 1809, and then returned to Alaska with two thousand sea otter skins (Ogden 1941:58-59).

The invasion by the Alaskans stimulated new Spanish interest in the lands on the north side of the Golden Gate. In 1809, after many years of shunning the waters of the Bay for purposes of transportation, the Spanish authorities finally constructed launches that were more seaworthy than the native tule balsas. Missionaries began going by sea to proselytize on the Marin Peninsula. A baptismal entry for October 12, 1809, documents the availability of the launch:

> Maria Bernardina...was born on October 12 on the other shore at the village of the Huymenes and baptized there on the same day by the Reverend Father Buenaventura Fortuni, minister of the Mission of San Jose, who had gone there with the launch (SFR-B 3794).

On October 17, ten Tamal adults were baptized at Mission San Francisco, and a small group of Olemaloques, including some orphans, went to the mission in the spring of 1810.

American contract ships again brought Alaskan hunters and their Russian overseers to Bodega Bay in the fall of 1810. By mid-September, Alaska natives were hunting in San Francisco Bay, as far south as the sloughs at the bottom of the Santa Clara Valley. Three Aleut hunters were captured by Spanish soldiers south of Mission San Francisco on September 24 (Arrillaga [1810], Appendix 5, 24).

Gabriel Moraga led a party of soldiers to Bodega Bay to meet with the Russians and Americans in late September, 1810. Since he did not have the manpower to force the newcomers to leave, he merely lodged a weak protest regarding their presence. By November, four American contract vessels were anchored at Bodega Bay. Some Omiomi people went down to San Francisco in the late fall, but it was not until 1811 and 1812 that the majority of the Omiomis and people further north migrated to Mission San Francisco.

The arrival of the Russians at Bodega Bay presented the tribal people of the Marin coast with an alternative source of western material goods and knowledge. They were probably surprised to discover that there were maritime powers who were not afraid of the Spaniards, and they must have been impressed by the ease with which the Alaska natives invaded San Francisco Bay. In addition, the Russian leadership wished to avoid conflict with the native Californians. Alexander Baranov in Alaska gave the first California expedition leader, Ivan Kuskov, the following instructions regarding interactions with California Indians:

> You must strictly prohibit even the slightest exploitation of the local natives either by Russians or by members of the hunting groups; they must not be either insulted or abused. You personally and your subordinates must make every effort to win their friendship and affection. You must not use fear because of the superiority of your firearms, which these people do not possess. Rather, seek to attract them through kind gestures based on humanity, and occasional gifts to win them over. Do not neglect any opportunity to gain future benefits (Baranov [1808] 1989:168).

In the field, things did not always work out according to plan. The Alaskan otter hunters were suddenly everywhere along the beaches of the western Marin Peninsula tribes.

One clash between Alaskans and Californians was documented in a Mission San Francisco death register entry in November, 1810. Two Olemoloque neophytes were killed in their homelands in an encounter with seven Onalasca natives:

> I have been assured by the neophytes Majen, Regulo, and Castor that the Indians of the Russian Establishments or of Onalasca were hunting sea otters around Point San Antonio. Seven of the Onalascas who fled to the land of the Olemus killed the neophyte Ciriaco and his son Elias (SFR-D 2885, 2886).

The Russian authorities were no more able to control the actions of their Alaskan hunters than the Spanish officers were able to control the actions of the colonists at San Jose, or of Mission Indians on *paseo* with grudges to settle.

Defeat of the Suisuns

The Suisuns, who had killed eleven Saclan and Jalquin neophytes in early 1804, were left alone by the Spanish military over the next few years. Prior to 1809, the Spaniards lacked the boats that would have been necessary to mount a major expedition northward across Carquinez Strait. During those years, the Carquin and Suisun areas were safe havens for escaped Saclan, Chupcan, and Carquin neophytes with family connections. There were sixty-two Mission San Francisco runaways hiding north of the bay as of February, 1807 (Abella [1807], Appendix 4, 20).

In early February of 1807, the Suisuns killed twelve Mission San Francisco men during a neophyte raid north of Carquinez Strait. The raid and subsequent slayings were part of the ongoing history of feuds among the Saclans, Chupcans, Carquins, and Suisuns that went back at least as far as 1804. However, the immediate provocation for the ill-fated neophyte raid on the Suisuns was an incident that occurred in January, 1807. On January 6, immediately after the death of a Tatcan neophyte boy, his parents and two other Tatcan couples fled Mission San Francisco (SFR-B 2384; SFR-D 2888). The Tatcan lands were empty at the time, so the three families joined relatives among the Chupcans, who had withdrawn into the territory of the Suisuns north of the Carquinez Strait. Within days, one of the runaway women either left her husband or was taken away from him.

The man whose wife had been taken, Octaviano Oloacse, returned to Mission San Francisco to get help from his relatives in getting her back. An enthusiastic group of neophyte men gathered to help Octaviano carry out his plan. Missionary Ramón Abella wrote:

> On February 3 the one who returned, whose name is Octaviano (and who has now run away again), and a friend of his got together a number of people from his homeland, about twenty or thirty men (Abella [1807], Appendix 4, 20).

Instead of halting the expedition, the missionaries helped to organize it. Presumably, they hoped that the Christian Indians would round up all the runaways throughout the Carquinez Strait region. Wrote Father Abella:

> As a result of their effort [Octaviano's relatives] more than one hundred men were soon gathered together, including the healthy and the not so healthy. Some were ill, and the majority had no weapons. I clearly remember telling one man not to go (who ended up being the first one killed.) It was

necessary to restrain some to keep them from going. Not one of them was forced to go (Abella [1807], Appendix 4, 20).

The mission posse, consisting of over a hundred men, ferried to the east shore of the bay across from Mission San Francisco on Wednesday, February 4, 1807:

> On Thursday they continued over land. On Friday they again went by water, across the Strait of the Karquines, the mouth of the rivers.... Sixty men remained right there at the village of the Karquines, gathering up all the runaways that were there, as well as some pagans. They had no trouble (Abella [1807], Appendix 4, 20).

A group of about forty men continued further north to the Suisun lands, in search of Octaviano's wife and the other runaway Tatcans:

> They had a number of run-ins along the trail, at which it is said that several people told the leader, who was the *alcalde* (who also died), that there were too many people in the area, that they should go back. Finally on Saturday morning thirty-nine of them got there. They found several runaways, who took the lead in firing arrows and urging the pagans to do the same. Even the old women were waiting with sticks when they arrived. Nevertheless, they still brought the village under control (Abella [1807], Appendix 4, 20).

The village which the neophyte posse was said to have brought under control may have been one composed of Chupcan refugees who had moved north across Suisun Bay from their Diablo Valley homeland a few years earlier. Octaviano and the other Tatcans had numerous documented marriage ties to the Chupcans, but none to the Suisuns.

The mission posse's control of the village was short-lived:

> Soon men joined in from neighboring *rancherías*, particularly from one called Suio Suiu (it is not yet known who told them, but it will be discovered in time), and began firing arrows. Then the neophytes took off running. A great many of them never stopped. I already mentioned that they had very few arrows. Others, in order to help their sick companions (who had been so foolish as to go along to the furthest area for no other reason than that they were from the same homeland as the *alcalde*) tried to hold out even though they were the

smallest group in number. Both Christians and pagans used up their arrows shooting at one another. Very close to the boat launching area in the Karquin village two were beaten to death, although I believe that they had already shot the *alcalde*, who was one of those killed, with an arrow (Abella [1807], Appendix 4, 20).

The names of the twelve neophytes who were killed in this running battle were listed in the Mission San Francisco *Libro de Difuntos* (Table 4).[4] It was not by

Table 4. Mission San Francisco men killed on the road between the Suisun and Carquin villages on February 7, 1807, along with information about their wives and any subsequent marriages of those wives.

Death #	Name	Bapt. #	Tribe	Age	Wife Bapt.#	Wife's Next Spouse Bapt.#	Tribe	Wedding
2418	Hilarion*	334	Pruristac	44	335	906	Lamchin	7-19-07
2419	Genaro	882	Lamchin	38	1016	1005	Oljon	8-30-07
2420	George*	298	Pruristac	49	668	**		
2421	Juan Santos	734	Oljon	48	919	793	Lamchin	2-16-08
2422	Efren	2379	Jalquin	24	1758	2926	Tatcan	5-31-07
2423	Henrique	2380	Jalquin	29	3005	611	Huchiun	9-10-07
2424	Bonifacio	925	Tatcan	25	2932	2320	Jalquin	5-31-07
2425	Fernando	2990	Tatcan	39	1735	**		
2426	Evaristo	873	Lamchin	27	(widower)			
2427	José Cupert.o	211	"otra banda"	42	(widower)			
2428	Yndalecio	603	Lamchin	28	(widower)			
2429	Geminiano	912	Chiguan	50	(widower)			

* These two men were the <u>alcaldes</u> of Mission San Francisco at the time of the incident.
** In these two cases the wife made no subsequent marriage.

---

[4] The following note preceded the Mission San Francisco *Libro de Bautismos* entries for the men who were killed north of Carquinez Strait in 1807: "On February 7 of said year [1807] on the other shore of the estuary of the Carquines, between the *ranchería* of Suyusuyu and said estuary of the Carquines, to the northeast of the mission, the following people died violently at the hands of the pagans, according to the word of their companions who went with them, of whom there were many" (SFR-D 2418-2429 [February 2, 1807, Ramón Abella]).

chance that certain of the raiders were killed and others spared, as missionary Ramón Abella noted:

> It was a dirty trick by one, or a few, of the neophytes, who could have defended them. Not all of them had good hearts. The neophytes who had relatives there had divided loyalties. For the most part they inclined to the side of the pagans and the runaways. The fact is that it looks like they chose the ones they would kill. Seven dead were from San Mateo and San Pedro and it is said that they were talking together in their southern language (Abella [1807], Appendix 4, 20).

This incident illustrates the fact that the violent incidents among Indians and between Spaniards and Indians did not take place in a vacuum. All seven of the southerners (that is to say, Costanoan speakers) that were killed had affiliations with either the Tatcans who had fled or the family of a Puichon man who had been killed in the abortive raid into the Suisun area back in 1804.

Hilarion and George, the two slain *alcaldes*, were long-time Christians from San Pedro Valley south of San Francisco who had a special relationship to the Tatcans in the mission community. The first two children in the Tatcan baptismal class of January, 1804 had been named Hilarion and George (SFR-B 2887, 2888). Also, Genaro, another southerner killed in this incident, had shared his name with the Tatcan boy whose death in January had caused his parents to flee, triggering this entire incident. Finally, all five of the other old Christians from the San Francisco Peninsula who died at this time were related by blood or marriage to Pedro Armengal, the Puichon man who had been killed in the Suisun incident back in 1804.

Additionally, five East Bay Christians from Bay Miwok-speaking tribes were among the dead. An examination of their baptismal and marriage relationships suggests a link between this 1807 incident and both the Chimenes killings of April 1795 *and* to the mysterious deaths of so many Saclan and Jalquin men in February, 1804. The documented interrelationships are as follows:

—Bonifacio Guaste, a Tatcan, had been in the same baptismal class in 1804 as the abducted wife of Octaviano, Sinforiana Tercete (SFR-B 2930).

—Fernando Chusacse, a Tatcan, was married to Teotica Cacnumaie (SFR-B 1735) a Saclan woman who had been baptized in 1795 with two of the Saclan men who had been killed north of Carquinez Strait in January of 1804.

—José Cupertino Petenacs, a man baptized back in 1781 from an unspecified East Bay tribe, was the brother of Juan José Lecmese (SFR-B 210), who had been one of those killed at the Chimenes village in April of 1795. José Cupertino was a widower five times over. His brother-in-law through his fourth wife, Bibiana (SFR-B 2384), had been the Jalquin man Aaron (SFR-B 2384) who was killed in the January, 1804 incident.

—Efren Tupursia, a Jalquin, had been baptized in 1802 with the punished Saclan/Jalquin resistance leaders from 1795—Carues, Cahuas, and Jovocsia. During their baptism, they had stood directly behind Aaron, the brother-in-law of José Cupertino who had died in the Suisun area in 1804.

—Henrique Elupacse, a Jalquin, was the brother of Efren (above). Following his death, Henrique's wife married Pascasio Tenéa (SFR-B 611), a Huchiun who had been baptized in 1787 along with one of the men killed in 1804; that man was the widower of Reginalda Sacnem, a Jalquin who had been the wife of Reginaldo, another man killed in February, 1804.

All of these ties point to the probability that the 1807 neophyte expedition against the Suisuns was partially an unsuccessful attempt at revenge against those who had taken part in the 1804 killings. The earlier 1804 confrontation itself may have been triggered by feuds that went back to the 1795 Chimenes affair between neophytes and runaway Saclans. The details of these interrelated stories are now beyond recovery; they may always have been beyond our comprehension.

Although the Spanish military authorities considered it to be both their right and their obligation to judge and punish those who had participated in the slayings of February, 1807, over the next three years the tribes living north of Carquinez Strait seem to have escaped Spanish harassment. Some fragments of correspondence suggest that the Spanish planned to search for "criminals" during the fall of 1807; one note, for example, mentions a plan to make a surprise attack across Carquinez Strait on specially made tule balsas that year (Arrillaga

[1807f]); there is no documentary evidence suggesting that the plan was carried out.⁵

The Carquin people finally moved to Mission San Francisco in June of 1809, after successfully resisting Spanish expansion for three or four years longer than might have been expected. Ten of the sixty Carquin children under the age of ten who were baptized that summer had parents who were deceased. None of the Carquins admitted to having been married to any of the Suisuns, which may merely reflect their desire to maintain some social distance from the Suisuns, who were considered by both the old neophytes and the Spaniards to be criminals.

By the spring of 1810, there were no buffer groups between the Suisuns and the Spanish establishments. On February 5, 1810, the Spanish governor and the commander of the San Francisco Presidio were preparing an expedition into Suisun territory (Arrillaga [1810]); at the same time, the missionaries at San Francisco were allowing new Carquin neophytes to go back home on "*paseo.*" The result was the third incident involving the murder of Mission San Francisco people in six years:

> On February 16 or 19, 1810 in the *ranchería* of the pagans called SuyuSuyu, they killed three neophytes. Seven people had gone on a "*paseo*" to the *ranchería* of the Karquines and four had remained there. The other three had gone on to said *ranchería* of SuyuSuyu, where they had friends. They were killed just as they were coming near. So swear their companions, who say the pagan Chupanes came and told them this (SFR-D 2768).

The three men killed were Leandro Lutes (SFR-B 3845), Laurentino Tocal (SFR-B 3850), and Agricola Geumpis (SFR-B 3852), all of whom were Carquins. They had just been baptized two months earlier, along with some

---

⁵ Some kind of Spanish punitive expedition did go into the interior in November of 1807 (Arrillaga [1807g]). However, that sortie seems to have been directed against Mission San Jose runaways and their non-Christian relatives in the Mt. Diablo area. It is documented only by a one-line paraphrase of Governor Arrillaga's ([1808]) note of February 8, 1808: "He writes about the capture of six Christians and four Indians by the corporal of the escort of Mission San José." The only Mission San Jose baptisms that occurred that winter were those of the last Livermore Valley vicinity couples, a Tatcan couple (Posscon at Mission San Jose), a Pelnen-Souyen couple, and a Seunen-Tatcan couple. The four non-Christians captured in November may or may not have been among these three couples.

Huchiun-Aguastos and a Saclan refugee married to a Carquin woman (SFR-B 3846).

This incident provoked the troops at the San Francisco Presidio to prepare for a major punitive expedition against the Suisuns. Arrillaga reported to the viceroy as follows:

> He ordered the commander of the San Francisco Presidio, Second-Lieutenant Gabriel Moraga, to go out in pursuit of pagans of the village called Sespesuyu to the north of the San Francisco Presidio. Over the past three years they have brought things to a sorry state, having killed over that time sixteen Christians (Arrillaga [1810a], Appendix 4, 24).

On May 22, 1810, the Suisuns with a force of 120 fighting men were attacked by a Spanish party, consisting of seventeen soldiers and an auxiliary force of Christian Indians of unknown size, under the command of Second Lieutenant Gabriel Moraga (Venegas [1811]):

> Said second-lieutenant...took as prisoners eighteen pagans. They were set free because they were gravely wounded and he had no way to transport them. He believes that not one of them could have avoided death. Toward the end of the action the surviving Indians sealed themselves in three brush houses, from which they made a tenacious defence, wounding the corporals and two soldiers. Those were the only injuries sustained by the troop. No one was killed. After having killed the pagans in two of the grass houses, the Christians set fire to the third grass house, as a means to take the pagans prisoner. But they did not achieve that result, since the valiant Indians died enveloped in flames before they could be taken into custody. The second-lieutenant says that he could not reason with the pagans, who died fighting or by burning (Arrillaga [1810a], Appendix 4, 24).

The soldiers returned to San Francisco with six boys and six girls, comprising a mixed group of Suisuns and Chupcans (SFR-B 3992-4001, 4002, 4004). In 1811, large groups of Chupcans and Suisuns moved to Mission San Francisco, and Suisuns continued to move to that mission through 1816.

Although the Suisun massacre was a small battle when judged by the standards of modern warfare, it had a devastating effect upon those who survived it. The Suisuns had been a counterweight to Spanish and Mission Indian dominance since 1804. When Spanish soldiers finally attacked them, the outcome was devastating. Eleven years later, in the fall of 1821, a Spanish force encountered a woman who had survived the massacre and was now living in the village of Chila, located in the Sacramento Valley forty miles north of Suisun Bay:

> [The village] offered a pleasant view, although the voices and yelling of its inhabitants were not so pleasant. It is worth mentioning the case of an old Suisuna that lived here. As soon as she saw the troop enter the woods near the village, she bravely came forward and made gestures of kindness. We really did not understand what she was saying, although her meaning was presumed. Punished by the experience of what had happened in her homeland, she came to implore the commander on behalf of her people here. She begged him to treat them kindly. The commander used this occasion, talking to her through the neophyte interpreter Rafael, to request of her that she try to pacify them before they give us occasion to carry out the punishment they deserved for their offense (Ordáz [1821] 1958: 233).

San Joaquin Valley Tribes Look West

The Cholvons in the San Joaquin Valley some thirty miles east of Mission San Jose found themselves on the mission frontier at the beginning of 1806. Only two hill tribes, the Juñas and the Tayssens, remained in the area of the Diablo Range far to the east of Mission Santa Clara. With the Coast Range villages almost empty, Spanish authorities began to formulate plans for a new series of missions in the San Joaquin Valley. They sent at least three survey expeditions into the valley in 1806 (Bancroft 1885:43-55), though the only extant diary is that stemming from Gabriel Moraga's trip of September-November 1806, in which various eastern tribes, ranging from the Nupchenche west of Merced north to the Moquelumnes at Lodi, were visited.[6]

---

[6] The San Joaquin Valley tribes had been visited by Spanish expeditions at various times during the thirty-year period prior to 1806. In September of 1776, José Joaquin Moraga and eight soldiers went into the San Joaquin Valley by way of the Livermore Valley and Altamont Pass. They crossed the three branches of the San Joaquin River northeast of Tracy, and probably went as far north as

Governor Arrillaga wanted his troops to act as goodwill messengers during these expeditions; this was clearly stated in the instructions which were given to Luís Argüello, who followed an undocumented route north or northeast of the Bay Area in May of 1806:

> The object of the expedition that you will undertake is to reconnoiter to the north to gain knowledge of the rugged lands adjacent to our establishments, as well as to make peace with the pagans. The goal is to relieve them of the horror with which they view our troops, for which they are not lacking in motives, since up to now we have never gone out except to punish them.
>
> The present concept is different, in that I intend to create a situation in which the pagans will not oppose our coming to their villages or into their lands, that they will see that our sorties are not made with the object of punishment, but with the object of friendship. Likewise let them understand that they are not to admit runaways or criminals, and certainly not to shelter our enemies, just as we would not admit theirs, and that we are quick to receive them into our friendship and commerce. Leave them of a peaceful disposition in their villages, and offer them sincerely that we will listen to their complaints and castigate any Christians who maltreat them or do them any damage. All of this the sergeant is to make them understand as best as he is able (Arrillaga [1806]).

Although the Spanish military wanted people to welcome them everywhere that they went, they had no intention of discontinuing their policy of responding with military force when their passage was opposed. Runaway Christians were no more to be tolerated in the San Joaquin Valley than they had been in the Coast Range hills.

The Tayssens of Orestimba Creek to the southeast of Santa Clara got another taste of Spanish policy in the summer of 1806:

---

the Mokelumne River in the Lodi area (Palóu [1773-1783] 1926:4:127-131). A report on the San Joaquin Valley written by Hermenegildo Sal in 1796 was probably a reminiscence about this earlier exploration, although Cook (1960:242) was under the impression that Sal conducted a new exploration of the San Joaquin Valley in that year.

> Due to a conspiracy among some Indians, according to what the ministers of Mission Santa Clára showed him, he [Governor Arrillaga] ordered a sortie under Sergeant Gervasio Argüello with a few members of the troop, with the object of arresting the promoters of this subversion. They have succeeded in capturing the ringleader, forty-two Christians and forty seven pagans (Arrillaga [1806b]).

The well-established Spanish strategy worked again, and forty-two Tayssen Christians were returned to the priests at Mission Santa Clara. Some of the non-Christians accompanying them were baptized on July 29, 1806, but many were not baptized until September 23. They may have been put to work at the pueblo of San Jose, to get the wheat and hemp harvests in, before being sent on to Mission Santa Clara. Eventually, forty-six Tayssen people joined the Mission Santa Clara population from July through September of 1806.

The townspeople at the pueblo of San Jose faced a serious problem after 1806. There were no more non-Christian villagers living in the Santa Clara Valley or in the nearby mountain valleys to the east to provide cheap wage labor (Arrillaga [1806a]). The priests at Mission Santa Clara complained in 1807 that the townspeople of the pueblo were luring Christian Indians from Mission Santa Clara to come to the town and work for them. Governor Arrillaga supported the traditional governmental position of giving full control over mission Indians to the Franciscans:

> In light of the repeated complaints made by the reverend Father ministers of Mission Santa Clara regarding the townspeople of the pueblo secreting away Indians of the mission, I advise you to give all such Indians, men or women, twenty-five lashes and then send them back to their mission, if they are over age twelve (Arrillaga [1807d]).

By July of 1807, the townspeople of San Jose were desperate for Indian labor to help bring in their wheat harvest and the commercial hemp crop. Governor Arrillaga agreed to an experiment; the townspeople were allowed to go to the San Joaquin Valley to the Cholvon villages to solicit non-Christian wage laborers.

The Cholvons were quite familiar with the missions. Fifteen of them had been baptized at Mission San Jose in the spring of 1806, just prior to the measles epidemic. At least six of the "San Antonio" people baptized at Mission Santa Clara on June 25, 1806 had been Cholvons. (They were noted as Bolbons in later Mission Santa Clara death records.) Some Cholvons accepted the 1807 offer to come to work for flannel, thread, needles, glass beads, and blankets:

> The work assignments are to be moderate. Because they are not accustomed to it, it will be difficult to put much on them for the present. I am aware of your knowledge of them. I hope and trust that they will be content as well as useful. Let them know that it is my desire that neither they nor their relatives should come to any harm. Rather, I want to maintain harmony. Let them know that they can come and go at will. I want no one to apply any violent pressure on them to become Christians. I desire that they enjoy their liberty, as they have done up until now. I also want them to be paid a just wage for their work (Arrillaga [1807b], Appendix 4, 21).

Governor Arrillaga emphasized the tribal people's freedom of choice, a necessity for continued cordial relations and an assured labor supply:

> If at the end of the projects some of these pagans want to remain in the service of someone in particular, you will take care to discover the circumstances and to inform me. But at all times they are to have complete freedom to leave at their own convenience (Arrillaga [1807b], Appendix 4, 21).

Despite the governor's orders that the visiting Cholvon workers be well treated, an incident occurred which almost erupted into a major disaster. A Mission Santa Clara Indian critically injured one of the children who had come with the work party:

> Regarding this incident I should tell you that although you have done very well to inform the pagans that they will receive just compensation for the transgression, it is important that you give them what you can. Given the situation, I order you to take the thug to the jail. If what you tell me is true, I will order you to punish him with twenty-five lashes for three or four mornings running, and if it be necessary, for still more days. If it seems they are not satisfied with that punishment, let the pagans know that I will banish him to a place where he will never do harm again. The

strongest necessary punishment will be given him, short of execution (Arrillaga [1807c], Appendix 4, 22).

A follow-up letter illustrates the Cholvons' conflict resolution strategy—incident, followed by negotiation, with group recompense for injury to the individual—a strategy typical of a feud-based society.

> I received your advice regarding the case and the petition from the two *capitanejos* that the delinquent be granted pardon. And so it seems that they feel recompensed for the injury done to them. That leaves me satisfied.
>
> I am not upset that the Santa Clara Indian is to be set free. But if it were possible I would have liked the little pagan who was abused to have been brought forth in order to clarify exactly what happened before the thug was put at liberty. It seems to me that it would have been better to have proceeded in that way. But it was a natural mistake to fail to do that. You proceeded as seemed best, but that method would have allowed all the pagans to see that the abused boy was recovering well. I am satisfied (Arrillaga [1807e], Appendix 4, 23).

The Cholvons returned to their villages on the San Joaquin River with their trade goods in early September of 1807. According to the governor, the hemp and wheat crops had been brought in and everyone was quite happy about the resolution of the situation (Arrillaga [1807e], Appendix 4, 23). Only one Cholvon was baptized during their stay at the pueblo that summer—the one-year-old daughter of Somes and Sosñute (SCL-B 5344).[7]

A steady stream of people from the easternmost Coast Ranges came in to Mission Santa Clara throughout 1808, 1809, and 1810. As the Luecha, Juñas, and Tayssen villages emptied, Cholvon families began to appear at Mission San Jose and Mission Santa Clara in greater and greater numbers. At the same time, the Spaniards sent more survey expeditions out into the San Joaquin Valley.

In September and October of 1808, Gabriel Moraga undertook the most ambitious exploration to date of the interior. Moraga crossed the San Joaquin

---

[7] Somes and Sosñute, who were definitely at Santa Clara in 1807, were not baptized until March of 1810. They migrated to Mission Santa Clara in that year along with Tepel, the Cholvon captain, and twenty-five other members of the tribe (SCL-B 5667, 5698).

east of Cholvon territory and marched north into the Sacramento Valley as far as the big Sacramento River village at Colusa, circled the Sutter Buttes, then swung all the way south to the mouth of the Merced River, before returning north to Cholvon country and then west to the Spanish settlements.

In 1809, fifty-eight Cholvons went to Mission San Jose and at least seventeen more to Mission Santa Clara. Many of the baptisms of infants took place in March, while most of the adult baptisms took place in September. This pattern suggests that the San Joaquin Valley people went west to help with plantings and harvests in 1809, and then stayed to join the missions. Cholvons again show up in the baptismal books at Mission San Jose and Mission Santa Clara in February and March of 1810. Captain Tepel, whose daughter had been baptized in August, 1808 (SCL-B 5664, SCL-B 5499), was among the new neophytes. Another large Cholvon or Josmite group from the San Joaquin Valley, composed of eighteen people of all ages and sexes, joined Mission Santa Clara on June 13, 1810 (they were identified as being from the "San Antonio" district, and many were labeled as being "Bolbon" in their later death records).

A Spanish intelligence-gathering party passed through tribal lands (extending from the mouth of the San Joaquin south to Los Banos Creek) in August of 1810 (Cook 1960:258-260). The party, under Gabrial Moraga and Father José Viader of Mission Santa Clara, included seven Spanish soldiers and four Mission Santa Clara neophyte interpreters.

The Julpuns at the mouth of the San Joaquin hid from the Spanish party, as did the Cholvons in the area of the present town of Tracy (Cook 1960:258).

> Here, in the village of the Cholvones, or Pescadero, we stayed all the rest of the day, and the night. We sent an interpreter to get in touch with the Cholvones. He returned with a heathen Indian called Guanats, together with a considerable quantity of fish. They say that the Christian fugitives from San Jose are on the opposite shore, between the river and a lake (Viader *in* Cook 1960:258).

Over the next few days, tribes further south along the San Joaquin River, the Lamames, Mayemes, Tauhalames, and Apelamames, variously greeted or avoided the Spanish detachment.

When Moraga and Viader returned to the Spanish settlements they organized a larger expedition to go after the fugitive Christians. While they were making their preparations in late September, another thirteen Cholvons became Christians at Mission Santa Clara (SCL-B 5731-5744).

On the night of October 20, 1810, a dance was taking place at the main Cholvon village on the San Joaquin River, the place called by the Spaniards *Pescadero* ("The Fishery"). Unbeknownst to the celebrants, Moraga and Viader had returned to the area with a large detachment of troops and mission Indian auxiliaries. In the early morning hours, the Spaniards attacked a subsidiary village:

> Before dawn we assaulted a village on this side of the river and only one person escaped, a San Jose Christian named Bernardo. He, having gone to sleep at a distance from the village, jumped into the water and swam in great haste to warn those at the dance. For this reason we immediately fell upon the other village, which was on the opposite side of the river, and took it entire. The prisoners in all included 15 San Jose Christians, 18 heathen men, and 51 heathen women. The latter were released by the lieutenant and went away very happy (Viader *in* Cook 1960:259).

The Spanish expedition then continued south along the San Joaquin River in search of other fugitive Christian neophytes. All along the River, tribal headmen now faced the same disagreeable choice that the coastal leaders had faced in earlier years, to either force neophyte fugitives to go back to the missions or face Spanish military raids. At the village of Mayem the Spanish missionary diarist wrote:

> Although they know that they have in their village Christians from Santa Clara, they deny it and furthermore declare that they will never again admit any. If it were not for the nuisance it would cause us, the Lieutenant says he would flog them... (Viader *in* Cook 1960:260).

On the same day, across the San Joaquin River from the Tauhalamnes lands, Viader wrote:

> I sent a boy to the village to carry a statement to the natives here of our purpose to call for Christian fugitives and offer them pardon. Six heathen Indians returned who, filled with apprehension, said that all the Christians had gone to the mission and would not be allowed to come back, but they were lying (Viader *in* Cook 1960:26).

There was a short lull in the baptism of San Joaquin Valley people following the retreat of the Moraga-Viader party to Santa Clara. However, the remaining Cholvons and their neighbors the Tamcans moved to Mission San Jose in large numbers in 1811 and 1812.

***

During the period between 1806 and 1810, all the contextual processes that had led the inner Bay Area people to join the missions were being experienced once again by others further from the missions. The period began with the most terrible epidemic ever experienced, an outbreak of measles that killed one quarter of the Bay Area mission population and unknown numbers of people in tribal areas. More tiny independent groups disappeared, as increasing numbers of people migrated to the missions from the central Marin Peninsula, the Carquinez Strait region, and the eastern Coast Ranges. The period saw new localized resistances to the expansion of Spanish control; an especially tenacious one centered around the Suisuns to the north of Carquinez Strait. And just as the period saw new resistances, it saw new proofs that Spanish soldiers, together with Mission Indian auxiliaries, could and would break them.

Chapter 10

Conclusion

> Twice in the year they receive permission to return to their native homes. This short time is the happiest period of their existence; and I myself have seen them going home in crowds, with loud rejoicings. The sick, who cannot undertake the journey, at least accompany their happy countrymen to the shore where they embark, and there sit for days together, mournfully gazing on the distant summits of the mountains which surround their homes; they often sit in this situation for several days, without taking any food, so much does the sight of their lost home affect these new Christians (Kotzebue [1816] 1932: 63).

As the period between 1806 and 1810 drew to a close, the remaining tribal people on the north side of San Francisco Bay and in the San Joaquin Valley found their world disrupted and their choices for reaction increasingly constricted. The Spanish missions continued to beckon, offering them access to a European vision of a meaningful life in exchange for cultural and political obliteration. Over the next two decades, the 1810s and 1820s, more and more people from tribes further and further to the north and east would struggle with the difficult choice this dilemma imposed; that struggle continued until the missions were closed as centers of proselytization in 1836.

Unquestionably, the tribal people loved their homelands and their traditional ways of life. In each tribal area, children grew up surrounded by an ideology and cosmology that was embodied in and made incarnate by the very form of the land itself. Individuals belonged to—and drew much of their personal identity from—specific places. The move to a mission inevitably resulted in deep emotional trauma. When people left their home valleys, they left behind a major portion of that identity.

Tribal people who considered the possibility of joining a mission must have known that they would not lead happy lives there. Yet they did move to the missions, one group after another. In the fall of 1816, scores of Coast Miwok-speaking Petalumas and Patwin-speaking Malacas went to Mission San Francisco. Otto von Kotzebue described their arrival at the mission:

Figure 15. Illustration of multiple sets of dancers performing in the plaza at Mission San Francisco in October of 1816, by L. Choris ([1816] 1932) (courtesy of The Bancroft Library).

> As we were leaving the Mission, we were surprised by two groups of Indians, which were also composed of different nations. They came in military array; that is, quite naked, and painted with gay colours: the heads of the most were adorned with feathers, and other finery (Kotzebue [1816] 1932:61).

Although specific centers of resistance to Spanish domination arose again and again, nothing stopped the stream of migrants south and west to the missions. By the end of 1817 the greater part of the Coast Miwok and Patwin speakers on the north side of San Francisco Bay and the Yokuts-speakers along the San Joaquin River to the east of the Bay Area had moved to the missions. By the time active proselytization came to a halt, in the early 1830s, all tribal lands within 40 miles to the north of San Francisco Bay and 80 miles to the east were empty of villages (see Phillips 1993).

One question that I have attempted to answer in this book is, "Why did people leave their homelands and move to the mission communities?" If I had to propose a single explanation, it would focus on people's loss of faith in the feasibility of continuing their traditional ways within the context of a new reality. Each new migration involved emotionally ambivalent people who had reached the conclusion that they had no other choice but to join a mission; they felt both dread and hope as they made their journey. Tribal people did not choose the new reality within which they made their decision. It was forced upon them by global processes that were expressed through the actions of officials of the Spanish Empire, representatives of the tightly organized, heavily armed society that had been expanding in the direction of California since Columbus' landing in 1492.

The conditions that existed during the period between 1777 and the early 1790s, when the earliest tribal recruits joined the missions, were somewhat less complex than those that provoked migrations in subsequent time periods. Two contextual factors played a significant role in the decisions made by the first teenagers to join the missions and by the first adult couples to bring their children for baptism: (1) the stunning material technology and complex social organization of the Spaniards challenged traditional criteria as to what constituted economic and social success; and (2) Spanish soldiers, with their muskets, steel swords, and lances, proved themselves to be the most dangerous fighting men in the region when they killed anyone who opposed them during the first weeks of Spanish settlement.

I suggest that some of the first mission recruits were spurred into taking their course of action by a naive desire to take part in something new and exciting, while others were sent by family elders who had made a calculated decision to ally themselves with the powerful newcomers. As the years went by the negative aspects of mission life became clear; these included high disease rates, an interference in personal lives, an oppressive organization of work, corporal punishment, and the forced return of runaways. However, new recruits continued to join mission communities despite these negative aspects. They made the difficult decision to move to the missions within the context of a steady deterioration in their physical, social, and psychological environment.

Environmental deterioration, significant loss in food resources—greens, bulbs, and seeds—came about in the Santa Clara Valley and the San Francisco Peninsula as a consequence of overgrazing by Spanish livestock. Seed crops were further reduced by the cessation of native fire management practices, which were banned by the Spanish authorities in order to protect their cattle. Furthermore, elk and antelope had to compete with livestock for browse, and the diversion of water for farming near the missions probably hurt fish populations.

The decline of native populations severely affected traditional village organization. The combination of epidemic and endemic diseases, most notably syphilis, caused an accelerated infant death rate in native villages, and emigration to the missions also induced a decline in village populations. Two related problems arose as a direct result of reduced village sizes: first, because such small groups relied heavily on teamwork, populations could quickly fall below the minimal size necessary for proper social functions to be carried out; second, talented community leaders might have been dying or moving away before younger people were available to replace them.

The new pressures probably exacerbated existing intertribal tensions and led to an increase in regional warfare. Only a minority of the tribal people ever got into direct physical confrontations with proselytizing Mission Indians, and still fewer ever fought against Spanish troops or even witnessed such a conflict. Every native Californian, on the other hand, had participated in or had witnessed an intertribal raid during their lifetime. Arguments over proper responses to the missions joined traditional grounds for feuds to become an important source of friction between factions within tribes, as well as between tribes as a whole. In addition, the epidemics may have been blamed on sorcerers in neighboring communities, and thus have provoked retaliatory raids. Those tribal people who blamed the Christian Indians, the soldiers, or the missionaries for the new diseases actually reinforced the image of power that the invaders presented. Fear and anger would have been more readily directed against traditional opponents—who could conceivably be defeated—rather than the seemingly invincible newcomers.

As the tribal village populations declined due to new diseases and migrations to the missions, the people remaining in those villages became vulnerable to attacks from stronger groups situated further away from the missions. The more the members of a village group felt vulnerable to attack, the more likely they were to join relatives already at a mission. The anti-mission factions who did not want to emigrate could not protect themselves once the population fell below a certain critical level. That level was probably reached when a tribal population dropped below fifty percent of its original size. At that point, the option to remain in the homeland ceased to exist. People either moved inland to join relatives in the villages of more cohesive neighboring tribes, or they joined their fellow tribespeople already at a mission.

Population losses also disrupted trade and festival networks; this led to a gradual "impoverishment" in lifestyle (according to traditional standards for success), and destroyed regional social cohesion. Once the tribes in the core areas around the missions were removed from their villages, regional trading networks linking the surrounding tribes were weakened. Because of changes in their lifestyle, mission people were no longer interested in the traditional commodities that they had once procured from the east: bows, arrows, basketry materials, paints, and feather blankets. Thus the inland groups could not get shells for ornaments and monetary exchanges from the coast. Furthermore, dances held by frontier area groups lost some of their power and efficacy when attendance dropped as a consequence of reduced populations and increased intertribal antagonisms.

Conclusion

The combination of psychological and socio-economic disintegration played into the Spanish Franciscan campaign of cultural denigration. The missionaries sought to make the native people feel ashamed of their traditional way of life and envious of Spanish culture. The missionary campaign of denigration, presumably motivated by good will, turned out to be a campaign involving protracted psychological violence.

The success of the Spanish assault on native culture is well illustrated by Father Palóu's comment regarding changes in the native attitude toward the naked human body:

> It is worthy of notice, that while before baptism, they had no sense at all of shame, these feelings are immediately dominant in them as soon as baptism is received, so that if it is necessary to change the clothing because they have outgrown them, they hide themselves nor will they show themselves naked before any one, and much less before the Fathers (Palóu [1786] 1913:211).

Many people internalized the belief that they deserved to be powerless, to be ordered about, and to be punished. Missionary president Lasuén wrote in 1793: "They hear Mass every day, and those who accept the Ten Commandments are now convinced that it is right to punish them for their defects" (Lasuén [1793]). The relentless disintegration of the physical and social environment undermined people's faith in the traditional patterns of knowledge and behavior, patterns passed down from one generation to another. That traditional body of knowledge taught one how to behave in a wide variety of situations—what postures to take, what songs to sing, when to speak and when to be silent, and so on. But it provided no answers in the context of the new social reality.

Feelings of comparative unworthiness cut so deeply into the psyches of many people that the Spanish word *gentile*, referring to an unbaptized Indian, was absorbed into some languages as a pejorative term.

> *híntil'* (from Spanish 'gentil')—Indian, unbaptized, person with no manners, native or wild of plants, animals, foods. Although *híntil* came into various Indian languages from the missions, it was earliest recognized as applying to everything native as opposed to everything Spanish or western. In this meaning it is opposed to *láyh*, "foreign, great, important" which came to designate western or Spanish as opposed to native or Indian (from *English-Wappo Vocabulary* by Jesse O. Sawyer 1965:55).

To accept a foreign culture as inherently superior to one's own is, in a sense, to deprecate one's self. Such self-deprecation can cut away at an individual's psychological foundations and internally injure that person.

Most people who chose to become Christian neophytes were acknowledging the existence of fears and doubts about the future and were hoping to acquire some healing power by identifying with the powerful invaders. They sought the familiar within the alien at the missions. They placed themselves in the hands of the Franciscan missionaries, and relied upon them—just as they had traditionally relied upon knowledgeable elders in their own lands—to guide them in proper ritual conduct and in respect for the supernatural. Mission life, which was organized around elaborate Roman Catholic rituals and had a power that was expressed through colorful dress, esoteric prayer, and ostentatious architecture, provided them with a sense of contentment and belonging.

Traditional culture included respect for, even awe and fear of, supernatural spirits. Those spirits with which the Franciscans were associated, many believed, clearly deserved that awe and fear. That attitude was illustrated by Louis Choris at a Mass at Mission San Francisco in 1816:

> All the Indians of both sexes, without regard to age, are obliged to go to church and worship. Children brought up by the superior (friar), fifty of whom are stationed around him, assist him during the service which they also accompany with the sound of musical instruments. These are chiefly drums, trumpets, tabors.... It is, indeed, the only means of producing an effect upon them. When the drums begin to beat they fall to the ground as if they were half dead. None dares to move, all remain stretched upon the ground without making the slightest movement until the end of the service and, even then, it is necessary to tell them several times that the mass is finished (Choris [1816] 1932:8-9).

Given the perceived failure of traditional ways of relating to the supernatural, I submit, many people sought a new identity built around Christian ceremony and the leadership of the missionaries. They became deeply committed to special mission roles, such as those involving church ceremonies, the leadership of work crews, or the acquisition of a mechanical knowledge of the loom or the lariat.

The Spanish missionaries at San Francisco in 1814 reported that the Indian people at their mission were docile and obedient (Abella and Sainz de Lucio [1814] 1976:31). The priests at Mission San Jose agreed that obedience was the most admirable quality shown by the Mission Indians (Durán and Fortuny [1814] 1976:45). On the surface at least, daily life at the missions seems to have been generally harmonious. Those individuals who had chosen to enter the confusing foreign world of the missions tended to assume that the gatekeepers of that world, the missionaries, best understood the appropriate rules of behavior: "They are so prone to lying that they almost always confess sins they have never committed" (Manríquez and Escudé [1814] 1976:104).

Some people at the missions, however, would not—and probably could not—relinquish the beliefs and behaviors of their youth. Older neophytes clung to their own language, and people often tried to retain other familiar aspects of life (such as dances, gambling games, and traditional foods) as well in order to feel a sense of continuity with the past. An unknown number of people continued to practice some aspects of their traditional ceremonial life, which the missionaries considered threatening. The missionaries used such behavior as a foil in their continuous efforts to remold peoples' consciousness. Native rituals and beliefs were identified as the work of the Devil, and proof that those who maintained them deserved punishment and hardships.

Well-documented fugitivism and near-rebellions indicate that the strain of maintaining a new identity sometimes became too much to bear. Overt resistance was rare at the missions themselves, although a group of Mission Santa Cruz men did poison a missionary in 1812 (Castillo 1989:383). A more common expression of protest was a listless attitude and a lack of cooperation toward work activities.

The tribal peoples of west Central California encountered in the Spaniards a people who were not so much interested in taking their land and its resources as they were in totally restructuring their lives. The Spanish Empire's main agency for the social control in California was the Franciscan mission system. The missionary representatives of the Church actively proselytized tribal peoples, using highly effective techniques that were designed to instill the contemporary cultural values of the Empire's Mediterranean homeland.

Tribal groups in Central California were never able to forge enduring regional military alliances to oppose the Europeans precisely because they did not consider themselves to be a single people. Even when they did begin to establish alliances with one another in the 1820s—after many years of constant European pressure—they had no access to the kinds of weaponry that might have given them parity with the Spanish soldiers. They were beyond the range of the French fur traders who were supplying guns to tribal peoples in the New Mexico area. Lacking effective weapons, without any regional organization, and without foreign allies, they had no power to dictate—or to even influence—the path that their interaction with the invaders might take.

* * *

The Bay Area villagers were tantalized with material products and denigrated for their traditional practices by the agents of western technological and organizational complexity. Soaring death rates and the continual threat of overwhelming military violence against any group that attempted to bar the mission proselytizers increased the pressure. Is it any wonder that the tribal people came to doubt the value of their native culture, and started to accept a definition of themselves as ignorant and unskilled, and deserving of a life of subordination in the new, caste-based social structure?

It should come as no surprise that the western world penetrated and destroyed the hopes and dreams of the native people around San Francisco Bay. The processes of westernization, by which highly organized, highly capitalized forces of world commercial society undermine simple lives and local spirits, stimulate material cravings, and constantly redefine appropriate standards of living, have worked to destroy local cultures time and time again in all parts of the world. In the grip of such processes people have very little choice.

Conclusion

Figure 16. Portraits of long-time Mission San Francisco neophytes by L. Choris ([1816] 1932), including (1,3) Huimens, (2) a Huchiun, and a Saclan (4,5) (courtesy of The Bancroft Library).

Figure 17. Portraits of some new Mission San Francisco neophytes by L. Choris ([1816] 1932), including (1) an Ululato, (2) a Numpali (may be alias for Caymus), (3) a Suisun, (4) an Olompali, and (5) a Cholvon (courtesy of The Bancroft Library).

Map 4. Tribal regions of the San Francisco Bay Area: northern perspective.

Map 5. Tribal regions of the San Francisco Bay Area: southern perspective.

Appendix 1

Encyclopedia of Tribal Groups

In this appendix I will discuss the evidence for the tentative tribal locations indicated on Maps 4-5 (pages 228-229). Franciscan mission registers are the main sources for the tribal group names, and lists of most of those names have been published (Merriam 1955, 1968, 1970). Unfortunately, the mission registers give few explicit clues about the locations of the tribes, and no clues whatsoever about their territorial boundaries. Some groups can be placed on the landscape from clues in military correspondence, some from information on early nineteenth century maps. For many tribes, however, no explicit locational references exist at all. Only their general location can be established through a study of their proximity to one another, as suggested by their patterns of intermarriage. Marriage network analysis and other methods of tribal area identification are explained more fully below.

Techniques Used To Assign Tentative Tribal Locations

Direct Identification. A few tribal areas can be identified because their names have been retained as the names of modern cities and geographic features. In the northern part of the San Francisco Bay area these names include Carquinez Strait, Napa, Sonoma, Petaluma, and Suisun. Farther south, on the San Francisco Peninsula, some Spanish place names continue to be used which derive from old appellations for tribal villages; examples are "Las Pulgas" and "San Francisquito," originally villages situated along creeks on the San Francisco Peninsula. The mission baptismal records did provide a few precise locations by giving distances to villages from known points. One new neophyte was described as the "son of Camcegmne, the captain of the place called Ssatumnúm, about three leagues south of *Las Almejas* [Moss Beach] and of his second wife, who gave birth to the child at Chagunte, about a league hither from said place" (SFR-B 337). Another was from "the village of *Nuestra Señora de los Remedios*, called Ssupichom by its natives, about three leagues to the south of the Arroyo of San Mateo" (SFR-B 127).

Historic Maps. Narciso Durán of Mission San Jose prepared a map in the year 1824, his *Plano Topográfico*, that showed the relative locations of tribes along the San Joaquin River, the eastern frontier with mission-controlled areas in the year 1810 (Bennyhoff 1977:166-167). A few Mexican-period land grant maps indicate tribes that once lived on their lands. One example is the *diseño* for Rancho Monte del Diablo, which showed the Chupucanes tribe in the lower Diablo Valley of the East Bay region (Land Case Map D-184, Bancroft Library, University of California, Berkeley).

"Domino Theory." In general, tribes whose members appeared early in the baptismal register of a given mission lived closer to the mission than tribes absorbed at a later date. This assumption helps make tentative relative placements of groups known to have come from a restricted area. For example, the first group to come to Mission San Francisco from the Marin Peninsula were the Huimens, followed a few years later by the Guaulens from Bolinas Bay and the Habastos, a group for whom no locational clues are given in any historical record. A few years after the first Guaulens and Habastos went to San Francisco, some of their relatives began showing up there with some new groups, Tamals identified with the Nicasio area, and Omiomis, whose captain gave his name to the town of Novato in the northeastern Marin Peninsula area. All of those groups except the Habastos could be placed on the landscape from direct clues. Only the San Rafael area was not assigned to any group by direct clues. That area is approximately as far from Mission San Francisco as is Bolinas Bay, the area from which the Guaulens moved to San Francisco during the same time period that the Habastos went to San Francisco. Therefore, I tentatively place the Habastos at San Rafael on the basis of the "domino" theory and a process of spatial elimination.

Marriage Networks. Marriage networks provide important clues to the relative location of groups. Tribes that intermarried heavily generally lived adjacent to one another. An examination of marriage networks works well in conjunction with the domino theory. Again I will use Marin Peninsula groups as examples. The Habastos were heavily intermarried with the Huimens, the Guaulens, and Omiomis. That fact lends confidence to the indirect placement of the Habastos as neighbors of those other three groups. In the East Bay, marriage networks alone provide clues for locating the Tatcans in the San Ramon Valley (see **Tatcan** in this appendix).

Appendix 1. Tribal Groups 233

Sources of Confusion. Two problems exist in building tribal geography from the information supplied by missionaries, the problem of scale and the problem of synonymy. The problem of scale arises because the priests used the word *ranchería* in reference both to specific village locations and to tribal aggregations of people. Occasionally the missionaries provided both the village and tribal identification of an individual, such as Uaricse at Mission San Francisco, for instance, "from Supichom, in the Nation they call the Lamchin" (Miguel Giribet, SFR-B 497). More commonly, villages near the missions were listed as *rancherías* without reference to their tribal affiliation. One must resort to indirect means to expose the relationships among such villages at the tribal level. The best tool for such a clarification is the study of village overlaps within nuclear families.

A second problem is that of synonymy. Each tribe was known to various neighbors by a variety of informal names; sometime this was a descriptive nickname, sometimes it was the name of a leader or the central village, or it was just a name referring to the direction from which some new group came to the mission. Synonyms used in mission records become obvious when the recorded homelands of various members of specific nuclear families are compared with one another, with a resultant pairing of two completely different homeland names.

The "District" Problem at Missions Santa Clara and San Jose. The biggest problem in reconstructing ethnogeography results from the failure of some missionary priests to pay any attention at all to tribal organization in their assignment of place names. The Mission Santa Clara registers from 1777 through 1806 are useless for the direct reconstruction of tribal groups and their locations, because the missionaries labeled people by Spanish designations, first for specific small villages (Santa Clara, San Francisco, San Francisco Solano, San Jose Cupertino, San Juan Bautista, Santa Ysabel) and later for four large artificial aggregations of village and tribal groups that represented the cardinal directions from the mission, east (San Antonio), west (San Bernardino), south (San Carlos), and north (Santa Agueda). However, beginning with the Luechas in 1805, and then with all San Joaquin Valley groups in 1810, tribal names were provided in Mission Santa Clara baptismal register entries.

At Mission San Jose, no tribal names were provided from the first baptismal entry in September 1797 until March 1803. During that period the 800+ newly baptized people were said to be from six general areas, the Alameda, *Estero*, *Palos Colorados* ("Redwood," the upper drainage of San Leandro Creek), as well as the *este* (east), *norte* (north), and *sur* (south). The tribal affiliations of many of the early converts have been discovered through cross-references to their later relatives.

Results. Maps 4-5 (pages 228-229) show tentative tribal locations. No information exists that could justify mapping specific boundary lines between the tribes in any part of the San Francisco Bay region. North Bay, San Francisco Peninsula, and East Bay tribal areas are mapped with a high degree of confidence. Unfortunately, due to the poor quality of the Mission Santa Clara locational data, specific tribal spaces in and around the Santa Clara Valley are open to question.

Tribes And Villages

Achistaca (Costanoan language). A tribe in the upper San Lorenzo River drainage in the Santa Cruz Mountains in the vicinity of the modern towns of Boulder Creek and Riverside Grove (location inferred from marriage ties). Eighty-five of them went to Mission Santa Cruz from 1791 to 1795. Four people from an unlocated group called Acsaggis were baptized at Mission San Francisco between 1787 and 1791. The first was fifteen year old Ssolcóm, married at the time to a thirty-nine year old Oljon man. She was "from the Acssagis *familia* in the vicinity of Soróntac at the source of San Francisquito Creek" (SFR-B 676). The last large group from the south coast baptized at San Francisco, in early May 1793, may have been Acsaggis (SFR-B 1290-1329). Among the otherwise unlocated group was the mother of one of the identified Acsaggis (SFR-B 1318). The timing of baptism and the distance north to San Francisco suggests that these people were from the Saratoga Gap area. However, their name is strikingly similar to the Achistacas of the upper San Lorenzo River. If they were Achistacas, they were probably moved north to San Francisco in 1793 at the end of the Charquin rebellion.

Acsaggis—see Achistaca.

Aguasto—see Habasto, Huchiun-Aguasto, and Yelamu.

Alaguali (Coast Miwok language). A tribe along the marshland borders on the north side of San Pablo Bay at the mouth of Sonoma Creek and Tolay Creek. Franciscans visited their village of Cholequebit by boat in August of 1811 (SFR-B 4414, 4415). Fifty Alaguali people went to Mission San Francisco between 1811 and 1817. Another seventy went to Mission San Jose in 1816 and 1817. Most of the survivors were later transferred back to Mission San Francisco Solano.

Appendix 1. Tribal Groups   235

Alson (Costanoan language). A tribe which held the low marshlands at the very southern end of San Francisco Bay, probably both north and south of the mouth of the Coyote River, now the cities of Newark, Milpitas, and Alviso. The name Alson does not appear in any of the early mission records, but it does appear in the Mission San Jose Padron of 1838 as the tribe name for some surviving Estero and Alameda people (SJO-B 6, 131, 151, 328, 384, 412). The pattern indicates that the Alsons went to Mission Santa Clara under the designation "Santa Agueda" and that they had been nearly depleted before Mission San Jose was opened. It is impossible to determine their contribution to mission populations.

Anizumne (Plains Miwok language). This group sent 244 people for baptism at Mission San Jose between 1812 and 1825. Durán's *Plano Topográfico* of 1824 places this group on the west side of the Sacramento River between the Ompins and the Chucumnes (Bennyhoff 1977:166). The map, intermarriages, and time of baptism place them in the present Rio Vista area. A descendent of this group who lived in Pleasanton was called a "Han-né-su" in 1910 (Merriam 1967:368).

Aptos (Costanoan language). The Aptos group held the shores of Monterey Bay from Aptos eastward about half way to the mouth of the Pajaro River. They appear in the Santa Cruz Mission Baptismal Register under the name "San Lucas" in the margin and Aptos in the text (for instance, SCR-B 4). They were one of the four early groups converted at Mission Santa Cruz, but were actually the last of those four nearby groups to be completely absorbed into the mission, in 1796. Although they had some marriages with their neighbors the Cotoni, Sayanta, and Uypi, they were completely mixed together with the Cajastaca, alias "San Antonio," people of the Corralitos area. So much mixing occurred within nuclear family groups that the idea arises that Aptos and Cajastaca were a single tribal group.

Asirin (Costanoan language). A tribe in the rugged, broken country in the Coast Ranges eastward from Mission San Jose and the Santa Clara Valley, probably on upper Alameda Creek, upper Arroyo del Valle, and Colorado Creek areas along the present Alameda-Santa Clara County border. Geiger (1969:58) incorrectly placed them on the east side of the San Joaquin Valley between the Calaveras and Stanislaus rivers, an impossible location for the group. Cook (1957:144) incorrectly guessed that Asirin territory was on the San Joaquin River, as did Bennyhoff (1977:164).

Only thirty Asirins who went to Mission San Jose from 1802 to 1805 were explicitly identified. They were intermarried with Taunans, but with no other group at Mission San Jose. That fact alone places them to the south of the

Taunans. By time of baptism they could not have been a San Joaquin Valley group. Furthermore, a small group of "Santa Agueda" people baptized at Mission Santa Clara in September of 1804 (SCL-B 4619-4632) cross-refer to the Asirins at Mission San Jose. Some of the "San Antonio" district people baptized at Mission Santa Clara between 1801 and 1805 may also have been Asirins.

Ausaima (Costanoan language). The core area of the Ausaima tribe is confidently placed on the east side of the San Felipe sink on Pacheco Creek. Five Ausaimas went to Mission San Carlos Borromeo in 1791. A total of 276 people from the group were baptized at Mission San Juan Bautista over the years 1797 through 1806. Their large village of Poytoquix (21 specific references) became the Mission San Juan Bautista ranch and chapel of San Felipe (Merriam 1967:391). Levy (1978:485) mislocated this tribe in the Aromas area to the west of the San Felipe sink. He was probably following some confused historical information regarding their location gathered by Merriam (1967:391). The village of Chipuctac, home of some people who went to Mission Santa Cruz, seems to have belonged to the Ausaimas (see Chipuctac).

Auxentac (Costanoan language). The village name Auxentac has been applied with reservations to people from the poorly known rugged country along Coyote Creek, including the present Gilroy Hot Springs and Henry Coe Park, east of the present town of Morgan Hill. Only 25 people were identified from Auxentac. They went to Mission Santa Cruz in 1800. Three of them can be tied to "San Carlos" district people baptized at Mission Santa Clara between 1792 and 1799 (SCR-B 992, 995, 1005; SCL-B 2053, 3803). No links can be found to those "San Carlos" families that were going to Mission Santa Clara at the same time, in early 1802. Nevertheless, the majority of people from the assigned area probably went to Mission Santa Clara as "San Carlos" people between 1802 and 1805. Other fragmentary groups noted at Mission Santa Cruz that may have been from this vicinity include Muistac (2 people in 1803) and Taratac (2 people in 1804, 2 people in 1805). Some of these villages may have been eastward of the area in which Auxentac has been placed on Map 5. Note that the Orestac group, placed by Levy (1978:485) in the Gilroy Hot Springs area, probably lived in the Los Banos Creek drainage on the eastern Coast Range slopes. See also Churistac.

Bitakomtara (Southern Pomo language). This tribe held the eastern side of the Santa Rosa Plain in the present area of Santa Rosa (Stewart 1943:53-54). At least 124 of them went to Mission San Rafael between 1821 and 1826 under the name Gualomi, presumably the Coast Miwok translation of their own name.

Bolbon. This group is not shown on Maps 4-5. The name Bolbon has been applied to at least two, and probably three, distinct groups. Members of the group called Volvon in the Mission San Francisco Book of Baptisms were called Bolbons by Father Abella in the Mission San Francisco Padron of 1822. The group called Cholvons in the Mission San Jose Book of Baptisms were identified as Bolbons by Father Abella on October 22, 1811, when he visited "the village of Pescadero, called also of the Bolbones" along a fork of the San Joaquin River north of the present city of Tracy (Argüello [1811] 1960:262). At Mission Santa Clara, 39 people identified as "San Antonio" people at baptism were listed as Bolbons in their death records. Intermarriage patterns of the Volvons at Mission Santa Clara and the "San Antonio" Bolbons of Mission Santa Clara are radically different. Perhaps then, the Mission Santa Clara Bolbons were the same people as the Cholvons at Mission San Jose. They certainly appeared for baptism during the same years that the Cholvons were going to Mission San Jose, 1806-1812. Yet in addition to Cholvons, there were three *"Volvon del Sur"* people baptized with Luechas and Cholvons at Mission San Jose (SJB-B 1360, 1657, 1935). All of this suggests that the "San Antonio" Bolbons at Mission Santa Clara may have been a separate Coast Range group living in the steep canyons of the Del Puerto Creek drainage to the east of the Santa Clara Valley. I have given that area to the Juñas group in this report (Figure 22), but this whole question is open to further study. The Mission Santa Clara Bolbons were intermarried with Juñas (three marriages), as well as Tugites (one marriage) and Lamames on the San Joaquin River. See also Cholvon and Volvon.

Caburan—see Pelnen.

Caguapatto—see Tolena.

Cajastaca (Costanoan language). The *"Cajastaca, alias San Antonio"* group, baptized at Mission Santa Cruz during the late 1790s, was from the lands just north or northeast of the present town of Watsonville, near the Pajaro River (cf. Levy 1978:485). They were clearly contiguous with the Aptos; Cajastaca was possibly a subgroup of the Aptos. Among the last 38 Aptos people baptized at Mission Santa Cruz were 11 people later identified in death records or census lists as Cajastacas.

Canicaymos—see Canijolmano, Caymus, and Huiluc.

Canijolmano (Wappo language). Intermarriage patterns place the Canijolmano group in the central Napa Valley in the vicinity of the modern town of St. Helena. Some of their members went to Mission San Francisco in 1820 together with their Caymus and Huiluc neighbors under the multitribal designation "Canicaymo," certainly in recognition of their common, and new at

Mission San Francisco, Wappo language. They were baptized at Mission San Francisco Solano from 1824 to 1831.

Carquin (Costanoan language). A tribe on both sides of the Carquinez Strait in the present Port Costa, Martinez, Benicia area. Father Abella of Mission San Francisco passed through the "*estrecho de los Carquines*" during an exploration of the Central Valley in 1811 (Cook 1960:261). The "*Estrecho de Karquines*" also appears on Father Duran's 1824 *Plano Topográfico* (Bennyhoff 1977:166). Bennyhoff (1977:137-144) felt strongly that they held only the southern side of Carquinez Strait, while the Aguastos, whom he identified as Patwin speakers, held the north side of the Strait. The specific Aguasto group of that area, the Huchiun-Aguastos, may have held the north side of Carquinez Strait from Glenn Cove west to Mare Island, but they were clearly Costanoan speakers and heavily intermarried with the Carquins (see Huchiun-Aguasto in this appendix). I see no evidence for any other group to the north of Carquinez Strait until one reaches the Napa and Suisun tribes, tribes definitely not located on Carquinez Strait. A total of 152 Carquins went to Mission San Francisco, most of them in 1809 and 1810.

Causen (Costanoan language). A tribe, or perhaps a single village, in the Sunol Valley area to the north of Mission San Jose, also known as Patlans, after the name of one of their older male members (SJO-B 35, 108, 111, 442, 462). They were intermarried with the Pelnens of the Livermore Valley and with the Tuibuns of the Fremont Plain. Only eleven people specifically identified as Causens and another seven identified as Patlans were baptized at Mission San Jose between 1803 and 1808.

Caymus (Wappo language). The Caymus held the present Yountville area of the Napa River Valley north of San Pablo Bay (Yount in Heizer 1953:312). The majority of them went down to Mission San Francisco in 1821, where they were among 240 Wappo-speaking people from four tribes all baptized under the generic term for all Wappo speakers, Canicaymus. Many of them were transferred north to help found Mission San Francisco Solano in the Napa Valley in 1823. It is in the mission registers of Mission San Francisco Solano that one can find evidence that the majority of Canicaymos that went to Mission San Francisco were in fact Caymus, and that only a few were Canijolmano, Huiluc, and Mayacma, other Wappo-speakers of the North Bay Area. Only five additional Caymus people were baptized after Mission San Francisco Solano opened.

Chaloctac (Costanoan language). The village or tribe of Chaloctac held the rough country around Loma Prieta Creek along the crest of the Santa Cruz Mountains. They went to Mission Santa Cruz between 1792 and 1795. Before

Mission Santa Cruz opened, however, some of them seem to have gone to Mission Santa Clara under the designation "*San Carlos de la Sierra*" and "*Rancho de la Sierra*." (The Chaloctac people that went to Mission Santa Cruz had an exceptionally frequent number of marriages with the Sayanta people (five marriages).

Chemoco (Mixed Wappo and Patwin languages). The Chemoco group appears occasionally in the baptismal registers for Mission San Francisco Solano from 1824 through 1834. Altogether only 34 of them were baptized. I have tentatively placed them in the Wooden Valley area, rugged hill country north and east of the Napa Valley, on the basis of their inter-marriages with the Tolenas, the Caymus, and the Aloquiome to the north.

Chiguan (Costanoan language). A tribe on the Pacific coast of the San Francisco Peninsula from Point Montara south to Pilarcitos Creek, the area presently known as Half Moon Bay (Brown 1973:20). They were baptized at Mission San Francisco between 1783 and 1791. Two specific village names appear in the Mission San Francisco Baptismal Register. One of those, Ssatumnumo, was said to be "about three leagues south of 'The Mussels' [in the vicinity of San Pedro Valley]," while the other, Chagúnte, was "about a league hither from said place" (SFR-B 337).

Chipuctac (Costanoan language). Chipuctac, tentatively located in the Cañada de los Osos area northeast of the present town of Gilroy, may have been the Mission Santa Cruz term for the Ausaimas tribe at Mission San Juan Bautista. Twenty of the "*parage de San Juan*" people baptized at Mission Santa Cruz in 1804 and 1805 were explicitly said to be from Chipuctac. Two men in that group had brought their children to Mission Santa Clara in 1798 under the "San Carlos" designation (SCL-B 3699, 3702; SJB-B 1140, 1143). Four Mission San Juan Bautista Ausaimas who moved to Mission Santa Cruz were identified as Chipuctacs in marriage and death records at Santa Cruz (SJB-B 311, 330, 311, 1501). Things are complicated, however, by the fact that Ausaimas were not the only people called Chipuctacs at Mission Santa Cruz. Some of the people identified in Mission Santa Cruz death records and censuses as Chipuctacs were first baptized there as Pitacs (SCR-B 661, 902, 1133), Chitactacs (SCR-B 625, 626, 630), and Aptos (SCR-B 285). Therefore, the place name Chipuctac came to be used as a catch-all term at Mission Santa Cruz for people from a wide area, perhaps all of the Santa Clara Valley corridor from San Martin south and east to Hollister.

Chitactac (Costanoan language). Although the Chitactac are placed on the upper reaches of Uvas Creek in the Santa Cruz Mountains on Map 5, they may just as easily have held lower lands further to the east in the Santa Clara

Valley corridor (cf. Levy 1978:485). Chitactac people were baptized at Mission Santa Cruz between 1795 and 1802. They were the first, and largest, of a number of groups at Santa Cruz identified with the "*parage de San Juan*". The parents of many children identified as Chitactacs in early 1796 were themselves baptized as Pitacs a few weeks later. Later death register entries for people from the two groups were also contradictory. This suggests either that the missionaries were confused about political and territorial relationships between them or that Chitactac and Pitac were two villages of a single tribe. In any case, the Pitac group is assumed to have lived further from Mission Santa Cruz than the Chitactac group, because most of them were baptized in 1798, after Chitactac conversion had dropped off.

Chocoay (Coast Miwok language). I have mapped the lower Petaluma River as though it were the territory of the Omiomi group (Figure 21). However, three small splinter groups which I did not map may possibly have lived along the sloughs in that area. In 1811 a woman was baptized from "*Poscuy al norte de Omiomi*" (SFR-B 4299). All told, 25 Puscuy people were baptized at San Francisco from 1811 through 1817. They have numerous family ties to two other splinter groups which first appeared in the winter of 1813-1814. The largest of the other groups was the Chocoay, with 53 people at Mission San Francisco in 1813-1817 and 2 people at Mission San Jose, one each in 1817 and 1818. The third splinter group was the Geluasibe, with 47 people appearing at San Francisco from 1812 to 1817. Of the three groups, only the Puscuy had extensive family ties to the Olompali. Study of the Mission San Rafael records should clarify the locations of these three groups through a reconstruction of all their family ties with the larger neighboring groups.

Choquinico—see Olompali.

Chocoime (Coast Miwok language). Also known as Sonomas and Chucuiens, this tribe held the valley of Sonoma Creek around the present town of Sonoma. The largest block from the tribe, 92 people, went to Mission San Jose in 1815 and 1816 under the name Chocoime (also spelled Choquoime). Forty-three others went to Mission San Francisco in 1814 and 1815 under the name Chucuien. Many of the people from the tribe who were still alive in 1823 moved back north to their Sonoma Valley homeland when Father José Altimira founded Mission San Francisco Solano. Among the Mission San Francisco converts from the tribe was a sixty year-old man named Sonoma, baptized on April 8, 1815 (SFR-B 5047). According to S.A. Barrett (1908:313) a man named Sonoma, alias Tolopo, was the captain of the people in the Sonoma Valley (see also Powers 1877:195). One Mission San Francisco entry actually labels a group of new neophytes "*Chucuiens llamados tambien Sonomas*" (SFR-B 4986-4993).

Cholvon (Northern Yokuts language). The Cholvons held the Old River channel of the lower San Joaquin River and the flat plains and seasonal lakes to the south, now the vicinity of the city of Tracy. They are placed confidently on the basis of time of baptism, marriage ties, and location on Duran's *Plano Topográfico* of 1824 (Bennyhoff 1977:166). At Mission San Jose, 164 Cholvons were baptized from 1806 through 1824, the preponderance of the group in 1810 and 1811. They were called "Tcholovones" by Kotzebue expedition members in 1816 (Chamisso [1816] 1932:88). Alphonse Pinart was told by a woman who spoke their language that the "Čolovomnes ... inhabited a 'rancheria' or village situated nearly where the little town of Bantas is today" ([1894] 1955:134). Banta is northeast of Tracy, probably at the very eastern edge of traditional Cholvon territory. See also Bolbon.

Chucumne (Plains Miwok language). This large group, 369 of which were baptized between 1816 and 1825, has been located on the west side of the Sacramento River delta at the juncture of Sutter Slough and Miner Slough (Bennyhoff 1977:77).

Chucuyen—see Chocoime.

Chupcan (Bay Miwok language). A tribe which held the lower Diablo Valley in the East Bay, occasionally called Yacumusmos in Mission San Francisco records. Some of them went to Mission San Francisco in 1804 in mixed nuclear family groups with Carquins and Tatcans. Their main village on lower Pacheco Creek at the present city of Concord was known as *Monte del Diablo* or "The Devil's Woodlot" to the Spaniards (Pacheco [1828] 1855). The great majority of the 146 Chupcans who went to Mission San Francisco and Mission San Jose were baptized in 1810 and 1811. With them were the Suisuns, with whom they were heavily intermarried.

Churistac (Costanoan language)—see also Auxentac. This group is not indicated on Maps 4-5. However, the village name Churistac, used in Mission Santa Cruz records, deserves special attention. No person was ever said to be from that place at the time of their baptism. All the references occurred after 1818, in marriage records, death records, and census records. The individuals had been baptized between 1800 and 1806 from the specific villages of Achachipe (SCR-B 1201), Auxentac (SCR-B 915), Muistac (SCR-B 1040), and Taui (SCR-B 1058), and from the general areas of San Juan (SCR-B 912, 980) and San Francisco Xavier (SCR-B 1058). Thus, this may be a cover term for a cluster of villages in the mountains eastward of the present town of Morgan

Hill, either in the area that I have assigned as Auxentac in the drainage of Coyote Creek or in the North Fork of Pacheco Creek.

Cotegen (Costanoan language). A tribe on Purisima Creek on the Pacific Coast, south of Half Moon Bay. One of their towns was "Ssalaime, the principal place of the Cotegenes" (SFR-D 216). Another was Torose (Milliken 1983:85). Forty-two people of this small group moved to the Mission San Francisco outstation of San Pedro during the late 1780s and early 1790s.

Cotoni (Costanoan language). The Cotoni group held the Pacific Coast in the vicinity of the present town of Davenport and probably the inland ridge in the Bonny Doone area as well. They were one of the four initial groups converted at Mission Santa Cruz, where 95 of them were baptized between 1792 and 1800. They appear in the Santa Cruz baptismal register under the designation "Santiago" on the margins of their baptismal entries, and Cotoni in the text (SCR-B 117).

Coybos (Northern Valley Yokuts language). The Coybos sent 91 people to Mission San Jose, most between 1811 and 1824. Shown on Duran's *Plano Topográfico* of 1824, this group seems to have held the San Joaquin River near where the San Joaquin River began to braid out into its delta, in the present Lathrop area (Bennyhoff 1977:166).

Geluasibe—see Chocoay.

Genau—see Huchiun.

Gualomi—see Bitakomtara.

Guaulen (Coast Miwok language). A tribe centered at Bolinas Bay along the Pacific Coast of the Marin Peninsula. The modern place name "Bolinas" is a corruption of the Mexican rancho name for the area, "Baulinas," which is itself a corruption of Guaulen. A total of 112 people from the group migrated to Mission San Francisco between 1801 and 1803.

Guaypem (Plains Miwok language). This group, also called Guaypemne, seems to have been situated on Tyler Island in the Sacramento-Mokelumne River delta (Bennyhoff 1977:73). They sent at least 41 people to Mission San Jose between 1821 and 1828. Merriam (1967:367) interviewed a descendant of this group, whom he called a "Wí-pa," at Pleasanton in 1910.

Guemelento—see Olpen.

Habasto (Coast Miwok language). The group that I am here calling Habasto held the eastern side of the Marin Peninsula, Point San Pedro, and the small valleys just to its north and south. Kelly (1978:415) published the names of villages in the area which were not named in the mission records: Shotomoko-cha at Miller Creek, Ewu at Gallinas Creek, and Awani-wi, the site of Mission San Rafael. They all probably belonged to the Habastos, as did sites on upper San Anselmo Creek to the west. The Habastos went to Mission San Francisco between 1800 and 1810. Many of them returned to their homeland as Mission Indians when Mission San Rafael was founded in late 1817.

Huchiun (Costanoan language). Huchiun lands seem to have extended over a large area along the East Bay shore, from Temescal Creek opposite the Golden Gate north at least to the lower San Pablo and Wildcat Creek drainages in the present area of Richmond. East Bay people who came to Mission San Francisco before 1787 were said to be from numerous specific villages in "Yacomui." The most commonly mentioned villages were Genau and Josquizara. Yacomui probably referred to "Easterners" in the Costanoan language of the San Francisco area (Heizer 1974:43). Family reconstitution evidence and one direct statement indicate that Genau was a Huchiun village (SFR-B 188-191, 194, 201, 203, 450, 541). The first explicit reference to the Huchiun involved an individual who was baptized in 1787 "from the village of Junchaque of the Juchiun nation" (SFR-B 581). The first large groups of Huchiuns came to Mission San Francisco in the fall of 1794. Missionary Antonio Dantí identified them as "Jutchiunes—All from the northeast of the mission" (SFR-B 1628). Between 1800 and 1805 they appeared in mixed groups with Huchiun-Aguastos. The missionaries were inconsistent in their identification of nuclear family members as Huchiun or Huchiun-Aguasto. Either it did not matter, because the two groups were a single tribe, or the missionaries found it impossible or unimportant to differentiate them. In addition to 384 Huchiun converts there were 95 Huchiun-Aguastos (see below).

Sometime before 1820 Mission San Francisco founded a cattle ranch in the Richmond, San Pablo area which they called "San Ysidro of the Juchiunes" (SFR-B 5875, 5879). That mission ranch, taken over during the 1820s by the Castro family, became the Mexican rancho called "San Pablo, alias Los Cuchiyunes." Temescal Creek in north Oakland, directly across the bay from San Francisco, was known in the Mexican era as the "Arroyo del Temescal o Los Juchiyunes" (Land Case Map E-214, Bancroft Library, Berkeley).

Huchiun-Aguasto (Costanoan language). The Huchiun-Aguastos held lands in the East Bay on the southeast shores of San Pablo Bay. The first member of the group identified in San Francisco baptismal records was Blandina Guaiamay from "the village of Ssogoreate on the port of the Assumption near the outlet of the great river of Our Father San Francisco, of the family of the Aguasajuchiun" (SFR-B 708). Groups of Huchiun-Aguastos went to Mission San Francisco between 1803 and 1811, usually with Carquins or Huchiuns. Many of the 384 Mission San Francisco people baptized merely as "Huchiuns" were probably Huchiun-Aguastos. Numerous nuclear families contain individuals from either named group.

Huiluc (Wappo language). The Huilucs held the upper valley of Sonoma Creek north of San Pablo Bay. The Mexican period land grant Los Guilicos, in the present Kenwood area, derives its name from this group. A significant portion of the 240 Canicaymos baptized at Mission San Francisco in 1821, perhaps as many as 100 people, were from the Huiluc tribe. Thirty-four "Guilucs" went to Mission San Rafael in 1822 and 1823. Another thirty-six Huilucs were baptized at Mission San Francisco Solano in the Napa Valley between 1825 and 1832.

Huimen (Coast Miwok language). The Huimens controlled the vicinity of Richardson Bay on the southern tip of the Marin Peninsula. They were the first group from "the other shore of the port" to go down to Mission San Francisco, beginning in 1783 (SFR-B 369). The first Huimen people to appear in Mission San Francisco records were from the large village of Liuaneglua (SFR-B 305, 532). C. Hart Merriam (1916:118) gathered information identifying Liuaneglua with the present location of the town of Sausalito (Merriam 1916:118). The first two persons expressly stated to be from the "Nación Huimen" at Mission San Francisco were an older woman and a middle aged man, both parents of persons earlier baptized from Liuaneglua (SFR-B 620, 623). Two other Huimen villages were mentioned in the *Libro de Bautismos* of Mission San Francisco, Naique "of the Uimen family to the north of the Presidio across from Angel Island" (SFR-B 843) and Anamás "of the far shore from the Presidio, the port called Huimenes" (SFR-B 1631). The Huimens spoke Coast Miwok as their primary language, although some have argued that they spoke Costanoan (Beeler 1972; A. Brown 1973a). The Huimen vocabulary that Father Arroyo de la Cuesta ([1821-1837]) recorded in 1821 is definitely a Coast Miwok word list (Beeler 1961:202).

Jalalon (Northern Valley Yokuts language). A small group, the Jalalon sent 30 people to Mission San Jose between 1811 and 1825. They are shown on Duran's *Plano Topográfico* of 1824 between the Tamcan and the Julpun (Bennyhoff 1977:166). They were a completely marsh-oriented group that seems to have lived in the vicinity of Indian Slough east of the present Brentwood area (Bennyhoff 1977:133).

Jalquin (Bay Miwok language). The Jalquins lived in the interior East Bay hills east of Oakland or San Leandro. Some evidence suggests that the Jalquins, who went to Mission San Francisco in 1801-1803, are the same group as the Yrgins, who went to Mission San Jose during the same period. In the text of this book I have treated the Jalquin/Yrgins as a single tribe, but in this section

Appendix 1. Tribal Groups 245

I have treated them separately. The possibility of their synonymy presents a very difficult problem, as the following evidence attests. In 1797, seven non-Christian men were arrested and punished for their involvement in the 1795 Saclan murder of seven Mission San Francisco men. At that time they were identified as Saclans (see Argüello [1797c], Appendix 4, 13). Four of those men, Otseit, Caguas, Carues, and Joguacsea, were baptized in 1802 as Jalquins (SFR-B 2319, 2372, 2374, 2375). The case of those four men suggests that the Jalquin were a Saclan subgroup. Furthermore, the mother of the Saclan resistance leader Potroy was baptized as a Jalquin in 1802 (SFR-B 2356). Also, Saclans joined Mission San Francisco before and after the 1801-1803 time period in which the Jalquins appeared, but not during that time, suggesting that they are the same people. However, Jalquins and Saclans were differentiated in the Mission San Francisco Padron of 1822.

At the time of the Jalquins' move to Mission San Francisco in 1801-1803, their only recorded exogamous family ties, other than to the Saclans, were to the Seunens (two marriages) and Tatcans (one marriage). That pattern suggests that the Jalquins were the southernmost East Bay group to go to Mission San Francisco. Predictably, any Jalquins who went to Mission San Jose would have been intermarried with the Seunens, with whom they went to San Francisco, and with the Yrgins, the northernmost bay shore group at Mission San Jose. However, there are no Jalquins directly identified at Mission San Jose. And by the same token, no Yrgins appeared at Mission San Francisco. This mutual absence of group names forces us to consider the possibility that Jalquin and Yrgin are synonyms.

The first missionaries at Mission San Jose muddied the data about relationships among tribes from the hypothesized Jalquin/Yrgin area by failing to note tribal designations between 1797 and mid-1803. They designated all new neophytes from north of San Lorenzo Creek as "Redwoods" in that period. Twenty-six people at Mission San Jose were identified as "Redwoods" area people. Six of them cross-refer to families that included subsequent Mission San Jose Yrgins. Six others cross-refer to "Alameda" area families, itself an ambiguous directional term that included Tuibuns, and maybe some Yrgins. Two "Redwoods" children at Mission San Jose were definitely Saclans (SJO-B 198, parents SFR-B 1557, 1575; SJO-B 218, listed as a Saclan in the Mission San Jose Padron of 1838). One "Redwoods" person at Mission San Jose gave her personal name as "Jalquin" (SJO-B 34), yet her name had been given as "Huyumute" at the baptism of her daughter one week earlier (SJO-B 33). Perhaps the missionary who baptized her mistook the name of her tribe for her personal name. A few years later a Seunen man was reported dead in his village by "los gentiles Yrgines" (SJO-D 253). He had been baptized with his Jalquin wife at Mission San Francisco (SFR-B 2313). Family reconstitution analysis shows marriage ties between Mission San Francisco Jalquin men and three Mission San Jose Yrgin women (SFR-B 2318, whose two wives were SJO-B 679—identified as Yrgin through SJO-B 868—and SJO-B 934, also a Yrgin; and SFR-B 2318, whose former wife was SJO-B 1168, also a Yrgin). Like the Jalquins who went to San Francisco, the Yrgins were strongly tied to the Seunens of the present Dublin-San Ramon area to the east. Taken as a whole, the perspective from Mission San Jose would suggest that Yrgin and Jalquin were either a single people or two contiguous groups. The last Jalquins joined at Mission San Francisco in 1802, but Yrgins were baptized at Mission San Jose as late as 1808 (see Yrgin).

Julpun (Bay Miwok language). The northernmost tribe along the Old River of the San Joaquin River, according to Father Duran's 1824 *Plano Topográfico* (Bennyhoff 1977:166). Three Julpuns went to Mission San Francisco with their Volvon neighbors in March 1806. Four went to Mission San Jose in 1807 and 1808 with Tamcan and Cholvon people. The largest group, 103 people, went to Mission San Jose during 1811. Another 50 people came to Mission San Jose through 1827. When John Marsh ([1846] 1890:213) took over the tribe's area in 1838, he found a few Indian people there whom he referred to as "Pulpunes." They were presumably Julpuns who had returned to the area following the secularization of Mission San Jose at the end of 1836.

Juñas (Costanoan language). This tribe appeared at Mission Santa Clara between 1804 and 1815. They probably came from the Hospital Creek drainage of the Diablo Range, overlooking the San Joaquin Valley. Alternatively, they were the people of the San Antonio Valley in the heart of the Diablo Range. The highest numbers of adult baptisms from the group were in 1807 and 1808.

Kabemali (Southern Pomo language). No Pomo name seems to have been handed down for the tribe along the Pacific Coast between Bodega Bay and the mouth of the Russian River. Their main village, at Duncan's Point, was Kabemali (Barrett 1908:232). Seventy-six people from this group were baptized at Mission San Rafael under the Coast Miwok version of their name, Lupuyomi, primarily in 1823 and 1824.

Konhomtara (Southern Pomo language). This tribe was centered in the Sebastopol area on the southwest side of the Santa Rosa Plain (Stewart 1943:54). They went to Mission San Rafael between 1820 and 1831 under their Coast Miwok tribal name, Livantolomi.

Lamaytu—see Partacsi.

Lamchin (Costanoan language). A tribe that held the portion of the bay shore of the San Francisco Peninsula from present day Belmont south to present day Redwood City, and adjacent interior valleys to the west. Their most important village, "Cachanigtac, alias Las Pulgas" was probably on Pulgas Creek in the present city of San Carlos (Brown 1973:16). Other villages mentioned in the Mission San Francisco Libro de Bautismos were Usséte, Guloisnistac, Oromstac, and Ssupichom.

Libantone—see Olema.

Licatiut (Coast Miwok language). A tribe which held the lands from the Cotati area west as far as Bloomfield and Two Rock in the northernmost part of the Bay Area (Slaymaker 1982:356-360). This area is a low watershed divide between steams which flow south into San Francisco Bay, north to the Laguna de Santa Rosa, and west through Estero Americano to the Pacific Ocean. The tribe moved to Mission San Rafael between 1820 and 1825, ninety-two people in all.

Lisyan. Mission San Jose descendants told J.P. Harrington ([1921]) that the Indian name for the Chocheños (Mission San Jose people) was "Lisjánes". On the basis of this entry, Levy (1978:485) placed the Lisyan group at the mouth of San Lorenzo Creek in the East Bay on his map of contact period tribe areas. The word does not appear in any Spanish mission period records.

Livantolomi—see Konhomtara.

Luecha (Costanoan and Yokuts languages). I place the Luechas on Corral Hollow and Arroyo Mocho in the rough lands southeast of the Livermore Valley. Cook (1957:144) and W. Egbert Schenck (1926:133), on the other hand, believed that they lived along the San Joaquin River. Marriage ties, time of baptism, José María Amador's statement during the 1860s that they had lived "four or five leagues" (twelve miles) east of Livermore (Cook 1957:144) make the foothill location most likely. The Luechas are of special note because they killed Mission San Jose steward Ygnacio Higuera and three Mission San Jose Indians, dismembering their bodies, in February of 1805 (SJO-D 537-540). Said incident may be the basis for the name Arroyo Mocho ("Creek of the Mutilated"), the creek southeast of the Livermore Valley. The preponderance of the 125 baptized Luechas went to Mission Santa Clara in 1805 and 1806. A smaller number were baptized at Mission San Jose during the same years.

Lupuyomi—see Kabemali.

Malaca (Patwin language). Only 64 Malaca people were ever baptized, most at Mission San Francisco between 1815 and 1821, and a few at Mission San Francisco Solano from 1827 to 1832. Time of baptism and marriage ties place them on the plains on the north side of Suisun Bay, east of the present town of Fairfield. They were closely tied to the Suisuns and many of the 326 Suisuns at San Francisco may actually have been Malacas.

Matalan (Costanoan language). The Matalan tribe held the Santa Clara Valley corridor from the present town of Coyote south to the present town of Morgan Hill. The group may have held the Chesbro Reservoir area on Llagas Creek to the west, and the Anderson Reservoir area in the hills to the east, as well. There are only eleven explicit references to persons from either Laguna Seca or Matalanes in mission registers, those being at Mission Santa Clara in 1789 and 1790. Relatives of the explicitly identified tribe members identified through family reconstitution continued to be baptized through 1799 (SCL-B 3788, 3795). The largest clusters of "San Carlos" district married couples went to Mission Santa Clara in 1802. Those groups may have been the last Matalans or they may have been from the Coyote Lake area east of San Martin, an area where one would expect proselytization from missions Santa Cruz and San Juan Bautista to have occurred.

Musupum (Plains Miwok language). This small group sent 46 people for baptism to Mission San Jose between 1818 and 1824. Bennyhoff (1977:76) placed them on Staten Island in the Sacramento-Mokelumne River delta, on the basis of marriage ties, time of missionization, and their location on Duran's *Plano Topográfico* of 1824.

Napa (probably Patwin language). The Napa tribe held the east side of the lower reaches of the Napa River below the present town of Napa. They had four marriages with the Huchiun-Aguastos, four with the Choquoimes, and two with the Tolenas. The overall regional pattern of intermarriages places the Napas as southern neighbors of the Caymus, even though I could find only one marriage between them. Some 221 Napa people were baptized. Fifty-seven went to Mission San Francisco from 1809 through 1815. A larger group, 164 people, went to Mission San Jose from 1814 to 1818.

Nototomne (Northern Valley Yokuts language). This group sent 106 people to Mission San Jose for baptism, most between 1816 and 1819. They appear on Duran's *Plano Topográfico* of 1824 in the middle of the delta lands of the San Joaquin River (see Bennyhoff 1977:132-133).

Olema (Coast Miwok language). The Olema tribe lived near the Pacific Coast of the Marin Peninsula to the north of Bolinas Bay. The majority of the tribe were baptized at Mission San Francisco in 1803 and 1805. Only two pre-mission intermarriages have been noted, one with the Tamals, and two with the Guaulens. The tribe gave its name to the modern village of Olema at the south end of Tomales Bay, yet it remains a question as to whether or not their main village was near the modern town (see Gudde 1969:227).

Forty people from an area called Olemaloque were baptized at San Francisco between 1807 and 1810. Isabel Kelly (1978:415) placed them at the town of Olema, indicating that they are synonymous with Olema. Gudde (1969:227) suggests that they may also be the same group as Olemochoe, a group placed by Samuel Barrett (1908:308) some ten miles north of the present town of Olema in Chileno Valley. My own research suggests that Chileno Valley was within the contact period area of another tribe, the Olompali.

A group of twenty-five adults baptized at Mission San Francisco on August 12, 1807 were identified as Libantones (SFR-B 3416-3441). The children of the group had been baptized on July 19, 1807, at which time they were identified as "Olemalocoe" (SFR-B 3405-3411). The relationship between Olemaloque, Olema, Olema-tamal, and Libantone can be cleared up through future family reconstitution research. In general, all such people were from the Point Reyes-Inverness-Olema area.

Oljon (Costanoan language). A tribe on the lower drainages of San Gregorio Creek and Pescadero Creek on the Pacific Coast west of the Santa Clara Valley. They joined Mission San Francisco between 1786 and 1793. Village names mentioned include Zucigim (SFR-B 569) and Pructaca (SFR-B 588). The term Ohlone, an alternative for Costanoan, may have derived from this tribe's name. Mission San Francisco descendant Pedro Alcantara reported in 1850 that the tribes of that mission were five in number, "the *Ah-wash-tes*, *Ol-hones* (called, in Spanish, Costanos or Indians of the Coast), *Al-tah-mos*, *Ro-mo-nans*, and *Tu-lo-mos*" (Schoolcraft 1860:2:506).

Olompali (Coast Miwok language). A tribe in the interior valleys of present Marin County, west of the Petaluma River. They were also known as Choquinicos, the tribal name under which their captain was baptized at Mission San Jose in 1817 (SJO-B 3470, see also SFR-B 5231). The specific territory of the group is a great question. Father Payeras visited San Antonio Creek in 1819, calling it "*Cañada de los Olompalis*" (Gudde 1969:228). Kroeber (1925:273-274) and Barrett (1908:310) considered the San Antonio Creek drainage to be the Olompali core area. Slaymaker (1982:109) placed them further east at the present Olompali State Park. See Geluasibe for a further discussion of the problems in determining tribal groups in that area, seemingly a border area between Olompali lands and those of the Omiomis of Novato. Eighty-three Olompalis went to Mission San Francisco from 1814 to 1819, and 120 to Mission San Jose in 1816 and 1817. See also Chocoay.

Olpen (Costanoan language). Also known as Guemelentos, this tribe held interior hill and valley lands of the Santa Cruz Mountains, the La Honda Creek portion of the San Gregorio watershed, and the Corte de la Madera Creek portion of the San Francisquito Creek watershed. Only ten individuals from the group can be identified in the Mission San Francisco baptismal records between

1786 and 1794, although many otherwise unassignable Peninsula baptismal entries may also have been Olpens. Mission Santa Clara probably absorbed the greater part of the tribe under the general area designation "San Bernardino". At Mission Santa Clara one "San Bernardino" district person was explicitly identified as a Guemerenta (SCL-B 256) and another as an Olpen (SCL-B 2429).

Omiomi (Coast Miwok language). A tribe that held the valley of Novato Creek on the northwest side of San Pablo Bay. The town of Novato derives its name from an Indian headman of the Mexican era (Merriam 1907:355). Nobato Gayuc, one of the earliest Omiomis baptized at Mission San Francisco, on February of 1802, was probably that individual (SFR-B 2649). Very few Omiomis went down to San Francisco until 1811. In that year 142 of them were baptized. They continued to supply neophytes to Mission San Francisco through 1817.

Ompin (Bay Miwok language). A tribe centered on both sides of the channel where the Sacramento and San Joaquin rivers meet to flow into Suisun Bay, across from the present town of Pittsburg (Duran's map *in* Bennyhoff 1977:166). The group probably used the lands on both the northern and southern shore of the river. The Ompins joined Mission San Jose in 1811 and 1812, ninety one people in 1811 and seventeen people in 1812.

Pala (Costanoan language). The Paleños inhabited the mountainous area of Hall's Valley between the east side of the Santa Clara Valley and Mount Hamilton. Their lands may also have reached down into the Santa Clara Valley itself in the Evergreen vicinity. The word "Paleño" is not a native tribal designation, but a Hispanic derivation from the personal name of the group's captain, Pala. A later Mexican land grant, Rancho Cañada de Pala, was centered at Hall's Valley, well within the Paleño territory, while another, Rancho Pala, lay within the territory of the Paleños' northwestern neighbors, the Santa Ysabel group. Most of the people baptized between 1777 and 1802 at Mission Santa Clara under the designation "San Antonio" were probably from Captain Pala's tribe.

Partacsi (Costanoan language). The name of the tribe that inhabited the Saratoga gap area in the high mountains and valleys of the upper Pescadero Creek, Stevens Creek, and Saratoga Creek watersheds west of the Santa Clara Valley is unknown. The village known as Partacsi in thirty-six Mission Santa Cruz records and as Paltrastach in one Mission Santa Clara baptismal record (SCL-B 2525), seems to have been in this rugged area which today lacks a single small town. Most of the people of the area went to Mission Santa Clara along with members of neighboring tribes under the general designation "San Bernardino" between 1787 and 1801. They are probably one of four "San

Bernardino" tribal groups whose names appear in the Mission Santa Clara vital registers without specific location, Pornen (SCL-B 2424, 2432), Lamaytu (SCL-B 2339, 2340, 2343, 2422, 2423), Muyson (SCL-B 2337, 2426), or Solchequis (SCL-B 2334, 2335, 2342).

Pelnen (Costanoan language). The Pelnen tribe held the western part of the Livermore Valley in the area of the present town of Pleasanton, north no farther than the present Dublin area, and south to the canyon leading to Sunol Valley. Another small group of about six families, the Caburans, seem to have inhabited a subsidiary village of the Pelnens, since a number of nuclear families at Mission San Jose had both Pelnen and Caburan members (children of SJO-M 328, 345, 385). The two groups joined Mission San Jose between 1798 and 1805.

Petaluma (Coast Miwok language). The Petalumas held the valley of Petaluma River to the north of the Marin Peninsula. Barrett (1908:310) said that the early nineteenth century native village of Petaluma was on a low hill on the east side of Petaluma Creek, across from the present city of Petaluma. The Petalumas were baptized at four missions, San Francisco from 1814 through 1817 (53 people), San Jose from 1815 to 1818 (72 people), San Rafael from 1818 through 1822, and San Francisco Solano in 1824.

Pitac (Costanoan language). The Pitacs were the second largest of the six groups baptized at Mission Santa Cruz who were identified with the "*parage de San Juan.*" (Chitactac was the largest.) At least 76 Pitacs were baptized at Santa Cruz, mainly in 1796 and 1798. Up to 20 other people identified merely as "*San Juan*" may also have been Pitacs. Time of baptism and intermarriage patterns with Chitactacs and with Unijaimas of Mission San Juan Bautista suggest that they held the present San Martin area in the Santa Clara Valley corridor. Alternatively, they were Unijaima people from the Gilroy area at Mission Santa Cruz under a different name. (See Chitactac for another interpretation.)

Posscon—see Tatcan.

Pruristac (Costanoan language). A village in San Pedro Valley on the Pacific Coast just south of San Francisco. Numerous Mission San Francisco baptismal entries name "Pruristac, alias San Pedro." Pruristac and Timigtac, just a few miles north on the coast at the present town of Rockaway Beach, were inhabited by small group of closely interrelated families. Like the people of nearby Urebure to the east, they seem to have been independent bands rather than members of a large multi-village tribe. The Mission San Francisco outstation of San Pedro was constructed at Pruristac during the mid-1780s.

Puichon (Costanoan language). A tribe on the west shore of San Francisco Bay between lower San Francisquito Creek and lower Stevens Creek, now the areas of Menlo Park, Palo Alto, and Mountain View. Puichons went to Mission San Francisco between 1781 and 1794. Their San Francisquito Creek village of Ssipùtca was mentioned six times in the Libro de Bautismos at Mission San Francisco. Being equidistant between Mission San Francisco and Mission Santa Clara, they appeared at both missions. They went to Mission Santa Clara from 1781 to as late as 1805. There they were noted as being from the "San Bernardino" district. Some of them were said, more specifically, to be from "San Francisquito" (SCL-B 1463, SCL-D 1065).

Puscuy—see Chocoay.

Quenemsia (Plains Miwok language). This tribe held Grand Island in the delta of the Sacramento River (Bennyhoff 1977:77). They went to Mission San Jose between 1811 and 1828, the majority in 1825.

Quiroste (Costanoan language). A tribe on the Pacific Coast from Bean Hollow Creek south to Año Nuevo Creek, and inland to Butano Ridge. Occasional Quirostes appeared among the earliest San Francisco Peninsula coastal groups baptized at Mission San Francisco. Sujute, wife of an Oljon, was "from Churmutcé, farther south than the Oljons" (SFR-B 679, October 27, 1787). Uégsém, wife of a Cotegen, was from "the family of the Quirogtes of the village of Mitine to the west of Chipletac" (SFR-B 711, October 19, 1788). A few of them went to Mission Santa Cruz under the designation "San Rafael, alias Mutenne." Most went to Mission Santa Clara from the "San Bernardino" district.

Ritocsi (Costanoan language). The upper drainage of the Guadalupe River and central portion of Coyote Creek in the Santa Clara Valley, from downtown San Jose south to New Almaden, was held by an unnamed tribe. The village designated "San Juan Bautista" in the Mission Santa Clara vital records was probably the northernmost village of the tribe. Only six married couples were baptized from San Juan Bautista village, all between 1780 and 1802. That is not enough couples to represent an entire tribe, and suggests that people from the "Santa Teresa Hills" tribe's other villages were labeled "San Carlos" (literally "southerners") at Mission Santa Clara. The name Ritocsi is applied to this tribe with great hesitation. At Mission Santa Cruz between 1793 and 1801 eight people were baptized from a fragmentary group called "San Jose, alias Ritocsi". Their ties were to groups between Santa Cruz and San Jose, and I suggest that they were from Mission Santa Clara's "San Juan Bautista" group. Thus, on a very weak basis, I have assigned the name Ritocsi to the area. Little more can be said about the people of this area until further in-depth family reconstitution analysis is done on the San Carlos district people at Mission Santa Clara.

Saclan (Bay Miwok language). The Saclans lived in the small inland valleys in the East Bay hills, to the east of present day Oakland. The earliest mention of the tribe is found in the Libro de Bautismos of Mission San Francisco in December of 1794, when baptisms were performed on seventeen juveniles, "Chaclanes from the other shore in front of the mission" (SFR-B 1531). Their parents and scores of other Saclans were baptized in the next few weeks. As Erwin Gudde (1969) has pointed out, the name of the Mexican-period land grant of Rancho Acalanes at the present town of Lafayette was derived from Sacalanes (see also Martinez [1855]). In the section about the Jalquin tribe I discuss the possibility that the Saclans and Jalquins were one people. Four men identified as Saclans during their hearings in August 1797 were baptized at Mission San Francisco as Jalquins in 1802. It is more likely that the Spanish at Mission San Francisco and the San Francisco Presidio during the 1790s lumped together all Bay Miwok speakers—the first Saclans, their Jalquin relatives baptized at the same time, and even some Chupcans and Tatcans baptized in the same period—under the name Saclan.

"Santa Ysabel" (Costanoan language). Extrapolation from better documented areas suggests that one tribe held both the eastern Santa Clara Valley and part of the upper Calaveras Creek drainage in the hills to the east, between the Taunans on the north and the *Paleños* on the south. The central part of their area was on Penitencia Creek where Alum Rock Park is today. Coyote Creek flows northward through the very western part of that area. The Mission Santa Clara district name Santa Ysabel initially referred to a single large village on that section of Coyote Creek, a village alternatively known to the Spaniards as "the village of Coyote" (SCL-B 3335, 3400, 3573, 3741, 3762, 4360). Two specific village names were mentioned in the Mission Santa Clara registers, Ottasimin (SCL-B 1608) and Socotach (SCL-B 3290). The Santa Ysabel people were absorbed into Mission Santa Clara over a very long period of time, from 1777 to 1808.

Sayanta (Costanoan language). This group, which went to Mission Santa Cruz between 1791 and 1795, gave its name to the present day Zayante Creek and Zayante village in the mountains between Santa Cruz and the Santa Clara Valley. The tribe held the Scotts Valley area and the Glenwood and Laural areas to the north and east, all in ocean-facing watersheds. The area is part of the Mexican land grant *Arrollo de Sayante* (Gudde 1969:373). Only 69 Sayanta people were baptized at Mission Santa Cruz. They were heavily intermarried with the Chaloctac group around Loma Prieta to the east, much more so than was typical for neighboring groups.

Segloque (Coast Miwok language). Seqloque is one of numerous spellings for a small village somewhere in the Tomales Bay area. The actual tribal name of the people on Tomales Bay, if they were even organized as a single tribe, is not known. Slaymaker (1982:333-340) included three tribe-sized areas, Tamal, Olema, and Segloque, as a single Tamales tribal area. But he also wrote, "The large size of the Tamales tribelet may indicate the former cohesion of three separate tribelets into one" (Slaymaker 1982:340). On the basis of an initial analysis of mission records and historical documents, he suggested that the following towns formed part of the "Segloque" constellation at the mouth of Tomales Bay: Copoloyomi, Cotomkowi, Echacumis, Juchi, Ocolom, Pattai, and Yoittaca. People from those villages moved to Mission San Rafael between 1817 and 1824.

Seunen (Costanoan language). A tribe that held a fairly small territory at the northwest side of the Livermore Valley in the hills east of San Francisco Bay. The main Seunen village may have been at the present town of San Ramon, or alternatively, farther south at the present town of Dublin. Most of the Seunens went to Mission San Jose between 1801 and 1804, although four of them went to Mission San Francisco in 1801 and 1802 as part of a large Jalquin group.

Siplichiquin—see Urebure.

Somontac (Costanoan language). Somontac has been tentatively assigned to the present Los Gatos region of the Santa Clara Valley. This is the single most speculative location assigned in this study. The name Somontac appears only in the Mission Santa Cruz records, where "*Somontac, alias Santa Clara*" people appeared from 1793 to 1801. The Los Gatos area seems to be too far south to have belonged to the Tamien group of the central Santa Clara Valley, and beyond the projected areas of other surrounding groups as well. Since very few Somontac people went to Mission Santa Cruz, and their alias name "*Santa Clara*" suggests that they were from the direction of that mission, I have placed them in the Los Gatos area. This is clearly pure speculation. Marriages and time of baptism suggest, alternatively, that Somontac was a Matalan village.

Sonomas—see Chocoime.

Souyen (Costanoan language). A tribe that held the north side of the marsh that once existed in the western Livermore Valley as well as the area northward from there up the Tassajara Creek drainage into the southern foothills of Mount Diablo. They are located only indirectly, but with confidence, on the

Appendix 1. Tribal Groups 255

basis of time of baptism and intermarriage patterns. They joined Mission San Jose from 1797 through 1805.

Ssalson (Costanoan language). The Ssalsons lived in at least three main villages along San Mateo Creek, near the west shore of San Francisco Bay and in the San Andreas Valley (see Brown 1973:9-12). The villages of Altagmu, Aleitac, and Uturbe were said to be along branches of the Arroyo of San Matheo in numerous baptismal entries (SFR-B 173, 175, 176, 177, 213). Tribe members were baptized at Mission San Francisco from 1780 through 1793.

Ssaoam (Costanoan language). The Ssaoam tribe lived in the dry hills and tiny valleys around Brushy Peak and Altamont Pass, hill lands which separated the Livermore Valley from the San Joaquin Valley. They went to Mission San Jose from 1802 through 1805, eighty-seven between October of 1804 and February of 1805. Only one Ssaoam went to Mission San Francisco, a man married into a large group of Bay Miwok-speaking Tatcans (SFR-B 2989). The Yuliens, a small group of nineteen people who went to Mission San Jose from 1803 to 1808, seem to have been a subgroup or alias name of the Ssaoams. Four of six young Yuliens baptized in February of 1804 had parents baptized a year later and identified as Ssaoams (SJO-B 1094, 1095, 1101, 1102), while two had parents baptized just six months later and identified as Yuliens (SJO-B 1095, 1096). The latter two had grandparents who were Ssaoams (SJO-B 903, 1263, 1279).

Suisun (Patwin language). The Suisuns lived on the north shore of Suisun Bay (Gudde 1969:324). Gabriel Moraga attacked their villages in May of 1810 (Chapter 9). His diary gives no details beyond the fact that the villages were north of Carquinez Strait. The route of Father Abella, who visited them in 1811, indicates a location in the present Fairfield area on the north side of Suisun Bay (Cook 1960:265). Suisuns were baptized at San Francisco between 1810 and 1816 (326 people). Francisco Solano, the Mexican-era associate of Mariano Guadalupe Vallejo, was a Suisun baptized at Mission San Francisco in July of 1810 at age 10 (SFR-B 4024).

Tamal (Coast Miwok language): Over 170 neophytes baptized at Mission San Francisco between 1802 and 1810 were identified as Tamals. The word seems to have been used by some priests to indicate a tribe, by other priests as a general term for "northerners." Twentieth century Indian people of the Marin Peninsula remembered a village called Etcha-tamal at Nicasio (Dietz [1976]). Most of the Tamal people who were baptized at Mission San Francisco in the period from 1802 to 1803, and who came in to San Francisco with Habastos and Olemas, were probably from that area. However, some people baptized later as Olema-Tamals, and other Tamals baptized in 1807-1809, may have come from areas farther north, on the east side of Tomales Bay.

Tamcan (Northern Valley Yokuts language). The Tamcan tribe is placed with confidence on the Old River branch of the San Joaquin River east of the present town of Byron, on the basis of time of baptism, marriage ties, and location on Duran's *Plano Topográfico* of 1824 (Bennyhoff 1977:166). They sent 138 people to Mission San Jose between 1806 and 1824, the majority in 1811. They are certainly the same people as the Tammukamnes of Alphonse Pinart ([1894] 1955:134).

Tamien (Costanoan language). I tentatively propose that the Tamien tribe held the central Santa Clara Valley along the Guadalupe River from Agnews to the present area of downtown San Jose, and the flat lands westward from the Guadalupe to the present town of Cupertino on upper Stevens Creek (cf. C. King 1978). Fathers Murguía and Peña of Mission Santa Clara noted in the title page of their Libro de Bautismos, and again in a letter of 1777, that the mission was built in an area known as Tamien. The Tamien boundaries with neighboring groups are not at all clear from the information in the Mission Santa Clara vital records.

Three of the twelve villages and villages/regions designated with Spanish names in the Santa Clara Mission vital registers probably made up the Tamien tribe: Our Mother Santa Clara, Our Patron San Francisco, and San Jose Cupertino. Those towns were empty by the end of 1795.

Tatcan (Bay Miwok language). The Tatcans held the San Ramon Creek in the central East Bay hills, just west of Mount Diablo. Their central village area may have been at the present town of Danville, or alternatively, at the present town of Walnut Creek. The first large group went to Mission San Francisco in the first months of 1804. The first entry for the group reads, "*Ranchería llamado Tatcan y Poscon*" (SFR-B 2887). At Mission San Jose the name Tatcan never appeared, but three Posscons went to Mission San Jose in 1808: a woman, her three children and her Seunen husband (SJO-B 1599, 1590, 1591, 1601). Another Posscon woman went to Mission San Jose in 1811 with her Chupcan husband (SJO-B 1812, 1811) as part of a large group.

Tauquimne (Northern Valley Yokuts language). Some 77 Tauquimne people were baptized at Mission San Jose between 1815 and 1825. Their location on Duran's *Plano Topográfico* of 1824, their marriage ties, and an historical diary suggest that they held the eastern margin of the Sacramento-San Joaquin delta at the mouth of Bear Creek, just north of present-day Stockton (Bennyhoff 1977:132; Cook 1960:275).

Taunan (Costanoan language). The Taunan tribe held mountainous reaches of Alameda Creek and Arroyo del Valle south of the Livermore Valley, probably as far south as the present Alameda-Contra Costa county line. An unknown number of Taunans went to Mission Santa Clara during the 1790s and early 1800s under the Santa Agueda district designation. Most of the group went to Mission San Jose from 1797 to 1803 under the designation "Este" ("easterners"). With the arrival of new missionaries to Mission San Jose, they began to appear in its baptismal book under their tribe name. They continued to come in to Mission San Jose through the year 1805. Four Taunans married at the Mission San Jose church to "Santa Agueda" people who had moved back north from Mission Santa Clara (SJO-M 14, 30, 82, 311). The clumping of tribes under the designations "Santa Agueda" and "Santa Ysabel" at Mission Santa Clara masks recognition of the Taunans who might have married and continued to live at Mission Santa Clara.

Tayssen (Costanoan language). The people identified by the Santa Clara missionaries as Tayssens comprised a very large group (274 people) that seems to have inhabited a large area of the central and eastern Coast Ranges east and southeast of the Santa Clara Valley. The Tayssens were baptized at Mission Santa Clara between 1803 and 1811, most of them in 1805 and 1806. A small number called Sumus, baptized at Mission Santa Cruz in 1806 and 1807, cross-tie to the Tayssens at Mission Santa Clara (SCR-B 1287, father SCL-B 5236; SCR-B 1302, father SCL-B 4746). The name Tayssen is probably a cover term used by the missionaries for all people from the Crow Creek, Orestimba Creek, and Garzas Creek drainages. Whether they were a cluster of two or three tribes, or a loose network of nomadic bands, is not known.

Tolena (Patwin language). The Tolenas lived on the very northern edge of the San Francisco Bay Area, in Green Valley just north of the Suisun Plain. The first of them to go to a mission, a small group of nine people, went down to Mission San Francisco with some Suisuns in 1812, at which time they were called Caguapattos and were said to speak the "lengua de Napa" (SFR-B 4439). A total of 138 people went to Mission San Jose from 1815 until 1820 under the name Tolena. Another 19 were baptized at Mission San Jose.

Tomoi (Costanoan language). This tribe held lands somewhere in the general vicinity of Pacheco Pass; it is unclear, however, exactly where. They may have been centered to the east of the pass in the valley of San Luis Creek (presently San Luis Reservoir). Alternatively, they may have held the upper reaches of the North Fork of Pacheco Creek and Mississippi Creek, north of Burra Peak, east to Pacheco Pass, but not down into the San Luis Valley. Tomoi people moved to Mission Santa Cruz between 1803 and 1807, although their homeland seems to have been much closer to Mission San Juan Bautista than to Mission Santa Cruz. A few Tomoi people also went to Mission Santa Clara, during the 1805-1809 period, under the "San Carlos" district designation. Tomoi people at Mission Santa Cruz were in mixed groups with small numbers from Acastaca (four people), Sitectac (seven people), and Uculi (two people). Two of the seven Sitectac were identified as Tomoi in later death and census records (SCR-B 1080, 1087), as was one of the Acastaca people (SCR-B 1114). This suggests that Acastaca and Sitectac were specific village sites within the Tomoi tribal area.

Tuibun (Costanoan language). The Tuibun tribe seem to have been located at the mouth of Alameda Creek and in the Coyote Hills area on the eastern shore of San Francisco Bay. Only twenty people from the group were identified in baptismal registers, all at Mission San Jose in 1803 and 1804. Those twenty people were relatives of neophytes baptized between 1797 and 1803 under the general designations of "Alameda" and "Estero." They also had some relatives who had been baptized at Mission Santa Clara during the 1780s and 1790s under the designation "Santa Agueda".

Ululato (Patwin language). The Ululatos lived in the present Vacaville area in the western Sacramento Valley. Ulatis Creek, which runs eastward from the hills through Vacaville and thence onto the plains, takes its name from these people, who were visited by Luís Argüello on October 23, 1821 (Argüello [1821] 1992:22). A total of 280 Ululato people were baptized at Mission San Francisco between 1815 and 1822, 215 in 1821 alone. Another 67 Ululatos were baptized at Mission San Francisco Solano between 1824 and 1833.

Unisumne (Plains Miwok language). Also called Junizumne, this group lived in the present Walnut Grove area in the Sacramento-Mokelumne River delta (Bennyhoff 1977:72-73). They were attacked by Spanish soldiers in 1813 for harboring runaway Christians (Cook 1960:265, 275, 290). They sent at least 119 people for baptism to Mission San Jose between 1813 and 1836.

Unijaima (Costanoan language). A tribe of the Gilroy and Carnadero areas, on the west side of the San Felipe sink. The Unijaimas (also spelled Uñijaimas) supplied 135 converts to Mission San Juan Bautista between 1797 and 1808; prior to that time they had sent two people south to Mission San Carlos Borromeo. Four explicitly identified Unijaima converts went to Mission Santa Cruz between 1798 and 1802, and perhaps scores more went to Mission Santa Cruz between 1796 and 1798 under the name Pitac (see Pitac).

Urebure (Costanoan language). The people of the San Bruno Creek area just south San Bruno Mountain on the San Francisco Peninsula seem to have been a single village group. The captain of this small group (43 people baptized) was said to be from "Urebure and other places" at baptism, while he was called "Captain of San Bruno" at his son's baptism (SFR-B 35, 40). Another member of the group was "born at San Bruno, the place called by the natives Siplichiquin" (SFR-B 34). The group was entirely absorbed into the Mission San Francisco community by the end of 1785. The Mexican land grant of Buriburi, patented in the year 1826, included lands from the present city of Millbrae north to the present city of South San Francisco.

Uypi (Costanoan language). The Uypi people held the mouth of the San Lorenzo River, the site of the present city of Santa Cruz. Two children of their captain, Suquel, were baptized at Mission Santa Clara in 1791 under the designation "San Carlos" (SCL-B 1894, 1907). Suquel and his wife were the second and third people baptized at Mission Santa Cruz (SCR-B 2, 3). All in all, 103 Uypi people were baptized at Mission Santa Cruz between 1791 and 1795. They were the first group to go in large numbers to Mission Santa Cruz for baptism and the first group completely absorbed into that mission population. Uypi people were called "Soquel" people in post-1810 Mission Santa Cruz death records and padrons. The present town of Soquel, just east of Santa Cruz, certainly derives its name from that of captain Suquel (the Spanish rendering of this man's name, which was also spelled Sugert and Suquer in various Spanish manuscripts).

Volvon (Bay Miwok language). The Volvons held the peak of Mount Diablo and the rugged lands to the east of the peak. Their villages were along the Marsh Creek drainage on the eastern side of that mountain. Some of the Mission San Jose priests referred to them as the Zuicuns. Forty-four Volvons were baptized at Mission San Jose in the spring of 1805, although one faction seems to have fled in the spring of 1805 after their children were baptized. Many of the parents of those children were sent to Mission San Francisco in August of 1805 (SFR-B 3153, 3154). Other parents were among the last large group of Volvon converts at Mission San Francisco, in the spring of 1806 (SFR-B 3327, 3334). Father Abella's 1811 diary referred to Mount Diablo as the "*Cerro Alto de los Bolbones*," the name by which it was known until the early 1840s (Gudde 1969:89). The variant spelling "Bolbon" was included in the title of a Mexican-period land grant, Rancho Nueces y Bolbones (Walnut trees and Bolbones [mountain or Indians]). The Volvons who went to Mission San Francisco and Mission San Jose from 1803 to 1806 should not be confused with the people labeled Bolbon in the death registers of Mission Santa Clara. The latter group have a number of family ties to the Cholvons of the Tracy area in the San Joaquin Valley, and absolutely no family ties to the Volvons of the Mount Diablo area.

Yelamu (Costanoan language). Yelamu is a tentative cover term for the tribe that held the northern tip of the San Francisco Peninsula. Father Cambon baptized four people from the *parage* or "locality" of Yelamu at San Francisco between 1777 and 1779 (SFR-B 15, 16, 21, 58). During the same years Father Palóu baptized two people from "Yalamu" and Father Santamaría baptized one person from the "*ranchería de Yalamú*" (SFR-B 26, 43; 52). Those Yelamu people had siblings and parents from the villages of Chutchui, Sitlintac, Amuctac, and Petlenuc, all within the later area of the city of San Francisco. The structure of the word is similar to that of "Yacamui," the generic directional term used in the early San Francisco registers for people from the east side of San Francisco Bay. Yelamu may have been a nearby village to Mission San Francisco in some specific direction. I am guessing, however, that it referred to the people of the geographic region at the head of the San Francisco Peninsula.

Sitlintac and Chutchui, only a mile or two apart in the valley of Mission Creek, seem to have been Yelamu sites used at different times of the year by one band of families. Another Yelamu band seems to have used the village sites of Amuctac and Tubsinte in the Visitation Valley area in the same way. Petlenuc, perhaps near the site of the Spanish presidio compound, seems to have been a third, small band (Milliken [1983]). The people from these villages joined Mission San Francisco from 1777 until 1787. Most of the teenagers joined in 1777 and 1778, while most older people were baptized from 1784 to 1787. Only twenty-six men and thirty-five women over the age of twenty were ever baptized. They had a number of marriage ties to the Huchiuns across San Francisco Bay to the east and with Pruristac village to the southwest.

Fathers Palóu and Cambón called the San Francisco people "Aguazios" in one report. "They [the Ssalsons] have married among those of this place, who are called Aguazios (which translates as 'Northerners')" (Palóu and Cambon [1783]). The words Habasto and Aguasto, applied by the missionaries to tribes on San Pablo Bay, probably also meant northerner. In fact, every tribe in the northern Costanoan-speaking area could have been called "Aguasto" by its southern neighbors.

Yoletamal (Coast Miwok language). The people of the Bodega Bay area have been called Yoletamal by Charles Slaymaker (1982:235-247). Their main settlements were at Bodega Bay, but they also had camps or settlements on Salmon Creek to the north and Estero Americano to the south. A few of them seem to have gone to Mission San Francisco under the vague rubric of "*de la Costa*" between 1808 and 1817. A Russian settlement was founded at Bodega Bay in 1812 (Dmytryshyn et al. 1989:207). Mission San Rafael began operation on the Marin Peninsula in December of 1817, after which time some Yoletamal people went to that mission under the village names Calupetamal, Geluatamal, and Yoletamal. These place names occur in the San Rafael Book of Baptisms through the year 1822.

    Yrgin (Costanoan and Bay Miwok languages). The Yrgins, who went to Mission San Jose, seem to have been the same group as the Jalquins, who went to Mission San Francisco. They held the bay shore in the present Hayward and Castro Valley areas, the watershed of San Lorenzo Creek. They went to Mission San Jose from 1799 to 1805. The Jalquins went to Mission San Francisco between 1801 and 1804 (see Jalquin in this appendix). Yrgins baptized before February, 1803 at Mission San Jose can be identified as such only by family reconstitution, because they were absorbed during the time period that Mission San Jose priests did not provide tribal labels. Many people who were labeled Yrgin at Mission San Jose after January 1803, the date that the missionaries began noting tribal names, had children and other relatives who had joined the mission as "Redwoods" people prior to that time (SJO-B 33, 34, 138, 312-314, 633-635).

    Yulien—see Ssaoam.

    Zuicun—see Volvon.

Appendix 2

Yearly Mission Population Totals
and
Crude Death Rates

The three tables in this appendix (Tables 5, 6, and 7) present the yearly totals for new neophyte baptisms, mission born baptisms, deaths, crude death rates, and year-end populations at Missions San Francisco, San Jose, and Santa Clara. The tables are based upon direct counts from the computerized database of all people baptized through December 31 of a given year, minus all in that group that were reported as dead by the same date.

Yearly totals for baptisms and deaths at the Bay Area missions have been published by Zepherin Engelhardt (1912), Jacob Bowman (1958), and Robert Jackson (1983,1984,1987). Their lists were based on aggregative statistics, year end mission population totals as reported by missionaries in their reports to Mexico. Such aggregative counts do not provide information on sectors of the populations, age and sex-defined subgroups, new recruits, or mission births. The family reconstitution database does allow such detailed analysis, some of which is reported in Tables 5, 6, and 7.

The counts presented in the following tables are at odds with those published by Engelhardt (1912), Bowman (1958) and Jackson (1983,1984) for some years. Many discrepancies occur between my year-end population figures, derived by linking individual baptism and death records, and those of the missionary annual reports. Although the priests who provided the annual report year-end counts were on the ground at the time, those counts are not necessarily always more accurate than mine.

I am aware of seven sources for the discrepancies between my year-end counts and those reported by the missionaries on the spot. Three of the sources are minor and self correcting over the years, while the other four could work

Causes Of Self-Correcting Discrepancies

(1) Bowman or the other researchers may have misread some numbers on Spanish period texts. Such errors would not carry over from year to year.

(2) A missionary may have made a minor counting error in a given year, then corrected it in a subsequent year.

(3) The death registers often include some year-end entries for people whose deaths as runaways had just recently been discovered, but who had died in earlier years. For instance, Father Martín Landaeta listed eighteen deaths in the *Libro de Difuntos* of Mission San Francisco on April 1, 1797, along with the statement "it is known that during the years '95, '96, and '97 the following Christians were killed on the other shore" (SFR-D 1056-1073). Other information shows that seven of those people (SFR-D 1056-1062) died on April 29, 1795. In my counts those seven individuals are included in the San Francisco death count for 1795, and the others randomly assigned dates of death over the years in question.

Causes Of Non-Correcting Discrepancies

(4) I treated all children born of local Indian women as part of the Mission Indian community, whether the father was a local Indian man or a Mexican Indian man. I am not certain whether all of the missionaries followed that practice or not.

(5) Some of the priests may have done direct counts every year, but others may have worked from their register figures and previous reports. If they made a mistake one year, they may have carried it over through time.

(6) According to Bowman (1958:140) the annual report year-end figures "include the neophytes of other missions sojourning at the missions in question and exclude the missions' own neophytes at or on their way to other establishments". However, I do not believe that he was correct in at least one significant case. A large number of people moved from Mission Santa Clara up to Mission San Jose at its founding in 1798, at least fifty and as many as seventy. They appear as parents in Mission San Jose baptisms, as spouses in Mission San Jose marriages, and their deaths are recorded in both the Mission San Jose and Mission Santa Clara death records. Yet the year-end report counts for Missions

Santa Clara and San Jose for the years 1798 through 1805 match my own year-end totals, which assume no re-aggregation.

(7) During especially stressful times some missionaries seem to have forgotten to record every death that occurred, so that the computer database indicates some people as alive who were actually dead at the time. The discrepancies between year-end reports and computer counts for Mission San Francisco in 1798, and Mission Santa Clara during the measles epidemic of 1806, probably result from such failures by the missionaries to record some deaths.

All in all, the year-end population totals produced from computer database counts of individuals are very close to the previously published missionary annual report totals. Unrecorded deaths (problem category seven) are probably the largest source of the discrepancies between my computer-generated year-end population counts and the missionaries' annual year-end reports. However, all of the other suggested sources of discrepancy discussed above occurred at one point or another over time.

Only two discrepancies between the computer generated counts and the year-end reports are significant, Mission San Francisco in 1798 and Mission Santa Clara in 1806. In the Mission San Francisco case, the annual reports from 1798 forward indicate that between fourteen and twenty more persons died there in 1798 than were individually reported. In the same way, the Mission Santa Clara annual reports suggest that some seventy persons died at that mission in 1806 who were not listed in its death register.

Table 5. Mission San Francisco Yearly Tribal Converts, Mission Births, Deaths, Crude Death Rates and Year-end Indian Populations through 1810.

Year	Tribal Converts	Mission Births	Deaths	Mid-year Pop.	Crude[a] Death Rate	Year-end Pop.	Annl.[b] Report
77	32	0	1	15.5	60	31	( )
78	42	2	2	52.0	40	73	( )
79	45	2	7	93.0	80	113	( )
1780	49	6	9	136.0	70	159	( )
81	33	3	19	167.5	110	176	( )
82	39	6	24	186.5	130	197	-9
83	37	1	14	209.0	70	221	-6
84	51	15	24	242.0	100	263	-3
1785	22	12	46	257.0	180	251	-1
86	120	10	26	303.0	90	355	-1
87	89	19	38	390.0	100	425	+1
88	10	19	31	424.0	70	423	+3
89	26	16	38	425.0	90	427	+2
1790	113	21	37	475.5	80	524	+1
91	104	18	52	559.0	90	594	-4
92	110	18	99	608.5	160	623	-1
93	166	25	101	668.0	150	713	-2
94	302	26	123	815.5	150	918	-5
1795	142	24	224	889.0	250	860	+12
96	3	10	101	816.0	120	772	+18
97	2	27	99	737.0	130	702	+ 8
98	10	28	81	680.5	120	659	-14
99	1	23	64	639.0	100	619	-16
1800	74	29	71	635.0	110	651	-16
01	179	38	68	725.0	90	800	-22
02	149	39	133	827.5	160	855	-41
03	305	30	115	965.0	120	1075	-24
04	162	38	150	1100.0	140	1125	-22
1805	156	46	161	1145.0	140	1166	( )
06	72	22	360	1033.0	350	900	-14
07	33	27	118	871.0	140	842	-16
08	152	32	104	882.0	120	922	-16
09	201	23	117	975.5	120	1029	-19
1810	160	37	150	1052.5	140	1076	-19

[a] Crude death rates per thousand have been rounded off. Note that they can exceed 1000 per 1000, as deaths can exceed the mid-year population.
[b] Divergence of year-end missionary annual report counts (Bowman 1958)   ( ) = no data

Appendix 2. Mission Population

Table 6. Mission Santa Clara Yearly Tribal Converts, Mission Births, Deaths, Crude Death Rates and Year-end Indian Populations through 1810.

Year	Tribal Converts	Mission Births	Deaths	Mid-year Pop.	Crude[a] Death Rate	Year-end Pop.	Ann.[b] Report
77	67	0	26	20.5	1270	41	0
78	50	1	2	65.5	30	90	+1
79	22	1	3	100.0	30	110	+1
1780	85	2	5	151.0	30	192	0
81	56	12	14	219.0	60	246	( )
82	79	14	35	275.0	130	304	( )
83	165	16	39	375.0	100	446	-112
84	63	18	62	455.5	140	465	+1
1785	102	13	101	472.0	210	479	-4
86	144	12	73	520.5	140	562	-5
87	138	9	61	605.0	100	648	-1
88	109	13	98	660.0	150	672	0
89	227	14	130	727.5	180	783	+4
1790	304	19	196	846.5	230	910	0
91	146	21	113	937.0	120	964	-7
92	182	23	159	987.0	160	1010	-9
93	165	28	138	1037.5	130	1065	
94	475	25	136	1247.0	110	1429	11
1795	242	50	176	1487.0	120	1545	-4
96	73	51	240	1487.0	160	1429	-5
97	77	41	182	1397.0	130	1365	-5
98	146	47	170	1376.5	120	1388	-6
99	113	43	194	1369.0	140	1350	-7
1800	92	41	161	1336.0	120	1322	-4
01	89	45	137	1320.5	100	1319	-3
02	185	39	248	1307.0	190	1295	-4
03	92	34	144	1286.0	110	1277	-6
04	67	34	126	1264.5	100	1252	-12
1805	289	47	109	1365.5	80	1479	( )
06	181	47	231(+70)[c]	1477.5	160(210)[c]	1476	-70
07	94	43	142	1473.5	100	1471	-70
08	93	45	132	1474.0	90	1477	-67
09	57	32	102	1470.5	70	1464	-66
1810	63	22	147	1433.0	100	1402	-70

[a] Crude death rates per thousand have been rounded off. Note that they can exceed 1000 per 1000, as deaths can exceed the mid-year population.
[b] Divergence of year-end missionary annual report counts (Bowman 1958). ( ) = no data
[c] Crude death rate in brackets assumes another seventy deaths in 1806.

Table 7. Mission San Jose Yearly Tribal Converts, Mission Births, Deaths, Crude Death Rates and Year-end Indian Populations through 1810.

Year	Tribal Converts	Mission Births	Deaths	Mid-year Pop.	Crude[a] Death Rate	Year-end Pop.	Ann.[b] Report
97	33	0	0	16.5	0	33	0
98	122	8	8	94.0	90	155	-1
99	57	9	33	171.5	190	188	+1
1800	119	16	46	232.5	200	277	0
01	221	23	63	367.5	170	458	+2
02	233	15	91	536.5	170	615	+7
03	181	36	109	669.0	160	723	+6
04	212	18	179	748.5	240	774	+5
1805	171	32	166	792.5	210	811	( )
06	26	14	233	714.5	330	618	+44
07	11	27	67	603.5	110	589	+48
08	15	11	70	567.0	120	545	-1
09	78	10	62	558.0	110	571	0
1810	15	16	58	557.5	100	544	+1

[a] Crude death rates per thousand have been rounded off. Note that they can exceed 1000 per 1000, as deaths can exceed the mid-year population.

[b] This column indicates how much higher or lower year-end missionary annual report counts were, as published by Bowman (1958). Brackets ( ) indicate that the year-end report was not available to Bowman.

Appendix 3

Yearly Baptisms by Tribal Group

Counts of year baptisms for San Francisco Bay Area tribal groups are presented in Tables 8-12 in this appendix. The summary counts of baptisms for specific tribes are often larger than those that have been published by C. Hart Merriam (1955,1968,1970). Merriam's village and tribe counts severely under-represent the number of people baptized from most groups. The problem lay in the fact that his counts were based on the number of times a locational name appeared in the records. Many missionary scribes entered the tribal name of a group of new neophytes from a specific place only in the first baptismal register entry of the day, with a comment such as "*todos de la rancheria de Omiomi*." Some other priests did not provide homeland location information in any of their baptismal entries.

I have verified aggregate tribal populations represented in mission baptisms through family reconstitution, using cross-checking techniques from tribal information in marriage or death record, sometimes relying on the tribal affiliation of siblings, parents or children of a problem ego. The updated counts of tribal baptisms are presented in the following tables for four geographic regions, the San Francisco Peninsula (Table 8), Marin Peninsula (Table 9), Carquinez Strait and northern East Bay Area (Table 10), and southern East Bay Area (Table 11).

Baptismal counts are not available for tribal groups near Mission Santa Clara, as the missionary priests at that mission ignored tribal affiliations in their baptism records until the 1805-1810 period. Table 12 indicates the yearly baptisms at Mission Santa Clara from ten districts defined by the missionaries. Six of those Mission Santa Clara districts were almost certainly specific villages (Santa Clara, San Francisco Our Patron Saint, San Jose Cupertino, San Juan Bautista, San Francisco Solano, and Santa Ysabel). Four other district names may have indicated specific villages during the 1770s and 1780s, but came to represent cardinal directions after the 1780s (San Bernardino = west, Santa Agueda = north, San Carlos = south, and San Antonio = east).

Table 8. Yearly Baptisms of San Francisco Peninsula Tribes at Mission San Francisco between 1777 and 1800.

Year	Unident. Peninsula	Yelamu	Urebure	Pruristac	Ssalson	Chiguan	Lamchin	Cotegen	Puichon[a]	Oljon[a]	Olpen[a]	Quiroste[b]
77		26	5				1					
78	2	35	2		1							
79		15	5	7	5	1	7					
1780	3	8	7	2	17							
81	2	2	2	5	4		7		6			
82	1	7	12	2	7		3	1	1			
83		5	3	12	7	5						
84	1	16	5	5	6	7	4	1				
1785		1	2	3	5	3	2		2			
86		8		7	45	10	7	10	1	10	1	
87		2			7	10	5	5	10	23	3	3
88					2		1	1	2	1	1	1
89	1				1		6	2	2	9		
1790	1				20	1	51	1	30		2	
91	10				3	4	6	19	3	19		25
92	5				3		18		5	33	2	8
93	55[c]				8		19	2	24	10		42
94	9				1		2		2	1	1	
1795												
96												
97												
98												
99												
1800	1											
Total	91	125	43	43	142	41	139	42	88	106	10	79

[a] In addition to these people, a significant but unknown number of San Bernardino district people at Mission Santa Clara were Puichons, Oljons, Olpnes, and Quirostes.

[b] Included in this Quiroste column for years 1790, 1791, and 1793 are some people identified only as "from the coast" and some Accsagis people.

[c] These fifty-five people were baptized with identifiable Ssalsons, Lamchins, and Puichons.

Appendix 3. Yearly Baptisms By Tribe

Table 9. Yearly Baptisms of Marin Peninsula Tribes at Mission San Francisco between 1777 and 1810.

Year	Unident.[a] Marin	Huimen	Habasto Guaulen	Tamal	Olema[b]	Olemaloque Omiomi[c]	Olemopas[d]	Costa[e]	Total
77									
78									
79									
1780									
81									
82									
83		2							2
84	3								3
1785									
86		7							7
87		5	1						6
88									
89		1							1
1790		5							5
91	1	2							3
92		1							1
93									
94		16	1						17
1795	12	29		1					42
96		1							1
97									
98	2	1							3
99									
1800		6	14	36					56
01	3	47	25	6	1				82
02	7	11	23	12	30	3	2		88
03	26	16	39	62	26	57	8		234
04		3			1				4
1805			7	4	37		1	4	1	54
06	3	4			9	3	2		1	22
07						26	7		33
08	5		2	2	91	7	19	11	2	139
09	2			2	13	5		16	27	65
1810	10			5	3	4	22	6	14	64
Total	74	157	112	130	173	143	53	41	4	45	932

[a] Unidentified Marin Peninsula people include individuals labeled *rumbo de los Huimenes* and people in groups identified as mixes of specific Marin tribes but lacking tribal labels on individuals.
[b] Includes 26 Libantone people baptized in 1807.
[c] Another 230 Omiomi people were baptized over 1811-1817.
[d] Olemopas may be an alias for "Olompali," a group that migrated to the missions in the mid-1810s.
[e] Another 90 *Costa* people were baptized in 1811-1817, as well as 25 *Punta del Reyes* and *Estero de S. Francisco* people in 1816-1817.

Table 10. Yearly Baptisms of the Carquinez Strait and Northernmost East Bay Area Tribes at Mission San Francisco and Mission San Jose between 1777 and 1810.

Year	General East Bay FR	Huchiun[a] FR	Hu.-Ag.[b] FR	Saclan FR JO	Jalquin FR	Tatcan[c] FR JO	Volvon[d] FR JO	Carquin FR	Chupcan[e] FR JO	Suisun[f] FR
77										
78										
79	1									
1780	8	1								
81	4									
82	4									
83	1									
84	3									
1785	1									
86	9	1								
87	1	10						1		
88			1							
89		2								
1790										
91	7	5								
92	2	33								
93		1								
94	24	165		65		1				
1795	5	5		78		8		3	2	
96		2								
97		2								
98				8						
99				1 2						
1800		14		3						
01		65		2	26					
02		5		1	46	3		4		
03		44	18		5	1	2			
04		5		1		127	2 6	7	12 1	
1805		22	43	5		5	20 44	1	5	
06		2				12	31		1	
07						2	4			
08			3	1		2	1	1		
09			23	3				99	7	
1810			7	1				33	30	19
Total	70	384	95	171	77	161	110	151	58	19

[a] Some of these people are probably Huchiun-Aguastos, especially after 1802.
[b] Huchiun-Aguasto.
[c] Includes Posscons at Mission San Jose in 1807 (2) and 1808 (2).
[d] Includes Zuicuns at Mission San Jose in 1803 (1), 1804 (6), 1807 (4), and 1808 (1).
[e] Includes Yacomusmo. Another 88 Chupcans were baptized at the missions in 1811.
[f] Another 284 Suisuns were baptized at Mission San Francisco through 1821.

Appendix 3. Yearly Baptisms By Tribe 273

Table 11. Yearly Baptisms of the Southernmost East Bay Area Tribes at Missions San Francisco and San Jose between 1795 and 1810.

Year	East[a] Bay JO	Tuibun Alson JO	JO	Yrgin JO	Taunan JO	Pelnen[c] Causen[b] JO	JO	Seunen FR JO	Souyen FR JO	Ssaoam[d] FR JO	Luecha[e] JO CL	Cholvon[f] JO
1795												
96												
97	1	11	10	3		2	1		3			
98	38	22	10	2	38	12					1	
99	24	15	1	2	5	5			4		2	
1800	48	7	18	6	26	7	1		6			
01	34	50	51	5	23	18	17	3 13	9			
02	7		31	66	9	25	35	1 33	16	3	1	
03			19	49	29	6	15	19	25	10		
04	2		1	14	19	10	49	11	2 20	1 62	4	
1805				5	4	1	4	1	46	51	14 66	
06								1 1			9 17	15
07						1			2	1	2	
08							2	1			3	5
09											5	58
1810											1	11
Total	154	105	141	152	154	87	124	84	133	128	125	84

[a] The East Bay column includes 2 Cusscuns as well as people from *Estero*, *Alameda*, *Norte*, and *Sur* who cannot be linked to a specific tribe.
[b] Includes Patlans.
[c] Includes Caburans.
[d] Includes Yuliens in 1800 (1), 1804 (13), 1805 (5), and 1807 (1).
[e] Note that the left-hand Luecha column lists baptisms at Mission Santa Clara.
[f] Includes Tamcans in 1806 (1), 1809 (15), and 1810 (3). Many more Cholvons were baptized later.

Table 12. Yearly Baptisms at Mission Santa Clara from the Rancheria Districts Designated by the Mission Santa Clara Missionaries between 1777 and 1810.

Year	N.M.[a] Santa Clara	N.P.[a] San Francisco	San[a] Jose Cuprtno	San[b] Juan Bautista	San[c] Francisco Solano	Santa[d] Ysabel	San[e] Brnrdno	San[f] Carlos	Santa[g] Agueda	San[h] Antonio	Tayssen
77	6	10	17	15	9	7	3			2	
78	7	15	6	3	13	6				1	
79	2	4	6		7		2	1			
1780	3	16	24	23	10	1	1		5	5	
81	4	5	10	6	7	3	11	10	2		
82			25	8	17	6	4	10		1	
83		4	12	2	17	5	32	34	25	36	
84		2	11	1	7	2	18	7	15	1	
1785	1	2	19	5	10	8	11	25	9	11	
86		3	11	3	11	11	29	20	21	19	
87	1	1	10	2	7	6	18	77	8	13	
88		2	10	3	5	8	26	27	27	5	
89	1	3	8	3	5	21	39	110	17	26	
1790		3	8	2	3	13	82	119	44	22	
91		1	7	2	5	9	37	61	21	6	
92		1	8	2	7	2	76	67	12	6	
93	1		3		5	8	86	37	8	8	
94			35	2	14	21	224	76	99	5	
1795			10	2	11	23	47	84	65	4	
96		1	1	3		8	3	22	11	22	
97			5		2	11	10	24	18	10	
98				2	1	13	21	45	37	26	
99			3	2	1	10	7	45	18	28	
1800				2	6	7	24	20	15	18	
01			1	1		5	5	30	14	33	
02				3		8	1	112	24	51	
03				1		1	1	27	4	63	
04							3	4	27	49	
1805						4		8	9	72	131
06						5		6	2	54	95
07						3		24	4	53	9
08						4				53	34
09								4		47	5
1810										62	
	26	73	250	98	180	239	821	1,136	561	812	274

[a] Probably part of the Tamien tribe.
[b] Probably formed Ritocsi group, toether with some San Carlos district people.
[c] Probably formed Alson tribe, together with some Santa Agueda district people.
[d] Penitencia Creek-Calaveras Creek tribe.
[e] Oljon, Olpen, Partacsi, Puichon, and Quiroste tribes.
[f] Large group of tribes south of Santa Clara as far as Santa Cruz and Gilroy.
[g] Alson, Causen, Taunan, Luecha and other tribes later represented at Mission San Jose.
[h] Juñas, Palas, and other tribes to the east of Santa Clara, including 30 Acirino at Mission San Jose.

Appendix 4

Pertinent Manuscripts
In Translation

This appendix includes translations of twenty-four documents written by members of the Spanish military and church hierarchies. The documents, not previously translated, shed light on specific incidents in native San Francisco Bay Area Indian history. Seven of the manuscripts are housed in the Archivo General de Nación in Mexico City, three in the Archives of the City of San Jose, California, and one at the Archives of the Archdiocese of San Francisco, California. The remaining thirteen manuscripts are part of the Archives of California collection in the Bancroft Library at the University of California, Berkeley.

The Archives of California collection deserves a special introduction. The manuscripts are neither originals nor true copies. They are paraphrases of original manuscripts, most of which are no longer available, having been destroyed in the San Francisco fire of 1906. The paraphrases were made in the late nineteenth century by employees of historian Hubert Howe Bancroft. For the most part, Bancroft's copyists introduced information with third person constructions such as "*Dice...*" ("It says...") and "*Enterado que ...*" ("It states that ..."). Details about Indian people, including the names of individuals and villages, were often omitted by the Bancroft copyists.

The relative loss of specific information about Indian people is made clear by comparing Archives of California documents with those few originals for which copies still exist today. For instance, the Archives of California contain a paraphrase version of document 14 in this appendix, a report on mission conditions by *Huchiun* fugitives in 1797 which still exists in the Archivo General de Nación in Mexico City. A sample entry from the full version in the Archivo General de Nación reads:

> Claudio—He declares that he fled because he was continually fighting with his brother-in-law Casimiro and because the *alcalde*, Valeriano, was clubbing him every time he turned

around, and when he was sick this same Valeriano made him
go to work.

A sample entry from the Archives of California version at the Bancroft Library reads:

Claudio—Because the *alcalde* constantly beat him and when he
was sick he had to go to work.

Bancroft's copyists, faced with stacks of documents to transcribe, omitted details about Indian people because those details were marginal to their interests.

The following translations were prepared by the author with extensive aid from Caroline Highley, and special help with difficult problems from Vivian Fisher, Luis Carlos Rodriguez-Leiva, and Francisco Santamarina. Sections of some documents, not relevant to Bay Area Indian people, have been omitted.

DOCUMENT 1.

EXCERPTS FROM A PARAPHRASE OF THE REPORT OF HERMENEGILDO SAL, PAYMASTER AT SAN FRANCISCO PRESIDIO, TO INTERIM GOVERNOR JOSE JOAQUIN DE ARRILLAGA. SAN FRANCISCO PRESIDIO. FEBRUARY 27, 1793.

[... Items 1 and 2 not pertinent to Indian people, skipped. ...]

Item 3. He communicates that some eighteen months ago a mountain Indian, who had been called Charquin as a pagan, was baptized at Mission San Francisco. He didn't even remain at the mission for eight days. Not even when the missionaries sent out messengers for him did he return. On two occasions endeavors were made to apprehend him. On one of them he retreated into the mountains and on the other he took up arms against the Christians of the mission. This has caused him to become insolent, inasmuch as he is increasingly fearsome in the eyes of the Indians.

On the fifteenth of this month Corporal Miguel Pacheco, in charge of the escort of Mission Santa Cruz, reported that there was no news except that two Indians of the Charquin's *ranchería*, who had been baptized, went back there with a license to visit. Because they had become Christians he wanted to kill them and take their wives. Although they fled that day, they returned by night to look for their wives. Upon discovering them, Charquin took away their weapons. They had to return alone to their mission.

On that same day the Reverend Father Baldomero López told him [Sal] that Charquin had finally given them more than they could endure. The commander of the presidio of San Francisco also concluded that he would no longer allow such excesses (which had continued, notwithstanding the consideration with which they had tolerated his behavior). He desires to go under cover of darkness to capture this Indian and give him what he deserves, regardless of the obstacles presented by the impregnable reaches of the mountains in which he pulls together his forces. It was known that said Charquin had in his power about twenty Christians of the Mission of San Francisco, including women and children, and allowed none to leave him. Consequently, in regard to what he has reported, he hopes to receive a directive for action as soon as possible.

DOCUMENT 2.

EXCERPTS FROM A PARAPHRASE OF A REPORT BY FORMER GOVERNOR PEDRO FAGES TO VICEROY MIGUEL DE LA GRUA TALAMANCA Y BRANCIFORTE REGARDING CONSTRUCTION AT MONTEREY. MEXICO. AUGUST 12, 1793[1]

Your Excellency—The account by Lieutenant José Argüello refers expressly to the expenditures for the restoration of the Monterey Presidio. The letter the interim governor of the Californias, Don José Joaquín de Arrillaga, forwarded with the account sheet under discussion says that it includes the disbursements for the reconstruction of the presidio as well as for the construction of the church, under my orders, from August 17, 1789 through the end of December, 1791.

These two projects originated under diverse circumstances. The walls of the first, the Monterey Presidio, had been completed earlier, although its roofs were merely tule thatching. About half of them burned up due to an unexpected accident on the August 11, 1789. It was I who, having run to and fro during the fire wherever my presence was needed, ended up suffering the greatest losses. I ordered an immediate start on reconstruction, with the idea of improving the buildings and liberating us from future problems.

The old church, besides being small, was poorly planned. It had occupied the center of the plaza, obscuring the customs house from the view of the place where the governor lives. So it occurred to me to begin a new church with the capacity, facade, and tower shown in the sketch made by the director of architecture of the Royal Academy of San Carlos, Don Antonio Velasquez,

---

[1] This report was attached to Viceroy Branciforte's December 12, 1795 letter to Governor Diego de Borica.

which is attached to this dispatch. After the presidio burned, I asked the advice of the commander general of the Interior Provinces, because at that time the Californias were subordinate to him, regarding the losses of some small belongings of the Treasury that had burned, and the expenses that would be incurred in the speedy rebuilding, expenses which Arrillaga has pointed out. I asked him from what funds or branches of government we were supposed to cover the existing losses and the ongoing costs during reconstruction.

The commander general did not answer my request, and it was necessary in those remote countries and in those circumstances to take advantage of the most convenient methods, or least hurtful, that necessity dictated and experience confirmed. The admirable proportions and liberal natural resources of the Californias, especially Alta California, provide an abundance of all the materials necessary for constructing the buildings—wood, stone, limestone, sand, and workers—more than enough to build whole cities. I realized upon considering the matter that by taking advantage of the opportunity, I could build the new church and repair the Presidio of Monterey at little cost to the Royal Treasury.

For instructors I made use of the three government stone cutters, and for laborers, the various servants left from one year to the next by the supply ships, together with the pagans of the villages in the vicinity of the pueblo of San Jose on the Guadalupe. To that end, I first called together their captains and leaders. I proposed that they send groups of five, ten, fifteen, or twenty, according to the number of people that they had and could do without for the defense of their lands. I promised to reward them with blankets, shirts, glass beads, and shells. They agreed to the pact, and in groups of eighty to one hundred they arranged with the commissioner of the town and the commander of the guard to give them an escort of a corporal and four soldiers to accompany the groups for security. The corporal gathered up and held the bows and arrows of each person, in order to avoid any trouble. The escort conducted them over the twenty leagues [fifty-four miles] which separates Monterey from the pueblo of San Jose, in order not to disquiet the pagans they encountered along the road. They made a specific request to the commissioner regarding the protection of the villages and the women left behind in those villages, to guard them against the tremendous abuse which they are in the habit of doing to one another whenever they see their spouses left behind. At their arrival provisions were given them on the king's account, but it was not much, because most of them brought seed meal, rabbits, fish, wild fruit and other foods from their homes. When they arrived they were allowed a day or two of rest and given food to relieve their fatigue, as were those who were leaving to return to their homes. The morning fare was a normal portion of beef, those at mid day and late afternoon a sauce pan of hot corn meal mush and beans.

To please them upon their return, I met with the captains of each group and asked them if they had experienced any problems, if things had gone well, and if they would come again when they were requested. All responded "yes" in one voice. Then they were given back the bows and arrows which I had kept in custody. I gave each person a small cotton blanket valued at five or six reals, on the king's account. And on my own account I gave four to six strings of glass beads to the captains and two or three strings of glass beads to the rest. I permitted them to go to the beach to gather shells, which they greatly value for working into the coinage with which they trade, and the adornments which they and their wives wear. They were sent off in this way. I appointed a corporal and four soldiers to escort them to their lands. One or two cattle were slaughtered for the road. And while they were pillaging the meat, two mules were loaded with the two half loads of shells, relieving them of the weight. The troop leader was advised to take whatever road they wished, and to treat them with the utmost humanity. In this way, so in conformity with the customs of these people, they were kept well pleased.

How fair it is to the Royal Treasury that I undertook the construction of the church and Monterey Presidio, which can be observed by comparing the costs to the much higher cost of similar works elsewhere. And now Your Excellency sees that over the two years and four months from August 17, 1789 until the end of December, 1791 covered by the account sheet of Lieutenant José Argüello, the cost totalled only 2,609 pesos, nine granos, supplied from the paymaster's fund. Notwithstanding that the quantity seems moderate, because I did not receive certified copies of items one through four, which Argüello seems to have presented to Governor Arrillaga as detailed accounts of the expenditures in four parts, I am unable to inform you regarding their accuracy. I would be able to verify them if your authority were used to order the above-mentioned governor to remit the referenced copies. Mexico, August 12, 1793. Señor Pedro Fages.

DOCUMENT 3.

PARAPHRASE OF A LETTER FROM COMMANDER JOSE MARIA PEREZ-FERNANDEZ TO GOVERNOR JOSE JOAQUIN DE ARRILLAGA REGARDING THE MACHINATIONS OF THE INDIANS. SAN FRANCISCO. MARCH 15, 1794.

Corporal Luís Peralta, having gone out with the troops to Mission Santa Clara regarding cattle, went in search of the pagan Indians who the Reverend Father Diego de Noboa had accused of taking cows, as I had informed Your Mercy in a dispatch on the first of the month. Because the Indian guides missed the road, they went past the village. When they turned back to it, they found it empty. So they returned.

After two days one of the Indians surrendered at the mission. Upon his having been questioned, he declared it true that he and his relatives ate a dead bull which a bear had been feeding on. Father Noboa said that some recently castrated young bulls had strayed off, that he was sure that this was one of them. So the summoned pagan was found innocent. However, he was held in the stocks for ten days in payment for the crime of failure to report the death of the steer.

At sunrise on the eleventh word arrived from the corporal of the same escort, Miguel Pacheco, that he has verified that four Christian Indians had taken some horses from the herd of the guard the previous night and gone to rob and kill livestock. The corporal took the meat from the village, brought it to the Reverend Fathers, and placed the four Christian Indians under detention.

He immediately sent Corporal Peralta with one man to bring them to the presidio. He arrived at the mission around midnight.

Sergeant Pedro Amador arrived shortly before that at Santa Clara, with the intent of going on to the pueblo to solicit pagans for work at the presidio [of San Francisco]. From there he advised me on the twelfth that the Christian Indian prisoners had incriminated fifteen pagans of being involved in the affair. He awaited my word in order to fall upon said pagans with the men he had there and with some auxiliaries from the pueblo. Losing no time, I dispatched another man with orders that he undertake the project, and once they are caught, to transfer them and the four Christians to the care of Corporal Peralta, then continue on his original commission. He returned today (with only twenty-two contract laborers, not having been able to get more). He told me that he went with fifteen men, between troops and townspeople, in search of the accused pagans, but found the village empty. They captured four of them in other villages that they came upon. They remain at the presidio, together with the Christian prisoners (who confessed to me that they had killed some livestock). The rest of them could not be caught.

They all applied to work on the fort. (But I lack shackles to secure them by day). In the meantime, please tell me what I ought to do regarding the above mentioned incident as well as the letter from the Reverend Father Noboa which is attached for your information.

DOCUMENT 4.

PARAPHRASE OF A LETTER FROM COMMISSIONER GABRIEL MORAGA TO LIEUTENANT JOSE ARGUELLO AT MONTEREY PRESIDIO. PUEBLO OF SAN JOSE. OCTOBER 30, 1794.

I give Your Mercy notice that, as a result of various trips made by the Reverend Father Manuel Fernández, minister of Mission Santa Clara, to the villages neighboring this town, the pagans have abandoned them and have retired into the mountains. It is common knowledge among the Indians, confirmed by remarks made by the soldiers that have escorted said religious, that Indians who refused to become Christians were severely threatened. In some cases he went beyond threat to actual punishment. Confirming this was he who the Father came upon at the cornfield of soldier Ygnacio Soto, and in whose presence the Father called to one of several pagans who were gleaning corn. Because the man did not come over immediately, he [Father Fernández] asked a soldier who accompanied him for a lance, then proceeded to horsewhip the Indian with it to the utmost. Following this and other incidents, the pagans really credited the threat of the Father to the effect that if those who told him (out of fear) that they would go to be baptized failed to fulfill this promise, he would have to burn their villages down.

One pagan inhabitant of this pueblo, called *El Mocho*, came to me to complain that said Father had gone to his village and, because he would not go to the mission and because he was accused of dissuading his relatives, had ordered him tied up and given many lashes, first with a halter rope and then with a leather riata. The Indian was left in such bad condition that he came in supporting himself by a cane, unable to stand upright, with waist and buttocks covered with swollen wounds.

Finally, it came to pass shortly after sunset last night that citizen Ygnacio Castro came upon, a short distance out behind his house, a pagan Indian armed with bow and arrows, whom he could not identify because he was completely covered with paint. Castro set about interrogating him. Among other things the Indian said, as if taking pity on him, that he should get his wife and children away from town, because the pagans were very angry. Many had gotten together, including those from very far off, and determined to come and kill all the people of the pueblo and the mission. This man was going that night to tell those pagans whom the Father had brought in not to become Christians. Then Castro commiserated with him and persuaded him by flattery to come and see me. When the Indian resisted this, Castro grabbed him by the hair and shouted to citizen Pedro Romero, who is his nearest neighbor. But the Indian's resistance was so strong that by the time Romero arrived, he had escaped. They both caught up with him down by the river. Although citizen Claudio saw this happening, he thought they were all Indians. Even after he recognized them, he did not go help because he did not know what was going on. So the Indian got away. All the above, I thought, should be put promptly to your attention so that you may take any measures that you may deem necessary. Keep in mind that we have here, with the exception of myself, only three soldiers of the escort and three citizens. All the rest are without arms. Of the small amount of powder I received, and the small number of balls, I am making cartridges with blank sheets of archival paper. For the use of the swivel-gun I will set aside some of the same. There is hardly enough for two discharges. So I hope that it will serve Your Mercy to guide me with all the care this matter demands. You well know the proportion of the munitions that go into reloading the swivel gun.

Soberanes and the previously mentioned Romero, who arrived yesterday, told me that from the Laguna Seca hither they observed tracks of many Indians heading toward the mountains to the east, and the same has been observed in this area.

I remain fully vigilant. Beginning tonight I will see that everyone keeps his horse saddled, that the few arms that are here are ready, that the pueblo is patrolled, and that everything is in such a condition that any surprise will be avoided until I receive supplies from you.

At the same time, I hope that you will tell me what to do with the wheat from last year's tithe. If it is not sent out quickly, it will certainly be lost. I will have no other choice but to sell it by weight in exchange for corn on account. And I tell you that we run the same danger with this year's crop if from now on we are not given a price that stimulates a proportional effort.

DOCUMENT 5.

PARAPHRASE OF A LETTER OF INSTRUCTIONS FROM LIEUTENANT JOSE ARGUELLO TO SECOND-LIEUTENANT HERMENEGILDO SAL AT SAN FRANCISCO PRESIDIO. MONTEREY. OCTOBER 31, 1794.

In view of the report which I just received from Corporal Gabriel Moraga, commissioner of the pueblo of San Jose, that the pagan Indians of that vicinity have become upset because one of the ministers of Mission Santa Clara, Father Manuel Fernández, has set upon them with violence to make them Christians, you should be briefed by said commissioner. To that end, go immediately to ascertain the circumstances of this development and satisfy yourself regarding the truth of the situation of the town. Then go immediately to the mission and make the ministers understand that the disturbances provoked by the temerity and lack of prudence of the aforementioned Father Manuel are likely to result in an insurrection by the neighboring pagans. Then get them to leave the mission immediately. To that effect you are given two soldiers to accompany them to San Francisco. Their exit is to be by night in order to avoid any incident that the pagans may plan. Upon completing this action you are to call upon the captains, with all due respect. When they know that the object of their restlessness has been withdrawn, they will calm down. In said case, convey a sincere statement to clarify the matter, to convince them that we do not intend to cause them trouble while they are not making trouble, that we do not want to make them Christians by force or by harshness, and that the governor has now ordered the Father who harassed them to leave.

Finally, take all measures necessary in order to calm them down, and admonish them regarding the mischief they caused by going away to the mountains, that they should have complained when problems first arose by sending two or three of their number to Monterey to talk with said governor. I count upon the efficacy with which you will apply the prudence and wisdom necessary in this case, so exceptional in its circumstances. As I have so few troops, and have nine dangerous prisoners, I can only send you two soldiers from the San Francisco Presidio. Tomorrow I will send another two or three of those who are now guarding the cattle at the royal ranch. I hope that you will advise me of the results so that I may report to the Governor.

If, Heaven forbid, the Reverend Father Manuel refuses to leave the mission, the corporal of the escort of his mission is not to give him an escort to go out anywhere, the commander of the San Francisco Presidio granting you that power, since it pertains to the cited mission of Santa Clara, which is within his jurisdiction.

DOCUMENT 6.

PARAPHRASE OF A LETTER FROM SECOND-LIEUTENANT HERMENEGILDO SAL TO LIEUTENANT JOSE ARGUELLO AT MONTEREY PRESIDIO. SAN JOSE. NOVEMBER 2, 1794.

I give you notice that I arrived at this pueblo at daybreak on the first of the month. As soon as they knew of my arrival some of the pagan Indians appeared. Immediately, I arranged to dispatch some of them to request the people and their captains to come in. Before mid-day three of the latter presented themselves. I spoke to them. It is said that they have been calming down their people, with the effect that some have calmed down. Today I hope that three or four captains are coming in with their people.

I have attempted to treat them kindly and I have entertained them as well as I have been able. They are content enough.

There is not a single indication among them that they think I believe there is a revolt afoot. And so, I am persuaded that the Indian that Ygnacio Castro says told him about it was not telling the truth.

In regard to what has transpired with the Reverend Father Manuel Fernández, it is not as has been reported. If he punished the Indian Mocho, I have reason to believe he had good reason to do so, although this punishment did stimulate the Indians to abandon their villages. I have delayed the delivery of Father Sanchez's letter. Tomorrow I will set out for the presidio.

DOCUMENT 7.

PARAPHRASE OF A LETTER FROM LIEUTENANT JOSE ARGUELLO TO GOVERNOR DIEGO DE BORICA REGARDING TRIBAL DISTURBANCES. MONTEREY. NOVEMBER 4, 1794.

This regards a communication submitted to me by Gabriel Moraga, commissioner of the pueblo of San Jose. Forwarded to your hands as attached Item Number One [see Appendix 4,4], it is about an imminent insurrection by the pagans of that vicinity who had abandoned their villages. In view of its content, I did not want to send the case along to Your Mercy until I was assured of the truth of the matter. So I decided to quickly dispatch the second-lieutenant of the district, Don Hermenegildo Sal, under orders, a copy of which I send to you as attached Item Number Two [see Appendix 4,5]. In addition to the verbal advise which was given, I sent a letter for the Reverend Father ministers of Mission Santa Clara, with instructions to give it to them if he was completely satisfied that there was an emergency, but if there was none, to return it to me. Said officer, having completed his commission, wrote to me from the town the report which I send along to you as Item Number Three [see Appendix 4,6]. It documents the conditions at the time of his arrival, namely, that the Indian population was quiet and in the villages. He left them clearly admonished and informed them that if they comport themselves poorly they will be punished and that any time they receive offense from any of our people they should come to Monterey to present their complaints to the Governor, since they all know the road. He reprimanded the corporal for the quickness with which he sent such a report, without checking the evidence. He holds the corporal and the mayor responsible for any omissions that may have been made during the exercise of their offices. I send all of this to Your Mercy for your information.

On the first of November, 1794, this matter was brought up verbally with the Reverend Father president Fermín Francisco de Lasuén. We are in accord that he should write to the Reverend Father who is the principal minister of Mission Santa Clara, to the effect that he moderate the zeal of Father Manuel Fernández.

DOCUMENT 8.

LETTER BY FATHER ANTONIO DANTI TO GOVERNOR DIEGO DE BORICA. MISSION SAN FRANCISCO. MAY 3, 1795.[2]

My Dear Sir.

I inform you that some newly converted Christian Indians, having received my permission to go to the far side of the Bay, stayed out longer than the time limit that I had set. I sent out some other Christian Indians, old-timers here, to go over to their villages and bring them back, with the understanding that they would not go forward to others if they did not find them. Well, they went out, and not finding them in their own villages, they went on until they arrived at an unknown village. Upon their asking if they had any Christians from this mission, a mob of armed pagans came out of a dance house, shouting that these people were their enemies and that they were going to shoot arrows at them until they killed them. Seeing this, the Christians took off running. Only eight stayed, with the idea of calming them down. I wish to God that they had fled as the others had. Well, the pagans satisfied their terrible fury with arrows and spears, until, as they had boasted, some were killed. Within an hour, only one of the eight was left alive. He says that as he was fleeing he saw them kill two or three and that they were trying to do the same to the rest. Lord save me. This news is such a great pain for me, that it is the most abundant harvest of sorrow that I could expect in my life. This terrible transgression took place on the twenty-ninth of last month, and they told me about it on the first of this month. I will be able to discuss it at greater length when you come up here.

May God our Lord grant you many years. Mission of Our Seraphic Father San Francisco. May 3, 1795. Antonio Dantí. Copy.

---

[2]The translated version is from a copy of the letter forwarded by the governor to the viceroy as an attachment to a subsequent report.

DOCUMENT 9.

PARAPHRASE OF A LETTER FROM SECOND-LIEUTENANT JOSE PEREZ- FERNANDEZ TO GOVERNOR DIEGO DE BORICA. SAN FRANCISCO REGARDING AN ATTACK ON CHRISTIAN INDIANS. MAY 29, 1795.

That the Indian Oton, having received the mandate of Father Dantí, crossed to the other side of the bay with two alcaldes and other Christians, old and new, a total of fourteen people, to look for the new Christian Xatlanes that had fled from this mission. He [Father Dantí] advised them to bring with them only some short ropes in order to tie up the Christians and so to bring them back. He did not permit them to bring their bows and arrows, assuring them that the pagans would not be able to do any harm to Christians.

That with this conviction they embarked for the other shore, where they encountered a large number of pagans waiting to attack them. Essentially, what took place was that all were killed except the bearer of this information.

That having presented himself to the Father, the Indian related what had happened. At this he [Father Dantí] replied that he was a liar. But as the Indian insisted on the truth of the sad occurrence, the Father said to him, "Then be careful about what you say to any soldier or the commander will find out. Be careful to say nothing." But the occurrence was already known to all, as the women were crying inconsolably.

DOCUMENT 10.

LETTER FROM GOVERNOR DIEGO DE BORICA TO VICEROY MIGUEL DE LA GRUA TALAMANCA Y BRANCIFORTE. MONTEREY. JUNE 23, 1795.

On the May 4 I informed you, under Item 96, that the pagans of the side of the bay opposite Mission San Francisco had killed seven Christians from the mission. I offered to go up to San Francisco to get a full briefing on the event and to take measures to avoid further disasters in the future.

Eventually I did go up to said mission. There I called forward the long-time Christian named Othon, who was one of the eight who had remained to appease the pagans, and who had the fortune to save his life by fleeing. He gave me the following report: "They left the mission of San Francisco, five veteran Christian Indians, including the Alcaldes Pasqual and

Rogerio, together with nine new Christians from the *rancherías* on the other side of the bay. They had orders from Father Antonio Dantí to bring back all the Christians who had fled. On the first day they crossed the estuary with their tule boats and slept on the beach. On the second day they left in the morning for the village of the Chaclanes, where they arrived at mid-day. Having found no one in it, some of them continued onward for the rest of the day and all through the night, traveling without sleep or rest, the rain notwithstanding. They arrived at the village of the Chimenes at about two in the afternoon, where they encountered a huge number of people, as many as there are at the mission (at the end of 1794 they had about nine hundred souls). Upon their arrival, men armed with bows and arrows emerged from the dance house with such force that they broke down its walls. They began at once to fire arrows, yelling, "These men are our enemies." Faced with such violence, the alcaldes tried to calm them down, telling them that they had come neither to fight nor to do any harm. They paid no attention, but continued to fire arrows until they killed the seven. Six of the new Christians had fled at the start of the altercation, upon the orders of the alcaldes. The declarant himself got away at great risk, inasmuch as arrows were flying all around him.

This same Othon and others informed me that the above-mentioned Chimenes are a rough and valiant lot, that they are continuously at war with neighboring groups, particularly the Tegunes. They live towards the coast to the north, in the vicinity of Bodega Bay. Their foods are bulbs, acorns, and seed meal. Their principal captains are Mule and Yuma.

This tragedy must be attributed to the failure of the alcaldes to follow the directions of their ministers, which, according to what they told me, was that they were to retire to the mission without going any farther in the case that runaway Indians were not found in the village of the Chaclanes.

Due to the number of the Chimenes, their rough and valiant character, the lands that they inhabit, and the great distance from the San Francisco Presidio to their villages, which I understand to be no less than thirty leagues [eighty miles—it would make more sense as thirty miles], I have decided to delay any dispatch of a force to punish them. My best efforts would allow me to send no more than twenty men from the various companies without neglecting other important responsibilities. Moreover, this was not an assault upon vassals of the king, but upon Indians by their enemies. For such do they seem to consider the recently baptized Chaclanes, because although it was thought that the runaways from the mission had gone for aid to the Chimenes, Othon says that he saw none of them [Chaclanes] at that village.

As for the argument against punishing the Chimenes, they live near Port Bodega, where in the course of time they could do quite a lot of harm to us as declared enemies, were some foreign nation to attempt to establish themselves there.

The measures that I have taken to avoid similar tragedies is to pray and insist to the missionaries of Mission San Francisco that in the future they not send any Christian Indians to the other shore in search of runaways. It has been made clear to me that the Father President has sent the same orders. No doubt this will eliminate the future possibility of a similar disaster. I have reiterated the charge to the commander of the San Francisco Presidio to watch with zeal over the fulfillment of this order or inform me of any transgression....

DOCUMENT 11.

PARAPHRASE OF A LETTER FROM SECOND-LIEUTENANT PEREZ-FERNANDEZ TO GOVERNOR BORICA. SAN FRANCISCO. SEPTEMBER 13, 1795.

He reports to the governor regarding the information he was told by the Reverend Father Martín Landaeta, that approximately 280 Christians of both sexes have abandoned Mission San Francisco. They have slipped out a few at a time, going off in various directions. It has come to such a pass that even the very natives of San Francisco, San Mateo [west bay shore], and San Pedro [Pacific coast], long-time Christians who have never before run away, are found to be missing from among the inhabitants.

That recently one of the runaways who had fled to the other shore, José Miguel, presented himself here. He said, "I came over to the beach with two pagans from my *ranchería*, but I left them and came to present myself here." He said, "Punish me as I deserve. I will gladly take it, only not at the mission." The two pagans went over to the mission. They were detained in the mission village and brought before the missionaries, who questioned them, as I heard from the commander of the guard. He arranged to send them over to me, which was done.

I questioned the two pagans regarding the matters at hand. One of the two, Somson, said that a runaway named Enrique had been killed on the other side of the Bay and that seven long-time Christian men, thirteen women, and their families are being sheltered at the village Pucat of the Juchiunes, where the captain is the pagan Oclese. Because of this, I decided to send one of the pagans to Oclese to tell him to come here in person and bring all the Christians which he has in his village. That when it is verified that this has been done, he will be given gifts and the pagan Somson will be allowed to leave with him.

DOCUMENT 12.

REPORT BY SERGEANT PEDRO AMADOR TO GOVERNOR DIEGO DE BORICA REGARDING A SORTIE AGAINST THE SACLANS, WITH ATTACHED DIARY AND LIST OF CRIMINALS. MISSION SAN JOSE. JULY 19, 1797.

I arrived on the eighteenth at Mission San Jose with eighty-three Christian Indians, men, women, and children ... eighty-three ... and nine pagans. The latter are under indictment, five Saclanes for the murder of the seven Christians, three Juchillones who tried to kill Raymundo, as well as four Christians of the same Sacalanes who are indicted in the murders. They do not give their Christian names because they do not know them. They do give their pagan names. Those on the attached annotated list which are marked with a cross say that they are Christians. The total brought in, between Christians and pagans, is ninety-four. Everything that occurred is documented in the diary which I am sending along, with this addition. The guides did not know, as dawn approached, exactly where the villages would be found. Only by accident did we come across the middle village. The greater part of the people fled at the noise, so that we were only able to seize the one [sub-village]. Had it been known to us [that there were three sub-villages] we would have divided our men and fallen upon all of them. It is certain, Sir, that in that one section we found them full of resistance. They had put themselves in a state of preparedness, with baskets full and piled bunches of their seed plants. I was not able to find out in my investigation who among them had advised them to challenge us, because they are very haughty Indians. It is not easy to make them confess, either by persuasion or by severe force. Given all the signs of their preparations for war, we could not be sure that anything they said was true.

Nor could we trust the Juchillones because some of them deny and others confess to that which has already been established. It is certain that they have numerous villages and large ones—and this [war preparation] is the reason they come together to hold their rebel councils and store up many seeds. This compels me to decide to pay visits to them from time to time, so that they completely reconsider their presumption that we fear them.

I received from Corporal Vallejo the twenty men that you ordered and have been quite happy with them because everyone contributed equally well. I tell you that they have brought in some young pagan Indians who came willingly with their parent's permission. You see, I convinced them [the parents] that they must not give them over out of fear, but only if they wanted to give them over. Some were given over and others were not given over, so those who came back did so voluntarily. The men who brought them are the townsman Benabides (1) - Larios (1) -Manuel Mesquita (1) - Linares (1) - Manuel Guitron (2) - Ygnacio Castro (1) - Manuel Yguera (1) - Aguila (1) - Dolores Mesa (1) - Ygnacio Archuleta (2).

The Father minister of this mission made some objection about food for the Indians, but I told him to make up his mind right there whether or not to provide it to them. As a result he is giving it to them, but he told me he would give it only for immediate consumption, so I will give it for immediate consumption as he desires.

It has been arranged with the commander of the pueblo of San Jose to order the townsmen who brought the little Indians with the blessing of their parents to treat them well and set good examples, and return them to their own relatives when and if they ask for them.

Pedro Amador

[The following diary was attached to the above letter.]

DIARY OF SERGEANT AMADOR REGARDING THE MATTER DISCUSSED ABOVE, NOTING THE VALOR AND MODE OF FIGHTING OF THE INDIANS.

July 6—I arrived at Santa Clara without incident.

July 7—I arrived at Mission San Jose and investigated what the Indians had been saying.

July 8—I wrote reports to the governor and to my superior officer.

July 9—I assigned work parties for the projects at this mission.

July 10—ditto

July 11—I sent soldier Sanchez to pueblo because he was sick. I continued with the same work projects.

July 12—I received the orders from the governor and sent a soldier to San Francisco to get guides to lead our company.

July 13. We set forth on the campaign in the evening. I traveled all that night until dawn and hid with the party in a brushy ravine throughout the day.

July 14. In the evening we arrived at the place where the village of the Sacalanes was located.

July 15. At dawn we attacked said village. We met much resistance from the Indians in it. Although we repeatedly told them that we did not wish to fight but only to take away the Christians, they admitted to no persuasion but began to shoot, killing one of our horses and wounding two others.

Seeing this opposition, we used our weapons in order to subdue them so that they would surrender. Seven were killed, for they refused for two hours to give up. Finally, it was necessary to dismount and throw them back with swords and lances, for they have some wells in the middle of the village which are like walls and which can be strongly defended. There may have been about fifty persons there, men and women.

There were three villages close together, and with the destruction of this one, the inhabitants of the others fled. We captured only two persons from the second village, although in the first the number captured was thirty, including both pagans and Christians. Having carried out an investigation and having ascertained the guilty ones and the Christians, I made it clear to the rest, through the interpreters, that we did not wish to do them any harm. They said they wanted to obey and that they well understood that we had no evil intentions. I liberated the pagans and we set forth toward the region of the Juchillones.

We had gone but a short distance when there began to assemble a great many Indians, uttering shrieks and cries, so that we had to go into line of battle again. Falling upon them, we killed one person, and with this they all retreated. We followed our course in the direction we were going and concealed ourselves in a ravine near the beach. It has much timber, water, and firewood, good for a settlement. There we spent all the day hidden until nightfall when we went on to the *ranchería* of the Juchillones.

[July 16.] At dawn we reached the place where were gathered all the Christians whom we wanted, together with those pagans who had participated in the attempt to kill Raymundo and his people. We struck the first, second, and third village during the same morning. As we reconnoitered the Indians of the last village, which is very large, the inhabitants were just about to open hostilities. But being admonished by the interpreters that we had not come to harm them but to hunt for Christians, they were pacified. We pointed out to them that we had punished the others because they had fought with us. Then we returned to the first village with the Christians and pagans and there assembled all those who had been concealed in the three villages. Having separated out all those we had caught and were taking with us, we set forth on our return journey. The pagans had been cautioned, as the preceding ones had been, that we did not wish to injure them if they did not harm us. We followed our course of retirement along the coast. We reached an arroyo with little water and much timber, in which we passed the night with sentinels in the camp and at two outlying posts.

July 17. At night we reached an arroyo which has much water, much timber and firewood, and also has nearby redwood, and very much good sand, and some long valleys.

July 18. We reached Mission San Jose at a distance of sixteen miles.

Pedro Amador   July 19, 1797

DOCUMENT 13.

TESTIMONY OF PAGAN SACLAN AND HUCHIUN REBELS TAKEN BY LIEUTENANT JOSE ARGUELLO. SAN FRANCISCO PRESIDIO. AUGUST 9, 1797.

The detailed statements which, due to a direct order from Governor and Inspector General Don Diego de Borica dated 21 June 1797, I, Don Josef Argüello, lieutenant and commander of the cavalry company of the garrison of the Royal presidio of San Francisco, in the presence of the four witnesses listed below, attest were declared by the pagan Sacalanes who took part in the murders of the seven Christians of Mission San Francisco in the year 1795, and by the Cuchillones Indians who tried to destroy Raymundo El Californio and his companions. Also [here are] the explanations from the rest of the runaways whom Sergeant Pedro Amador conducted back in the round-up which he made, regarding the reasons and motivations they had for abandoning their mission. Their statements, with a note regarding the name of each one and the class of his crime, are as follows.

[margin] The declaration of Potroy, a Christian of the Mission of San Francisco, whose name is not recollected. *The main instigator*. He confesses to helping to kill the Christians during the year 1795...[illegible] ...in the same...[illegible]...he knows as a pagan Joquaja, Mercunta, as pagans...[illegible]...Otseit, Caguas, Tuma.

> [text] Potroy: Potroy was called and by means of two interpreters, in the presence of the witnesses Sergeant Joaquín Pico, corporals Claudio Galindo, José Miranda, and the soldier José Gonzalez, four members of the Company of Catalonian Volunteers, he was asked by me how he was called and from which village he comes. He responded that his name is Potroy, that he is a Christian of Mission San Francisco and is a native of the village of Jussent, where Sergeant Pedro Amador found them. I asked him what his Christian name is and how long he had been a fugitive. He responded that he does not recollect his Christian name, nor

how long he has been a fugitive. I asked him why he cooperated in the murders that had been committed during the year 1795 against the seven Christians of his mission. He responded that he knew nothing about it nor had he cooperated in said murders. Upon my pointing out that his relatives and countrymen in the village where he had been arrested accused him of having been the prime instigator of the killings, he responded that it is true that he had helped to kill the seven Christians and that he had also helped to set fire to Rogerio, one of the seven. They did it because they thought the deceased had come in search of pagans in order to convert them. That made them angry. He adds that it is true that the pagans had been uniting in order to go attack the new mission of San Jose. The ringleader in that was the captain called Ojyugma of the village of Juuquili, which is about three leagues [eight miles] away from the place Sergeant Amador went. He had nothing more to say, nor did he know his age, which looks to be about twenty-five years. [Restituto Potoróe, baptized in 1795 at age twenty-two, a Saclan (SFR-B 1765).]

Declaration of Joguoja, a Christian of the same mission called Cesario. He denies having joined in the murder of the seven Christians.

The same questions were asked of Joguoja, under the same circumstances as the last interrogation. He responded that he was called Joguaja as a pagan; that he is a Christian of the Mission San Francisco with the name Cesario, that he is of the Saclan nation as was the previous man, that he did not take part in the murders of which his relatives accused him because he was at another village when they took place. Although he repeated that what he had said was the truth, he had nothing more to add regarding the matter, except that he had abandoned his mission two and one half years ago. Asked about his motive for leaving, he responded that he had been very fearful and became terrified upon seeing that they always whipped his companions. He asserts that the above mentioned Potroy was one of the principals in carrying out the said seven murders. He does not know his age, which looks to be about twenty-two years. [Cesario Tiguacse, baptized in 1795 at age twenty, group not listed (SFR-B 1835). He was listed as a Carquin or Napa in the 1822 Mission San Francisco Padron.]

Declaration of Juscule, whose Christian name was said to be Mercunta. He attacked the Christians who fled.

> Juscule, who was given the same questions as the previous people, declared that he was called as a pagan Juscule, that he is a Christian of said mission of San Francisco, and that his name is Mercunta. It is true that when they were killing the seven deceased, he states that he went to cut off the rest of the Christian party in order that they not escape. He also repeated the information regarding the rumor that people under the leadership of captain Ojyugma were going to attack the new mission. He had no other motive for abandoning his mission than that he had grown tired of seeing that his relatives were doing the same thing. He also accused Potroy of being one of the motivators in the killing of the seven Christians. He seems to be about forty years old. [Verecundo Jusculé, baptized in 1795 at age fifty, a Saclan (SFR-B 1738).]

Declaration of Otseit, pagan of the Sacalanes.

> Otseit was given the same questions as the others. He responded that he is called Otseyt, that he is a pagan. Everything he says is in conformity with the above cited Juscule. He had intercepted, or gone to intercept, the Christians as they were being killed. In the rest he agrees with Potroy, except regarding the gathering of pagans to attack the new mission, of which he knew nothing. He would be about twenty-two years old. [Salvio Otscei, baptized in 1802 at age forty, a Jalquin (SFR-B 2319).]

Declaration of Caguas, pagan of the same nation, he killed a Christian.

> Caguas, who was interrogated as were the last. He responded that he was called Caguas, that he is a pagan of the village of Joussent. It is true that when one of the seven deceased, named Ventura, fled, he intercepted him and killed him with a single arrow. He also declares that Potroy was the principal motivator and instigator in the killing of the seven Christians and that captain Ojyugma wanted to attack the new mission and kill all of its inhabitants. He looks to be about twenty-three years old. [Clemente Cahuas,

baptized in 1802 at age twenty-four, a Jalquin (SFR-B 2375).]

Declaration of Joxanssea, Christian of said mission who does not remember his name. He confesses to nothing.

> Joxanssea, who was subjected to the same interrogation as the previous, responded that he is called as a pagan Joxanssea, that he is a Christian, and that he does not remember his name. He fled Mission San Francisco three years ago, for no specific reason. His village is closer to here than the place where the Christians were killed, and that they only found out about it after it happened. His countrymen had not considered attacking the new mission, and as soon as Sergeant Amador arrived, they all fled. He claims that he did not flee because he was looking after his seed meal. He had nothing more to say. He does not know his age, but seems to be about fifty years old. [Graciano Lumanacse (analysis of Document 22A indicates that this man was known by two names), baptized in 1795 at age fifty, a Saclan (SFR-B 1554).]

Declaration of Carues, pagan of the Sacalanes, that he joined in going out against the Christians, who were already dead.

> Carues, who was questioned as were the previous, responded that he is called Carues, that he is a pagan from the village of Juquili. It is true that he went with the other pagans to intercept the Christians in order to kill them, but that he did not arrive in time. They had already been killed. In regard to wanting to attack the new mission, he neither knew nor had heard anything. He had nothing more to say. He is about forty-five years old. [Arcadio Carues, baptized in 1802 at age thirty-five, a Jalquin (SFR-B 2372).]

Declaration of Jolassilla, pagan of the same nation.

> Jolassilla, to whom were given the same questions as were given the previous men, responded that he is called Jolassilla, a pagan of the village of Gequigmu, that he did not participate in the murders of the seven Christians because he was at another village. Having been challenged as to the truth of his testimony, because, as he himself heard, his

> own relatives accused him, he responded that what they impute is without merit. As to the desire to attack the new mission, he responded that he neither knew nor had heard spoken anything about it. He had nothing more to say. He appears to be about twenty-eight years old. [No man of this name is identifiable in Mission San Francisco or Mission San Jose baptismal records].

Declaration of Joguacsea of the same Nation, who attacked the Christians who had fled.

> Joguocsea, who was questioned in the same manner as the previous men, responded that he is called Joguocsea, a pagan of the village of Ogsente, that the truth is that he tried to intercept the Christians, but that he did not kill anyone because he was always behind everybody. Asked again whether or not he was telling the truth, he responded that he had nothing more to say. Nor did he know that the pagans wanted to attack the new mission. As he offered nothing more, I again challenged him regarding the truth of his testimony. He responded that what he had stated is nothing other than the truth regarding what took place. He would be about thirty years old. [Benjamin Jovocsia, baptized in 1802 at age thirty, a Jalquin (SFR-B 2374).]

Declaration of Tuma, pagan of the same nation, who helped attack the Christians that fled.

> Tuma, who was interrogated in the same manner as the previous men and responded that he was called Tuma, a pagan of the village of Jussenti, that it is true that he went to intercept the Christians in order to kill them, but that he did not kill anyone. He accused Potroy of being among the ring-leaders in the murder of said Christians. Being asked again if he were telling the truth, he responded that what he had said is what took place, nothing more. He does not know his age, which appears to be about twenty-two years old. [This man may be Respicio Toma, baptized at Mission San Jose in 1800 at age twenty-seven, from the "Redwoods" (SJO-B 212).]

Declarations of the Accomplices in the Persecution of Raymundo and his Group

Declaration of Massigse, pagan of the Cuchillones. He denies everything.

> Massigse was asked his name and the name of his village. He responded that he is called Massigse, and that he is a pagan of the village of Jupui of the Uchiunes. He was asked about his motive for wanting to jump Raymundo and those of his party who had come to look for Christians, as his relatives had charged. He responded that he was not on the beach when Raymundo arrived in search of the Christians, because he was at a dance at another village. When I challenged him regarding the truth of his assertions and reiterated the accusations of his own countrymen, he responded that he had spoken the truth, that he had left nothing out, and that he had not even seen Raymundo when he had come to their land. I got nothing more out of him, including his age, of which he is ignorant. He looks to be about seventy years old. [This man has not been identified in mission registers].

Declaration of Hichu, Christian of the mission, called Bibiano.

> Hijchu, who was asked the same questions as the previous man, responded that he was called Hijchu as a pagan, that he is a Christian with the name Bibiano, baptized at Mission San Francisco, of the nation Cuchillon. Raymundo arrived at the beach where the declarant was hunting sea otters. The minute he saw him he became angry, saying that he was a brave man and that he greatly regretted that he did not have his bow and arrows with him. He told them that he [Raymundo] was going to die as soon as they could tie him up and hang him. He said all this because he believed that they had entered his hut and stolen his gear. As soon as Raymundo and his companions ordered him to shut his mouth, he did so. Presently he went away to his hut to look for his weapons. At that time the pagan villagers began to arrive. By the time he got back Raymundo and his party had already embarked. Asked why he wanted to purchase the murder of said Raymundo, offering glass beads and other goods for his death, he responded that he had not done that, and that all the pagans had wanted to try to kill him. Asked

> his reasons for abandoning his mission without any intention of returning, he answered that he did it because he had been starving. Moreover, they wanted to make his father work when he was sick, even kicking him various times, until he went down to the beach, where he died. He had nothing more to say, and did not know his age. He was about thirty-eight years old. [Bibiano Guitchú, baptized in 1795 at age thirty, with Saclans (SFR-B 1767).]

Declaration of Lajus, pagan of the same nation. He confesses that he went down to the beach to kill Raymundo.

> Lajus, when questioned as had been the previous man, responded that he was called Lajus, that he is a pagan of the village called Abasto, that it is true that when they came to advise the people that Raymundo was on the beach he immediately left to see for himself, with the intention of killing them. By the time he got there Raymundo and his companions were already embarked. Asked again whether or not he spoke the truth and whether or not he had made any threats with weapons, he responded that he had not done anything. What he said is what happened and he had nothing more to say. He would be about thirty years old. [He cannot be identified in mission registers].

Declaration of Oquema, pagan of the same nation.

> Oquema, who was subjected to the same interrogation as the previous man, responded that he is called Oquema, that he is a pagan of the village of Orocorocay, that it is true that when he was told that Raymundo was in his land, his brother went there and began shooting arrows at a member of Raymundo's party. The man took off swimming along the shore, at which time the declarant came up with a spear in one hand and a machete in the other hand that he had made from a barrel hoop he had found washed up on the beach. He accompanied his brother, but had not brought along any arrows. Asked again as to whether or not he was telling the truth, he declared that what he had said was the truth. He had nothing more to say. He would be about twenty years old. [He has not been identified in mission registers].

Having concluded the preceding declarations, gathered legally and in conformance with the statements of the interpreters, and in recognition of their accuracy, I and my witnesses sign at the San Francisco Presidio on August 9, 1797.

Josef Argüello
Joaquín Tico
Claudio Galindo
Josef Miranda
José Gonsalez

DOCUMENT 14.

TESTIMONY OF RUNAWAY CHRISTIAN INDIANS TAKEN BY LIEUTENANT JOSE ARGUELLO. SAN FRANCISCO. AUGUST 12, 1797.

In fulfillment of the decree of Governor and Inspector General Don Diego de Borica, calling for testimony from the runaway Christian Indians of Mission San Francisco captured by Sergeant Pedro Amador during the recent campaign, on this day, July 21, 1797, I brought them before me. Once I figured out who was capable of testifying, I separated them out. By means of the interpreters and in the presence of the witnesses Sergeant Joaquín Pico, Corporal Claudio Galindo, Corporal José Miranda and soldier José Gonzalez, four members of the Catalonian Volunteers, I questioned each one regarding the causes and motives they had for running away from their mission without wanting to return. To these interrogations they responded in the following way:

Tiburcio—He testified that after his wife and daughter died, on five separate occasions Father Dantí ordered him whipped because he was crying. For these reasons he fled. [Tiburcio Obmusa, age fifty-five, a Huchiun (SFR-B 1108). His wife (SFR-B 1109) had been buried on February 15, 1795 (SFR-D 744).]

Marciano—He offered no other reason for fleeing than that he had become sick. [Marciano Muiayaia, age forty-three, a Huchiun (SFR-B 1501). Both his wife (SFR-B 1512), and his two children (SFR-B 1414, 1417) lived through the epidemic of 1795.]

Macario—He testified that he fled because his wife and one child had died, no other reason than that. [Macario Uncatt, age thirty-three, group not named at baptism, probably Huchiun (SFR-B 1480). His daughter Cirila Zutismain was buried on March 22, 1795 (SFR-B 1457, SFR-D 769). Maura

Tolempa, his wife, was buried on April 17, 1795 (SFR-B 1493, SFR-D 806).]

Magin—He testified that he left due to his hunger and because they had put him in the stocks when he was sick, on orders from the *alcalde*. [Magin Llucal, age forty-three, group not named at baptism, probably Huchiun (SFR-B 1484). His wife and a child born in 1788 lived through the 1795 epidemic and flight (SFR-B 1416, 1454).]

Tarazon—He declared that he had no motive. Having been granted license to go on *paseo* to his land, he had felt inclined to stay. [Trason Yapilis, age forty-eight, group not named at baptism, Saclan or Huchiun (SFR-B 1805). His daughter, Xantipa Ssaquenmaie, never did return after fleeing the mission in 1795 (SFR-B 1785). She was reported dead "*en la otra banda*" in 1800 (SFR-D 1332).]

Ostano—He testified that his motive for having fled was that his wife, one child, and two brothers had died, and because he had fought with another Indian who had been directing their work group. [Ostano Guilicsse, age fifty-three, Huchiun (SFR-B 1505). He was one of the eight men whose names had been written down on the ship *San Carlos* in August of 1775. Ostano's wife, Ostana Elimain, died on March 4, 1795 (SFR-B 1516, SFR-D 757).]

Roman—He testified that he left because his wife and a son had gone back to their land, because of the many whippings, and because he did not have anyone to feed him. [Roman Ssumis, age fifty, group not named at baptism, probably Huchiun (SFR-B 1065). His first wife, Candida Jalilite, was buried during the epidemic on May 9, 1795. He stayed at Mission San Francisco long enough to marry again on September 30, 1795, with Jobita Pispite, a Huchiun or Saclan (SFR-B 1775, SFR-M 519).]

Claudio—He declares that he fled because he was continually fighting with his brother-in-law Casimiro and because the *alcalde* Valeriano was clubbing him every time he turned around, and when he was sick this same Valeriano made him go to work. [Claudio Ssojorois, age sixty-one, from the "*otra banda*" (SFR-B 463). The brother-in-law Casimiro was a Ssalson, as was the *alcalde* Valeriano (SFR-B 490, 442). Bonifacio, one of the two ferrymen who drowned while transporting Huchiun people across the bay in November of 1794, was Claudio's son (SFR-D 704).]

José Manuel—He testifies that when they went to bring wood from the mountains Raymundo ordered them to bring him water. When the declarant wouldn't do it, this same Raymundo hit him with a heavy cane, rendering one hand useless. He showed his hand. It was a little puffed up, but had movement. That was his reason for having left the mission. [José Manuel Tolensa, age twenty-nine, a Huchiun (SFR-B 1158). His wife had returned to the mission in September of 1796, at which time their three month old child was baptized (SFR-B 1882).]

Homobono—He testifies that his motive for fleeing was that his brother had died on the other shore and when he cried for him at the mission they whipped him. Also, the alcalde Valeriano hit him with a heavy cane for having gone to look for mussels at the beach with Raymundo's permission. [Homobono Sumipocsé, age forty-one, from Josquizara, an unlocated East Bay village (SFR-B 504). One of his two children, Diego, had died at the very beginning of the 1795 epidemic, on January 20 (SFR-B 758, SFR-D 730).]

Malquiedes—He declares that he had no more reason for fleeing than that he went to visit his mother who was on the other shore. [Melquiades Eyumele, age twenty-three, tribe not identified at baptism, probably a Huchiun (SFR-B 1481). A son died November 24, 1794. His wife was reported dead as a runaway at the "*otra banda*" on April 1, 1797 (SFR-B 1494, SFR-D 1073).]

Liborato—He testifies that he left because his mother, two brothers, and three nephews died, all of hunger. So that he would not also die of hunger, he fled. [Liberato Yrec, age thirty-three, tribe not identified at baptism, probably a Huchiun (SFR-B 1478). His wife and two children lived through this time period (SFR-B 1406,1413,1491). The mother and brothers cannot be identified from the limited mission register information.]

Migilo—He declared that his motive for fleeing was that Lorenzo, who had been at the house of La Sargenta, took him along with him. [Miguel Jacobo, no native name given at baptism, age nineteen, a Huchiun (SFR-B 189). Miguel had not yet married in 1795. Lorenzo was also a Huchiun (SFR-B 1477).]

Nicolas—He says that he ran away only because his father had died. He had no other motive. [Nicolas Ennót, age twenty-seven, Huchiun (SFR-B 1504). His father cannot be identified from the limited mission register information. His wife, Nicolasa Factora Ssacnem, also lived through the period (SFR-B 1515).]

Timoteo—He declares that the *alcalde* Luís came to get him while he was feeling poorly, and whipped him. After that Father Antonio hit him with a heavy cane. For those reasons he fled. [Timoteo Guecusia, age twenty-seven, not identified by tribe at baptism, probably Huchiun (SFR-B 1159). His wife, Pia Guimum, had died during the epidemic on February 23, 1795 (SFR-B 1271, SFR-D 750).]

Otolon—He reports that he fled because his wife did not care for him or bring him food. The vaquero Salvador had sinned with her. Then Father Antonio ordered him whipped because he was not looking out for said woman, his wife. [Odilon Eunucse, twenty-four, probably Huchiun (SFR-B 1160). His wife, Leocadia, was from an East Bay family, but had been raised at the mission (SFR-B 191). Years later, after Odilon had died, she married

Manuel Conde, son of the former headman of Pruristac (SFR-B 93). Leocadia's sister was the wife of Casimiro, the Ssalson man who had been giving the declarant Claudio so much trouble. These women seem to have been part of the inner clique at Mission San Francisco. Salvador was a young Yelamu man, one of the earliest converts, married at the time to an East Bay woman nine years his senior (SFR-B 14, 484, SFR-M 157).]

Milan—He declared that he was working all day in the tannery without any food for either himself, his wife, or his child. One afternoon after he left work he went to look for clams to feed his family. Father Dantí whipped him. The next day he fled to the other shore, where his wife and child died. [Milan Alas, age twenty-seven, not identified by tribe at baptism, probably Huchiun (SFR-B 1479). Milan's wife Manuela Eyumain and five year old son were entered in the San Francisco burial register on June 10, 1798 as having died at the "*otra banda*" (SFR-B 1492,1436, SFR-D 1180,1181).]

Patabo—He says that he fled just because his wife and children died and he had no one to take care of him. [Patavio Guecuéc, age forty-three, a Huchiun (SFR-B 1631). His wife Patabia died on March 24, 1795 and their daughter Tara Guequectole died a week after that, April 1, 1795 (SFR-B 1656,1609, SFR-D 789).]

Orencio—He declared that his father had gone several times with a little niece of his to get a ration of meat. Father Dantí never gave it to him and always hit him with a cudgel. Because his niece died of hunger, he ran away. [Orencio Caustole, age thirty-three, a Huchiun (SFR-B 1507). His father cannot be identified from mission register evidence. A daughter born away from the mission in 1796 was baptized on the day of his return to Mission San Francisco, July 20, 1797 (SFR-B 1910).]

Toribio—He stated that the motive for his having fled was that he was always very hungry, and that he went away together with his uncle. [Toribio Eyúnú, age twenty-seven, Huchiun (SFR-B 1642). He and his wife had no children when they fled in 1795. A son born in 1796 was baptized at San Francisco on August 23, 1797, soon after this testimony was taken (SFR-B 1912). Toribio and his wife seem to have run away again later, as another child, age one, was baptized on January 13, 1800 (SFR-B 2010).]

Lopez—He explained that his reason for having run away was the following: He went one day over to the presidio to look for something to eat. Upon returning to the mission he went to get his ration. But Father Dantí did not want to give it to him, saying that he should go to the countryside to eat herbs. [No person named Lopez was ever listed in the San Francisco *Libro de Bautismos* up through the year 1810. It is certainly the man's nickname.]

Magno—He declared that he had run away because, his son being sick, he took care of him and was therefore unable to go out to work. As a result he was given no ration and his son died of hunger. [Magno Cuegila, age thirty-nine, not identified by tribe at baptism, probably a Huchiun (SFR-B 1500). His son Benedicto died and was buried at age four on February 17, 1795 (SFR-B 1424, SFR-D 746).]

Prospero—He declared that he had gone one night to the lagoon to hunt ducks for food. For this Father Antonio Dantí ordered him stretched out and beaten. Then, the following week he was whipped again for having gone out on *paseo*. For these reasons he fled. [Prospero Chichis, age forty-three, from his children's baptisms he is identified as the captain of the Huchiuns (SFR-B 1628). One of Prospero's daughters married Marín, the Huimen man for whom Marin County was named, in 1802 (SFR-B 1603,2182, SFR-M 738).]

Having concluded the preceding declarations that were legally gathered and which follow the testimony of the interpreters, and in the belief that they represent the truth, I and my assistants sign it at the San Francisco Presidio on August 12, 1797.

José Argüello
José Miranda
Joaquín Pico
José Gonzalez
Claudio Galindo

DOCUMENT 15.

PARAPHRASE OF JUDGEMENT RENDERED BY GOVERNOR DIEGO DE BORICA AGAINST CONVICTED SACLAN AND HUCHIUN INDIANS. MONTEREY. AUGUST 26, 1797.

Sentences For Indian Criminals

These sentences reflect the involvement of each man, as their testimony, taken by Lieutenant José Argüello's on August 9, 1797, documents:

Potroy (Christian)—who has forgotten his Christian name, will suffer the penalty of seventy-five lashes portioned over three distinct occasions, one year in shackles on rations and without wages, and after that to be given over to his ministers well cautioned that if he runs away again and behaves badly the punishment will be yet more severe.

Cesareo, as a pagan Joquoja—two months at labor in shackles, on rations and without wages, and after being warned to be given over to his ministers.

Juscule (Christian) - Verecundo—twenty-five lashes and four months in shackles.

Otseit—twenty-five lashes and four months in shackles, during which time work with delicacy to attract him into the folds of our religion. If he will agree he is to be given over to the reverend Fathers of Mission San Francisco. If the contrary he is to be put at liberty, being well warned that if he returns to actions against the Christians he will be apprehended and punished more severely.

Caguas (pagan)—fifty lashes portioned over two occasions, eight months in shackles, and the rest like the above.

Toxanssea (Christian) who does not remember his Christian name—two months in shackles, well warned, and given over to his reverend Father ministers.

Carues (pagan)—Like Otseit in all respects.

Jolassilla (pagan)—two months in shackles, and the rest like Otseit.

Joguaocsea (pagan)—in everything like Otseit.

Tuma (pagan)—in everything like Otseit.

Punishment to be suffered by the Christian Indians and pagans who in 1797 beat up those neophytes of Mission San Francisco that had crossed the bay in search of runaways, at the direction of their Fathers:

Massigse (pagan)—one month in shackles and in other respects like Otseit.

Bibiano (Christian), as a pagan Hijchu—in everything as the above except that he is to be given over to his Father ministers.

Lapiz (pagan)—two months in shackles and in other respects the same as Otseit.

Oquema (pagan)—two months in shackles, and in other respects the same as Otseit.

The sentences will commence this coming September 1. Their rations are to be paid for from governmental expense account in an amount that will keep them from suffering hunger. They are to be employed on the king's projects for only as many hours of the day as their state of health and their strength allow. They are to be treated with humanity.

DOCUMENT 16.

LETTER FROM GOVERNOR DIEGO DE BORICA TO VICEROY MIGUEL DE LA GRUA TALAMANCA Y BRANCIFORTE. MONTEREY. AUGUST 30, 1797.

In my reports of May 4 and June 23 in the year of 1795, under the numbers 96 and 122, I advised you that the pagan Sacalanes who inhabit the other shore of the port of San Francisco violently murdered seven Christian Indians who were sent with others of the same mission by their Father ministers in search of several runaways, and about the measures I had taken to avoid the occurrence of such tragedies in the future. Those measures were approved by Your Mercy in the ordinance of September 18 of the same year.

Notwithstanding the fact that one of those measures was to implore and charge the ministers of said Mission San Francisco verbally and in writing to abstain from sending Christian Indians to the other shore in search of fugitives, more than thirty individuals went out to bring them back last June, without the knowledge of the governor. Upon their arrival on the other shore they found in three villages of the pagan Cuchillones some Christians of all ages and sexes. They retreated to the beach with them, concerned that the rest of the Indians, who were away at a dance, would soon be returning. Just as they were ready to embark, these same Christian runaways whom they had gathered up impeded them by force. In the meanwhile, the rest of the Indians arrived from the dance. Although our people were threatened, they succeeded in getting to their tule balsas; but two who remained behind were attacked by the pagans and obliged to jump into the bay. They were picked up by their companions after one of them had received a flesh wound to the head.

In view of this opposition Raymundo El Californio resolved to order the Christians to retreat to their mission. But a storm came upon them which dispersed the balsas. He had to turn back in order to escape the danger, as did four others, and land again on the enemy shore. Observing that the balsas were falling apart, he found it necessary to abandon them. They went on foot along the shore of the bay until they came opposite San Francisquito, where they came upon a village of pagans who supplied them with tule from their own houses in order to make new balsas. With these they had the good fortune to arrive at their mission, where over the next few days the remainder of the party arrived, with the rest of the Christians, <u>without anyone having been lost</u>.

To avoid the possibility that in the future the Indians of San Francisco will be put at risk of being sacrificed to the pagans of the other shore, or perish during the dangerous passage across the strong currents on their miserable tule balsas, I asked the commander of the presidio, Don José Argüello, to bring together all the neophytes on a feast day and give them notice that while they should obey their ministers in all things and respect them as their spiritual and temporal fathers, they are to be exempted from going to the other shore in balsas in search of renegades, even though the missionaries order it.

In the same month of June in which the above-described event occurred between the Christians of Mission San Francisco and the pagans of the other shore, Mission San Jose was founded, as I have told Your Mercy, between the former mission and that of Santa Clara, on the right hand side of the estuary that reaches inland almost as far as the latter. It is in the direction of, and almost precipitously near, the lands of the Cuchillones and Sacalanes, of whom we have been speaking. <u>A very few</u> days after the founding of Mission San Jose, the corporal in command of the escort received two notices to the effect that the nearby pagans, who were participating in the construction, were informed that the group that had attacked Raymundo and his companions said they were getting ready to attack the mission and kill any pagans who were planning to become Christians or work on the buildings.

These rumors caused me some concern. I arranged for the sergeant of the company of San Francisco, Pedro Amador, to take three men as back up and go to the new establishment to investigate the truth of the matter, then get word back to me without losing any time. This he did, informing me in a letter of July 8 last, that the pagans who in the year of 1795 killed the seven Christian Indians of San Francisco Mission and those who this year beat up Raymundo El Californio and his companions were continuing their threats against those who lived near Mission San Jose. If they become Christians or come to help the construction, they will kill them. To that end they have formed an alliance and are preparing a great number of arrows. To avoid the fatal consequences that this might have for the conquest, both spiritual and temporal, as much from the mere threats of the Sacalanes and Cuchillones, as from any blow which a greatly swollen number might contemplate landing against the new mission of San Jose, and with the purpose of retrieving the many Christians who were hidden in their villages, I granted Amador twenty retired soldiers and citizens from the pueblo of San Jose (so as not to tie-up the experienced troops). I arranged for him to leave some of them watching over the mission, under command of the corporal in charge there, and to move out with the rest of them and with the soldiers of the escort to the villages of the above-mentioned pagans. He was to fall upon them at daybreak, gather up all the Christians that he could, and bring into custody the principle ringleaders and culprits in the aforementioned deaths. He was to bring them, the Christians and culprits, but leave free any others, with the warning that in the future they are to conduct themselves in peace and good will with the Spaniards and Christian Indians, for if they did not they would be dealt with harshly. He was to bring along two good interpreters and guides in order to minimize the risk of confrontation, by explaining to them [the pagans] the reason for his presence, which was to take back the Christians and to arrest the delinquents. That if at any time he used his arms, he should first be so prudent as to make the pagans understand clearly and distinctly, through the interpreters, that he was not going to hurt them if they handed over the fugitives and the culprits. If they did not appreciate his logic, he should try to explain himself several times over. Only if they insisted on taking up arms against his party should he make use of his own arms, and then only with the greatest reserve, so that as little blood as possible would be spilled.

    Amador left with his party under these orders from Mission San Jose on July 13. On the fifteenth he came upon a pagan village. He told them several times that he did not want to fight, but only to take away the Christians. But he was unable to persuade them to turn them over. On the contrary, sheltered by some steep-walled wells and trenches which they had prepared in their village with defence in mind, they began shooting arrows at our men, who had done nothing to harm them. They managed to kill a horse and injure two others. Amador, seeing their stubbornness, used his arms to try to get them under control and to make them give up. He had part of his detachment dismount. With sword and lance they attacked the pagans, who defended themselves for two hours. At last they gave up after seven Indians had died. He arrested over thirty Christians that they found there, and then continued on through two other villages, whose people were aroused by the noise from the confrontation. From these latter they were only able to capture two neophytes. Once the culprits and Christians were tied up, he set the rest free, telling them that the Spaniards did not want to do them any harm. Rather they wanted to do all the good possible for them, that is, so long as they kept themselves calm and under control. But if they harmed Christian Indians or those who intended to become Christians, he would proceed to punish them.

Later he began to march toward the land of the Cuchillones. After a short distance a great number of pagans were gathered, making a great hue and cry and feigning attacks. It was necessary to form ranks. Falling upon them, one was killed, and all the rest fled.

On the sixteenth he came upon three villages of those who had attacked Raimundo and his companions. Noting a great number of Indians who were resolved to fight in the third one, he got them to understand, through the interpreters, that he was not there to harm them, but rather to look for Christians. Having told them this and that he had punished the Indians at the other village because they had shot arrows at the Spaniards, he got them to calm down and hand over the three Christians who were among them, as well as the culprits that had offended the
Spaniards. He warned them to live in peace without upsetting the Spaniards or the Indians under their protection.

On the nineteenth Amador arrived at the new mission of San Jose, bringing along eighty-three Christians of all types and ages from the Mission of San Francisco, as well as nine pagan leaders and culprits in the aforementioned deaths and beatings. The first were turned over to their Father ministers. The second group were given punishment according to the part they had played in the affronts. We will work at converting them through kindness into the pale of our sacred religion. If they accede they will be given over to the same ministers. If they do not they will be set free after being well informed of the manner in which they will be expected to comport themselves in the future in order to avoid our wrath and punishment.

Having suppressed in this way the insolence and arrogance which the Cuchillones and Sacalanes manifested, I am persuaded that they will not dare again to offend us or the other pagans who are being converted at the missions. I am persuaded that with this blow they will remain quiet for many years, although I will not fail to take precautions, nor to take advantage of any available method, to draw them little by little into intercourse and friendship with us, through the troop at Mission San Jose, which borders their lands. Some favorable results are already apparent. On the third of this month three Indians arrived at that mission from the neighborhood of the rivers, asking if we were angry with them. They were told that we were not, that if they did not do us harm they would be looked upon as friends. According to reports from a San Francisco Christian who went out with permission, it seems that many pagans are thinking about coming to Mission San Jose to be baptized.

I bring all of this to Your Mercy's attention in compliance with my duty. May Our Lord grant you a long life.

Monterey, August 30, 1797
Your Servant, Diego Borica

DOCUMENT 17.

EXCERPTS FROM A PARAPHRASE OF INSTRUCTIONS FROM LIEUTENANT JOSE ARGUELLO TO SERGEANT LUIS PERALTA. SAN FRANCISCO. JUNE 6, 1798.

You will turn over command of the guard to Corporal Manuel Boronda and go without delay to Mission San Jose with six soldiers under your command. You will get the facts regarding the rumors circulating to the effect that the pagans want to attack. If you find substance to the insurrection, while awaiting further orders, you will observe the movements of the pagans, maintain double guards by night and take care that everyone has arms at the ready and horses saddled.

If you find it necessary to make any sortie, and it should be to the Sacalanes, put together a party of twenty or twenty-five capable well-armed men.

In the case that you should enter any village, you will take special care that your command operates prudently and as a unit. Only if the Indian population takes up arms and you are unable to control them through reasoning will you respond with yours [arms] so as to scare them. Arresting the guilty ones, you will return to the mission. After reporting to the governor, you will wait there with your men until you receive further orders. In everything you will move with prudence, according to the unfolding of events.

Your mission concluded, the pagans pacified, you will find out from the reverend Fathers of said mission whether all the individuals of the guard and their families have been faithful to the Church. If anyone has not, put him under arrest and make him look into himself. Until you can be sure he has, do not set him free.

At the same time you will check the information regarding the discord between Father Barcenilla and Corporal Miranda, in order to report to our Chief...

DOCUMENT 18.

INTERROGATION OF CHRISTIAN INDIANS REGARDING A CONSPIRACY AGAINST MISSION SAN JOSE, MADE BY SERGEANT LUIS PERALTA. MISSION SAN JOSE. JUNE 21, 1804.

I, Sergeant Luís Peralta, found myself at the guard station of Mission San Jose on June 14, 1804, under orders of Captain José Argüello to investigate and apprehend the Indians who intended to kill the fathers and soldiers and to burn the mission, according to the statement of Don Gervasio Argüello, head of the guard. He got the information from the Indian Abundio, who told him that the Christian Indians Ugenio, Primerio, Cisco, Constantino, Luminato, Donato, Hulario, Herasmo, Luís Antonio, Leuterio, Bruno, Andres, Proseso, José Manuel, Melchor, Salbador and Lion wanted to commit this offense. With this notice he imprisoned all of them except José Manuel, Proseso, Melchor, and Salvador, who were in the mountains cutting wood. While waiting for the soldiers to arrest those four Indians, I began to take the statements of those already imprisoned. Through an interpreter that I requested from the Fathers, and in the presence of the two soldiers Apolinario Bernal and Frutuoso Amador, I ordered the following prisoners called forward.

Declaration of Crico. I asked Crico what motives he had for wanting to kill the Fathers and the soldiers and burn the houses. He responds that he never considered it, that only today had he talked to José Manuel, Proseso, Melchor, and Salvador about it. They wanted to burn the houses and kill the Fathers. I asked if he had heard them say why they wanted to kill them. He responded "no". I asked if he knew that they had invited other Christians or any pagans to join them. He responded "no" and had nothing more to say. He was sent back to the guardhouse. [This may be Ciriaco Uniacse, age thirty-three, a Causen (SJO-B 519).]

Declaration of Lion. I ordered Lion called and I questioned him through an interpreter as I did the other man. He responded that he had not attempted anything, that Proseso, José Manuel, Melchor, and Salbador had asked him to join. They sent him a message through Primerio. He sent back [a message] that they should drop it, that he did not want to do it because he was frightened of the Fathers and soldiers, and that they ought to keep quiet because someone might hear about it. Although he told them that he would help them, in his heart he said, "If they go to burn the houses I will run to warn the Fathers." I asked if he had invited other Christians or pagans to join. He responded "no", that he only told four members of his own family about it, because he had no desire to help. Having nothing more to say, he was returned to the guardhouse. [León Tumiun, "adult" at baptism, a Taunan (SJO-B 1135).]

Declaration of Primerio. I called Primerio forward, and asked him the same questions as above. He responded that he was invited to join by Donato, but that he told them that he did not want [to get involved] because he feared the Fathers and soldiers. Disregarding them, he went off to his own house. This conversation took place in the house of Lion. I asked him if any others tried to recruit him or if he invited other pagans to join. He responded "no". I asked him if it were true that José Manuel, Proseso, Melchor, and Salbador sent him to recruit Lion and what message Lion sent back. He responded that it was true that Lion told him to tell them "yes". Having nothing more to say, I ordered him back to the guardhouse. [Pimerio Uitus, age thirty-one, a Taunan (SJO-B 94).]

Declaration of Donato. I had Donato called forward. Through the interpreter I questioned him the same as the others. He responded that he hadn't considered doing anything, that José Manuel had not said anything to him, that he did not know anything about it, and that José Manuel is a great dissembler. As he had nothing more to say, I sent him back. [Donato Taucucse, age thirty-seven, a Taunan (SJO-B 1007).]

Declaration of Constantino. I ordered Constantino called forward and asked him the same questions. He responded that he knew nothing nor had considered doing anything. No one had said anything to him. He is quite content at the mission. He was asked if he had heard anyone else say anything or knew if any others had recruited any pagans. He responded in the negative. Having nothing more to say, I ordered him retired to the guardhouse. [Constantino, age forty-four, Taunan (SJO-B 1003), step-father of Pimerio, brother-in-law of Donato.]

Declaration of Luminato. I had Luminato called forward and went over the same questions. He responded that he did not know anything about it, nor had he heard anything spoken, nor had he recruited anyone. Having nothing more to say, I ordered him retired to the guardhouse. [Yluminato Pulujtiz, age thirty-eight, "Redwoods", probably a Yrgin (SJO-B 742).]

Declaration of Ujencio. I had Ujencio called and questioned him like the others. He answered that Lion and Donato had invited him to join. He had told them "yes" because he feared them, but in his heart he did not want to [be involved]. Asked if he had invited any others, he answered "no". Asked if he knew that some pagans were to come to help the Christians, he answered "no". Having nothing more to say, I had him sent back to the guardhouse. [No such name found among Mission San Jose baptisms. This may be Eugenio Liuicsse, a Taunan (SJO-B 281).]

The following day, the soldiers returned, bringing the Indians José Manuel, Proseso, Melchor, and Salvador under guard. Said soldiers told me that on the road they had encountered Pedro Bojorques, the mission steward. He told them, and was on his way to tell the mission guard, that while they were in the mountains cutting wood he had overheard one of the four Indians, who were brothers, say "It will not be long before we kill the soldiers and the Fathers. Then we will have plenty of livestock and wheat to eat." The steward gave me the same information, saying he had come in only for that purpose, leaving the rest of the Indians cutting wood. On the basis of that information, said four Indians were kept imprisoned. From among them I had José Manuel called. In the presence of the two soldiers who served as witnesses I questioned him through an interpreter.

Declaration of José Manuel. I asked him what his motives were for wanting to murder the Fathers and soldiers and burn down the mission, who suggested this, and what person or persons had recruited him. He responded that he had no motive, that Donato, Constantino, and Bernardo had invited him to join, but that he did not want to join, nor had he recruited others. Asked if he knew whether some pagans were coming to help or had been called to come, he responded "no". As he had no more to say, I ordered him back to the guardhouse. [José Manuel Queucher, age thirty-three, "Redwoods" at baptism, probably Yrgin (SJO-B 194)—his father was a Tuibun (SJO-B 975).]

Declaration of Proseso. I ordered Proseso called forward and asked him the same questions as to the other. He responded that he had not considered doing anything, that he had just heard some talk from Luminato and Genaro. Then he recanted and said that he had not heard anything or talked about anything. Nor did he know anything. Asked if he had heard others saying anything, he responded in the negative. As he had nothing more to say, I ordered him taken back. [Proceso Quesuesi, age forty, Tuibun (SJO-B 698)]

Declaration of Melchor. I called Melchor and questioned him as I had the others. He answered that he was not guilty, he had not even considered doing anything, nor had he recruited anyone else, nor did he know anything. He had merely heard Illuminato and Genaro talking. Then he said that they told him they wanted to kill the Fathers, but that they did not say why. Asked if he had heard others talk or if he knew whether any pagans had come to help them, he responded in the negative. As he had nothing more to say, I ordered him retired to the guardhouse. [Melchor Toquila, age thirty-three, "Alameda" at baptism (SJO-B 539), son of a Tuibun (SJO-B 977)—probably a cousin of José Manuel.]

Declaration of Salvador. I ordered Salvador called and asked him the same questions. He answered that he had entered no scheme, but only heard Constantino, Bernardo, and Donato saying that they wanted to burn the houses of the Fathers and the troops because they punished them so much.

Asked if they recruited him or if they had recruited any pagans, he answered "no". Having nothing more to say, I had him sent back to the guardhouse. [Salvador Ollema, age thirty-eight, group not listed at baptism (SJO-B 836)—brother of Tuibun/Yrgin José Manuel.]

Through other investigations and inquiries which I made I absolutely verified that the principal ringleaders of the scheme were José Manuel, Proseso, Melchor, and Salvador. The rest, on the other hand, carry no great guilt. I followed the instructions which my commander, Don Argüello gave me, to punish the minor culprits with nine days of whippings in front of the assembled Indians, and release them well admonished to the reverend Fathers of the mission. Each day that I did this I warned all the Indians that they were to be good Christians. I made them understand that the Fathers and soldiers were there for their own good. I directed other warnings toward the maintenance of good order and quit at the mission. As for those that, I am certain from all the inquiries I made, clearly had intentions to do something and to recruit others, they deny it, as is customary, even though accused by everyone else. Instructing the Indian population to remain in peace without the least trouble, I decided to return to my presidio, bringing as prisoners José Manuel, Proseso, Melchor, and Salvador as the principal ringleaders. Apart from them, I imprisoned Lion (although I could not prove him guilty of anything more than being invited to join, he is esteemed among his relatives and he has a lot of influence among them) in order to keep things under some manner of control.

And therefore I sign this with the two witnesses at said mission on June 21, 1804.

Luís Peralta
José Fructuoso Amador
Apolinario Bernal

DOCUMENT 19.

PARAPHRASE OF A REPORT FROM JOSE ANTONIO SANCHEZ TO LIEUTENANT JOSE ARGUELLO. MISSION SAN JOSE. JANUARY 16, 1805.

He states that Father Cueva asked for an escort to visit the sick and to hear confession at a village of Christian Indians. He was given the soldiers Ygnacio Alviso and Joaquín Higuera. Mayordomo Ygnacio Higuera and several Indians also accompanied them on foot, to carry the sick. Ygnacio Alviso was given orders not to go beyond the village, even if the Father would want to do so. Yet, according to what Alviso said, there was a dense fog and the guide led them to a village of pagans, telling them they were Christians. Those from the village began to fire arrows with great enthusiasm—soon they got support from two other villages. They killed Ygnacio Higuera and two of our Indians. Father Cueva took an arrow in the eye and Joaquín Higuera another in the thigh. The pagans killed all the saddle horses, and those of the remuda as well. They kept firing arrows at the Father and the soldiers from midday until about dusk. The soldiers lost everything but their leather jackets, shields, and muskets. This took place yesterday, and some Indians brought back word on foot. This morning the Father and soldiers arrived on horses that had been sent out for them from here.

He asks that the governor order the commissioner at San Jose Pueblo to stand ready to grant the commander at San Francisco anything and everything he needs in order to make sorties against the hostile Indians, in as much as the force at the presidio is so small. He entreats also that they arrange with the commander at Monterey to send all the auxiliaries that are asked for to San Francisco without excuse or delay, in case they are needed for sorties against the Indians.

The horse herd which Sergeant Peralta brought back is badly maimed, and it will not be possible to return it to the company for some time. That notwithstanding, the Indians here remain peaceful.

DOCUMENT 20.

LETTER FROM FATHER RAMON ABELLA TO GOVERNOR JOSE JOAQUIN DE ARRILLAGA. MISSION SAN FRANCISCO. FEBRUARY 28, 1807.

I give you the cursed news that the pagan natives and runaway Christians have killed between eleven and thirteen neophytes of this mission. I dare say it was twelve, because one remains a runaway or dead. Nothing is known about him. He could be with two others that I know for sure fled. It happened like this. In the middle of January a young boy died a natural death. Because of that death, his parents and two other married couples fled (six people). The pagans kidnapped the wife of one of them, who returned alone to tell his relatives about it. On February 3 the one who returned, whose name is Octaviano (and who has now run away again), and a friend of his got together a number of people from his homeland, about twenty or thirty men. As a result of their effort more than a hundred men were soon gathered together, including the healthy and the not so healthy. Some were ill, and the majority had no weapons. I clearly remember telling one man not to go (who ended up being the first one killed.) It was necessary to restrain some to keep them from going. Not one of them was forced to go. On Wednesday, February 4, they embarked. On Thursday they continued over land. On Friday they again went by water, across the Strait of the Karquines, the mouth of the rivers. All of this is to the northeast of the mission. On that Friday afternoon they split up, and that was their ruin. Sixty men remained right there at the Karquin village, gathering up all the runaways that were there, as well as some pagans. They had no trouble. The other forty men went further inland. They had a number of run-ins along the trail, at which it is said that several people told the leader, who was the alcalde (who also died), that there were too many people in the area, that they should go back. Finally on Saturday morning thirty-nine of them got there. They found several runaways, who took the lead in firing arrows and urging the pagans to do the same. Even the old women were waiting with sticks when they arrived. Nevertheless, they still brought the village under control. But soon men joined in from neighboring *rancherías*, particularly from one called Suio Suiu (it is not yet known who told them, but it will be discovered in time), and began firing arrows. Then the neophytes took off running. A great many of them never stopped. I already mentioned that they had very few arrows. Others, in order to help their sick companions (who had been so foolish as to go along to the furthest area for no other reason than that they were from the same homeland as the *alcalde*) tried to hold out even though they were the smallest group in number. Both Christians and pagans used up their arrows shooting at one another. Very close to the boat launching area in the Karquin village two were beaten to death, although I believe that they had already shot the *alcalde*, who was one of those killed, with an arrow. But it was a dirty trick by one, or a few, of the neophytes, who could have defended them. Not all of them had good hearts. The neophytes who had relatives there had divided loyalties. For the most part they inclined to the side of the pagans and the runaways. The fact is that it looks like they chose the ones they would kill. The seven dead were from San Mateo and San Pedro and it is said that they were talking together in their southern language. On Sunday the eighth, thirty men came to the mission to tell us what happened.

You can imagine the confusion here. I myself thought about running away so that I would not have to face it. Nonetheless, I realized that such an action would be the least appropriate thing to do. They were all discussing a variety of schemes, such as going to kill them [the enemy] secretly one at a time. But they have finally calmed down.

What I am asking Your Mercy is that you regard the mission, its neophytes, and my successors with compassion, exerting your influence to put together an expedition when the time is right. Otherwise all is finished here, because the runaways will never return. There is one runaway, who I don't know, who fled again the minute the troops brought him in. Many will now flee to that haven. Only he who seeks it will know his own loss, which is a matter for God and for the King, Our Lord, may God protect him. I have heard from many that it is not difficult [to get there]. One only needs to cross the heads of the estuaries. It is also said that they must swim the horses and move the men in balsas. There is a large amount of tule there, a narrow strait, and calm waters. The second-lieutenant and the sergeants of the presidio know about this. Now I will cease pestering Your Mercy.

Ramón Abella

P.S. Also in that vicinity are other villages in which there are some runaways, called Omiomi. There are a total of sixty-two runaways.

DOCUMENT 21.

LETTER FROM GOVERNOR JOSE JOAQUIN DE ARRILLAGA TO THE COMMISSIONER OF THE PUEBLO OF SAN JOSE. MONTEREY. JULY 23, 1807.

I note the success resulting from the expedition of the townsmen of the pueblo to solicit pagan Indians to bring in the present harvest. I am very happy with the way it was done and I hope to God that this example will lead to more help in the future. With pleasure I order that you be given what you ask for in clothing for these pagans.

[The following list is written along the left margin.]

40 yards of flannel—2 bundles of thread—50 needles—4 bundles of glass beads—cloth for blankets

I wish them to be treated with all possible consideration so that, seeing the treatment that they receive, they will feel like coming in to reside in the future.

The work assignments are to be moderate. Because they are not accustomed to it, it will be difficult to put much on them for the present. I am aware of your knowledge of them. I hope and trust that they will be content as well as useful. Let them know that it is my desire that neither they nor their relatives should come to any harm. Rather, I want to maintain harmony. Let them know that they can come and go at will. I want no one to apply any violent pressure on them to become Christians. I desire that they enjoy their liberty, as they have done up until now. I also want them to be paid a just wage for their work.

There should be no special consideration for any of the townsmen who went with my permission to look for them. Rather, the work shall be divided up with complete equality. Everyone should contribute to the on-going enterprise. Pay should be the same for everyone who goes out to do the work.

Regarding Dolores Mesa, let him know that his claim regarding what he should receive in relation to the rest of the townsmen is ridiculous, completely crazy. The governor did not concede him any privileges because he went out to bring in said pagans. Nor would he even have gotten them if you had not made the request on behalf of the these townsmen. Like a good citizen he should contribute to the general welfare of the entire pueblo, and not even mention any claim that he be given preference.

If the projects of those who went to look for the pagans are concluded, and someone then wants to make use of them, he must first get the agreement of everyone, but I advise you to first get them finished and in the meanwhile keep them from the townspeople, that they not take advantage of them for any reason, not even to do acts of kindness, because such actions will lead to the failure of the projects. Well, my goal is that everyone who went to get these pagans benefits as equally as possible, and for that reason I grant you whatever could be salvaged from the warehouse.

If at the end of the projects some of these pagans want to remain in the service of someone in particular, you will take care to discover the circumstances and to inform me. But at all times they are to have complete freedom to leave at their own convenience.

José Joaquín de Arrillaga

DOCUMENT 22.

LETTER FROM GOVERNOR JOSE JOAQUIN DE ARRILLAGA TO THE COMMISSIONER OF THE PUEBLO OF SAN JOSE. MISSION SOLEDAD. AUGUST 17, 1807.

Today I forewarned the commander of San Francisco Presidio that he will receive from you a disposition from the neophyte Indian of Mission Santa Clara who unjustly maltreated and injured a pagan that was working for militiaman Rafael Gomez, about which you informed me in your letter of the twelfth of this month, when you also told me that you had reported to your commander. He has also passed word to me.

Regarding this incident I should tell you that although you have done very well to inform the pagans that they will receive just compensation for the transgression, it is important that you give them what you can. Given the situation, I order you to take the thug to the jail. If what you tell me is true, I will order you to punish him with twenty-five lashes for three or four mornings running, and if it be necessary, for still more days. If it seems they are not satisfied with that punishment, let the pagans know that I will banish him to a place where he will never do harm again. The strongest necessary punishment will be given him, short of execution.

I inform you also that whether the little pagan dies or not, well, in the former case, over and above the punishment that you would be able to mete out, it will be necessary to proceed in a more formal manner against the thug.

Finally, with regard to what you have offered, in my name, as recompense to the pagans, it is important that you pay them fully. I give you my full authorization to take care of the matter as you see fit. I want the pagans to remain content and to know that the governor and those he commands detest such goings on and punish them. As I have said, do as you see fit and advise me of your decision.

José Joaquín de Arrillaga

DOCUMENT 23.

LETTER FROM GOVERNOR JOSE JOAQUIN DE ARRILLAGA TO MACARIO CASTRO, COMMISSIONER OF THE PUEBLO OF SAN JOSE. MONTEREY. SEPTEMBER 5, 1807.

I received your dispatch of August 30, regarding the results of the punishment given to the Christian Indian of Santa Clara who mistreated a pagan Indian. I received your advise regarding the case and the petition of the two *capitanejos* that the delinquent be granted pardon. And so it seems that they feel recompensed for the injury done to them. That leaves me satisfied.

I am not upset that the Mission Santa Clara Indian is to be set free. But if it were possible I would have liked the little pagan who was abused to have been brought forth in order to clarify exactly what happened before the thug was put at liberty. It seems to me that it would have been better to have proceeded in that way. But it was a natural mistake to fail to do that. You proceeded as seemed best, but that method would have allowed all the pagans to see that the abused boy was recovering well. I am satisfied.

In regard to what you told me concerning the other two boys about whom the Father spoke, I must point out to you that you did not tell me whether they were Christians or not. If they are not, send them off to their village, and if they do not want to be, send them also. If they are now Christians, and they want to live in the pueblo with some citizens without going back to the mission except to hear Mass, allow them to remain, and inform me. Make it clear to them that they are under no compulsion to do anything except have a good attitude toward the patron whom they serve. You will charge the patron with instructing them in the Catholic Doctrine, little by little. However, I cannot believe that in such fashion they can be made into good Christians. If they want to live in the pueblo, whether they be pagans or Christians, they are to live without anyone abusing them. Their patron should take care that they hear Mass on feast days.

It does my heart good that the pagans who came here comported themselves well, and that they completed their work on the wheat and hemp harvests without the slightest problem.

José Joaquín de Arrillaga

DOCUMENT 24.

PARAPHRASE OF A REPORT FROM GOVERNOR JOSE JOAQUIN DE ARRILLAGA TO VICEROY FRANCISCO JAVIER VENEGAS. MONTEREY. JUNE 28, 1810.

He says that he ordered the commander of the San Francisco Presidio, Second-Lieutenant Gabriel Moraga, to go out in pursuit of pagans of the village called Sespesuyu to the north of the San Francisco Presidio. Over the past three years they have brought things to a sorry state, having killed over that time sixteen Christians. Said village lies on the other side of the estuary of San Francisco. The troops lack launches, but he found one very small one in which the second lieutenant and his troops and horses embarked under trying conditions. They made several passages. Said second-lieutenant ... took as prisoners eighteen pagans. They were set free because they were gravely wounded and he had no way to transport them. He believes that not one of them could have avoided death. Toward the end of the action the surviving Indians sealed themselves in three brush houses, from which they made a tenacious defence, wounding the corporals and two soldiers. Those were the only injuries sustained by the troop. No one was killed. After having killed the pagans in two of the grass houses, the Christians set fire to the third grass house, as a means to take the pagans prisoner. But they did not achieve that result, since the valiant Indians died enveloped in flames before they could be taken into custody. The second-lieutenant says that he could not reason with the pagans, who died fighting or by burning. There was no room for compassion in this disaster wrought upon them by our troops, because of their resistance. It is calculated that 120 pagans were fighting.

He commends the comportment of the troop and asks that the second-lieutenant be promoted to lieutenant, the wounded corporals to sergeant, and the [wounded] soldiers be granted one month extra pay.

Bibliographic Practices

Bibliographic references are cited in the text of this study according to a modified version of the common format of anthropological publications (author, date, page number). For unpublished manuscripts, the date is bound in brackets. I follow a non-standard procedure for published letters and manuscripts, indicating the manuscript date before the publication date, as follows:

manuscripts	—	(author, [manuscript date])
published manuscripts	—	(author, [manuscript date] publication date)
books and articles	—	(author, publication date)

This technique has the advantage of giving primacy to the date upon which an early historical document was generated, rather than to some later date at which it may have been translated and placed into print. It allows the bibliophile the luxury of perusing the bibliographic listings for the works of, say, Pedro Fages, in the order in which they were produced.

Specific entries from the registers of Missions San Francisco, San Jose, and Santa Clara are cited in the text of this report as follows:

Mission	*Baptism*	*Marriage*	*Death*
Santa Clara	SCL-B ____	SCL-M ____	SCL-D ____
Santa Cruz	SCR-B ____	SCR-M ____	SCR-D ____
San Francisco	SFR-B ____	SFR-M ____	SFR-D ____
San Jose	SJO-B ____	SJO-M ____	SJO-D ____

The unique sequential entry number from the cited register book follows the letter code in the citations.

Bibliography

Mission Register References[1]

SCA-D   Mission San Carlos Borromeo *Libro de Difuntos, 1777-1858.* Chancery Office, Diocese of Monterey, 580 Fremont Blvd., Monterey, California.

SCL-B   Mission Santa Clara *Libro de Bautismos, 1778-1863* (3 vols.) University of Santa Clara Archives, Santa Clara, California.

SCL-M   Mission Santa Clara *Libro de Casamientos, 1778-1863* (1 vol.) University of Santa Clara Archives, Santa Clara, California.

SCL-D   Mission Santa Clara *Libro de Entierros, 1777-1866* (2 vols.) University of Santa Clara Archives, Santa Clara, California.

SCR-B   Mission Santa Cruz *Libro de Bautismos, 1791-1857* (2 vols.) Chancery Office, Catholic Diocese of Monterey, Monterey, California.

SFR-B   Mission San Francisco *Libro de Bautismos, 1776-1870* (2 vols.) Archives of the Catholic Archdiocese of San Francisco, Mountain View, California.

SFR-M   Mission San Francisco de Asís *Libro de Casamientos, 1777-1859* (1 vol.) Archives of the Archdiocese of San Francisco, Mountain View, California.

SFR-D   Mission San Francisco de Asís *Libro de Difuntos, 1776-1856* (2 vols.) Archives of the Archdiocese of San Francisco, Mountain View, California.

SFR-P   Mission San Francisco *Padron, 1818-1822.* Mission Archives, 1769-1856 (C-C4, Item 68). The Bancroft Library, University of California, Berkeley.

---

[1]For mission register citation format, see Bibliographic Practices (page 321).

SJO-B   Mission San José *Libro de Bautismos, 1797-1859* (2 vols.) Archives of the Archdiocese of San Francisco, Mountain View, California.

SJO-M   Mission San José *Libro de Casamientos, 1797-1859* (1 vol.) Archives of the Archdiocese of San Francisco, Mountain View, California.

SJO-D   Mission San José *Libro de Difuntos, 1797-1837* ((1 vol.) Archives of the Archdiocese of San Francisco, Mountain View, California.

General References

Abbreviations

AGN   Archivo General de la Nación. Palacio Nacional, Mexico City.
ASJ   Archives of the City of San Jose. Manuscripts on file with the San Jose Historical Society.
C-A   Archives of California. [Paraphrases of Spanish and Mexican Period manuscripts destroyed in the 1906 San Francisco fire.] The Bancroft Library, University of California, Berkeley
UCPAAE   University of California Publications in American Archaeology and Ethnology. Berkeley.

References

Abella, Ramón
   [1807]   Carta al Gobernador José Joaquín de Arrillaga. San Francisco. February 28, 1807. Cartas de los Misioneros, No. 317. Archives of the Catholic Archdiocese of San Francisco, Mountain View, California.
   [1818-1822]   *Padron*. Mission San Francisco. Alphabetical List of Indian People at Mission San Francisco at the end of 1818, augmented through 1822. C-C 4-5, Number 68.

Abella, Ramón and Juan Sainz de Lucío
   [1814] 1976   Reply to the Interrogatory of 1812 from Mission San Juan Bautista. November 11, 1814. *In* As the Padres Saw Them: California Indian Life and Customs as Reported by the Franciscan Missionaries, 1813-1815. Maynard Geiger and Clement Meighan, eds. Santa Barbara, CA: Santa Barbara Mission Archives.

Ackerknecht, Irwen H.
   1965   *History and Geography of the Most Important Diseases*. New York: Hafner Publishing.

Alberni, Pedro
   [1796]   Informe sobre la causa que tengan los Indios para huirse. September 12, 1796. AGN, Ramo Californias 65:111-116.
   [1800]   Alberni al Gobernador Arrillaga sobre depradaciones de Indios. Monterey. July 2, 1800. C-A 11:33-34.

Alvarado, Juan Bautista
 [1876] Historia de California. Bancroft Library, University of California, Berkeley.
Amador, Pedro
 [1797] Amador al Gobernador Diego de Borica. Mission San Jose. July 8, 1797. C-A 8:371-373.
 [1797a] Amador al Gobernador Diego de Borica. San Jose. July 19, 1797. AGN, Ramo Californias, Tomo 65, Doc. 93.
 [1797b] Nombres Indios. San Jose. July 19, 1797. C-A 8:323.
 [1797c] Diario. Mission San Jose. July 28-August 16, 1797. C-A 8:368-370.
 [1797d] Amador al Gobernador Borica. Mission San Jose. August 17, 1797. C-A 8:365-368.
 [1797e] Amador al Gobernador Borica. San Jose. September 3, 1797. C-A 8:317-318.
 [1798] Amador al Gobernador Diego de Borica. Mission San Jose. April 11 [19], 1798. C-A 10:101.
 [1798a] Amador al Teniente José Argüello. Mission San Jose. April 17, 1798. C-A 10:100.
 [1800] Diario. San Francisco Presidio. May 15, 1800. C-A 16:130-132.
Amorós, Juan
 [1814] 1976 Reply to the Interrogatory of 1812 from Mission San Carlos. February 3, 1814. *In* As the Padres Saw Them: California Indian Life and Customs as Reported by the Franciscan Missionaries, 1813-1815. Maynard Geiger and Clement Meighan, eds. Santa Barbara, CA: Santa Barbara Mission Archives.
Anza, Juan Bautista de
 [1776] 1930 Anza's Diary of the Second Anza Expedition, 1775-1776. Pp. 1-200 in *Anza's California Expeditions*, Volume 3. Herbert Bolton, editor. Berkeley and Los Angeles: University of California Press.
Applegate, Richard B.
 1978 *'Atishwin: The Dream Helper in South-Central California*. Ballena Press Anthropological Papers No. 13. Lowell John Bean and Thomas C. Blackburn, series editors. Socorro, New Mexico: Ballena Press.
Argüello, Gervasio
 [1811] 1960 Diario de Un Registro de los Ríos Grandes, October 15-31, 1811.
Argüello, José
 [1788] Argüello al Gobernador Pedro Fages sobre pelea de Indios. San Francisco Presidio. April 30, 1788. C-A 4:261-262.

[1790]	Argüello al Gobernador Fages. San Jose. April 19, 1790. C-A 5:218-219.
[1790a]	Argüello al Gobernador Fages sobre persecución a unos Indios que se huiron llevandose unos caballos. San Francisco Presidio. May 1, 1790. C-A 5:215.
[1793]	Instrucciones a Macario Castro. Monterey. September 23, 1793. ASJ, 1793, Doc.19.
[1794]	Instrucciones al Alférez Hermenegildo Sal. Monterey Presidio. October 31, 1794. C-A 7:130-132.
[1794a]	Informe al Gobernador Diego de Borica sobre alborotes de gentiles. Monterey Presidio. November 4, 1794. C-A 7:125-126.
[1797]	Argüello al Gobernador Borica. San Francisco Presidio. June 14, 1797. C-A 8:210.
[1797a]	Argüello al Gobernador Borica. San Francisco Presidio. July 6, 1797. C-A 9:90-91.
[1797b]	Argüello al Gobernador Borica. San Francisco Presidio. July 31, 1797. C-A 9:90.
[1797c]	Relación de los gentiles Sacalanes y los Indios Cuchillones. San Francisco Presidio. August 9, 1797. AGN, Ramo Californias, Tomo 65, Doc. 101.
[1797d]	Declaraciones de Indios Cristianos, huidos de la Misión de San Francisco. San Francisco Presidio. August 12, 1797. AGN, Ramo Californias, Tomo 65, Doc. 106.
[1798]	Argüello al Gobernador Borica. San Francisco Presidio. April 6, 1798. C-A 10:97.
[1798a]	Argüello al Sargento Pedro Amador. Prevenciones sobre gentiles. San Francisco Presidio. April 12, 1798. C-A 10:124.
[1798b]	Argüello al Gobernador Borica sobre Indios que volvieron. San Francisco Presidio. May 28, 1798. C-A 10:93.
[1798c]	Instrucciones al Sargento Luís Peralta. San Francisco Presidio. June 6, 1798. C-A 10:107-108.
[1800]	Argüello al Gobernador José Joaquín de Arrillaga. San Francisco Presidio. May 20, 1800. C-A 11:32-33.
[1800a]	Estado de Jurisdicción. San Francisco Presidio. December 31, 1800. C-A 16:132-133.
[1804]	Argüello al Gobernador Arrillaga. San Francisco Presidio. June 30, 1804. AGN, Ramo Californias, Tomo 9:439-441.
[1804a]	Argüello al Gobernador Arrillaga. San Francisco Presidio. October 26, 1804. C-A 11:358-359.
[1805]	Argüello al Gobernador Arrillaga. San Francisco Presidio. January 31, 1805. C-A 12:36-37.
[1805a]	Argüello al Gobernador Arrillaga. San Francisco Presidio. February 28, 1805. C-A 12:39-40.

[1805b]   Argüello al Gobernador Arrillaga. San Francisco Presidio. May 30, 1805. C-A 12:42.
[1805c]   Argüello al Gobernador Arrillaga. San Francisco Presidio. May 31, 1805. C-A 12:43.
[1805d]   Argüello al Gobernador Arrillaga. Expedición entre gentiles. San Francisco Presidio. June 25, 1805. C-A 16:251-252.

Argüello, Luís
[1805]   Informe a Teniente José Argüello sobre un plan de Indios para quemar la Misión de Santa Clara y matar a los Padres. Mission San Jose. May 10, 1805. C-A 12:30.
[1821] 1992   *The Diary of Captain Luis Antonio Argüello: The Last Spanish Expedition in California.* Translated by Vivian Fisher. The Friends of the Bancroft Library, University of California, Berkeley.

Arrillaga, José Joaquín de
[1793]   Arrillaga al Alférez José Perez-Fernández sobre persecución de Indios. Monterey. December 17, 1793. C-A 14:176.
[1794]   Instrucciones al Alférez Hermenegildo Sal. Monterey. May 7, 1794. C-A 22:364.
[1794a]   Informe al Alférez Perez-Fernández. Monterey. July 29, 1794. C-A 22:367.
[1794b]   Informe al Gobernador Diego de Borica sobre estado de las Californias. Monterey. August 1794. C-A 7:188-200.
[1804]   Arrillaga al Virrey José de Iturrigaray. Monterey. May 11, 1804. AGN, Ramo Californias, Tomo 9:433.
[1805]   Arrillaga al Virrey Iturrigaray. Monterey. March 11, 1805. AGN, Ramo Californias, Tomo 9:452-453.
[1806]   Arrillaga al Alférez Luís Argüello. Monterey. May 20, 1806. C-A 26:262-265.
[1806a]   Arrillaga al Virrey Iturrigaray. Monterey. June 30, 1806. C-A 25:330.
[1806b]   Arrillaga al commandante de San Francisco. Monterey. July 17, 1806. C-A 26:491.
[1807]   Arrillaga al commandante de San Francisco. Santa Barbara Presidio. February 14, 1807. C-A 26:494.
[1807a]   Arrillaga al commandante de San Francisco. May 6, 1807. C-A 26:496.
[1807b]   Arrillaga al comisionado del pueblo de San José. July 23, 1807. ASJ, 1807, Doc. 21.
[1807c]   Arrillaga al comisionado del pueblo de San José. August 17, 1807. ASJ, 1807, Doc. 22.

[1807d]	Arrillaga al Macario Castro, comisionado del pueblo de San José. September 4, 1807. ASJ, 1807, Doc. 24.
[1807e]	Arrillaga al comisionado del pueblo de San José. September 5, 1807. ASJ, 1807, Doc. 25.
[1807f]	Arrillaga al commandante de San Francisco. September 25, 1807. C-A 26:499.
[1807g]	Arrillaga al commandante de San Francisco. November 4, 1807. C-A 26:500.
[1808]	Arrillaga al commandante de San Francisco. February 5, 1808. C-A 26:502.
[1809]	Arrillaga al commandante de San Francisco. Monterey. February 9, 1809. C-A 26:511.
[1810]	Arrillaga al commandante de San Francisco. Monterey. February 5, 1810. C-A 26:430.
[1810a]	Arrillaga al Virrey Francisco Javier Venegas. Monterey. June 28, 1810. C-A 25:371-372.
[1810b]	Arrillaga al Commandante de San Francisco. Monterey. September 24, 1810. C-A 26:431.

Arroyo de la Cuesta, Felipe
[1814] 1976   Reply to the Interrogatory of 1812 from Mission San Juan Bautista. May 1, 1814. *In* As the Padres Saw Them: California Indian Life and Customs as Reported by the Franciscan Missionaries, 1813-1815. Maynard Geiger and Clement Meighan, eds. Santa Barbara, CA: Santa Barbara Mission Archives.
[1821-1837]   Lecciones de Indios. (Notebook of Grammers and Vocabularies taken between 1821 and 1837 at several missions.) 50p. H.H. Bancroft Collection (C-C 63:1). Bancroft Library, University of California, Berkeley.

Asisara, Lorenzo
[1878] 1989   The Assassination of Padre Andres Quintana by the Indians of Mission Santa Cruz in 1812: The Narrative of Lorenzo Asisara. Translated and introduced by Edward D. Castillo. *California History* 68(3):116-125.
[1878] 1989a   An Indian Account of the Decline and Collapse of Mexico's Hegemony over the Missionized Indians of California. Translated and introduced by Edward D. Castillo. *American Indian Quarterly* 13(4):391-408.
[1890] 1892   Narrative of a Mission Indian. Lorenzo Asisara with E.L. Williams. Pp. 45-48 in *The History of Santa Cruz County, California*. Edward S. Harrington, editor and principal author. San Francisco, CA.: Pacific Press.

Ayala, Juan Manuel de
[1775] 1971　From the Journal of Juan Manuel de Ayala, 1775. Pp. 78-87 in *The First Spanish Entry into San Francisco Bay*. John Galvin, editor. San Francisco: John Howell Books.

Bancroft, Hubert H.
1884　*The History of California*. Volume 1, 1542-1800 San Francisco: A.L. Bancroft and Company.
1885　*The History of California*. Volume 2, 1801-1824 San Francisco: A.L. Bancroft and Company.
1888　*California Pastoral*. San Francisco: A.L. Bancroft and Company.

Baranov, Aleksandr A.
[1808] 1989　Instructions from Aleksandr A. Baranov to his Assistant, Ivan A. Kuskov, Regarding the Dispatch of a Hunting Party to the Coast of Spanish California. Pp. 165-174 in *To Siberia and Russian America: The Russian American Colonies 1798-1867*, Volume 3. Basil Dmytryshyn, E.A.P. Crownhart-Vaughan, and Thomas Vaughan, editors. Oregon Historical Society Press.

Barcenilla, Ysidoro
[1799]　Barcenilla al Gobernador Diego de Borica. Mission San Jose. June 30, 1799. Cartas de los Misioneros. Archives of the Catholic Archdiocese of San Francisco, Mountain View, California.

Barrett, Samuel A.
1908　The Ethnogeography of the Pomo and Neighboring Indians. UCPAAE 6(1):1-332.
1933　Pomo Myths. *Bulletin of the Public Museum of the City of Milwaukee*, Volume 15. Milwaukee, Wisconsin.

Bates, Craig
1984　Miwok Dancers of 1856: Stereographic Images from Sonora, California. *Journal of California and Great Basin Anthropology* 6(1):6-18.

Bean, Lowell J.
1976　Power and its Applications in Native California. Pp. 407-420 in *Native Californians: A Theoretical Retrospective*. Lowell J. Bean and Thomas C. Blackburn, editors. Ramona, CA: Ballena Press.

Beeler, Madison S.
1955　Saclan. *International Journal of American Linguistics* 21(3):201-209.
1959　Saclan Once More. *International Journal of American Linguistics* 25:67-68.
1961　Northern Costanoan. *International Journal of American Linguistics* 27(3):191-197.

1972 Extension of San Francisco Bay Costanoan? *International Journal of American Linguistics* 38:49-54.

Beilharz, Edwin A.
1951 Felipe de Neve: Governor of California and Commandant General of the Interior Provinces. Ph.D. Dissertation in History, University of California, Berkeley.

Benedict, Ruth F.
1923 The Concept of the Guardian Spirit in North America. *Memoirs of the American Anthropological Association*, No. 29.

Bennyhoff, James A.
1977 The Ethnohistory of the Plains Miwok. *Center for Archaeological Research at Davis Publication*, No. 2. University of California, Davis.

Bettelheim, Bruno
1958 Individual and Mass Behavior in Extreme Situations. In *Readings in Social Psychology*. E.E. Maccoby, T.M. Newcomb and E.L. Hartley, editors. New York: Henry Holt and Co.

Blackburn, Thomas C. and Kat Anderson, editors
1993 *Before the Wilderness: Environmental Management by Native Californians*. Ballena Press Anthroplogical Papers No. 40. Thomas C. Blackburn, series editor. Menlo Park, CA: Ballena Press.

Boehm, Christopher
1984 *Blood Revenge: The Anthropology of Feuding in Montenegro and Other Tribal Societies*. University Press of Kansas.

Borica, Diego de
[1794] Instrucciones al commandante de San Francisco sobre negativa de auxilio de soldados a los misioneros. Monterey. December 3, 1794. C-A 24:32.
[1795] Borica al commandante de San Francisco. Monterey. May 6, 1795. [Paraphrase of destroyed original, month incorrectly copied as July.] C-A 24:58.
[1795a] Sobre persecución de Indios Cristianos. Monterey. May 29, 1795. C-A 7:48-490.
[1795b] Borica al Alférez José Perez-Fernández. Monterey. June 2, 1795. C-A 24:56.
[1795c] Borica al Virrey Miguel de la Grúa Talamanca y Branciforte. Monterey. June 23, 1795. AGN, Ramo Californias, Tomo 65, Doc. 79.
[1795d] Borica al comissionado del Pueblo de San José. Monterey. July 29, 1795. C-A 44:51.

[1795e] Borica al commandante de Santa Clara sobre aprehensión de un Indio. Monterey. June 10, 1795. C-A 24:53.
[1796] Borica al commandante de San Francisco Presidio. Monterey. June 21, 1796. C-A 24:89.
[1796a] Informe al commandante general. Monterey. August 24, 1796. C-A 50:206-208.
[1797] Borica al Ygnacio Vallejo, comisionado del pueblo de San José. July 2, 1797. C-A 44:82.
[1797a] Borica al Sargento Pedro Amador. Monterey. July 10, 1797. C-A 9:71-72.
[1797b] Borica al Ygnacio Vallejo, comisionado del pueblo de San José. August 26, 1797. C-A 44:84.
[1797c] Castigos de criminales Indios. Monterey. August 26, 1797. C-A 9:77-79.
[1797d] Borica al Virrey Talamanca y Branciforte. Monterey. August 30, 1797. AGN, Ramo Californias, Tomo 65, Doc. 468.
[1798] Borica al Virrey Talamanca y Branciforte. Monterey. July 1, 1798. AGN, Ramo Californias, Tomo 65, Doc. 118.
[1798a] Borica al commandante del escolta de San José. Monterey. October 22, 1798. C-A 24:115.
[1799] Borica al Virrey Miguel José de Azanza. Monterey. March 14, 1799. C-A 24:443-444.

Bowman, Jacob N.
1958 The Resident Neophytes of the California Missions, 1769-1834. *Quarterly of the Historical Society of Southern California* 40(2):138-148.

Brown, Alan K.
1973 Indians of San Mateo County. *La Peninsula: Journal of the San Mateo County Historical Association* 17(4).
1973a San Francisco Bay Costanoan. *International Journal of American Linguistics* 39(3):184-189.

Burnet, Frank M. and David O. White
1972 *Natural History of Infectious Disease*. 4th edition. London: Cambridge University Press.

Callaghan, Catherine A.
1970 Bodega Miwok Dictionary. *Univ. of Cal. Pubs. in Linguistics* 60. Berkeley.
1971 Saclan: A Reexamination. *Anthropological Linguistics* 13(9):448-456.

Cambón, Pedro and Diego García
[1787] Informe de la Misión de N.S.P. San Francisco. December 31, 1787. AGN, Archivo Historico de Hacienda. Documentos para la Historia de Mexico, Segunda Serie, Tomo 2, Doc. 63.

Cambón, Pedro and Miguel Giribet
[1786] Informe sobre la Misión de N.S.P. San Francisco. December 31, 1786. AGN, Archivo Historico de Hacienda. Documentos para la Historia de Mexico, Segunda Serie, Tomo 2, Doc. 47.

Campa, Miguel de la
[1775] 1943 Colección de Diarios y Relaciones para la Historia de los Viajes y Descubrimientos, Tomo 2. Centro Superiór de Investigaciones Cientificas, Instituto de la Marina, Madrid.

Cañizares, José de
[1775] 1971 The Report of José de Cañizares, First Sailing Master of the San Carlos, to Captain Ayala. Pp. 94-98 in *The First Spanish Entry into San Francisco Bay*. Translated and edited by John Galvin. San Francisco: John Howell Books.

Castillo, Edward D.
1989 The Native Response to the Colonization of Alta California. Pp. 377-394 in *Columbian Consequences: Archaeological Perspectives on the Spanish Borderlands West*. David Hurst Thomas, editor. Washington: Smithsonian Institution.

Catalá, Magín and José Viader
[1797] Informe al Gobernador Diego de Borica. Santa Clara Mission. August 6, 1797. C-A 52:279.
[1814] 1976 Reply to the Interrogatory of 1812 from Mission San Juan Bautista. November 4, 1814. *In* As the Padres Saw Them: California Indian Life and Customs as Reported by the Franciscan Missionaries, 1813-1815. Maynard Geiger and Clement Meighan, eds. Santa Barbara, CA: Santa Barbara Mission Archives.

Chamisso, Adelbert von
[1816] 1932 Chamisso's Observations. Pp. 71-90 in *The Visit of the "Rurik" to San Francisco in 1816*. Translated and edited by August Mahr. Stanford University Press.

Choris, Louis
[1816] 1932 Choris's Description of San Francisco. Pp. 91-102 in *The Visit of the "Rurik" to San Francisco in 1816*. Translated and edited by August Mahr. Stanford University Press.

Colson, Elizabeth
1986 Political Organizations in Tribal Societies: A Cross-Cultural Comparison. *American Indian Quarterly* 10(1):5-20.

Cook, Sherburne F.
1940 Population Trends among the California Mission Indians. *Ibero-America* 17:1-48. (Reprinted in 1976 in *The Conflict between the California Indian and White Civilization*. Berkeley and Los Angeles: University of California Press.)
1943 The Indian versus the Spanish Mission. *Ibero-America* 21. (Reprinted in 1976 in *The Conflict between the California Indian and White Civilization*. Berkeley and Los Angeles: University of California Press.)
1943a The Physical and Demographic Reaction of the Nonmission Indians in Colonial and Provincial California. *Ibero-America* 22. (Reprinted in 1976 in *The Conflict between the California Indian and White Civilization*. Berkeley and Los Angeles: University of California Press.)
1957 The Aboriginal Population of Alameda and Contra Costa Counties, California. *University of California Anthropological Records* 16(4):131-156. Berkeley.
1960 Colonial Expeditions to the Interior of California: Central Valley, 1800-1820. *University of California Anthropological Records* 16(6):239-292. Berkeley.
1976 *The Population of the California Indians, 1769-1970*. Berkeley and Los Angeles: University of California Press.

Costansó, Miguel
[1769] 1969 Excerpts from the Journal of Miguel Costansó during the Portolá Expedition. Pp. 70-109 in *Who Discoverd the Golden Gate?* Frank M. Stanger and Alan K. Brown, editors. San Mateo, CA: San Mateo County Historical Association.

Costo, Rupert and Jeanette Costo, editors
1988 *The Missions of California: A Legacy of Genocide*. San Francisco: The Indian Historian Press.

Crespí, Juan
[1769] 1969 Excerpts from the Journal of Juan Crespí during the Portolá Expedition of 1769-1770. Pp. 70-109 in *Who Discoverd the Golden Gate?* Frank M. Stanger and Alan K. Brown, editors. San Mateo, CA: San Mateo County Historical Association.
[1772] 1927 *Fray Juan Crespí: Missionary Explorer on the Pacific Coast 1769-1774*. Robert E. Bolton, editor. Berkeley and Los Angeles: University of California Press.
[1772] 1969 Excerpts from the Journal of Juan Crespí during the Fages and Crespí Exploration of 1772. Pp. 120-128 in *Who Discovered the Golden Gate?* Frank M. Stanger and Alan K. Brown, editors. San Mateo, CA: San Mateo County Historical Association.

Cutter, Donald C.
1950 The Spanish Exploration of California's Central Valley. Ph.D. Dissertation in History, University of California, Berkeley.

Dantí, Antonio
[1795] Dantí al Gobernador Diego de Borica. Mission San Francisco. May 3, 1795. AGN, Ramo Californias, Tomo 65, Doc. 75(2).

Decker, Jody F.
1991 Depopulation of the Northern Plains Natives. *Social Science and Medicine* 33(4):381-393.

Dietz, Stephen A.
[1976] Echa-Tamal: A Study of Coast Miwok Acculturation. Masters Thesis in Anthropology, San Francisco State University.

Dmytryshyn, Basil, E.A.P. Crownhart-Vaughan, and Thomas Vaughan
1989 *The Russian American Colonies, 1798-1867: A Documentary Record.* Oregon Historical Society Press.

Dobson, Mary J.
1989 The Last Hiccup of the Old Demographic Regime: Population Stagnation and Decline in Late Seventeenth and Early Eighteenth-century South-east England. *Continuity and Change* 4(3):395-428. Cambridge.

Dobyns, Harold F.
1966 Estimating Aboriginal American Population: An Appraisal of Techniques with a New Hemispheric Estimate. *Current Anthropology* 7:395-416.
1983 *Their Number Become Thinned: Native American Population Dynamics in Eastern North America.* Knoxville: University of Tennessee Press.

Driver, Harold
1936 Wappo Ethnology. UCPAAE 36(3):179-220. Berkeley.

Durán, Narciso and Buenaventura Fortuny
[1814] 1976 Reply to the Interrogatory of 1812 from Mission San Juan Bautista. November 7, 1814. *In* As the Padres Saw Them: California Indian Life and Customs as Reported by the Franciscan Missionaries, 1813-1815. Maynard Geiger and Clement Meighan, eds. Santa Barbara, CA: Santa Barbara Mission Archives.

Engelhardt, Zephyrin
1909 *The Holy Man of Santa Clara or Life, Virtues, and Miracles of Fr. Magin Catalá, O.F.M.* San Francisco: James H. Barry.
1912 *The Missions and Missionaries of California. Volume 2. Upper California.* San Francisco: James H. Barry.

1924   *San Francisco or Mission Dolores.* Chicago: Franciscan Herald Press.

Espí de Valencia, José de la Cruz and Martín de Landaeta
[1797]   Informe a Teniente José Argüello. San Francisco Mission. July 26, 1797. C-A 9:89.

Estudillo, José María
[1809]   Causa Criminal. San Francisco Presidio. April 15, 1809. C-A 17:2-11.

Fages, Pedro
[1770] 1969   A Letter to the Viceroy, and excerpts from the journal of his brief expedition of 1770, by Lt. Pedro Fages. Pp. 118-120 in *Who Discovered the Golden Gate?* Frank M. Stanger and Alan K. Brown, editors. San Mateo, CA: San Mateo Historical Society.

[1772] 1969   Excerpts from the Journal of Pedro Fages during the Fages-Crespí Explorations of 1772. Pp. 120-128 in *Who Discovered the Golden Gate?* Frank M. Stanger and Alan K. Brown, editors. San Mateo, CA: San Mateo County Historical Association.

[1775] 1937   *A Historical, Political, and Natural Description of California.* Herbert I. Priestley, translator and editor. Berkeley and Los Angeles: University of California Press.

[1782]   Carta al Teniente José Joaquín Moraga. Monterey. December 2, 1782. C-A 23:154-156.

[1782a]   Carta al Teniente José Joaquín Moraga. Monterey. December 12, 1782. C-A 23:153-154.

[1784]   Informe al Commandante General. Monterey. May 30, 1784. C-A 22:173.

[1784a]   Informe al Commandante General. Monterey. June 3, 1784. C-A 22:173

[1784b]   Informe al Commandante General. Monterey. June 4, 1784. C-A 22:173.

[1785]   Instrucciones al Director de San José, Ygnacio Vallejo. Monterey. July 18, 1785. C-A 22:338-341.

[1786]   Informe al Commandante General. Monterey. May 11, 1786. C-A 22:353.

[1787]   Informe General de Misiones. Monterey. December, 1787. C-A 52:121-151

[1790]   Fages a Macario Castro. Monterey. January 2, 1790. C-A 44:27.
[1790a]   Fages a Macario Castro. Monterey. April 23, 1790. C-A 44:31.
[1790b]   Fages a Macario Castro. Monterey. May 7, 1790. C-A 44:32.
[1790c]   Fages a Macario Castro. Monterey. May 31, 1790. C-A 44:37.
[1790d]   Fages a Macario Castro. Monterey. July 22, 1790. C-A 44:39.

[1790e]	Fages a Macario Castro. Monterey. August 22, 1790. C-A 44:41.
[1790f]	Fages a Macario Castro. Monterey. August 30, 1790. C-A 44:42.
[1791]	Sobre Puntos del Govierno de la Peninsula de California. Monterey. February 26, 1791. C-A 6:151-168.
[1793]	Sobre Obras de Monterey. August 12, 1793. Attached to Viceroy Branciforte's December 12, 1795 letter to Governor Diego de Borica. [Paraphrase of original.] C-A 7:405-413.

Fernández, José María
[1797]   Frey Fernández al Gobernador Diego de Borica. San Francisco Mission. June 21, 1797. C-A 8:218-220.

Fogel, Daniel
1988   *Junípero Serra, the Vatican, and Enslavement Theology.* San Francisco: Ism Press.

Font, Pedro
[1776] 1930   *Font's Complete Diary of the Second Anza Expedition. Anza's California Expeditions, Volume 4.* Herbert E. Bolton, editor. Berkeley and Los Angeles: University of California Press.

Forbes, Jack D.
1965   *Warriors of the Colorado: The Yumas of the Quechan Nation and Their Neighbors.* Norman: University of Oklahoma Press.

Freire, Paulo
1970   *Pedagogy of the Oppressed.* New York: Seabury Press.

Fried, Morton
1975   *The Notion of Tribe.* Cummings: Menlo Park.

Galvan, Michael
1968   "People of the West": The Ohlone Story. *The Indian Historian* 1(2):9-13.

Galvin, John
1971   *The First Spanish Entry into San Francisco Bay, 1775.* John Galvin, editor. San Francisco: John Howell Books.

Garr, Daniel
1972   Planning, Politics, and Plunder: The Missions and Indian Pueblos of Hispanic California. *Southern California Quarterly* 54(4):291-311.

Gayton, Anna H.
1935   Areal Affiliations of California Folktales. *American Anthropologist* 37(4):582-599.

Geiger, Maynard
1969   *Franciscan Missionaries in Hispanic California, 1769-1848. A Biographical Dictionary*. San Marino, California: Huntington Library.

Geiger, Maynard and Clement Meighan, editors
1976   *As the Padres Saw Them: California Indian Life and Customs as Reported by the Franciscan Missionaries, 1813-1815*. Santa Barbara, CA: Santa Barbara Archives.

Gibson, Charles
1988   Spanish Indian Policies. Pp. 96-102 in *Handbook of North American Indians*, Volume 4. Washington, D.C.: Smithsonian Institution.

Gifford, Edward W.
1916   Miwok Moieties. UCPAAE 12(4):139-194.
1917   Miwok Myths. UCPAAE 12(8):283-338. Berkeley.
1955   Central Miwok Ceremonies. *University of California Anthropological Records* 14(4):261-318. Berkeley.

Gudde, Erwin
1969   *California Place Names: The Original Etymology of Current Geographical Names*. Third edition. Berkeley and Los Angeles: University of California Press.

Guest, Francis F.
1973   *Fermin Francisco de Lasuen*. Washington, D.C.: Academy of American Franciscan History.
1979   An Examination of the Thesis of S.F. Cook on the Forced Conversion of Indians in the California Missions. *Southern California Quarterly* 61(1):1-77.
1983   Cultural Perspectives on California Mission Life. *Southern California Quarterly* 65(1).
1988   The Franciscan World View. Pp. 24-33 in *New Directions in California History: A Book of Readings*. James J. Rawls, editor. Washington, D.C.: Academy of American Franciscan History.

Harrington, John P.
[1921]   Chochenyo Fieldnotes. Manuscript on file in the National Anthropological Archives, Smithsonian Institution, Washington, D.C.

Heizer, Robert F.
1953   The Archaeology of the Napa Region. *University of California Anthropological Records* 12(6). Berkeley.
1974   The Costanoan Indians. *Local History Studies*, Volume 18. Robert F. Heizer, editor. Cupertino, CA: California History Center at DeAnza College.

1974a *The Destruction of California Indians*. Robert F. Heizer, editor. Santa Barbara: Peregrine Smith.

1974b *Elizabethan California: A Brief and Sometimes Critical Review of Opinions on the Location of Francis Drake's Five Weeks' Visit with the Indians of Ships Land in 1579*. Ramona, CA.: Ballena Press.

1978 *Handbook of North American Indians*, Volume 8 (California). Robert F. Heizer, editor. Washington, D.C.: Smithsonian Institution.

Holmes, King K., Per-Anders Mardh, P. Frederick Sparling, and Paul J. Wiesner

1984 *Sexually Transmitted Diseases*. New York: McGraw-Hill.

Hoover, Robert L.

1989 Spanish-Native Interaction and Acculturation in the Alta California Missions. Pp. 395-406 in *Columbian Consequences: Archaeological and Historical Perspectives on the Spanish Borderlands West*. David Hurst Thomas, editor. Washington: Smithsonian Institution.

Hurtado, Albert

1988 *Indian Survival on the California Frontier*. New Haven: Yale University Press.

Hutchinson, C. Alan

1969 *Frontier Settlement in Mexican California; the Hijar-Padres Colony and its origins, 1769-1835*. New Haven: Yale University Press.

Jackson, Robert H.

1983 Disease and Demographic Patterns at Santa Cruz Mission, Alta California. *Journal of California and Great Basin Anthropology* 5(1,2):33-57.

1984 Gentile Recruitment and Population Movements in the San Francisco Bay Area Missions. *Journal of California and Great Basin Anthropology* 6(2):225-239.

1987 Patterns of Demographic Change in the Missions of Central Alta California. *Journal of California and Great Basin Anthropology* 9(2):251-272.

Johnson, John R.

1988 Chumash Social Organization: An Ethnohistoric Perspective. Ph.D Dissertation in Anthropology, University of California, Santa Barbara.

1989 The Chumash and the Missions. Pp. 365-376 in *Columbian Consequences: Archaeological and Historical Perspectives on the*

Spanish Borderlands West. David Hurst Thomas, editor. Washington: Smithsonian Institution.

Kelly, Isabel
[1931-1932] 1991 Interviews with Tom Smith and Maria Copa. *Miwok Archeological Preserve of Marin Occasional Papers* Number 6. San Rafael, California.
1978 Coast Miwok. Pp. 414-425 in *Handbook of North American Indians*, Volume 8. Robert F. Heizer, editor. Washington, D.C.: Smithsonian Institution.
1978a Some Coast Miwok Tales. *Journal of California Anthropology* 5(1):21-41.

King, Chester
1978 Historic Indian Settlements in the Vicinity of the Holiday Inn Site. Pp. 436-469 in Archaeological Investigations at CA-SCL-128, The Holiday Inn Site. Joseph Winter, editor. Prepared for the City of San Jose by the Holiday Inn Corporation. (Limited distribution.)

Kirkby, Dianne
1980 Frontier Violence: Ethnohistory and Aboriginal Resistance in California and New South Wales, 1770-1840. *Journal of Australian Studies*, June, pp. 36-48.
1984 Colonial Policy and Native Depopulation in California and New South Wales, 1770-1840. *Ethnohistory* 31(1):1-16.

Kniffen, Fred B.
1939 Pomo Geography UCPAAE 36(6):353-400.

Kotzebue, Otto von
[1816] 1932 Extract from Kotzebue's Diary. Pp. 321-335 in *The Visit of the "Rurik" to San Francisco in 1816*. August C. Mahr, editor. Stanford, CA: Stanford University Press.

Kroeber, Alfred L.
1925 Handbook of the Indians of California. *Bureau of American Ethnology Bulletin* 78. Washington.
1932 The Patwin and their Neighbors. UCPAAE 29(4):253-423.

La Pérouse, Jean Francois de Galaup
[1786] 1989 *Monterey in 1786: The Journals of Jean Francois de la Perouse*. Malcolm Margolin, editor. Berkeley: Heyday Books.

Landaeta, Martín
[1801] 1949 Landaeta al Frey Tomás de la Peña. Mission San Francisco. September 30, 1801. Pp. 36 in Noticias Acerca del Puerto de San Francisco (Alta California). J.C. Valadéz, editor. Mexico City: Antigua Librería Robrado.

[1802] 1949 Landaeta al Frey Tomás de la Peña. Mission San Francisco. February 27, 1802. P. 39 in Noticias Acerca del Puerto de San Francisco (Alta California). J.C. Valadéz, editor. Mexico City: Antigua Librería Robrado.

[1806] Landaeta al Frey Tomás de la Peña. Mission San Francisco. April 28, 1806. California Mission Letters (C-C 201) 1:2. Bancroft Library, University of California, Berkeley.

[1807] Landaeta a José Viñals. Mission San Francisco. September 30, 1807. California Mission Letters (C-C 201) 1:6. Bancroft Library, University of California, Berkeley.

Langsdorff, George H. von
[1806] 1814 *Voyages and Travels in Various Parts of the World during the Years 1803, 1804, 1805, 1806, and 1807.* Part 2. London: Henry Colburn.

Lasuén, Fermín F. de
[1785-1803] 1965 *The Writings of Fermín Francisco de Lasuén.* Finbar Kenneally, editor. Richmond, Virginia: Academy of American Franciscan History.

[1793] Ynforme del Estado Espirituál de los Misiones de la Nueva California en el fin del año 1792. Mission San Francisco. March 6, 1793. AGN, Archivo Historico de Hacienda. Documentos para la Historia de Mexico, Segunda Serie, Tomo 2, Misiones de la Alta California, Documento 146.

Levy, Richard
1978 Costanoan. Pp. 485-495 in *Handbook of North American Indians*, Volume 8. Robert F. Heizer, editor. Washington, D.C.: Smithsonian Institution.

1978a Eastern Miwok. Pp. 398-413 in *Handbook of North American Indians*, Volume 8. Robert F. Heizer, editor. Washington, D.C.: Smithsonian Institution.

Lewis, Henry
1973 *Patterns of Indian Burning in California: Ecology and Prehistory.* Ballena Press Anthropological Papers No. 1. Lowell John Bean, series editor. Ramona, CA: Ballena Press. (Reprinted in 1993 in *Before the Wilderness: Environmental Management by Native Californians.* Thomas C. Blackburn and Kat Anderson, editors. Ballena Press Anthropological Papers No. 40:55-116. Thomas C. Blackburn, series editor. Menlo Park, CA: Ballena Press.)

Librado, Fernando
[1912-1913] 1979 *Breath of the Sun: Life in Early California as told by a Chumash Indian, Fernando Librado, to John P. Harrington.* Travis Hudson, editor. Banning, CA.: Malki Museum Press.

Manríquez, Marcelino and Jayme Escudé
[1814] 1976 Reply to the Interrogatory of 1812 from Mission San Juan Bautista. April 30, 1814. *In* As the Padres Saw Them: California Indian Life and Customs as Reported by the Franciscan Missionaries, 1813-1815. Maynard Geiger and Clement Meighan, eds. Santa Barbara, CA: Santa Barbara Mission Archives.

Margolin, Malcolm
1978 *The Ohlone Way: Indian Life in the San Francisco and Monterey Bay Areas.* Berkeley: Heyday Books.

Marsh, John
[1846] 1890 Letter to Lewis Cass, February 1846. *Overland Monthly*, Second Series 15:213-216.

Martinez, José
[1855] Testimony in the Case of Rancho Acalanes. English translation on page 119 in the Transcripts of the Record from the Board of United States Land Commissioners, 1855, United States District Court, Northern District of California. Case ND 276. Bancroft Library, University of California, Berkeley.

Mason, William H.
1975 Fages' Code of Conduct toward Indians, 1787. *Journal of California and Great Basin Anthropology* 2(1):90-100.

McCarthy, Francis F.
1958 *The History of Mission San Jose, California, 1797-1835.* Fresno, CA: Academy Library Press.

Meighan, Clement
1987 Indians and California Missions. *Southern California Quarterly* 69(3):187-201.

Meighan, Clement and Robert Heizer
1952 Archaeological Exploration of Sixteenth-Century Indian Mounds at Drake's Bay. *Quarterly of the California Historical Society* 31:98-108. San Francisco.

Menzies, Archibald
[1792] 1924 Menzies' California Journal. *Quarterly of the California Historical Society* 2:265-340. San Francisco.

Merriam, C. Hart
1907 Distribution and Classification of the Mewan Stock in California. *American Anthropologist* 9(2):338-357.
1910 *The Dawn of the World: Myths and Weird Tales told by the Mewan Indians of California.* Cleveland: Arthur H. Clark.
1916 Indian Names in the Tamalpais Region. *California Out-of-Doors*. April, 1916, p.118.

1955	California Mission Baptismal Records. Pp. 188-225 in *Studies in California Indians*. [C.Hart Merriam materials.] Berkeley and Los Angeles: University of California Press.
1967	Ethnographic Notes on Central California Indian Tribes. Robert F. Heizer, editor. *University of California Archaeological Survey Reports*, No. 68(3). Berkeley.
1968	Village Names in Twelve California Mission Records. *University of California Archaeological Survey Reports*, No. 74. Berkeley.
1970	Indian Rancheria Names in Four Mission Records. Pp. 29-58 in *Contributions of the University of California Archaeological Research Facility*, number 9. Department of Anthropology, University of California, Berkeley.

Milliken, Randall

[1978]	Ethnohistory of the Lower Napa Valley. Pp. 2.1-2.43 in Report of Archaeological Excavations at the River Glen Site (CA-Nap-261) Thomas Jackson, editor. U.S. Army Corps of Engineers, San Francisco District (limited distribution).
[1983]	The Spatial Organization of Human Population on Central California's San Francisco Peninsula at the Spanish Arrival. Masters Thesis in Cultural Resource Management, Sonoma State University, Rohnert Park, California.

Miranda, Alejo

[1797]	Miranda al Teniente José Argüello. Mission San Jose. June 29, 1797. C-A 9:92.
[1797a]	Miranda al Teniente José Argüello. Mission San Jose. July 3, 1797. C-A 9:91.
[1797b]	Miranda al Teniente José Argüello. Mission San Jose. July 29, 1797. C-A 9:90.

Moraga, Gabriel

[1794]	Informe al Teniente José Argüello. San Jose. October 30, 1794. C-A 7:125-133.
[1797]	Informe al Gobernador Diego de Borica. San Jose. January 8, 1797. C-A 8:201.

Moraga, José Joaquín

[1782]	Instrucciones al cabo de la escolta del pueblo de San José. San Francisco Presidio. December, 1782. C-A 2:160.
[1783]	Moraga al Gobernador Pedro Fages. San Francisco Presidio. January 20, 1783. C-A 2:355.
[1783a]	Moraga al Gobernador Pedro Fages. San Francisco Presidio. February 13, 1783. C-A 2:27.

Murguía, Antonio and Tomas de la Peña
[1777]   Informe al R.P. Presidente Frey Junípero Serra. Mission Santa Clara. December 30, 1777. Archives of the Mission of Santa Barbara 9:505-509.
[1778]   Informe al R.P. Presidente Frey Junípero Serra. Mission Santa Clara. December 31, 1778. AGN, Archivo Historico de Hacienda. Documentos para la Historia de Mexico, Segunda Serie, Tomo 2, Misiones de la Alta California, Informes 1769-1809.
[1782] 1955 Letter to Governor Pedro Fages. Mission Santa Clara. November 1, 1782. Pp. 397-398 in *The Writing of Junípero Serra*, Volume 4. Antonine Tibesar, translator and editor. Washington: Academy of American Franciscan History.
[1782a] 1955 Letter to Father President Junípero Serra. Mission Santa Clara. November 2, 1782. Pp. 398-401 in *The Writing of Junípero Serra*, Volume 4. Antonine Tibesar, translator and editor. Washington: Academy of American Franciscan History.

Nandy, Ashis
 1983   *The Intimate Enemy: Loss and Recovery of Self under Colonialism*. Delhi: Oxford University Press.

Neve, Felipe de
[1782]   Instrucción del Ex. Gobernador Neve a su sucesor Pedro Fages en el Gobernador de Californias. Saucito. September 7, 1782. C-A 54:74-82.
[1783]   Informe a Juan Bautista de Anza. December 10, 1783. New Mexico Archives, volume 47, section 873.

Noboa, Diego
[1794]   Informe sobre una situación muy critica. Mission Santa Clara. March 14, 1794. C-A 7:54.

Noboa, Diego and Tomas de la Peña
[1784]   Padron de los Indios Neofitos de esta Misión de la S. M. Santa Clara de Thamien existentes in 31 del mes de Diciembre del 1783. AGN, Documentos para la Historia de Mexico, Segunda Serie, Tomo 2, Doc. 33. Archivo Historico de Hacienda.
[1788]   Informe del estado de esta Misión de N.S. Madre Santa Clara de Thamien. January 5, 1788. AGN, Documentos para la Historia de Mexico, Segunda Serie, Tomo 2, Doc. 71. Archivo Historico de Hacienda.

Ogden, Adele
 1941   The California Sea Otter Trade, 1784-1848. *University of California Publications in History*, Volume 26. Berkeley and Los Angeles: University of California Press.

Ordáz, Blas
[1821] 1958 La Ultima Exploración Española en America. Donald Cutter, editor. *Revista de Indias*, Volume 18 (April-June). Madrid.

Ortiz, Beverly
1989 Mount Diablo as Myth and Reality: An Indian History Convoluted. *American Indian Quarterly* 8(4):457-470. Berkeley.

Pacheco, Salvio
[1828] 1855 Petition of October 30, 1828 for Rancho Monte del Diablo. English translation on page 19 in Transcripts of the Record from the Board of United States Land Commissioners, 1855, United States District Court, Northern District of California. Case ND 20. Bancroft Library, University of California, Berkeley.

Palóu, Francisco
[1774] 1969 Excerpts from Palóu's Journal during the Exploration of 1774. Pp. 131-146 in *Who Discovered the Golden Gate?* Frank M. Stanger and Alan K. Brown, translators and editors. San Mateo, CA: San Mateo County Historical Association.
[1773-1783] 1926 *Historical Memoirs of New California*. 4 Volumes. Berkeley and Los Angeles: University of California Press.
[1786] 1913 *The Life and Apostolic Labors of the Venerable Father Junípero Serra*. George Wharton James, translator and editor. Pasadena, CA: Private press of George Wharton James.
[1786] 1955 *Palou's Life of Fray Junípero Serra*. Maynard J. Geiger, translator and editor. Washington, D.C.: Academy of American Franciscan History.

Palóu, Francisco and Pedro Cambón
[1782] Informe de la Mission de Nuestro Serafico Padre San Francisco. December 31, 1782. AGN, Documentos para la Historia de Mexico, Segunda Serie, Tomo 2, Doc. 25. [Attachment.] Archivo Historico de Hacienda.
[1783] Informe de la Mission de Nuestro Serafico Padre San Francisco, del Puerto del Propio Nombre, desde su Fundación hasta el año de 1781 inclusiva. San Francisco. December 31, 1783. AGN, Documentos para la Historia de Mexico, Segunda Serie, Tomo 2, Doc. 25. Archivo Historico de Hacienda.

Peña, Tomas de la
[1786] Peña a al R.P. Presidente Fermín Francisco de Lasuén. Mission San Carlos Borromeo. November 25, 1786. AGN, Ramo Provincias Internas, Tomo 1 (6), folio 45-62.

Peralta, Luís
[1798] Peralta al Gobernador Diego de Borica. Mission San Jose. June 9, 1798. C-A 10:106.

[1798a]   Peralta al Teniente José Argüello. Mission San Jose. June 17, 1798. C-A 10:121.
[1804]   Declaraciones de Indios Cristianos. Mission San Jose. June 21, 1804. AGN, Ramo Californias, Tomo 9:437-439.
[1804a]   Peralta a un capitán (no dice cual). Mission Santa Clara. September 27, 1804. C-A 11:334.
[1805]   Diario del Expedición a la Sierra. Mission San Jose. January 30, 1805. C-A 12:33-34.

Perez-Fernández, José
[1794]   Informe al Gobernador José Joaquín de Arrillaga sobre los trabajos del Castillo. San Francisco Presidio. January 3, 1794. C-A 7:66.
[1794a]   Informe al Gobernador Arrillaga sobre prisión de Indios. San Francisco Presidio. February 1, 1794. C-A 7:55-56.
[1794b]   Informe al Gobernador Arrillaga sobre prisión y aprestos. San Francisco Presidio. February 1, 1794. [misdated February 1, 1793.] C-A 6:336.
[1794c]   Informe al Gobernador Arrillaga sobre tejas y ladrillos. San Francisco Presidio. February 28, 1794. C-A 7:65-66.
[1794d]   Informe al Gobernador Arrillaga sobre Indios ladrones. San Francisco Presidio. March 1, 1794. C-A 7:50.
[1794e]   Informe al Gobernador Arrillaga sobre tramas de los Indios. San Francisco Presidio. March 15, 1794. C-A 7:50-54.
[1794f]   Informe al Gobernador Arrillaga sobre fuga de Indios. San Francisco Presidio. April 1, 1794. C-A 7:54.
[1794g]   Informe al Gobernador Diego de Borica sobre nuevas conquistas y muerte de dos Indios. San Francisco Presidio. November 30, 1794. C-A 7:29-30.
[1794h]   Informe al Gobernador Borica sobre inquietud entre gentiles de San José. San Francisco Presidio. December 1, 1794. C-A 7:34.
[1795]   Informe al Gobernador Borica sobre persecución de Indios Cristianos. San Francisco Presidio. May 29, 1795. C-A 7:489-490.
[1795a]   Informe al Gobernador Borica. San Francisco Presidio. September 13, 1795. C-A 7:361-362.

Phillips, George H.
1974   Indians and the Breakdown of the Spanish Mission System in California. *Ethnohistory* 21(4):291-302.
1975   *Chiefs and Challengers: Indian Resistance and Cooperation in Southern California*. Berkeley and Los Angeles: University of California Press.

1993 *Indians and Intruders in Central California, 1769-1849.* Norman and London: University of Oklahoma Press.

Pinart, Alphonse
[1894] 1955 Etudes sur les Indiens Californiens. Pp. 133-138 in *Studies of California Indians.* [C.Hart Merriam Material.] Berkeley: University of California Press.

Portolá, Gaspár de
[1769] 1969 Journal of Gaspár de Portolá. Pp. 70-104 in *Who Discovered the Golden Gate?* Frank Stanger and Alan K. Brown, editors. San Mateo, CA: San Mateo County Historical Association.

Powers, Stephen
1877 Tribes of California. *Contributions to North America Ethnology*, Volume III. Department of the Interior, U.S. Geographical and Geological Survey of the Rocky Mountain Region. J.W. Powell, editor. Washington, D.C.: Government Printing Office.

Radin, Paul
1924 Wappo Texts; First Series. UCPAAE 19(1):1-147. Berkeley.

Ramenofsky, Ann F.
1987 *Vectors of Death: The Archaeology of European Contact.* Albuquerque: University of New Mexico Press.

Rawls, James
1984 *Indians of California: The Changing Image.* Norman: University of Oklahoma Press.

Rivera y Moncada, Fernando
[1774] 1969 Excerpts from the Journal of Captain Fernando Rivera y Moncada during the Exploration of 1774. Pp. 132-146 in *Who Discovered the Golden Gate?* Frank M. Stanger and Alan K. Brown, eds. San Mateo: San Mateo County Historical Assoc.

Rollins, M.
[1786] 1798 Philological and Pathological Memoir on the Americans, by M. Rollins, M.D. Surgeon Major of the Boussole Frigate. Pp. 260-279 in *The Voyage of La Pérouse round the World, in the Years 1785, 1786, 1787, and 1788, with the Nautical Tables.* Volume 2. London: J. Stockdale.

Ruíz, Francisco
[1805] Ruíz al Gobernador Arrillaga. San Vicente, Baja California. July 8, 1805. C-A 12:44. Bancroft Library, University of California, Berkeley.

Sainz de Lucio, Juan
[1809] Sainz de Lucio al Frey José Viñals. San Francisco Mission. March 31, 1809. California Mission Letters (C-C 201) 1:10.

Sal, Hermenegildo
[1791]   Instrucción al cabo de la escolta de Santa Cruz. San Francisco Presidio. September 21, 1791. C-A 54:274-280.
[1791a] Reconocimiento de la Misión de Santa Cruz. San Francisco Presidio. October 18, 1791. C-A 54:270-272.
[1793]   Informe a Gobernador interino Joaquín de Arrillaga. San Francisco Presidio. February 27, 1793. C-A 55:160-164.
[1794]   Informe al Gobernador interino Arrillaga sobre Indios y Obras. San Francisco Presidio. April 30, 1794. C-A 7:74-75.
[1794a] Informe al Teniente José Argüello. San Jose. November 2, 1794. C-A 7:132-133.
[1795]   Informe al Gobernador Diego de Borica. Monterey. November 30, 1795. C-A 8:30.
[1796]   Informe al Gobernador Borica. Monterey. January 31, 1796. C-A 8:4.
[1796a] Sal al comissionado del pueblo de San José. Monterey. April 29, 1796. ASJ, 1796, Doc. 37.
[1796b] Sal al comissionado del pueblo de San José. Monterey. May 18, 1796. ASJ, 1796, Doc. 41.
[1796c] Sal a Gabriel Moraga, comissionado del pueblo de San José. Monterey. September 10, 1796. ASJ, 1796, Doc. 54.
[1796d] Lista de asuntos pendientes, a José Argüello. Monterey. April 20, 1796. C-A 8:176-178.
[1800]   Sal a Macario Castro, comissionado del pueblo de San José. Monterey. July 6, 1800. ASJ, 1800, Doc. 45.
[1800a] Sal a Macario Castro. Monterey. October 7, 1800. ASJ, 1800, Doc. 62.

Sanchez, José Antonio
[1805]   Sanchez al Teniente José Argüello. Mission San Jose. January 16, 1805. C-A 12:34-35.

Sandos, James A.
1991   Christianization among the Chumash: An Ethnohistoric Perspective. *American Indian Quarterly* 15(1):65-89.

Santa María, Vicente de
[1775] 1971   The Journal of Father Vicente de Santa María. Pp. 11-74 in *The First Spanish Entry into San Francisco Bay, 1775*. John Galvin, editor. San Francisco: John Howell Books.

Sawyer, Jesse O.
1965   English-Wappo Dictionary. *University of California Publications in Linguistics* 43. Berkeley.

Schenck, W. Egbert
   1926   Historic Aboriginal Groups of the California Delta Region. UCPAAE 23:123-146. Berkeley.

Schoolcraft, Henry Rowe
   1860   *Archives of Aboriginal Knowledge.* 6 Volumes. Philadelphia: J.B. Lippencott and Company.

Serra, Junípero
   [1748-1784] 1955-56   *The Writing of Junípero Serra.* 4 Volumes. Antonine Tibesar, translator and editor. Washington: Academy of American Franciscan History.

Shipley, William F.
   1978   Native Languages of California. Pp. 80-90 in *Handbook of North American Indians,* Volume 8. Robert F. Heizer, editor. Washington, D.C.: Smithsonian Institution.

Slaymaker, Charles M.
   1982   A Model for the Study of Coast Miwok Ethnogeography. Ph.D. Dissertation in Anthropology. University of California, Davis.

Smith, Jedediah S.
   [1827] 1934   *The Travels of Jedediah Smith.* Maurice S. Sullivan, editor. Fine Arts Press, Santa Ana, California.

Snow, Dean R. and Kim M. Lanphear
   1988   European Contact and Indian Depopulation in the Northeast: The Timing of the First Epidemics. *Ethnohistory* 35(1):15-33.

Stewart, Omer C.
   1943   Notes on Pomo Ethnography. UCPAAE 40(2):29-62.

Tac, Pablo
   [1835] 1958   *Indian Life and Customs at Mission San Luis Rey.* Mina and Gordon Hewes, translators and editors. San Luis Rey, CA.: Old Mission.

Talamanca y Branciforte, Miguel de la Grúa
   [1795]   Branciforte al Gobernador Borica. Mexico City. October 8, 1795. C-A 7:308-314. Bancroft Library, University of California, Berkeley.

Tanner, Susan
   [1971]   The Marin Peninsula: The Impact of Inhabiting Groups on the Landscape from the Indian to the Railroad. Masters Thesis in Geography, University of California, Berkeley.

Tápis, Estévan
   [1803]   Carta al Gobernador Arrillaga. Santa Barbara. June 26, 1803. Santa Barbara Mission Archives.

Thornton, Russell, Tim Miller, and Jonathan Warren
  1991   American Indian Population Recovery following Smallpox Epidemics. *American Anthropologist* 93:28-45.
Valle, Rosemary
  1973   Medicine and Health in the Alta California Missions. Ph.D. Dissertation in Public Health, University of California, San Francisco.
Vallejo, Ygnacio
  [1797]   Vallejo al Gobernador Diego de Borica. San Jose. July 9, 1797. C-A 8:333-335.
  [1797a] Vallejo al Gobernador Borica. San Jose. July 23, 1797. C-A 8:337.
  [1797b] Vallejo al Gobernador Borica. San Jose. August 20, 1797. C-A 8:335.
  [1797c] Vallejo al Gobernador Borica. San Jose. September 1, 1797. C-A 8:341-342.
  [1797d] Vallejo al Gobernador Diego de Borica. San Jose. September 26, 1797. C-A 8:345.
Vancouver, George
  [1792] 1798 *A Voyage of Discovery to the North Pacific Ocean, and Round the World: In Which the Coast of North-West America has been Carefully Examined and Accurately Surveyed ... Performed in the Years 1790-1795 in the Discovery Sloop of War and Armed Tender Chatham, under the Command of Captain George Vancouver.* Volume 2. London: G.G. and J. Robinson.
Vayda, Andrew
  1967   Pomo Trade Feasts. Pp. 494-500 in *Tribal and Peasant Economies.* G. Dalton, editor. Garden City, New York: Natural History Press.
Venegas, Francisco Javier
  [1811]   Informe al Gobernador José Joaquín de Arrillaga. November 12, 1811. C-A 26:223-224.
Wagner, Henry Raup
  1931   The Last Spanish Exploration of the Northwest Coast and the Attempt to Colonize Bodega Bay. *California Historical Society Quarterly* 10(4):313-345.
Wallace, Anthony F.C.
  1957   Mazeway Disintegration: The Individual's Perception of Socio-Cultural Disorganization. *Human Organization* 16:23-27.
Webb, Edith
  1952   *Indian Life at the Old Missions.* Los Angeles: Warren F. Lewis.

Weber, Francis J.
   1986   *The Patriarchal Mission: A Documentary History of Mission San Jose*. Los Angeles: Archdiocese of Los Angeles Archives.

Index

Abasto tribe 298
Abella, Father Ramón 204, 237, 238, 255, 259
Accsagis tribe 118, 234
Achachipe tribe 241
Achistaca tribe 109, 234, 258
Agnews 256
Aguasajuchiun (see Huchiun-Aguasto tribe)
Aguastos 234, 238, 242, 260
Aguazios 260
Ah-wash-tes 249
Al-tah-mos 249
Alaguali tribe 234
Alameda 233, 235, 245, 258
Alameda Creek 36, 54, 235, 257, 258
Alaskan Natives 200-201
alcaldes 78, 300, 301
Aleitac 21, 255
Aleut 202
Aloquiome tribe 239
Alson tribe 54, 66, 70, 78, 147, 153, 162, 168, 170, 235, 273
Altagmu 21, 255
Altamont Pass 255
Alum Rock Park 253
Alviso 235
Amador, Pedro 119, 155, 156, 157, 158, 159, 161, 280, 306
Americans 201
Amuctac 61, 63, 260
Anamás 21, 244
Anderson Reservoir 248
Angel Island 41, 42, 45, 49, 58, 201, 244
Anizumne tribe 235
Año Nuevo Creek 252

Anza, Juan Bautista de 7, 52
Apelamame tribe 216
Aptos tribe 235, 237, 239
Aqui 69, 78, 94
Argüello, José 99, 107, 124, 127, 128, 143, 162
Aromas 236
Arroyo de la Cuesta, Father Felipe 26, 244
Arroyo del Valle 186, 235, 257
Arroyo Mocho 186, 247
Arroyo of San Mateo 232, 255
Asirin tribe 180, 186, 235, 236
Asisara, Lorenzo 7
Ausaima tribe 236, 239
Auxentac 236, 241, 242
Awani-wi 242
Ayala, Juan Manuel de 41, 42
Ayala Cove 45, 50
Baja California Indians 70, 72, 93-94, 102, 308
Bay Miwok language group 13, 24, 26, 153, 179, 207, 241, 244, 246, 250, 253, 255, 256, 259, 261
Bean Hollow Creek 252
Bear Creek 256
Belmont 52, 246
Benicia 238
Bitakomtara tribe 236
Blandina Guaiámay 103, 243
Bloomfield 247
Bodega 142
Bodega Bay 28-29, 142, 176, 201, 202, 203, 260, 287
Bolbon 237
Bolinas Bay 232, 242, 248
Bonifacio 103, 131

Bonny Doone 242
Borica, Diego de 123, 131, 132, 135, 139, 141, 143
Boulder Creek 234
Brentwood 244
Brushy Peak 255
Buriburi 259
Butano Ridge 252
Byron 256
Caburan tribe 237, 251, 273
Cachanigtac 247
Caguapatto 237, 257
Caguas 141, 245, 294, 304
Cajastaca 235, 237
Calaveras Creek 235, 253
Calendaruc 35
Calupetamal 261
Cambón, Father Pedro 62, 260
Canijolmano tribe 237, 238, 244
Cañada de los Olompalis 249
Cañada de los Osos 239
Carmel River 37
Carnadero 189, 258
Carquin tribe 24, 37, 56, 103, 134, 181, 191, 204, 205, 206, 209, 210, 238, 241, 243, 272, 293
Carquinez Strait 19, 24, 37, 56, 131, 139, 158, 180, 191, 204, 208, 218, 231, 238, 255, 269, 272
Carues 245, 295, 304
Castro Valley 261
Catalá, Magín 83, 124, 125, 152
catechism (see mission life)
Causen tribe 147, 155, 162, 238, 273, 310
Caymus tribe 237, 238, 239, 248
Central Valley 57
Cerro Alto de los Bolbones 259
Chaclanes (see Saclan tribe)
Chagúnte 231, 239
Chaloctac tribe 238, 239, 254
Chamis of Chutchui 68, 70
Charquin, resistance leader 115, 116, 117, 118, 119, 123, 234, 276, 277

Chemoco tribe 239
Chesbro Reservoir 248
Chiguan tribe 32, 108, 206, 239, 270
Chileno Valley 249
Chimenes 139, 141, 142, 146, 287
Chipletac 118, 252
Chipuctac 236, 239
Chitactac 239, 240, 251
Chocheños 24, 247
Chocoay 240, 249
Chocoime tribe 240-241, 248
Cholequebit 234
Cholvon tribe 193, 211, 213, 214, 215, 216, 218, 237, 241, 246, 259, 273
Choquinico tribe 240, 249
Choquoime (see Chocoime tribe)
Chucuyen (see Chocoime tribe)
Chucumne tribe 235, 241
Chupcan tribe 37, 57, 134, 181, 190, 191, 204, 205, 232, 241, 253, 256, 272
Churistac 236, 241
Churmutcé 252
Chutchui 53, 61, 62, 64, 260
Coast Miwok language group 24, 26, 28, 46, 176, 179, 219, 220, 234, 236, 240, 242, 244, 246, 247, 248, 249, 250, 251, 254, 255, 260
Coast Ranges 57, 184, 189, 215, 218, 235, 236, 237, 257
colonial expansion 2
Colorado Creek 235
Colorado River 72, 95
Colos, Angela 7
Čolovomnes (see Cholvon tribe)
Colusa 216
Concord 241
conversion (see mission recruitment, tribal disintegration)
Copoloyomi 254
Corral Hollow 247
Corralitos 235
Corte de la Madera Creek 249

Costanoan (Ohlone) language group 13, 24, 26, 46, 49, 153, 179, 207, 234, 235, 236, 237, 238, 239, 241, 242, 243, 244, 246, 247, 248, 249, 250, 251, 252, 253, 255, 256, 257, 258, 259, 260, 261
Cotati 247
Cotegen tribe 32, 40, 108, 242, 252, 270
Cotomkowi tribe 254
Cotoni tribe 235, 242
Coybos tribe 242
Coyote Creek 151, 236, 242, 252, 253
Coyote Hills 258
Coyote Lake 248
Coyote River 66, 72, 235
Crespí, Father Juan 32, 36
Crow Creek 257
Cuchillones (see Huchiun tribe)
Cueva, Father Pedro de la 143, 186, 188, 198
Cupertino 256
Dantí, Father Antonio 139, 141-142, 143, 144
Danville 256
Davenport 242
Del Puerto Creek 237
Diablo Range 246
Diablo Valley 13, 37, 57, 185, 205, 232, 241
disease, general 4, 67
    diphtheria 174
    dolor del costado 173
    epidemic 67, 90-91, 138, 173, 193-195, 199-200
    measles 193, 194, 199
    peste 174, 175, 176, 179
    scarlet fever 174
    syphilis 4, 172, 173, 176, 179
    tuberculosis 4
    typhus 138
Dublin 246, 254
Duncan's Point 246
Durán, Father Narciso 232, 235, 238

East Bay 14, 21, 24, 26, 35, 42, 47, 49, 54, 62, 64, 80, 102, 103, 110, 129, 134, 154, 156, 168, 170, 171, 178, 180, 184, 189, 191, 208, 232, 234, 241, 243, 244, 253, 256, 269, 272, 273
Eastern Miwok language groups 28
Economic interactions (see Indian labor)
El Calvo 123
El Mocho 126, 281
environmental deterioration 72-74, 98-99, 135-136, 148, 221
Estero 233, 235, 258
Estero Americano 247, 260
Etcha-tamal 255
Evergreen 250
Fages, Pedro 7, 20, 36, 57, 76, 80, 92, 93, 96, 97, 98, 100, 104, 106, 197
Fairfield 247, 255
Farallon Islands 131, 200
Fernández, Father José María 142, 145
Fernández, Father Manuel 124, 125, 126, 127, 128
firearms 98, 165
first contact situations 31-51, 54-58, 62, 113, 177
forced mission recruitment (see mission recruitment)
Fort Point 121
Fremont Plain 36, 129, 147, 153, 170, 238
frontier (see tribal frontier)
fugitivism (see mission life, forced return of runaways)
Gallinas Creek 242
Garzas Creek 257
Geluasibe 240, 242
Geluatamal 261
Genau 9, 131, 242, 243
Gequigmu 21, 295
Gilroy 189, 239, 258
Gilroy Hot Springs 236

Glenn Cove 238
Glenwood 253
Golden Gate 121, 177, 202, 243
Grand Island 252
Green Valley 257
Guadalupe River 66, 71, 74, 129, 152, 153, 252, 256
Gualomi 236, 242
Guaulen tribe 168, 176, 178, 179, 232, 242, 248, 271
Guaypem tribe 242
Guemelento tribe 242, 249, 250
Guilicos (see Huiluc tribe)
Guimas 62, 69, 81, 140
Guloisnistac 247
Habasto tribe 168, 178, 179, 232, 242, 255, 260, 271
Halchis 102
Half Moon Bay 239, 242
Hall's Valley 250
Han-né-su (see Anizumne tribe)
Hayward 261
hemp production (see tribal labor)
Henry Coe Park 236
Hollister 239
Horseshoe Cove 50
Hospital Creek 246
Huchiun tribe 36, 46, 47, 48, 49, 56, 64, 110, 129, 131, 134, 139, 140, 143, 147, 153, 154, 156, 157, 158, 159, 160, 164, 168, 170, 176, 178, 206, 208, 243, 260, 272, 282, 288, 291, 297, 303, 305, 307
Huchiun-Aguasto tribe 37, 45, 55, 103, 131, 156, 180, 191, 210, 238, 243, 248, 272, 298
Huiluc tribe 237, 238, 244
Huimen tribe 21, 40, 42, 41, 43, 46, 49, 50, 134, 168, 176, 178, 179, 200, 232, 244, 271
Indian Slough 244
Jalalon tribe 244

Jalquin tribe 102, 103, 141, 156, 160, 162, 171, 180, 204, 206, 208, 244, 245, 253, 254, 261, 272, 295, 296
Josmite tribe 216
Josquizara 243
Juchillones (see Huchiun tribe)
Julpun tribe 244, 246
Junizumne tribe 258
Juñas tribe 184, 215, 237, 246
Juscule 181, 294, 304
Kabemali 246
Karkin (see Carquin tribe)
Karquin (see Carquin tribe)
Kenwood 244
Konhomtara tribe 246
La Honda Creek 249
Lafayette 157, 253
Laguna de Santa Rosa 247
Laguna Seca 127, 170, 171, 248
Lamames tribe 216, 237
Lamaytu tribe 246, 251
Lamchin tribe 34, 38, 52, 53, 110, 118, 206, 233, 246, 270
Landaeta, Father Martín de 142, 143
Langsdorff, George von 8, 23, 195, 196, 197
Language groups 13, 24-26 (see also Costanoan, Miwok, Patwin, Wappo, Yokuts)
Lasuén, Father Fermín Francisco de 77, 86, 87, 119, 143
Laurel Creek 52
León Tumiun 183, 311, 313
Libantone 247, 249
Licatiut tribe 247
Lisyan 247
Livaneglua 21, 40, 50, 244
Livantolomi 246, 247
Livermore Valley 37, 155, 165, 179, 180, 184, 185, 186, 188, 238, 247, 251, 254, 255, 257

Livestock raids (see tribal livestock raids)
Llagas Creek 59, 108, 248
Loma Prieta Creek 238
Los Banos Creek 216, 236
Los Gatos 254
Los Gatos Creek 129
Luecha tribe 23, 184, 185-191. 193, 215, 233, 237, 247, 273
Lupuyomi 246, 247
Malaca tribe 219, 247
Mare Island 238
Marin 178, 303
Marin County 249
Marin Peninsula 10, 13, 18, 19, 21, 22, 24, 26, 40, 50, 134, 168, 170, 176, 178, 179, 180, 191, 200, 201, 202, 203, 218, 232, 242, 248, 251, 255, 261, 269, 271
Marsh Creek 259
Martinez 238
Matalan tribe 36, 38, 52, 99, 165, 170, 171, 248, 254
Mayacma tribe 238
Mayemes tribe 216
Menlo Park 252
Menzies, Archibald 110
Merced River 216
Military
  apparel 66
  control of firearms 98, 165
  conflict with missionaries 126, 143, 145, 163, 281-285, 306
  expeditions
    against Alaskan hunters 201
    against Charquin 117-118
    against Luechas 187-188
    against Saclans 157-159, 169-170
    against Suisuns 210-211
    against Tayssens 212
    into Central Valley in 1808 215-218
    into Coast Ranges in 1805 189-191
    into East Bay in 1804 184-185

punishment of Indians 5-6, 64-65, 66-67, 73-74, 99-101, 141-142, 159, 170, 183, 187-188, 208-209, 280, 292, 303-305
refusal to escort missionaries 80, 131-133, 163
return of fugitive Christian Indians 4, 5, 97-98, 117-120, 156, 164, 184, 190-191, 212, 216-218, 289-292
strategy for regional control 109, 183, 208, 210, 212
use of Indian auxiliiaries 119, 210
Millbrae 259
Miller Creek 242
Milpitas 235
Miner Slough 241
Mission Bay 64
Mission Creek 53, 61, 63, 68, 260
Mission Dolores (see Mission San Francisco)
Mission of Our Patron San Francisco (see Mission San Francisco)
mission life
  alcaldes 79, 92, 155, 168, 174
  ambivalence toward, 1-2, 125-126, 146, 156, 184, 219, 222
  catechism 126, 127, 129, 193, 197
  culture shock 4, 112, 219-226
  death rates 266-268
  diet 86-88, 142-144, 196
  forced return of runaways 4-5, 95-97, 101, 138, 142, 164, 168, 181-182, 185, 197, 204, 216-217, 276-277, 288
  health conditions and mortality 4, 90-92, 146, 172-176
  in general 3-4, 86, 110-112, 195
  labor 86, 88-89, 93, 195
  marriage 79-81, 119, 134-135, 178, 181, 188
  monjerías 89-90
  paseo 95, 180, 203, 209, 300
  populations 266-268
  punishment 197
  sex ratio 173, 193-200

traditional religion and, 196, 198-199
social control 67, 79, 89, 92-95, 98, 155, 197
mission recruitment
disease and, 200
in general 1, 2, 11, 68-69, 71, 76-77, 78-84, 101, 124-125, 131, 220-226
lack of compulsary, 1, 82-84, 135-136
launches used in, 202
mission Indians used in, 99, 139-141, 153-155, 180-181, 190, 204-209
proselytization 39-40, 51, 83-84, 124-125, 186
Mission San Antonio 107
Mission San Carlos Borromeo 2, 35, 37, 236, 258
Mission San Francisco
abuse of Indians investigated 142-146, 299-303
disease 91-92, 138, 145, 172-175, 199-200
first baptism 68
foundation 2, 62-64
population change 69-70, 78-79, 110, 179, 200
structure and contents 110-111
Mission San Francisco Solano 10, 238, 239, 240, 244, 247, 258
Mission San Jose
disease 172, 175, 194-198
first baptism 162
foundation 153
survey for site 147
threatened with attack 155, 159-160, 162, 182-183, 310-313
Mission San Juan Bautista 26, 236, 239, 258
Mission San Rafael 10, 236, 242, 243, 244, 246, 247, 254, 260
Mission Santa Clara
disease 66-67, 90, 92, 172-175, 195

districts, general 66, 103, 233, 269
Our Seraphic Mother Santa Clara Village 3, 66-67, 78, 233, 256
Our Patron San Francisco Village 66, 71, 78, 94, 256
San Antonio Multi-tribal District 77, 103, 233, 235-237, 250
San Bernardino Multi-tribal District/Village 103, 117, 126, 233, 250, 252
San Carlos Multi-tribal District 40-41, 42, 45-47, 50-51, 55-56, 58, 64, 103, 131, 179, 233, 236, 239, 247-248, 252-253, 258-259
San Francisco Solano Tribal District/Village 66, 69-70, 78, 103, 233
San Jose Cupertino Tribal District/Village (usually abbreviated San Jose) 66, 68, 129, 233, 256
San Juan Bautista Village 68, 233, 252
Santa Agueda Multi-tribal District 103, 126, 233, 235-236, 257-258
Santa Ysabel Tribal District/Village 66, 71, 77, 93, 126, 165, 233, 250, 253, 257
first baptisms 67
foundation 3, 65-66
population change 69, 71, 110
structure and contents 110-112
threatened with attack 126-127, 189, 281-285
Mission Santa Cruz
attacked 5, 118-119
districts
San Antonio Tribal District 235

Index 359

San Francisco Xavier Multi-
    tribal District 241
San Juan Multi-tribal District
    241
San Lucas Tribal District 235
San Rafael Tribal District 252
Santiago Tribal District 242
    foundation 108-109
Mission Valley, San Francisco County
    62, 64
mission vital records 8-9, 20, 195,
    231-232, 264-268
Mississippi Creek 257
Mitenne 31, 32, 117, 252
Miwok language family (see Bay
    Miwok, Coast Miwok, Eastern
    Miwok, Plains Miwok, Sierra
    Miwok)
Monte del Diablo 185, 241
Monterey 36, 37, 40, 46, 51, 57, 62,
    65, 98, 106
Monterey Bay 35, 235
Monterey Peninsula 35, 37
Monterey Presidio 2, 104-107, 170,
    277
Moraga, Gabriel 124, 152, 255
Moraga, José Joaquín 74, 75, 80
Morgan Hill 236, 241-242, 248
Moss Beach 231
Mount Diablo 185, 189, 191, 194,
    254, 256, 259
Mount Hamilton 250
Mount Tamalpais 13, 178
Mountain Lake 53
Mountain View 252
Muistac 236, 241
Murguía, Father José 68, 256
Musupum tribe 248
Muyson tribe 251
Naique 21, 244
Napa tribe 238, 248, 293
Napa River 248
Napa Valley 10, 237, 238, 239, 244
New Almaden 252
Newark 235
Nicasio 232, 255

Nototomne tribe 248
Novato 232, 249, 250
Oakland 36, 244, 253
Ochole 119, 120
Ocolom 254
Ohlone 13, 24, 26, 249
Ojyugma 160, 161, 162, 293, 294
Olbera, Diego 102, 143, 175
Olema tribe 179, 180, 201, 248, 249,
    254, 255, 271
Olema-tamal 249, 256
Olemaloque 200, 201, 202, 248, 249,
    271
Olemochoe 249
Olemopas 271
Oljon tribe 32, 110, 115, 116, 206,
    234, 249, 252, 270
Olompali tribe 240, 249
Olompali State Park 249
Olpen tribe 34, 118, 125, 249, 250,
    270
Omiomi tribe 179, 180, 201, 202,
    232, 240, 249, 250, 269, 271, 316
Ompin tribe 235, 250
Orestac 236
Orestimba Creek 185, 212, 257
Oromstac 247
Oroysom 153
Oton 140, 141, 286
Pablo Tac 7
Pacheco Creek 236, 241, 242, 257
Pacheco Pass 189, 257
Pacheco Slough 184
Pajaro River 35, 235, 237
Pala, Captain 150, 151, 250
Paleños 165, 170, 253
Palo Alto 252
Palos Colorados 233
Palóu, Father Francisco 17, 20, 39,
    40, 51, 62, 63, 64, 66, 67, 69, 82,
    260
Paltrastach 250
Partacsi 250
Patlan tribe 238, 273
patron-client relationships 76, 78-79,
    150-151

Patwin language group 13, 24, 26, 28,
    180, 219, 220, 238, 239, 247,
    248, 255, 257, 258
Pedro Alcantara 249
Pelnen tribe 170, 180, 238, 251, 273
Penitencia Creek 253
Peña affair 93-95
Peña, Father Tomás de la 67, 88, 93,
    94, 101, 256
Pérouse, Jean François de La 86
Pescadero 188, 216, 217, 237
Pescadero Creek 20, 249, 250
Petaluma tribe 251
Petaluma River 240, 249, 251
Petlenuc 62, 260
Pilarcitos Creek 239
Pinart, Alphonse 256
Pitac 239, 240, 251, 258
Plains Miwok 13, 235, 241, 242, 252,
    248, 258
Pleasanton 235, 242, 251
Point Año Nuevo 18, 19, 31, 102,
    108, 115, 116
Point Montara 239
Point Reyes 249
Point San Pedro 242
Pomo, Southern 26, 236, 246
Pornen 251
Port Costa 238
Portolá, Gaspár de 7, 31
Posscon (see Tatcan tribe)
Potroy 160, 172, 245, 292, 296, 303
Poyl 189
Poytoquix 236
presidios (see specific presidios)
Pructaca 249
Pruristac 68, 79, 80, 81, 102, 116,
    206, 251, 270
psychological disintegration (see tribal
    disintegration)
Puichon tribe 34, 38, 79, 110, 118,
    168, 181, 207, 252, 270
Pulgas Creek 247
punishment of Indians 93-95, 120,
    122-123, 144-149, 160, 220-221
Purisima Creek 242

Puscuy 240, 252
Quenemsia tribe 252
Quiroste tribe 5, 31, 115, 116, 117,
    118, 119, 125, 129, 252, 270
Ramaytush 24
Rancho Acalanes 253
Rancho Cañada de Pala 250
Rancho de la Sierra 239
Rancho Monte del Diablo 232
Rancho Nueces y Bolbones 259
Rancho Pala 250
Raymundo El Californio 144, 153,
    154, 155, 160, 289, 297, 298,
    306, 308
Redwood City 247
religious conversion (see mission
    recruitment)
resistance (see mission life, also tribal
    resistance)
Richardson Bay 21, 41, 42, 244
Richmond 171, 243
Rio Vista 235
Ritocsi 71, 103, 252
Rivera y Moncada, Fernando 38
Ro-mo-nans 249
Rockaway Beach 251
Rumsen 35, 62
Russians
    at Bodega Bay 200-203
    Indian policy 203
    Rezanov expedition 195, 197-200
Sacalanes (see Saclan tribe)
Saclan tribe 9, 21, 138, 139, 140,
    142, 146, 147, 155, 157, 158,
    159, 160, 164, 165, 168, 180,
    181, 204, 209, 210, 245, 253,
    272, 286, 287, 289, 294, 295,
    307, 309
Sacramento River 216, 235, 250, 252
Sacramento Valley 35, 258
Sacramento-Mokelumne River delta
    242, 248, 258
Sal, Hermenegildo 108, 116, 117,
    122, 123, 127, 128, 129, 147
Salmon Creek 260
San Andreas Valley 255

San Anselmo Creek 243
San Antonio Creek 249
San Antonio Mission (see Mission San Antonio)
San Antonio Valley 246
San Bruno 201, 259
San Bruno Creek 258
San Bruno Mountain 258
San Carlos Borromeo Mission (see Mission San Carlos Borromeo)
San Diego Presidio 120
San Francisco 53, 61, 233, 251, 260
San Francisco de Asís Mission (see Mission San Francisco)
San Francisco Mission (see Mission San Francisco)
San Francisco Peninsula 2, 4, 20, 21, 24, 29, 35, 36, 38, 42, 52, 61, 62, 80, 102, 107, 110, 118, 129, 207, 234, 239, 246, 252, 258, 260, 269, 270
San Francisco Presidio 2, 65, 66, 72, 74, 77, 87, 98, 120, 121, 135, 151, 183, 209, 210
San Francisco Solano Mission (see Mission San Francisco Solano)
San Francisquito Creek 38, 79, 129, 231, 234, 249, 252
San Gregorio 249
San Gregorio Creek 32, 115, 249
San Joaquin River 188, 193, 215, 216, 217, 232, 235, 237, 241, 242, 246, 247, 248, 250, 256
San Joaquin Valley 10, 11, 26, 181, 194, 211, 212, 213, 233, 235, 236, 246, 255, 259
San Jose, pueblo of
  in general 3, 71-72
  land disputes 73-74, 98-99, 151-153
  local tribes 233-234, 252, 256
  influence on Indians 75-77, 104, 165, 213, 316-319
  threatened with attack 126-127, 156

San Jose Mission (see Mission San Jose)
San Juan Bautista Mission (see Mission San Juan Bautista)
San Juan, parage de 239, 240, 251
San Leandro 244
San Leandro Creek 172
San Lorenzo Creek 54, 172, 233, 245, 247, 261
San Lorenzo River 108, 109, 234, 259
San Luis Creek 257
San Luis Reservoir 257
San Martin 239, 249, 251
San Mateo 63
San Mateo Creek 53, 107-108, 255
San Pablo 243
San Pablo Bay 10, 13, 36, 42, 45, 55, 158, 180, 234, 238, 243, 244, 250, 260
San Pedro Outstation 102, 108, 115, 116, 242
San Pedro Valley 102, 108, 239, 251
San Rafael, Marin County 179, 232
San Rafael Mission (see Mission San Rafael)
San Ramon Valley 37, 180, 232, 246, 254, 256
Santa Clara 3, 67, 233
Santa Clara Mission (see Mission Santa Clara)
Santa Clara Valley 3, 13, 21, 24, 29, 36, 37, 38, 52, 53, 57, 59, 65, 66, 67, 68, 71, 73, 75, 77, 78, 81, 85, 104, 107, 108, 110, 112, 121, 125, 127, 129, 135, 147, 150, 152, 162, 167, 170, 180, 182, 185, 202, 234, 235, 237, 239-240, 248, 249, 250, 251, 252, 253, 254, 256, 257
Santa Cruz 252, 253, 259
Santa Cruz Mission (see Mission Santa Cruz)
Santa Cruz Mountains 5, 6, 13, 103, 118, 121, 129, 234, 238, 239, 249
Santa María, Father Vicente de 42, 43, 44, 46, 48, 49, 50, 58, 260

Santa Rosa Plain 26, 236, 246
Santa Teresa Hills 252
Saratoga Creek 250
Saratoga Gap 234
Sausalito 244
Sayanta tribe 235, 239, 253
Scotts Valley 253
sea otters 98, 200, 202, 297
Sebastopol 246
Segloque 177, 254
Serra, Father Junípero 4, 35, 81, 92, 95
Sespesuyu 319
Seunen tribe 171, 180, 189, 245, 246, 254, 256, 273
sexual abuse 4, 77
Sierra Miwok dances 199
Sierra Nevada foothills 29
Siplichiquin 254, 259
Sitlintac 61, 63, 68, 260
Smith, Tom 7, 28
Socotash 253
Solchequi 129, 251
Somontac 254
Sonoma, Captain 231
Sonoma Creek 234, 240, 244
Sonoma Valley 240
Sonomas (see Chocoime tribe)
Soquel 259
Soróntac 234
South San Francisco 259
Souyen tribe 162, 165, 170, 180, 184, 189, 254, 273
Spanish world view
   colonial 5, 58
   Franciscan 51, 58, 69, 83-84, 125
Ssalaime 242
Ssalson tribe 21, 23, 34, 38, 40, 52, 53, 63, 64, 69, 79, 118, 255, 260, 270
Ssaoam tribe 184, 185, 255, 273
Ssatumnumo 231, 239
Ssipùtca 252
Ssogoréate 103, 243
Ssupichom 232, 247
St. Helena 237

Staten Island 248
Stevens Creek 53-54, 120, 250, 252, 256
Stockton 256
Suio Suiu (see Suyusuyu)
Suisun tribe 180, 181, 204, 205, 207, 208, 209, 210, 231, 238, 241, 247, 255, 257, 272
Suisun Bay 24, 42, 184, 205, 247, 250, 255
Suisun Plain 10, 257
Sujute 252
Sumu, Captain 49
Sumu tribe 257
Sunol Valley 37, 238, 251
Supichom 233
Suquel, Captain 108, 109, 259
Sutter Buttes 216
Sutter Slough 241
Suyusuyu 181, 205, 209, 215
Tamal tribe 178, 179, 180, 201, 202, 232, 248, 254, 255, 256, 271
Tamcan tribe 218, 244, 246, 256, 273
Tamien tribe 3, 36, 65, 66, 68, 69, 71, 78, 129, 254, 256
Tammukamnes (see Tamcan tribe)
Tamyen 24
Taratac 236
Tassajara Creek 254
Tatcan tribe 34, 134, 180, 204, 205, 206, 207, 232, 241, 245, 251, 253, 255, 256, 272
Tauhalame tribe 216, 217
Taui village 241
Taunan tribe 162, 163, 164, 165, 168, 170, 182, 235, 236, 253, 257, 273, 311
Tauquimne tribe 256
Tayssen group 180, 182, 184, 191, 193, 212, 213, 215, 257
Tcholovones (see Cholvon tribe)
Tciménukme 139
Tegunes 287
Temescal Creek 243
Timigtac 251
Tolay Creek 234

Tolena tribe 239, 248, 257
Tomales Bay 248, 254, 256
Tomoi 257
Torose 242
Tracy 237, 241, 259
tribal disintegration, general 3, 100-101, 113, 135-136, 191, 221-222, 232
  ecological pressure 99, 148, 221
  psychological aspects 2, 4, 10, 82-84, 101, 112, 135-136, 181, 221
  role of disease 176, 179, 222-223
  winter of 1794-1795 5-6, 7, 125-136, 146, 168
tribal frontier 107-108, 146-147, 165, 170-171, 185, 191, 218-220, 232
tribal geography 231-234
tribal labor,
  hemp production 150-151, 213, 215
  for Presidios 104-107, 121-123, 147-148, 213, 278-280
  for settlers 75-77, 104, 149-151, 213-215, 316-319
  (see also patron-client relationships)
tribal leaders 116, 181, 183, 189, 216
  (see also Aqui, Guimas, Juscule, León Tumium, Ochole, Ojyugma, Pala, Potroy, Sumu, Suquel)
tribal life
  conflict resolution 23, 188
  foreign policy 23, 24, 42-43, 47-49, 96, 129, 159-160, 166, 197
  leadership 21, 22, 48-50, 53
  intermarriage 23, 24, 79, 181, 209, 232
  population density 19, 20
  warfare 22-23, 52-53, 63, 150
  world view 26-29, 43-44, 48-49, 58-59
tribal livestock raids 72-74, 120-122, 148, 156, 163, 279-280
tribal resistance
  Charquin 115-120, 123, 276-277
  Jorge of Santa Clara killed 184, 185, 190, 207
  Luecha 185-189, 313-314
  Saclan 138-141, 146, 156-160, 168, 171-172, 285-288, 289-292, 306-309
  Suisun 180-181, 204, 314-316, 319-320
tribal women 10, 22, 53
tribelet concept 13
Tu-lo-mos 249
Tubsinte 61, 260
Tugite tribe 237
Tuibun tribe 23, 36, 54, 147, 153, 170, 188, 238, 245, 258, 273, 312
Tyler Island 242
Uchiunes (see Huchiun tribe)
Uculi tribe 258
Uimen (see Huimen tribe)
Ulatis Creek 258
Ululato tribe 258
Unijaima tribe 251, 258
Unisumne tribe 258
Urebure 79, 80, 81, 98, 251, 258, 259, 270
Utian Language Family 24
Uturbe 21, 255
Uvas Creek 239
Uypi tribe 108, 235, 259
Vacaville 258
Valdez, Anecleto 93
Vancouver, George 8, 88, 90, 110, 111, 112, 142
violent encounters
  Alaskans-tribal Indians 203
  Americans-tribal Indians 201
  military-tribal Indians 3, 63-65, 102, 117-118, 157-159, 184-185
  mission Indians-tribal Indians 99, 139-141, 153-155, 168, 204-209
  missionaries-tribal Indians 93-95, 124, 126, 142-145, 185-186, 281
Visitation Valley 62, 260

Volvon tribe 184, 185, 189, 191, 194, 237, 246, 259, 272
Walnut Creek 256
Walnut Grove 258
Wappo language group 24, 26, 237, 238, 239, 244
Watsonville 237
Wí-pa (see Guaypem tribe)
Wildcat Creek 243
women 10, 22, 53, 70, 72, 79, 86, 89-90, 96, 100, 103, 117, 119, 129-130, 140, 143, 162, 174, 181-182, 187-188, 194, 204-206
Wooden Valley 239
Xatlanes (see Saclan tribe)
Yacomui 243
Yacumusmo 241, 272
Yelamu tribe 2, 3, 23, 53, 61, 62, 63, 64, 68, 69, 79, 80, 139, 140, 176, 260, 270
Yoittaca 254
Yokuts language group 26, 241, 242, 244, 247, 248, 256
Yoletamal 177, 260, 261
Yountville 238
Yrgin tribe 54, 55, 244, 245, 246, 261, 273, 311
Yulien 255, 261, 273
Yuman victories 72, 75, 95
Zayante Creek 253
Zuicun 259, 261, 272

Editorial:
Ballena Press
823 Valparaiso Avenue
Menlo Park, CA 94025
Tel. (415) 323-9261
Fax: (415) 321-2529

Orders: Ballena Press Publishers Services
P.O. Box 2510
Novato, CA 94948
Tel. (415) 883-3530
Fax: (415) 883-4280

OTHER BALLENA TITLES

Bean: THE OHLONE: PAST AND PRESENT	paper	$22.95
	cloth	$29.95
Bean: SEASONS OF THE KACHINA	paper	$21.95
Bean and Blackburn: NATIVE CALIFORNIANS	paper	$21.95
Bean: CALIFORNIA INDIAN SHAMANISM	paper	$27.50
	cloth	$33.00
Bean, Vane and Young: CAHUILLA LANDSCAPE	paper	$14.95
	cloth	$19.95
Blackburn and Anderson: BEFORE THE WILDERNESS	paper	$31.00
	cloth	$41.50
Chamberlain: WHEN STARS COME DOWN TO EARTH	paper	$17.95
Ericson et al.: PEOPLING OF THE NEW WORLD	paper	$19.95
Great Basin Foundation: WOMAN, POET, SCIENTIST	paper	$30.00
Heizer: FEDERAL CONCERN/CALIFORNIA INDIANS	paper	$ 7.95
Heizer: SOURCES OF STONES/MESOAMERICAN SITES	paper	$ 7.95
Hudson/Blackburn: THE MATERIAL CULTURE OF THE CHUMASH INTERACTION SPHERE.		
Vol. II. FOOD PREPARATION AND SHELTER	paper	$24.95
	cloth	$39.95
Vol. III. CLOTHING, ORNAMENTATION, AND GROOMING	cloth	$39.95
Vol. V. MANUFACTURING PROCESSES, METROLOGY, AND TRADE	paper	$28.95
Five Volume Series. Autographed Special Edition	cloth	$300.00
Hudson/Underhay: CRYSTALS IN THE SKY	paper	$18.95
Jewell: INDIANS OF THE FEATHER RIVER	paper	$12.95
Knack: LIFE IS WITH PEOPLE	paper	$ 6.95
Miller, J. SHAMANIC ODYSSEY	paper	$28.95
Sherer: BITTERNESS ROAD	paper	$13.95
Shipek: DELFINA CUERO	paper	$12.00
	cloth	$16.00
Stewart: A VOICE IN HER TRIBE	paper	$ 8.95
Stickel: NEW USES OF SYSTEM THEORY IN ARCHAEOLOGY	paper	$ 9.95
Sutton: INSECTS AS FOOD	paper	$17.95
Vane/Bean: CALIFORNIA INDIANS: PRIMARY RESOURCES	paper	$16.50
	cloth	$22.50
Wilke: PREHISTORY OF YUHA DESERT REGION	paper	$ 7.95